"Enlightening, uplifting, and meaningful . . . [*Reading Ruth*] reveals open doors where many see only stone walls, and presents an engaging example of the beauty and meaning which can be found in the Bible by modern men and women."

—*Hartford Jewish Ledger*

"For a long time I've wished I could be a fly on the wall at a women's Bible study group. *Reading Ruth* takes me right into the room for a discussion so rich and wonderful that I am not just a voyeur but a student hungry to learn."

—Ari L. Goldman
Author of *The Search for God at Harvard*

Reading Ruth

Reading Ruth

Contemporary Women Reclaim a Sacred Story

Edited by JUDITH A. KATES and
GAIL TWERSKY REIMER

BALLANTINE BOOKS • NEW YORK

Introduction and compilation copyright © 1994 by Judith A. Kates
and Gail Twersky Reimer

Illustrations copyright © 1994 by Diane Palley

Owing to limitations of space, permission acknowledgments
can be found on pages 385–386.

Library of Congress Catalog Card Number: 95-94989

ISBN: 0-345-38032-0

Cover design by Ruth Ross
Cover background by Diane Palley. Inset art, *The Story of Ruth*,
1876–77 by Thomas Matthews Rooke, courtesy of The Gallery/Art Resource

Manufactured in the United States of America

First Trade Paperback Edition: February 1996
10 9 8 7 6 5 4 3 2 1

To the memory of my mother,
Natalia Geizhals Twersky

כִּי יוֹדֵעַ כָּל־שַׁעַר עַמִּי כִּי אֵשֶׁת חַיִל אָתְּ:

For my husband,
William Wolfe Kates

אִישׁ גִּבּוֹר חַיִל

Contents

A Note about the Illustrations

Diane Palley has created a series of original papercuts for *Reading Ruth*. Papercutting is a traditional Jewish folk art which originated in Eastern Europe and the Middle East several hundred years ago. Incorporating biblical verses and traditional symbols, papercuts played a part in many holidays, including Passover and Shavuot. Usually only men and boys, literate and educated, were capable of making them because they required extensive knowledge of Hebrew texts and rituals. But women and girls did create papercuts for Shavuot, the holiday on which the Book of Ruth is read. The papercuts here, created by a contemporary woman who has embraced the full range of this traditional art form, visually represent the enterprise of this book. Following are explanations of each papercut.

1. "But Ruth Clung to Her"

In Eastern Europe, the papercuts women made to decorate houses on Shavuot were called *roiselech* (yiddish for roses), because their circular, symmetrical designs were often abstract roses or other flowers. In these illustrations, the rose becomes the symbol of both women, Ruth and Naomi, and of their descendant, King David, traditionally represented in the Jewish mystical system by a rose. The rose on the left stands for Naomi, while a smaller rose, Ruth, winds around and clings to the larger rose. A closed bud, Obed, branches off from the rose on the right, bringing forth an unfolding bud (Jesse), and then the open flower, David. Ruth's rose grows out of a hill labeled Moab, while Naomi's springs from the Land of Israel, the two hills separated by a stream of water, the Jordan river.

2. *"For Wherever You Go, I Will Go"*

The complete text of this most famous quotation from the Book of Ruth is intensely rhythmic, especially in Hebrew. This rhythmic quality is reflected in the alternating black and white words of the written verse. Just as Ruth seeks to join the life and God of her beloved mother-in-law, so the deer seeks water; "As a deer thirsts for water, so I thirst for You" (Psalms 42.1).

3. *"I Went Away Full, and the Lord Has Brought Me Back Empty"*

These words, spoken in grief by Naomi, are found above and below the arc of moons waning from full to empty. The names of her husband and two sons (Elimelech, Chilion, and Mahlon), are written in Hebrew in the hills, which support three stunted, dead trees.

4. *"Your Latest Act of* Chesed*"*

The moons at the top, showing a complete cycle, represent the completion of Naomi's line through Ruth's marriage to Boaz. The mother deer protecting a vulnerable fawn represents the most basic sense of *chesed*—selfless and generous lovingkindness. The wheat below the deer recalls the harvest time during which Ruth approached Boaz. The intermixing of Naomi's and Ruth's fate is again portrayed by the two sheaves of wheat interwoven at the bottom of the image.

5. *"Like Rachel and Leah, Both of Whom Built Up the House of Israel"*

These words are found across the top and around the arch of a house. The names of the twelve sons of Rachel and Leah, who became the House of Israel, are written on the walls surrounding the arch. The large flower in the opening of the wall is a mandrake, a plant that plays a significant role in the story of the two sisters' marriage to Jacob. The hills at the bottom supporting the House of Israel are interwoven, comparing the alliance between Rachel and Leah to the loving relationship between Ruth and Naomi.

6. "A Son Is Born to Naomi"

The waxing moons in this illustration complete the cycle of waning moons found in the illustration to section three. The son, Obed, is portrayed by a young lion, symbol of the monarchy which his grandson David would inherit. The lion plays with a dove, symbol of the messianic age to be inaugurated by a descendant of David. In contrast to the barren hills in the illustration to section three, the land in this illustration is teeming with the seven fruits of ancient Israel; barley, wheat, dates, figs, pomegranates, olives, and grapes.

7. "Ruth the Moabite . . . Begot David"

The two phrases of this section title, separated by most of the text of the Book of Ruth, are likewise separated by a row of crowns, symbols of the kingship of David through whose line the Messiah will be born. The messianic age is illustrated by the peacefully reclining animals, the lion with the lamb (Isaiah 11:7) and by the vine and fig tree under which "everyone . . . shall live in peace and not be afraid" (Micah 4:4). Midrashic tradition tells us that after the Messiah arrives, even the sun and moon, which both appear in this image, will no longer compete but will share the same sky.

Poetic Movements

The papercuts illustrating the poetic interludes in this book are based on the *roiselech*, the traditional woman-made art. The circular design contains four intertwined roses, representing the four mothers of Judaism, in whose names girls are blessed each week by their parents. The words of this blessing are written around the outside of the circle: "May the Lord bless you like Sarah, Rebecca, Leah, and Rachel."

Cover

The papercut in the background of the cover and on the title page brings together many of the central motifs used throughout the illustrations in *Reading Ruth*: intertwined roses, cycles of the moon, grains of the harvest, and fruits of the land of Israel, two sets of eighteen fish (symbols of life and survival), and the verses of sections one and two.

Acknowledgments

We acknowledge with thanks the many people who encouraged us as we developed the idea for this book. We thank our agent Charlotte Sheedy, who immediately saw its value, and Joëlle Delbourgo of Ballantine Books, for her enthusiastic reception of our proposal. If not for the equally enthusiastic response of all the contributors to the volume, the proposal would have remained merely an idea. We are particularly grateful to Vanessa Ochs for connecting us to Avivah Zornberg and to Avivah for generously cooperating with our unconventional presentation of her work. Special thanks also to Merle Feld, Marianne Hirsch, and Nessa Rapoport for wise counsel and supportive friendship along the way. We happily acknowledge the interest and encouragement of many other friends, among them Joyce Antler, Bella Brodzki, Esther Broner, Edward Feld, Evelyn Fox-Keller, Carol Gilligan, Arthur Green, Patricia Herzog, Barry Holtz, Judy Hurwich, Rachel Jacoff, Norman Janis, Frances Malino, Lawrence Rosenwald, Margery Sabin, George Savran, Patricia Spacks, Shelly Tenenbaum, and Avi Weinstein. We received able editorial help from Abigail Gillman, Erica Brunwasser, and Maryanne Payne. David Tebaldi's flexibility enabled the book to be completed in a timely fashion. Joanne Wyckoff, our editor at Ballantine Books, has contributed enormously to the final shaping and presentation of this diverse collection of voices.

The Worship-Study Minyan at Harvard-Radcliffe Hillel not only drew us together but provided an atmosphere of serious and sympathetic study of Jewish texts that has supported our own commitments. And our most constant sustenance has come from our families, most especially from William Kates and Joseph Reimer, who have lovingly, with excitement and devotion, "gone where we have gone."

Introduction

At the end of this collection, Norma Rosen sets the stage for an intensely engaged encounter with the Book of Ruth:

> *Scene:* Five women, their ages spanning the decades from late twenties to fifties, are meeting in a Manhattan living room. It is early evening; they have carried coffee to chairs and sofa. Comfortable with one another, they are members of an ongoing group facetiously acronymed WGTDTB: Women Gathered to Deplore the Bible. One or two of them secretly wish the initials more innocently connoted Women Gathered to Discuss the Bible. However, when mailings went out under the latter rubric, too few responded.

Reading Ruth had its genesis in a Boston living room. We, like Rosen's characters, had been gathering for years with other women to create "a room of our own" in the house of study. As we came to feel more like permanent, albeit uneasy inhabitants, the time seemed ripe to begin filling its shelves with works of our own. Our call to women to join us in creating Jewish women's commentary based on serious study of a specific biblical text generated a level of excitement suggested by the number of pieces gathered in this collection.

The house of study, standing figuratively at the center of the Jewish religious and cultural tradition, beckons us as we affirm that tradition. Yet we understand that the biblical commentaries and interpretations that fill it represent the origins of Western cultural and religious traditions that exclude women's voices and therefore feel alien to women's experiences. No wonder Rosen's characters respond to the urge to "deplore" the Bible. How could mere "discussion" generate enthusiasm in women caught up in such tensions? Yet our involvement in communities of Jewish learning open to feminist and literary perspectives has convinced us that women do engage with full intensity in "discussion" that creates the possibility of new commentary based on serious study.

We began discussing the Bible over a dozen years ago. Though one of us was preparing for the bar mitzvah of her younger son and the other had just celebrated the naming of her first daughter, we were both struggling to shape Jewish lives informed by our feminist concerns. As women trained in academic literary study, we naturally gravitated to the study of texts. Allowing our own experiences and concerns to shape the questions we asked of the text, we began to discover women's voices where we had once heard only those of men. Listening to, responding to, and elaborating upon one another's interpretations we began to envision a gathering of Jewish women's interpretations of biblical texts through which we could claim the text as our own.

Although the texts of the Hebrew Bible have been shaped by male authors and editors, we believe that it is interpretive traditions more than biblical texts that leave women feeling excluded. Too often, women recognize ways in which a traditional text speaks to their experience as women, but when they turn to commentary, they find little that speaks to either their experiences as women or their experiences as women reading/confronting a biblical text. It is our hope that, just as Ruth enabled Naomi to read her life as full rather than barren, women who bring their own questions and points of view to the interpretive and hermeneutic process will enable other women to feel nourished by these texts. And by entering a twenty-five-hundred-year Jewish tradition of dynamic interaction with text through commentary and interpretation, Jewish women will redefine a space initially created by other hands, creating a space in which other women can feel they belong.

The Book of Ruth seems like a particularly fruitful place to begin to explore the riches women's points of view might yield when brought to bear on traditional Jewish texts. So many experiences, qualities, dilemmas, and issues traditionally of concern to women surface in this text. Its central figures are women, its central story (or stories) is relationship. It tells the story of marriage and childbirth, of widowhood and childlessness, from within women's experience. It evokes the experience of mothers and daughters, while highlighting the tensions in a mother-in-law's relationship to her daughter-in-law. It focuses on the experience of being "other"—the other as foreigner and the other as woman. It addresses the problems of women's powerlessness and vulnerability in a man's world and illustrates the power generated when women mobilize their resources. It is a story of women caring and women plotting, women mourning and women rejoicing. And perhaps more than anything else, the story is an emblem of women like ourselves seeking to feel at home in a patriarchal tradition and discovering support and sustenance in both the resources of that tradition and the voices of other women.

Focusing on Ruth seems especially appropriate because of its traditional connection to the central event of Jewish covenantal history, commemorated annually at the holiday of Shavuot: Matan Torah, the giving of the Torah to the entire Jewish people at Sinai. If we understand Torah, the gift of God "who brought you out of the land of Egypt," as directed centrally to the sustenance and liberation from suffering of the *ger, yatom, vealmana*—"the stranger, the orphan, and the widow"—then the Book of Ruth, the protagonists of which embody all those vulnerable figures, speaks to the essence of Torah. Its women characters challenge the Jewish world to live up to Torah ideals and, in so doing, make manifest to us what sort of society—what sort of people—Torah is supposed to create. By representing women at the heart of Torah, the Book of Ruth speaks particularly to the connection between women and traditional Jewish texts that we hope to foster in this book.

Text study, which for almost two thousand years has occupied the center of intellectual and spiritual life for Jewish men, has come to define a distinctively Jewish way of life. The traditional mode of study is graphically represented in the rabbinic edition of the Bible called Mikraot Gedolot (literally "big scriptures"). In its volumes, the biblical text is literally surrounded on the page by commentaries from many centuries engaged with every detail of the text and with each other. To study within such a tradition is to enter a room filled with intense conversation and take one's place at the table, listening and adding one's own voice in affirmation, disagreement, excitement. Revelations and insights are generated by the very process of interaction. But until now the occupants of the room have been male. We envision a new Mikraot Gedolot, in which the voices surrounding the text would include those of women and the conversation would include women's perspectives and interactions with the traditions of commentary.

To "deplore" the problem of sacred scriptures that seem to relegate

women's experiences to subordinate or marginal positions remains a first
step. But, as a number of contributors note, simply deploring leaves us
with a sense of loss, an uneasy awareness that potential connections to
a valued tradition are being abandoned. In this volume we move beyond that stage, not just to discussion, but to study. We offer the fruits
of women's scholarship, literary sensitivity, professional expertise, and
personal insight to enrich the ongoing process of interpretation through
which Jews have made the Bible a living text. The writers in this volume all engage with the Book of Ruth as modern women. A significant
number of them contrast their current interpretations to childhood
memories of a book they had dismissed as reinforcing repressive stereotypes of docile and angelically "good" women. In returning to the text
as adults, they have discovered in it complexities and depths that both
resonate with their own lives and render its teaching effective because it
springs from a more encompassing truth. Their experience might serve
as a paradigm for readers of this volume. The complexity and depth
created by the array of responses assembled here will, we hope, draw
women and men sensitive to women's concerns to new ways of perceiving not only the Book of Ruth but other biblical texts as well.

The writers we have gathered in this volume are all, to varying de-
grees, students of the Bible. Only a handful are what we might call
traditional students—scholars of Bible and/or Jewish studies or scholars
who devote a significant part of each day to Torah study. Others bring
to their readings the fruits of their work in women's studies, literary
studies, psychology, and sociology. Still others draw upon their professional and personal experience as psychiatrists and rabbis, mothers and
daughters, friends and lovers. All are Jewishly involved women who
have written in ways that indicate their interest and enthusiasm for
women's perspectives in Judaism. By including women from outside the
academy, we hope to provide models for thoughtful, engaged, lay
women to appropriate the sources of their tradition for themselves.

Reading Ruth brings together women from a wide spectrum of Jewish
practice and affiliation. It also brings together women who write in a
variety of forms. Thus, in addition to essays, we've included poetry,
autobiographical meditations, fiction, midrash, and other variations on
traditional Jewish forms. The collection opens with a verse-by-verse
commentary on Ruth modeled on that of the best-known medieval
commentator, Rashi. While adopting Rashi's method of posing to the

text questions raised by structure, grammar, word choice, etc., Ruth Sohn asks strikingly different questions and thus creates new interpretations. Later in the volume, we include an edited version of Avivah Zornberg's *shiur* (oral teaching), which offers an opportunity to observe a woman's refashioning of this traditional form of teaching through reflections on a classical Jewish text.

These new voices, speaking in both traditional and new modes, have been organized in a form inspired by the traditional Mikraot Gedolot. The aim of the collection is not to present a unified voice, but to surround the text with many different voices, allowing them to play off one another.

We begin with a woman's version of the traditional style of commentary because we intend to position this book as continuous yet innovative within the Jewish tradition. Norma Rosen's dramatic rendering of a women's study group, with which we close the volume, recapitulates the activity of the book, bringing together a range of women's voices discussing and interpreting the Book of Ruth. The almost ritualized affirmation and celebration of women's engagement with the Bible that closes Rosen's drama seems an appropriate finale for *Reading Ruth.*

Within this frame we have organized the pieces into seven sections, each of which develops a theme or motif suggested by a specific verse (or partial verse), from the Book of Ruth. Although most pieces engage the Book of Ruth as a whole, we have drawn a connection between each author's central focus or approach and one particular verse. At the start of each section we briefly discuss the interrelationships we see among the pieces in that section and its particular verse. Two creative interludes surround section 4.

The sections follow the sequence of verses as they appear in Ruth, yet readers will notice that six of the seven quotations are from the first and fourth chapters. This reflects a collective revision of the usual focus of interpretation of the Book of Ruth. The central relationship for almost all our writers is not that between Ruth and Boaz, but that between Ruth and Naomi. Daughter-in-law and mother-in-law, two women who care for each other, displace the more common Western love story of older man marrying younger woman. We consider this shift of focus one of the most striking results of our invitation to women to interpret this text.

The verses that structure our book are not always verses that have engaged commentators in the past. And even those verses that have received considerable attention in traditional commentary are illuminated here in new ways. Women found special resonance in the phrase "but Ruth clung to her" (Ruth 1:14). This verse inspires a series of pieces on friendship, including both Gloria Goldreich's novelistic re-creation of the friendships among Ruth, Orpah, and Naomi, and Ruth Anna Putnam's philosophical investigation of the nature of friendship in the Bible.

As we might expect, the most famous verse in the book, perhaps in the whole Bible, "For wherever you go, I will go," stirs the interest and imagination of several contributors. All return the verse to its original context and insist on the significance of these words being spoken by one woman to another. Yet for each writer, the identity of the women and what they represent is different.

Naomi's bitter cry, "I went away full, and the Lord has brought me back empty," creates the central motif of the third section, which brings together a group of writers who read Ruth as a story of women's responses to loss. The fourth section takes its title from Boaz's praise of Ruth, "Your latest deed of *chesed* [lovingkindness] is greater than the first." It includes pieces that bring a variety of women's perspectives to the understanding of "lovingkindness," traditionally considered the central value taught by the Book of Ruth.

Around the marriage blessing that invokes other biblical narratives, "May the Lord make the woman who is coming into your house like Rachel and Leah, both of whom built up the House of Israel," we bring together several essays connecting the Book of Ruth to narrative and thematic patterns in the Bible as a whole. The surprising statement by the women of Bethlehem after Ruth gives birth, "A son is born to Naomi," arouses contradictory responses regarding women's self-sacrifice and self-assertion in relationships.

For the title of the seventh section we bring together phrases from chapter 1 and chapter 4—"Ruth the Moabite [1:22] . . . begot David [4:22]." We purposely disturb the sequence of the actual text, which ends with a male genealogy from which women's names and roles have been erased. Our gerrymandered verse restores Ruth to her central position, as do the essays in this section which focus on the connections between Ruth's Moabite origins and her place in the engendering of the Messiah, envisioned by Jewish tradition as the descendant of David.

This restoration of Ruth's centrality, like the emphasis on the relationship of Ruth and Naomi, reveals how women's commentary gives voice to experiences which have been marginalized, ignored, or subordinated. Readers of this collection are likely to find unexpected and provocative new readings. For instance, Lois Dubin combines traditional commentary with lyric meditation to read Naomi as a female Job, probing the depths of female suffering. She sees Naomi's pain and feelings of "emptiness" as inextricably linked to Naomi's physical body, a body intended to be fertile and produce offspring. Naomi's pain is the pain of women—women who have suffered infertility, loss of a pregnancy, or loss of childbearing capacity in menopause. Women reading Ruth, Dubin and others suggest, may find in it a story that speaks to experiences of our own bodies.

While a focus on Naomi puts the desire for offspring at the heart of the book, a focus on Ruth leads to a radically different understanding of what women want. For Gail Reimer, Ruth stands out from other biblical heroines because of her singular lack of interest in motherhood. Reimer questions the conflation of Naomi and Ruth, and carefully distinguishes between the maternal desires of the one and the desires for sisterhood of the other. Implicit in her reading is a celebration of a text that can allow two strikingly different versions of women's desire to coexist.

Other writers emphasize the centrality of women to the biblical vision of continuity and intergenerational survival. While commentary has emphasized the Book of Ruth's representation of *chesed* (lovingkindness) as a central value, shifting the focus to Ruth and Naomi's relationship allows several writers to examine versions of *chesed* that grow out of mutuality, rather than the more hierarchical relationship of benefactor and recipient.

Women's commentary also brings the other women in the story into the foreground. The women of Bethlehem become more than a traditional chorus. As Patricia Karlin-Neumann understands them, for example, these women play a pivotal role in Naomi's healing, providing her with the living community necessary to draw a mourner back from her immersion in death and loss.

Allusions in the text of Ruth to other women in the Bible draw the attention of a number of our writers. They demonstrate the significance within the Book of Ruth and the Jewish tradition as a whole, of the troubling and often suppressed stories of Tamar's seduction of Judah and the incest initiated by the daughters of Lot. One emerges from their essays with radically new understandings of biblical stories, heroes, and heroines. Even a well-known story like that of Rachel and Leah looks different after Francine Klagsbrun reveals the complexity of the relationship between the two sisters. We recognize that what has traditionally been read as a predominantly competitive relationship is also filled with mutual understanding and shared goals.

The collection of women's voices addressing a single text occupies a special place in contemporary feminist criticism. Essay collections have become an established genre of feminist analysis and one to which readers interested in feminist issues have grown accustomed. Most collections involve a number of women looking at a variety of texts. What happens, we asked ourselves, when a group of women focuses on one text? Our collection, by focusing on a single book of the Bible, embodies and verifies a familiar axiom of feminist criticism, namely, that when women are involved, reading is not a singular enterprise. Among other things, this volume demonstrates that there is indeed a multiplicity of voices. Not only do our writers have strikingly different things to say, but they say them in diverse forms. While many present their readings in the familiar form of the essay, others like Gloria Goldreich retell the story in narrative, like Barbara Helfgott Hyett retell part of it in poetry, or like Sylvia Rothchild reflect upon it through memoir.

In recent years we have witnessed a renaissance of interest in the Bible. For intellectuals seeking traditional moorings for their personal lives, and literary critics working within the academy, the Bible has become a touchstone against which theoretical and personal beliefs and commitments are measured and understood. For the common reader the Bible has become a place where s/he can search for personal meanings.

By opening the interpretive tradition to the voices of those who have not been heard, a collection like this offers women and men the possibility of finding new meanings in a biblical book and provides a model to those looking for alternative pathways into the Bible. For people who have been stimulated by secular literary critics or who take an interest in how contemporary writers or thinkers engage with the Bible, this volume's diversity of voices and genres responds to that interest. People grappling with questions related to women and Judaism and the host of Jews and non-Jews looking for women-centered interpretations of texts can find a wealth of interpretive possibilities here.

In addition Jewish women and men encounter the Book of Ruth annually during the holiday of Shavuot, the festival of the Jewish year on which this text is traditionally read. This collection offers guidance to synagogue and adult education groups, as well as to individual learners, and stimulates consideration of the place of this book in the biblical canon, its role in Jewish liturgy, and the role of women in interpreting the books of the Bible.

Given the diversity of perspectives and approaches collected in this volume, readers of all kinds can expect to discover new meanings. While the book can be read from cover to cover, we believe it is best savored in small sections. We have designed the sections as discrete units, although we use the introduction to each section to point to related pieces elsewhere in the collection. Reading a whole section will enable the reader to hear the interplay of voices that mirrors the traditional Mikraot Gedolot, the rabbinic Bible with commentaries. Nevertheless each individual piece stands on its own and will draw the reader into new interpretive possibilities.

Women readers, in particular, are likely to be surprised by the many and different ways in which these women-centered readings resonate with their experiences. And we hope that the excitement generated by women who expand the questions and subjects of textual commentary will encourage them to engage more freely and fully in study that leads to their own discoveries.

Reading Ruth

The Book of Ruth

RUTH

Iɴ the days when the chieftains ruled, there was a famine in the land; and a man of Bethlehem in Judah, with his wife and two sons, went to reside in the country of Moab. ²The man's name was Elimelech, his wife's name was Naomi, and his two sons were named Mahlon and Chilion—Ephrathites of Bethlehem in Judah. They came to the country of Moab and remained there.

³Elimelech, Naomi's husband, died; and she was left with her two sons. ⁴They married Moabite women, one named Orpah and the other Ruth, and they lived there about ten years. ⁵Then those two—Mahlon and Chilion—also died; so the woman was left without her two sons and without her husband.

⁶She started out with her daughters-in-law to return from the country of Moab; for in the country of Moab she had heard that the Lᴏʀᴅ had taken note of His people and given them food. ⁷Accompanied by her two daughters-in-law, she left the place where she had been living; and they set out on the road back to the land of Judah.

⁸But Naomi said to her two daughters-in-law, "Turn back, each of you to her mother's house. May the Lᴏʀᴅ deal kindly with you, as you have dealt with the dead and with me! ⁹May the Lᴏʀᴅ grant that each of you find security in the house of a husband!" And she kissed them farewell. They broke into weeping ¹⁰and said to her, "No, we will return with you to your people."

¹¹But Naomi replied, "Turn back, my daughters! Why should you go with me?

This translation of the Book of Ruth is reprinted from *The Five Megilloth and Jonah* (Philadelphia: Jewish Publication Society, 1969). Many of the contributors to this volume quote other published translations or have consulted other translations in preparing their own; the sources each author has used are identified in a footnote at the beginning of her selection.

רות
RUTH

1 וַיְהִ֗י בִּימֵי֙ שְׁפֹ֣ט הַשֹּׁפְטִ֔ים וַיְהִ֥י רָעָ֖ב בָּאָ֑רֶץ וַיֵּ֨לֶךְ אִ֜ישׁ מִבֵּ֧ית לֶ֣חֶם יְהוּדָ֗ה לָגוּר֙ בִּשְׂדֵ֣י מוֹאָ֔ב
2 ה֥וּא וְאִשְׁתּ֖וֹ וּשְׁנֵ֥י בָנָֽיו׃ וְשֵׁ֣ם הָאִ֣ישׁ אֱ‍ֽלִימֶ֡לֶךְ וְשֵׁם֩ אִשְׁתּ֨וֹ נׇעֳמִ֜י וְשֵׁ֥ם שְׁנֵֽי־בָנָ֣יו ׀ מַחְל֤וֹן וְכִלְיוֹן֙ אֶפְרָתִ֔ים מִבֵּ֥ית לֶ֖חֶם יְהוּדָ֑ה וַיָּבֹ֥אוּ שְׂדֵי־מוֹאָ֖ב
3 וַיִּֽהְיוּ־שָֽׁם׃ וַיָּ֥מׇת אֱלִימֶ֖לֶךְ אִ֣ישׁ נׇעֳמִ֑י וַתִּשָּׁאֵ֥ר הִ֖יא וּשְׁנֵ֥י
4 בָנֶֽיהָ׃ וַיִּשְׂא֣וּ לָהֶ֗ם נָשִׁים֙ מֹֽאֲבִיּ֔וֹת שֵׁ֤ם הָֽאַחַת֙ עׇרְפָּ֔ה וְשֵׁ֥ם הַשֵּׁנִ֖ית ר֑וּת וַיֵּ֥שְׁבוּ שָׁ֖ם
5 כְּעֶ֥שֶׂר שָׁנִֽים׃ וַיָּמ֥וּתוּ גַם־שְׁנֵיהֶ֖ם מַחְל֣וֹן וְכִלְי֑וֹן וַתִּשָּׁאֵר֙ הָֽאִשָּׁ֔ה מִשְּׁנֵ֥י יְלָדֶ֖יהָ וּמֵאִישָֽׁהּ׃
6 וַתָּ֤קׇם הִיא֙ וְכַלֹּתֶ֔יהָ וַתָּ֖שׇב מִשְּׂדֵ֣י מוֹאָ֑ב כִּ֤י שָֽׁמְעָה֙ בִּשְׂדֵ֣ה מוֹאָ֔ב כִּֽי־פָקַ֤ד יְהֹוָה֙ אֶת־
7 עַמּ֔וֹ לָתֵ֥ת לָהֶ֖ם לָֽחֶם׃ וַתֵּצֵ֗א מִן־הַמָּקוֹם֙ אֲשֶׁ֣ר הָיְתָה־שָּׁ֔מָּה וּשְׁתֵּ֥י כַלֹּתֶ֖יהָ עִמָּ֑הּ וַתֵּלַ֣כְנָה בַדֶּ֔רֶךְ לָשׁ֖וּב אֶל־
8 אֶ֥רֶץ יְהוּדָֽה׃ וַתֹּ֤אמֶר נׇעֳמִי֙ לִשְׁתֵּ֣י כַלֹּתֶ֔יהָ לֵ֣כְנָה שֹּׁ֔בְנָה אִשָּׁ֖ה לְבֵ֣ית אִמָּ֑הּ יעש יַ֣עַשׂ יְהֹוָ֤ה עִמָּכֶם֙ חֶ֔סֶד כַּֽאֲשֶׁ֧ר עֲשִׂיתֶ֛ם
9 עִם־הַמֵּתִ֖ים וְעִמָּדִֽי׃ יִתֵּ֤ן יְהֹוָה֙ לָכֶ֔ם וּמְצֶ֣אןָ מְנוּחָ֔ה אִשָּׁ֖ה בֵּ֣ית אִישָׁ֑הּ וַתִּשַּׁ֣ק לָהֶ֔ן וַתִּשֶּׂ֥אנָה
10 קוֹלָ֖ן וַתִּבְכֶּֽינָה׃ וַתֹּאמַ֖רְנָה־לָּ֑הּ כִּי־אִתָּ֥ךְ נָשׁ֖וּב לְעַמֵּֽךְ׃
11 וַתֹּ֤אמֶר נׇעֳמִי֙ שֹּׁ֣בְנָה בְנֹתַ֔י לָ֥מָּה

5

Have I any more sons in my body, who might be husbands for you? ¹²Turn back, my daughters, for I am too old to be married. Even if I thought there was hope for me, even if I were married tonight and I also bore sons, ¹³should you wait for them to grow up? Should you on their account debar yourselves from marriage? Oh no, my daughters! My lot is far more bitter than yours, for the hand of the LORD has struck out against me."

¹⁴They broke into weeping again, and Orpah kissed her mother-in-law farewell. But Ruth clung to her. ¹⁵So she said, "See, your sister-in-law has returned to her people and her gods. Go follow your sister-in-law." ¹⁶But Ruth replied, "Do not urge me to leave you, to turn back and not follow you. For wherever you go, I will go; wherever you lodge, I will lodge; your people shall be my people, and your God my God. ¹⁷Where you die, I will die, and there I will be buried. Thus and more may the LORD do to me if anything but death parts me from you." ¹⁸When [Naomi] saw how determined she was to go with her, she ceased to argue with her; ¹⁹and the two went on until they reached Bethlehem.

When they arrived in Bethlehem, the whole city buzzed with excitement over them. The women said, "Can this be Naomi?" ²⁰"Do not call me Naomi," she replied. "Call me Mara, for Shaddai has made my lot very bitter. ²¹I went away full, and the LORD has brought me back empty. How can you call me Naomi, when the LORD has

רות
RUTH
1.12

הֲלָהֵן עַמִּי הָעוֹד־לִי בָנִים
בְּמֵעַי וְהָיוּ לָכֶם לַאֲנָשִׁים:
¹² שֹׁבְנָה בְנֹתַי לֵכְןָ כִּי זָקַנְתִּי
מִהְיוֹת לְאִישׁ כִּי אָמַרְתִּי יֶשׁ־
לִי תִקְוָה גַּם הָיִיתִי הַלַּיְלָה
לְאִישׁ וְגַם יָלַדְתִּי בָנִים:
¹³ הֲלָהֵן ׀ תְּשַׂבֵּרְנָה עַד אֲשֶׁר
יִגְדָּלוּ הֲלָהֵן תֵּעָגֵנָה לְבִלְתִּי
הֱיוֹת לְאִישׁ אַל בְּנֹתַי כִּי־
מַר־לִי מְאֹד מִכֶּם כִּי־יָצְאָה
¹⁴ בִי יַד־יְהֹוָה: וַתִּשֶּׂנָה קוֹלָן
וַתִּבְכֶּינָה עוֹד וַתִּשַּׁק עָרְפָּה
לַחֲמוֹתָהּ וְרוּת דָּבְקָה־בָּהּ:
¹⁵ וַתֹּאמֶר הִנֵּה שָׁבָה יְבִמְתֵּךְ
אֶל־עַמָּהּ וְאֶל־אֱלֹהֶיהָ שׁוּבִי
¹⁶ אַחֲרֵי יְבִמְתֵּךְ: וַתֹּאמֶר רוּת
אַל־תִּפְגְּעִי־בִי לְעָזְבֵךְ
לָשׁוּב מֵאַחֲרָיִךְ כִּי אֶל־אֲשֶׁר
תֵּלְכִי אֵלֵךְ וּבַאֲשֶׁר תָּלִינִי
אָלִין עַמֵּךְ עַמִּי וֵאלֹהַיִךְ
¹⁷ אֱלֹהָי: בַּאֲשֶׁר תָּמוּתִי אָמוּת
וְשָׁם אֶקָּבֵר כֹּה יַעֲשֶׂה יְהֹוָה
לִי וְכֹה יֹסִיף כִּי הַמָּוֶת יַפְרִיד
¹⁸ בֵּינִי וּבֵינֵךְ: וַתֵּרֶא כִּי־
מִתְאַמֶּצֶת הִיא לָלֶכֶת אִתָּהּ
וַתֶּחְדַּל לְדַבֵּר אֵלֶיהָ:
¹⁹ וַתֵּלַכְנָה שְׁתֵּיהֶם עַד־בֹּאֲנָה
בֵּית לָחֶם וַיְהִי כְּבֹאֲנָה בֵּית
לֶחֶם וַתֵּהֹם כָּל־הָעִיר עֲלֵיהֶן
וַתֹּאמַרְנָה הֲזֹאת נָעֳמִי:
²⁰ וַתֹּאמֶר אֲלֵיהֶן אַל־תִּקְרֶאנָה
לִי נָעֳמִי קְרֶאןָ לִי מָרָא כִּי־
²¹ הֵמַר שַׁדַּי לִי מְאֹד: אֲנִי
מְלֵאָה הָלַכְתִּי וְרֵיקָם הֱשִׁיבַנִי

dealt harshly with me, when Shaddai has brought misfortune upon me!"

²²Thus Naomi returned from the country of Moab; she returned with her daughter-in-law, Ruth the Moabite. They arrived in Bethlehem at the beginning of the barley harvest.

2 Now Naomi had a kinsman on her husband's side, a man of substance, of the family of Elimelech, whose name was Boaz.

²Ruth the Moabite said to Naomi, "I would like to go to the fields and glean among the ears of grain, behind someone who may show me kindness." "Yes, daughter, go," she replied; ³and off she went. She came and gleaned in a field, behind the reapers; and as luck would have it, it was the piece of land belonging to Boaz, who was of Elimelech's family.

⁴Presently Boaz arrived from Bethlehem. He greeted the reapers, "The LORD be with you!" And they responded, "The LORD bless you!" ⁵Boaz said to the servant who was in charge of the reapers, "Whose girl is that?" ⁶The servant in charge of the reapers replied, "She is a Moabite girl who came back with Naomi from the country of Moab. ⁷She said, 'Please let me glean and gather among the sheaves behind the reapers.' She has been on her feet ever since she came this morning. She has rested but little in the hut."

⁸Boaz said to Ruth, "Listen to me, daughter. Don't go to glean in another field. Don't go elsewhere, but stay here close to my girls.

רות
Ruth
1.22

א יְהֹוָה לָמָּה תִקְרֶאנָה לִי נָעֳמִי וַיהֹוָה עָנָה בִי וְשַׁדַּי הֵרַֽע־ 22 לִי: וַתָּשָׁב נָעֳמִי וְרוּת הַמּוֹאֲבִיָּה כַלָּתָהּ עִמָּהּ הַשָּׁבָה מִשְּׂדֵי מוֹאָב וְהֵמָּה בָּאוּ בֵּית לֶחֶם בִּתְחִלַּת קְצִיר שְׂעֹרִים:

ב א וּֽלְנָעֳמִי מוֹדַע לְאִישָׁהּ אִישׁ גִּבּוֹר חַיִל מִמִּשְׁפַּחַת אֱלִימֶלֶךְ 2 וּשְׁמוֹ בֹּֽעַז: וַתֹּאמֶר רוּת הַמּוֹאֲבִיָּה אֶל־נָעֳמִי אֵלְכָה־ נָּא הַשָּׂדֶה וַאֲלַקֳטָה בַשִׁבֳּלִים אַחַר אֲשֶׁר אֶמְצָא־חֵן בְּעֵינָיו 3 וַתֹּאמֶר לָהּ לְכִי בִתִּי: וַתֵּלֶךְ וַתָּבוֹא וַתְּלַקֵּט בַּשָּׂדֶה אַחֲרֵי הַקֹּצְרִים וַיִּקֶר מִקְרֶהָ חֶלְקַת הַשָּׂדֶה לְבֹעַז אֲשֶׁר מִמִּשְׁפַּחַת 4 אֱלִימֶֽלֶךְ: וְהִנֵּה־בֹעַז בָּא מִבֵּית לֶחֶם וַיֹּאמֶר לַקּוֹצְרִים יְהֹוָה עִמָּכֶם וַיֹּאמְרוּ לוֹ 5 יְבָרֶכְךָ יְהֹוָה: וַיֹּאמֶר בֹּעַז לְנַעֲרוֹ הַנִּצָּב עַל־הַקּוֹצְרִים 6 לְמִי הַנַּעֲרָה הַזֹּאת: וַיַּעַן הַנַּעַר הַנִּצָּב עַל־הַקּוֹצְרִים וַיֹּאמַר נַעֲרָה מוֹאֲבִיָּה הִיא הַשָּׁבָה עִם־נָעֳמִי מִשְּׂדֵי 7 מוֹאָב: וַתֹּאמֶר אֲלַקֳטָה־נָּא וְאָסַפְתִּי בָעֳמָרִים אַחֲרֵי הַקּוֹצְרִים וַתָּבוֹא וַתַּעֲמוֹד מֵאָז הַבֹּקֶר וְעַד־עַתָּה זֶה 8 שִׁבְתָּהּ הַבַּיִת מְעָֽט: וַיֹּאמֶר בֹּעַז אֶל־רוּת הֲלוֹא שָׁמַעַתְּ בִּתִּי אַל־תֵּלְכִי לִלְקֹט בְּשָׂדֶה אַחֵר וְגַם לֹא תַעֲבוּרִי מִזֶּה

⁹Keep your eyes on the field they are reaping, and follow them. I have ordered the men not to molest you. And when you are thirsty, go to the jars and drink some of [the water] that the men have drawn."

¹⁰She prostrated herself with her face to the ground, and said to him, "Why are you so kind as to single me out, when I am a foreigner?"

¹¹Boaz said in reply, "I have been told of all that you did for your mother-in-law after the death of your husband, how you left your father and mother and the land of your birth and came to a people you had not known before. ¹²May the LORD reward your deeds. May you have a full recompense from the LORD, the God of Israel, under whose wings you have sought refuge!"

¹³She answered, "You are most kind, my lord, to comfort me and to speak gently to your maidservant—though I am not so much as one of your maidservants."

¹⁴At mealtime, Boaz said to her, "Come over here and partake of the meal, and dip your morsel in the vinegar." So she sat down beside the reapers. He handed her roasted grain, and she ate her fill and had some left over.

¹⁵When she got up again to glean, Boaz gave orders to his workers, "You are not only to let her glean among the sheaves, without interference, ¹⁶but you must also pull some [stalks] out of the heaps and leave them for her to glean, and not scold her."

וְכֹה תִדְבָּקִין עִם־נַעֲרֹתָי:

9 עֵינַיִךְ בַּשָּׂדֶה אֲשֶׁר־יִקְצֹרוּן
וְהָלַכְתְּ אַחֲרֵיהֶן הֲלוֹא צִוִּיתִי
אֶת־הַנְּעָרִים לְבִלְתִּי נָגְעֵךְ
וְצָמִת וְהָלַכְתְּ אֶל־הַכֵּלִים
וְשָׁתִית מֵאֲשֶׁר יִשְׁאֲבוּן
10 הַנְּעָרִים: וַתִּפֹּל עַל־פָּנֶיהָ
וַתִּשְׁתַּחוּ אָרְצָה וַתֹּאמֶר אֵלָיו
מַדּוּעַ מָצָאתִי חֵן בְּעֵינֶיךָ
11 לְהַכִּירֵנִי וְאָנֹכִי נָכְרִיָּה: וַיַּעַן
בֹּעַז וַיֹּאמֶר לָהּ הֻגֵּד הֻגַּד לִי
כֹּל אֲשֶׁר־עָשִׂית אֶת־חֲמוֹתֵךְ
אַחֲרֵי מוֹת אִישֵׁךְ וַתַּעַזְבִי
אָבִיךְ וְאִמֵּךְ וְאֶרֶץ מוֹלַדְתֵּךְ
וַתֵּלְכִי אֶל־עַם אֲשֶׁר לֹא־
12 יָדַעַתְּ תְּמוֹל שִׁלְשׁוֹם: יְשַׁלֵּם
יְהוָה פָּעֳלֵךְ וּתְהִי מַשְׂכֻּרְתֵּךְ
שְׁלֵמָה מֵעִם יְהוָה אֱלֹהֵי
יִשְׂרָאֵל אֲשֶׁר־בָּאת לַחֲסוֹת
13 תַּחַת־כְּנָפָיו: וַתֹּאמֶר
אֶמְצָא־חֵן בְּעֵינֶיךָ אֲדֹנִי כִּי
נִחַמְתָּנִי וְכִי דִבַּרְתָּ עַל־לֵב
שִׁפְחָתֶךָ וְאָנֹכִי לֹא אֶהְיֶה
14 כְּאַחַת שִׁפְחֹתֶךָ: וַיֹּאמֶר לָהּ
בֹּעַז לְעֵת הָאֹכֶל גֹּשִׁי הֲלֹם
וְאָכַלְתְּ מִן־הַלֶּחֶם וְטָבַלְתְּ
פִּתֵּךְ בַּחֹמֶץ וַתֵּשֶׁב מִצַּד
הַקֹּצְרִים וַיִּצְבָּט־לָהּ קָלִי
וַתֹּאכַל וַתִּשְׂבַּע וַתֹּתַר:
15 וַתָּקָם לְלַקֵּט וַיְצַו בֹּעַז אֶת־
נְעָרָיו לֵאמֹר גַּם בֵּין הָעֳמָרִים
16 תְּלַקֵּט וְלֹא תַכְלִימוּהָ: וְגַם
שֹׁל־תָּשֹׁלּוּ לָהּ מִן־הַצְּבָתִים
וַעֲזַבְתֶּם וְלִקְּטָה וְלֹא תִגְעֲרוּ־

17She gleaned in the field until evening. Then she beat out what she had gleaned—it was about an *ephah* of barley—18and carried it back with her to the town. When her mother-in-law saw what she had gleaned, and when she also took out and gave her what she had left over after eating her fill, 19her mother-in-law asked her, "Where did you glean today? Where did you work? Blessed be he who took such generous notice of you!" So she told her mother-in-law whom she had worked with, saying, "The name of the man with whom I worked today is Boaz."

20Naomi said to her daughter-in-law, "Blessed be he of the LORD, who has not failed in His kindness to the living or to the dead! For," Naomi explained to her daughter-in-law, "the man is related to us; he is one of our redeeming kinsmen." 21Ruth the Moabite said, "He even told me, 'Stay close by my workers until all my harvest is finished.' " 22And Naomi answered her daughter-in-law Ruth, "It is best, daughter, that you go out with his girls, and not be annoyed in some other field." 23So she stayed close to the maidservants of Boaz, and gleaned until the barley harvest and the wheat harvest were finished. Then she stayed at home with her mother-in-law.

3 Naomi, her mother-in-law, said to her, "Daughter, I must seek a home for you, where you may be happy. 2Now there is our kinsman Boaz, whose girls you were close to. He will be winnowing barley on the thresh-

17 בָּהּ: וַתְּלַקֵּט בַּשָּׂדֶה עַד־
הָעֶרֶב וַתַּחְבֹּט אֵת אֲשֶׁר־
לִקֵּטָה וַיְהִי כְּאֵיפָה שְׂעֹרִים:
18 וַתִּשָּׂא וַתָּבוֹא הָעִיר וַתֵּרֶא
חֲמוֹתָהּ אֵת אֲשֶׁר־לִקֵּטָה
וַתּוֹצֵא וַתִּתֶּן־לָהּ אֵת אֲשֶׁר־
19 הוֹתִרָה מִשָּׂבְעָהּ: וַתֹּאמֶר לָהּ
חֲמוֹתָהּ אֵיפֹה לִקַּטְתְּ הַיּוֹם
וְאָנָה עָשִׂית יְהִי מַכִּירֵךְ בָּרוּךְ
וַתַּגֵּד לַחֲמוֹתָהּ אֵת אֲשֶׁר־
עָשְׂתָה עִמּוֹ וַתֹּאמֶר שֵׁם הָאִישׁ
אֲשֶׁר עָשִׂיתִי עִמּוֹ הַיּוֹם בֹּעַז:
20 וַתֹּאמֶר נָעֳמִי לְכַלָּתָהּ בָּרוּךְ
הוּא לַיהוָה אֲשֶׁר לֹא־עָזַב
חַסְדּוֹ אֶת־הַחַיִּים וְאֶת־
הַמֵּתִים וַתֹּאמֶר לָהּ נָעֳמִי
קָרוֹב לָנוּ הָאִישׁ מִגֹּאֲלֵנוּ
21 הוּא: וַתֹּאמֶר רוּת הַמּוֹאֲבִיָּה
גַּם כִּי־אָמַר אֵלַי עִם־
הַנְּעָרִים אֲשֶׁר־לִי תִּדְבָּקִין
עַד אִם־כִּלּוּ אֵת כָּל־הַקָּצִיר
22 אֲשֶׁר־לִי: וַתֹּאמֶר נָעֳמִי אֶל־
רוּת כַּלָּתָהּ טוֹב בִּתִּי כִּי תֵצְאִי
עִם־נַעֲרוֹתָיו וְלֹא יִפְגְּעוּ־בָךְ
23 בְּשָׂדֶה אַחֵר: וַתִּדְבַּק
בְּנַעֲרוֹת בֹּעַז לְלַקֵּט עַד־
כְּלוֹת קְצִיר־הַשְּׂעֹרִים וּקְצִיר
הַחִטִּים וַתֵּשֶׁב אֶת־חֲמוֹתָהּ:

1 וַתֹּאמֶר לָהּ נָעֳמִי חֲמוֹתָהּ בִּתִּי ג
הֲלֹא אֲבַקֶּשׁ־לָךְ מָנוֹחַ אֲשֶׁר
2 יִיטַב־לָךְ: וְעַתָּה הֲלֹא בֹעַז
מֹדַעְתָּנוּ אֲשֶׁר הָיִית אֶת־
נַעֲרוֹתָיו הִנֵּה־הוּא זֹרֶה

ing floor tonight. ³So bathe, anoint yourself, dress up, and go down to the threshing floor. But do not disclose yourself to the man until he has finished eating and drinking. ⁴When he lies down, note the place where he lies down, and go over and uncover his feet and lie down. He will tell you what you are to do." ⁵She replied, "I will do everything you tell me."

⁶She went down to the threshing floor and did just as her mother-in-law had instructed her. ⁷Boaz ate and drank, and in a cheerful mood went to lie down beside the grainpile. Then she went over stealthily and uncovered his feet and lay down. ⁸In the middle of the night, the man gave a start and pulled back—there was a woman lying at his feet!

⁹"Who are you?" he asked. And she replied, "I am your handmaid Ruth. Spread your robe over your handmaid, for you are a redeeming kinsman."

¹⁰He exclaimed, "Be blessed of the LORD, daughter! Your latest deed of loyalty is greater than the first, in that you have not turned to younger men, whether poor or rich. ¹¹And now, daughter, have no fear. I will do in your behalf whatever you ask, for all the elders of my town know what a fine woman you are. ¹²But while it is true I am a redeeming kinsman, there is another redeemer closer than I. ¹³Stay for the night. Then in the morning, if he will act as a redeemer, good! let him redeem. But if he does not want to act as redeemer for you, I will do so myself, as the LORD lives! Lie down until morning."

רוּת
Ruth
3.3

אֶת־גֹּ֥רֶן הַשְּׂעֹרִ֖ים הַלָּֽיְלָה׃

³ וְרָחַ֣צְתְּ ׀ וָסַ֗כְתְּ וְשַׂ֧מְתְּ שִׂמְלֹתַ֛יִךְ עָלַ֖יִךְ וְיָרַ֣דְתְּ הַגֹּ֑רֶן אַל־תִּוָּדְעִ֣י לָאִ֔ישׁ עַ֥ד כַּלֹּת֖וֹ

⁴ לֶאֱכֹ֥ל וְלִשְׁתּֽוֹת׃ וִיהִ֣י בְשָׁכְב֗וֹ וְיָדַ֙עַתְּ֙ אֶת־הַמָּקוֹם֙ אֲשֶׁ֣ר יִשְׁכַּב־שָׁ֔ם וּבָ֛את וְגִלִּ֥ית מַרְגְּלֹתָ֖יו וְשָׁכָ֑בְתְּ וְהוּא֙ יַגִּ֣יד

⁵ לָ֔ךְ אֵ֖ת אֲשֶׁ֥ר תַּעֲשִֽׂין׃ וַתֹּ֖אמֶר אֵלֶ֑יהָ כֹּ֛ל אֲשֶׁר־תֹּאמְרִ֥י ֵ ֵ ׃

⁶ אֶֽעֱשֶֽׂה׃ וַתֵּ֖רֶד הַגֹּ֑רֶן וַתַּ֕עַשׂ כְּכֹ֥ל אֲשֶׁר־צִוַּ֖תָּה חֲמוֹתָֽהּ׃

⁷ וַיֹּ֨אכַל בֹּ֜עַז וַיֵּ֤שְׁתְּ וַיִּיטַ֣ב לִבּ֔וֹ וַיָּבֹ֕א לִשְׁכַּ֖ב בִּקְצֵ֣ה הָעֲרֵמָ֑ה וַתָּבֹ֣א בַלָּ֔ט וַתְּגַ֥ל מַרְגְּלֹתָ֖יו

⁸ וַתִּשְׁכָּֽב׃ וַיְהִי֙ בַּחֲצִ֣י הַלַּ֔יְלָה וַיֶּחֱרַ֥ד הָאִ֖ישׁ וַיִּלָּפֵ֑ת וְהִנֵּ֣ה

⁹ אִשָּׁ֔ה שֹׁכֶ֖בֶת מַרְגְּלֹתָֽיו׃ וַיֹּ֖אמֶר מִי־אָ֑תְּ וַתֹּ֗אמֶר אָנֹכִי֙ ר֣וּת אֲמָתֶ֔ךָ וּפָרַשְׂתָּ֤ כְנָפֶ֙ךָ֙ עַל־

¹⁰ אֲמָ֣תְךָ֔ כִּ֥י גֹאֵ֖ל אָֽתָּה׃ וַיֹּ֗אמֶר בְּרוּכָ֨ה אַ֤תְּ לַֽיהוָה֙ בִּתִּ֔י הֵיטַ֛בְתְּ חַסְדֵּ֥ךְ הָאַחֲר֖וֹן מִן־הָרִאשׁ֑וֹן לְבִלְתִּי־לֶ֗כֶת אַחֲרֵי֙ הַבַּ֣חוּרִ֔ים אִם־דַּ֖ל וְאִם־

¹¹ עָשִֽׁיר׃ וְעַתָּ֗ה בִּתִּי֙ אַל־תִּ֣ירְאִ֔י כֹּ֥ל אֲשֶׁר־תֹּאמְרִ֖י אֶֽעֱשֶׂה־לָּ֑ךְ כִּ֤י יוֹדֵ֙עַ֙ כָּל־שַׁ֣עַר עַמִּ֔י כִּ֛י אֵ֥שֶׁת חַ֖יִל אָֽתְּ׃

¹² וְעַתָּה֙ כִּ֣י אָמְנָ֔ם כִּ֥י אִ֛ם גֹּאֵ֖ל אָנֹ֑כִי וְגַ֛ם יֵ֥שׁ גֹּאֵ֖ל קָר֥וֹב מִמֶּֽנִּי׃

¹³ לִ֣ינִי ׀ הַלַּ֗יְלָה וְהָיָ֤ה בַבֹּ֙קֶר֙ אִם־יִגְאָלֵ֥ךְ טוֹב֙ יִגְאָ֔ל וְאִם־לֹ֨א יַחְפֹּ֤ץ לְגָֽאֳלֵ֗ךְ

¹⁴So she lay at his feet until dawn. She rose before one person could distinguish another, for he thought, "Let it not be known that the woman came to the threshing floor." ¹⁵And he said, "Hold out the shawl you are wearing." She held it while he measured out six measures of barley, and he put it on her back.

When she got back to the town, ¹⁶she came to her mother-in-law, who asked, "How is it with you, daughter?" She told her all that the man had done for her; ¹⁷and she added, "He gave me these six measures of barley, saying to me, 'Do not go back to your mother-in-law empty-handed.'" ¹⁸And Naomi said, "Stay here, daughter, till you learn how the matter turns out. For the man will not rest, but will settle the matter today."

4 Meanwhile, Boaz had gone to the gate and sat down there. And now the redeemer whom Boaz had mentioned passed by. He called, "Come over and sit down here, So-and-so!" And he came over and sat down. ²Then [Boaz] took ten elders of the town and said, "Be seated here"; and they sat down.

³He said to the redeemer, "Naomi, now returned from the country of Moab, must sell the piece of land which belonged to our kinsman Elimelech. ⁴I thought I should disclose the matter to you and say: Acquire it in the presence of those seated here and in the presence of the elders of my people. If you are willing to redeem it, redeem! But if you will not redeem, tell me, that I may know. For there is no one to redeem but you, and I come after you." "I am willing to

רות
RUTH
3.14

וְנֵאלָתִיךְ אָנֹכִי חַי־יְהֹוָה
14 שְׁכְבִי עַד־הַבֹּקֶר: וַתִּשְׁכַּב
מַרְגְּלוֹתָו עַד־הַבֹּקֶר וַתָּקָם
בְּטֶרֶום יַכִּיר אִישׁ אֶת־רֵעֵהוּ
וַיֹּאמֶר אַל־יִוָּדַע כִּי־בָאָה
15 הָאִשָּׁה הַגֹּרֶן: וַיֹּאמֶר הָבִי
הַמִּטְפַּחַת אֲשֶׁר־עָלַיִךְ
וְאֶחֳזִי־בָהּ וַתֹּאחֶז בָּהּ וַיָּמָד
שֵׁשׁ־שְׂעֹרִים וַיָּשֶׁת עָלֶיהָ וַיָּבֹא
16 הָעִיר: וַתָּבוֹא אֶל־חֲמוֹתָהּ
וַתֹּאמֶר מִי־אַתְּ בִּתִּי וַתַּגֶּד־
לָהּ אֵת כָּל־אֲשֶׁר עָשָׂה־לָהּ
17 הָאִישׁ: וַתֹּאמֶר שֵׁשׁ־הַשְּׂעֹרִים
הָאֵלֶּה נָתַן לִי כִּי אָמַר
אַל־תָּבוֹאִי רֵיקָם אֶל־
18 חֲמוֹתֵךְ: וַתֹּאמֶר שְׁבִי בִתִּי
עַד אֲשֶׁר תֵּדְעִין אֵיךְ יִפֹּל
דָּבָר כִּי לֹא יִשְׁקֹט הָאִישׁ כִּי
אִם־כִּלָּה הַדָּבָר הַיּוֹם:

ד 1 וּבֹעַז עָלָה הַשַּׁעַר וַיֵּשֶׁב שָׁם
וְהִנֵּה הַגֹּאֵל עֹבֵר אֲשֶׁר דִּבֶּר־
בֹּעַז וַיֹּאמֶר סוּרָה שְׁבָה־פֹּה
2 פְּלֹנִי אַלְמֹנִי וַיָּסַר וַיֵּשֵׁב: וַיִּקַּח
עֲשָׂרָה אֲנָשִׁים מִזִּקְנֵי הָעִיר
וַיֹּאמֶר שְׁבוּ־פֹה וַיֵּשֵׁבוּ:
3 וַיֹּאמֶר לַגֹּאֵל חֶלְקַת הַשָּׂדֶה
אֲשֶׁר לְאָחִינוּ לֶאֱלִימֶלֶךְ
מָכְרָה נָעֳמִי הַשָּׁבָה מִשְּׂדֵה
4 מוֹאָב: וַאֲנִי אָמַרְתִּי אֶגְלֶה
אָזְנְךָ לֵאמֹר קְנֵה נֶגֶד הַיֹּשְׁבִים
וְנֶגֶד זִקְנֵי עַמִּי אִם־תִּגְאַל גְּאָל
וְאִם־לֹא יִגְאַל הַגִּידָה לִּי
וְאֵדְעָ כִּי אֵין זוּלָתְךָ לִגְאוֹל

redeem it," he replied. [5]Boaz continued,
"When you acquire the property from Naomi and from Ruth the Moabite, you must
also acquire the wife of the deceased, so as
to perpetuate the name of the deceased
upon his estate." [6]The redeemer replied,
"Then I cannot redeem it for myself, lest I
impair my own estate. You take over my
right of redemption, for I am unable to exercise it."

[7]Now this was formerly done in Israel in
cases of redemption or exchange: to validate
any transaction, one man would take off his
sandal and hand it to the other. Such was
the practice in Israel. [8]So when the redeemer
said to Boaz, "Acquire for yourself," he drew
off his sandal. [9]And Boaz said to the elders
and to the rest of the people, "You are witnesses today that I am acquiring from Naomi all that belonged to Elimelech and all
that belonged to Chilion and Mahlon. [10]I
am also acquiring Ruth the Moabite, the
wife of Mahlon, as my wife, so as to perpetuate the name of the deceased upon his estate, that the name of the deceased may not
disappear from among his kinsmen and
from the gate of his home town. You are
witnesses today."

[11]All the people at the gate and the elders
answered, "We are. May the LORD make the
woman who is coming into your house like
Rachel and Leah, both of whom built up
the House of Israel! Prosper in Ephrathah
and perpetuate your name in Bethlehem!
[12]And may your house be like the house of
Perez whom Tamar bore to Judah—through

וְאָנֹכִי אַחֲרֶיךָ וַיֹּאמֶר אָנֹכִי

5 אֶגְאָל: וַיֹּאמֶר בֹּעַז בְּיוֹם־
קְנוֹתְךָ הַשָּׂדֶה מִיַּד נָעֳמִי וּמֵאֵת
רוּת הַמּוֹאֲבִיָּה אֵשֶׁת־הַמֵּת
קָנִיתָ לְהָקִים שֵׁם־הַמֵּת עַל־

6 נַחֲלָתוֹ: וַיֹּאמֶר הַגֹּאֵל לֹא
אוּכַל לִגְאָול־לִי פֶּן־אַשְׁחִית
אֶת־נַחֲלָתִי גְּאַל־לְךָ אַתָּה
אֶת־גְּאֻלָּתִי כִּי לֹא־אוּכַל

7 לִגְאֹל: וְזֹאת לְפָנִים בְּיִשְׂרָאֵל
עַל־הַגְּאֻלָּה וְעַל־הַתְּמוּרָה
לְקַיֵּם כָּל־דָּבָר שָׁלַף אִישׁ
נַעֲלוֹ וְנָתַן לְרֵעֵהוּ וְזֹאת

8 הַתְּעוּדָה בְּיִשְׂרָאֵל: וַיֹּאמֶר
הַגֹּאֵל לְבֹעַז קְנֵה־לָךְ וַיִּשְׁלֹף

9 נַעֲלוֹ: וַיֹּאמֶר בֹּעַז לַזְּקֵנִים
וְכָל־הָעָם עֵדִים אַתֶּם הַיּוֹם
כִּי קָנִיתִי אֶת־כָּל־אֲשֶׁר
לֶאֱלִימֶלֶךְ וְאֵת כָּל־אֲשֶׁר
לְכִלְיוֹן וּמַחְלוֹן מִיַּד נָעֳמִי:

10 וְגַם אֶת־רוּת הַמֹּאֲבִיָּה אֵשֶׁת
מַחְלוֹן קָנִיתִי לִי לְאִשָּׁה
לְהָקִים שֵׁם־הַמֵּת עַל־
נַחֲלָתוֹ וְלֹא־יִכָּרֵת שֵׁם־הַמֵּת
מֵעִם אֶחָיו וּמִשַּׁעַר מְקוֹמוֹ

11 עֵדִים אַתֶּם הַיּוֹם: וַיֹּאמְרוּ
כָּל־הָעָם אֲשֶׁר־בַּשַּׁעַר
וְהַזְּקֵנִים עֵדִים יִתֵּן יְהוָה אֶת־
הָאִשָּׁה הַבָּאָה אֶל־בֵּיתֶךָ
כְּרָחֵל ׀ וּכְלֵאָה אֲשֶׁר בָּנוּ
שְׁתֵּיהֶם אֶת־בֵּית יִשְׂרָאֵל
וַעֲשֵׂה־חַיִל בְּאֶפְרָתָה וּקְרָא

12 שֵׁם בְּבֵית לָחֶם: וִיהִי בֵיתְךָ
כְּבֵית פֶּרֶץ אֲשֶׁר־יָלְדָה תָמָר

the offspring which the LORD will give you by this young woman."

¹³So Boaz married Ruth; she became his wife, and he cohabited with her. The LORD let her conceive, and she bore a son. ¹⁴And the women said to Naomi, "Blessed be the LORD, who has not withheld a redeemer from you today! May his name be perpetuated in Israel! ¹⁵He will renew your life and sustain your old age; for he is born of your daughter-in-law, who loves you and is better to you than seven sons."

¹⁶Naomi took the child and held it to her bosom. She became its foster mother, ¹⁷and the women neighbors gave him a name, saying, "A son is born to Naomi!" They named him Obed; he was the father of Jesse, father of David.

¹⁸This is the line of Perez: Perez begot Hezron, Hezron begot Ram, Ram begot Amminadab, ²⁰Amminadab begot Nahshon, Nahshon begot Salmon, ²¹Salmon begot Boaz, Boaz begot Obed, ²²Obed begot Jesse, and Jesse begot David.

לִיהוּדָה מִן־הַזֶּרַע אֲשֶׁר יִתֵּן
יְהֹוָה לְךָ מִן־הַנַּעֲרָה הַזֹּאת:

13 וַיִּקַּח בֹּעַז אֶת־רוּת וַתְּהִי־לוֹ
לְאִשָּׁה וַיָּבֹא אֵלֶיהָ וַיִּתֵּן יְהֹוָה
לָהּ הֵרָיוֹן וַתֵּלֶד בֵּן:

14 וַתֹּאמַרְנָה הַנָּשִׁים אֶל־נָעֳמִי
בָּרוּךְ יְהֹוָה אֲשֶׁר לֹא הִשְׁבִּית
לָךְ גֹּאֵל הַיּוֹם וְיִקָּרֵא שְׁמוֹ

15 בְּיִשְׂרָאֵל: וְהָיָה לָךְ לְמֵשִׁיב
נֶפֶשׁ וּלְכַלְכֵּל אֶת־שֵׂיבָתֵךְ כִּי
כַלָּתֵךְ אֲשֶׁר־אֲהֵבַתֶךְ יְלָדַתּוּ
אֲשֶׁר־הִיא טוֹבָה לָךְ מִשִּׁבְעָה

16 בָּנִים: וַתִּקַּח נָעֳמִי אֶת־הַיֶּלֶד
וַתְּשִׁתֵהוּ בְחֵיקָהּ וַתְּהִי־לוֹ

17 לְאֹמֶנֶת: וַתִּקְרֶאנָה לוֹ
הַשְּׁכֵנוֹת שֵׁם לֵאמֹר יֻלַּד־בֵּן
לְנָעֳמִי וַתִּקְרֶאנָה שְׁמוֹ עוֹבֵד
הוּא אֲבִי־יִשַׁי אֲבִי דָוִד:

18 וְאֵלֶּה תּוֹלְדוֹת פָּרֶץ פֶּרֶץ
19 הוֹלִיד אֶת־חֶצְרוֹן: וְחֶצְרוֹן
הוֹלִיד אֶת־רָם וְרָם הוֹלִיד

20 אֶת־עַמִּינָדָב: וְעַמִּינָדָב
הוֹלִיד אֶת־נַחְשׁוֹן וְנַחְשׁוֹן

21 הוֹלִיד אֶת־שַׂלְמָה: וְשַׂלְמוֹן
הוֹלִיד אֶת־בֹּעַז וּבֹעַז הוֹלִיד

22 אֶת־עוֹבֵד: וְעֹבֵד הוֹלִיד
אֶת־יִשַׁי וְיִשַׁי הוֹלִיד אֶת־
דָּוִד:

Verse by Verse
A Modern Commentary

Ruth H. Sohn

Nachmanides, Rabbi Moshe ben Nachman (1194–1270), once wrote that the relationship between *pshat* (the "plain sense" meaning of a biblical text) and *drash* (its interpretation) is analogous to the relationship between the letters and the vowels of the Torah. The Torah scroll consists of Hebrew letters on parchment; the vowels do not appear. And yet, without the vowels the letters remain only black ink on parchment, unpronounceable. To read the text aloud—to make it a spoken, *living* text—requires that we add the vowels.

So too with *pshat* and *drash*. The plain sense of the text—the literal meaning—is apparent on the surface of the page. But alone it is incomplete. To make the text comprehensible and meaningful to people in changing life situations, to make it a *living* text, we must infuse it with the life of *drash*—interpretation—both the interpretation that has come down to us through the many centuries and the interpretation that is born out of our own engagement with the text.

Drash has undoubtedly accompanied Hebrew Scripture from the moment it was committed to writing. The basic verbal form of the word, *lidrosh*, means "to ask or enquire," "to explain," or "to search out the meaning." To engage in the *process* of midrash, or "interpretation," is to

---

The author used her own translation of the Book of Ruth; she also consulted *Tanakh: A New Translation of the Holy Scriptures* (Philadelphia, New York, and Jerusalem: Jewish Publication Society, 1985).

dig deeper into the text—into the specific wording and even into the spaces between the words—and to discover deeper, more meaningful answers to the questions the text raises than those which had been apparent upon first reading. The *content* of midrash consists of the comments and interpretative stories that accompany the written text. For centuries these stories and comments have been carried within Judaism as an evolving tradition, reflecting the questions and experiences of succeeding generations.

Biblical commentary or *parshanut* is a genre of Jewish literature which has also accompanied Hebrew Scripture for centuries. Rashi, Rabbi Shlomo Yitzchaki (1040–1105), is the best known of the medieval commentators. Rashi's commentary includes both his own interpretations of the text as well as his frequent citation of classic midrashim of the earlier rabbinic period, which he feels shed light on the true meaning of the biblical text.

My commentary below is presented in a *form* reminiscent of Rashi's commentary, with both explanation of words and phrases and "citation" of midrashim. The *content* of my commentary, however, is not traditional. These interpretations and midrashim emerged out of my own encounter with the text. As is often done in traditional midrash and commentary, I sometimes point out connections between a given passage and a verse from elsewhere in Hebrew Scripture, the Midrash, the Talmud, or the liturgy. These traditional sources are always cited. Otherwise the material is my own. I have also translated the biblical verses myself so as to reveal the linguistic nuances that generated my comments.

May what follows encourage other women to add their voices to our evolving tradition. I look forward to the day when bookshelves will be filled with the commentaries and collections of midrash of Jewish women.

Ruth 1:3 **And she was left, and her two sons.**

Why does the verse not say Naomi was left *with* her two sons? Because at the time of Elimelech's death, Naomi and her sons were not of one mind:

"Why should I stay here in a foreign land, a woman alone with her two sons, so far away from family and friends?" Naomi said to herself when the period of mourning for Elimelech had passed.

"I still do not feel at home here. And the boys will soon be old enough to get married. Shouldn't I bring them back home so they will not have to marry foreigners?"

Later that night Naomi spoke with Mahlon and Chilion.

"We hear the famine is still raging in Judah," they reminded her. "Here at least we can eat. And besides, *we're* at home here. We want to stay. We'll take care of you, Ima, don't you worry. We'll all be fine."

"But in Judah we would at least be with our own people, we'd be home." Naomi's voice rose in intensity. "With your father's death, I realize these are not our people. They don't even know how to help us mourn. I feel so alone here." Naomi looked down at her feet. Could her sons understand? They had come to Moab as young boys. What did they remember of home?

Mahlon and Chilion tried to comfort her.

"Ima, you're still in mourning. You're not yourself. You have friends here. It will be okay. We'll take care of you. And when the famine ends we can go back to Judah if you still want to."

"Alright," Naomi agreed. But she was uneasy. They felt so at home here in Moab. Was that good? Maybe she should try harder to fit in. Or maybe she should take them back to Judah now before it was too late, despite the famine. And yet, would it be better to be hungry? Wasn't that why they had left in the first place? What would Elimelech want her to do? Naomi started to cry. She did not know how to answer that question. She only knew that in the face of her loss **she was left** with the strong desire to return home **and her two sons** wanted to remain in Moab. Naomi sighed. They would stay, for now.

Ruth 1:4 **They married Moabite women, one named Orpah and the other Ruth, and they dwelt there about ten years.**

When Mahlon and Chilion married, Naomi resigned herself to staying in Moab. "Orpah and Ruth are good women," Naomi said to herself with satisfaction. She took her daughters-in-law into her home and taught them the traditions of her family as passed down from mother to daughter. For the first time since Elimelech's death, Naomi did not feel so alone.

At the time of Mahlon's and Chilion's marriages they had already been in Moab for ten years. After their marriages, **they dwelt** there for another ten years. Here the Torah uses the word *vayesh'vu*, "they dwelt."* Earlier this word is not used. This is to teach that only after their marriages did Mahlon, Chilion, and their mother Naomi *dwell* in Moab with the intention of staying.

Ruth 1:5 **Then those two—Mahlon and Chilion—also died.**

Why does the verse say **then those two—Mahlon and Chilion** *(Vayamutu gam shneihem Mahlon v' Chilion)*? Isn't this repetitious? This is to teach us that they died together on the same day. And how did they die? They died as a result of a fall, when the roof they were building for their new house collapsed.

Ruth 1:6 **For she had heard in the field of Moab how Adonai had remembered His people in giving them bread.**

During the period of mourning for Mahlon and Chilion, Naomi's grief was intense. "If we hadn't stayed this never would have happened," she said to herself. "I should have taken them back to the land of Judah when Elimelech died. Now I've lost them all. Why, God, why?" They had both made good marriages. Even if Orpah and Ruth were Moabites, they had been good wives and good to her too. Mahlon and Chilion had been building a new house for them all; they had been building a life here in Moab for themselves. Was God punishing them, punishing her for staying in Moab? After all, it had been ten years since the marriages, twenty years in all. Was this how God worked? If this was God's way, why had they been "rewarded" with such wonderful wives? Naomi's thoughts swirled. Had God been testing them? Had they somehow failed the test? Naomi was not sure. But once again, facing loss, Naomi's thoughts turned to her old home.

After the period of mourning had ended, Naomi went out to the fields

---

*Ruth 1:1 tells us the family went to Moab *lagur*, "to sojourn," or "to dwell temporarily there." In verse 2, we read *vay'hi-yu*, "they were there." *Yashav*, in the *Hebrew and English Lexicon of the Old Testament* by Brown, Driver, and Briggs, is defined as "dwell, remain . . . stay or tarry." There are many such usages in Hebrew Scripture, such as 1 Samuel 1:22: "For when he has appeared before the Lord, he must *remain* there for good." *Gur* is defined as "sojourn," often with the specific sense "to dwell as a newcomer." See for example Genesis 19:9, Deuteronomy 18:6, and, referring to exile, Ezra 1:4.

with Orpah and Ruth to help them with the work. She could not resist asking some of the laborers, "What is the news from the land of Judah?"

"The rains finally came and the winter wheat was plentiful for the first time in years. We haven't heard anything yet about the barley crop," they answered. Naomi could not believe her ears.

"May the God who **remembered** our mother Sarah be praised for **remembering Her people and giving them bread**!" Naomi rejoiced, her decision final. She was going home.

This is similar to what the Talmud tells us Resh Lakish said in the name of Bar Kappara:

" 'Withholding' is applied to rain and 'withholding' is applied to a woman; 'withholding' is applied to a woman as it is said *For the Lord has shut up every womb* [Genesis 20:18] and 'withholding' is applied to rain, as it is written *And He will shut up the skies so that there will be no rain* [Deuteronomy 11:17]. . . .

"**Remembering** is applied to a woman and **remembering** is applied to rain; **remembering** is applied to a woman, as it is written *And the Lord* **remembered** *Sarah* [Genesis 21:1] and **remembering** is applied to rain, as it is written *You have* **remembered** *the earth, and watered her, greatly enriching her with the river of God that is full of water* [Psalm 65:10]" (Babylon Talmud, Ta'anit 8a–8b).

And in the land of Judah **remembering** is applied at one and the same time to rain and to the people of Israel, as it is said, **For she had heard in the field of Moab how Adonai had remembered His people in giving them bread.**

Ruth 1:6 **She started out with her daughters-in-law to return** (*vatashov*) **from the country of Moab**

This is the first of eleven appearances in the first chapter of the Book of Ruth of one or another form of the verb *lashuv*, "to return." From here we learn that *teshuva*, "repentance" or "return," is not a single event in time but a process. *Teshuva* is a turning toward God that always involves a journey, with many acts of turning on the way.

Ruth 1:7   She left the place where she had been living . . . to return to the land of Judah.

Why in verse 6 is **the country of Moab** (*s'dei Moav*) named twice as the place Naomi is leaving, while the place to which Naomi is returning is not referred to by name? And why does verse 7 refer to **the land of Judah** (*eretz Yehuda*) by name, but to Moab instead as **the place** (*hamakom*)?

In the first verse, Naomi is at the very beginning of her return journey. It is much clearer to her what she is leaving than to what she will eventually return. Therefore in verse 6 we read that Naomi wants to return **from Moab**, but the land to which she is returning is not named. In the next verse, Naomi has already moved forward. As soon as she leaves Moab, it ceases to be her home. Moab is now only the place she has left behind. The hold of Moab falls from her as a garment draped loosely over one's shoulders might drop suddenly to the ground. And now, the place that is named is **the land of Judah**, the land to which she is returning. Now Naomi can turn even more fully to the future, with the image of the land of Judah burning brighter before her eyes.

From Naomi we learn that *teshuva*, "repentance" or "return," is a process that seizes upon hope, affirms life, and moves toward redemption. Naomi, overwhelmed by the death and loss of her husband and sons, seizes upon the glimmer of hope present in the report that God has remembered Her people and is providing them with bread.

"God can still provide sustenance for the body," thinks Naomi. "Perhaps also for the soul." With this hope, Naomi begins her journey home.

Naomi's **return** finds its fulfillment in the marriage of Ruth and Boaz and the birth of a grandson, Obed, who will one day be the grandfather of David. From here we learn that *teshuva* moves toward new life and, ultimately, redemption.

But the path of *teshuva* is not always a clear ascent; there are dips and valleys. Naomi's hope gives way to despair before finding fulfillment in the birth of a grandson. And so it is with us: the process of *teshuva* is often one of overcoming obstacles and feelings of hopelessness as we move slowly toward the hope of renewed life and redemption.

Ruth 1:8 **Go return each of you to her mother's house.**

Why does Naomi tell Orpah and Ruth to return to their *mothers'* houses and not their fathers'? Throughout the Book of Ruth great emphasis is placed on the relationships between women. Now that their husbands have died the focus is on Orpah and Ruth's relationship with Naomi, their mother-in-law. The question becomes this: To whom do they feel a greater bond, their own mothers or Naomi? Which way of life will they choose, the way of the Moabites or the way of the Jews? For Orpah and Ruth, these two questions are bound up together.

Ruth 1:19 **The two of them went on until they came to Bethlehem.**

In this verse, Naomi and Ruth are not referred to by name. They are two women—any two women—making a journey together. A journey that means different things for each of them but which neither could make alone. For Naomi the journey is one of return, through old memories and loss and grief and eventually to the renewed light of hope. For Ruth it is a journey to a place still unknown, a journey to a people, a God, and a way of life she had only begun to know in Moab. For both Naomi and Ruth, because of the other the journey will prove fruitful: they will arrive in Bethlehem at the beginning of the barley harvest. As **the two of them** continue to interweave their lives, their shared journey will yield great and distinctive harvests for them both.

Ruth 1:19–21 **When they arrived in Bethlehem, the whole city buzzed with excitement over them. . . . I went away full and Adonai has brought me back empty.**

Naomi came back empty?! Did she not come back with Ruth? When Naomi returns to the land of Judah, she is suddenly flooded with memories: Elimelech, with his easy laugh, so loving, so strong and hardworking in the early years of their marriage. Mahlon and Chilion, always hungry as babies, hands grasping with impatient fingers. As young boys, they had both been sweetly affectionate in their own ways, eyes filled with wonder and curiosity. Scenes she thought she had forgotten, vivid with color and feeling, sweep over her. So much life and love and hope. Despite the famine, they had left the land of Judah certain they would one day return.

And now she has returned. But where Naomi had hoped to find comfort, her searing sense of loss tears at her all the more strongly in the face of her memories. She is blinded by her grief. "My babies," she moans. "I've lost my babies."

"Naomi, is it really you?" her friends cry when they see her. They hug her fiercely amid laughter and tears, touching the lines on her face with tenderness.

"I am not the same woman as when I left," she answers, seeming to take no pleasure in their recognition and loving welcome. "They're gone. Elimelech, Mahlon, Chilion, all gone. And no grandchildren."

"Do not call me Naomi," she says very quietly, tears of sorrow matching their tears of happiness. **"Call me Mara, for the Almighty has dealt very bitterly with me. I went away full and Adonai has brought me back empty"** (1:20–21).

Naomi does not even mention or introduce Ruth, who stands behind her in the shadows. At this moment she does not see Ruth; she does not see that because of Ruth and Ruth's love she is not in fact returning home empty.

"Do I have hope?!" (1:12) she had said earlier to her daughters-in-law, urging them to return to their own families. The love she shares with Ruth is her hope. For love always bears fruit and new life. As Naomi's friends will later tell her, upon hearing of the birth of Naomi's grandchild, **"Your daughter-in-law, who loves you and is better to you than seven sons has borne him"** (4:15). But upon her return to the land of Judah, Naomi is blind to this hope and love for she is overwhelmed with grief.

Ruth 1:22   **So Naomi returned from the country of Moab; she returned with her daughter-in-law Ruth the Moabite.**

For Naomi, the journey to the land of Judah, once her home, is clearly a return. But in what way is this a return for Ruth? For Ruth, isn't this journey a venture into unknown territory? From here we learn that any time a person turns toward the Holy One it is experienced as a return, as coming home.

Ruth 2:11 **How you left your father and your mother and the land of your birth and how you came to a people you had not known before.**

So too did our father Abraham journey in response to God's command: *Go forth from your land, the land of your birth and from your father's house to a land I will show you* (Genesis 12:1). This is to teach us that Ruth's journey is like Abraham's and Sarah's before her. Like Abraham and Sarah, Ruth left all that was familiar to take a journey to a land she had never seen, to embrace a people, a God, and a way of life not her own.

But who commanded Ruth to make this journey? To what voice did she respond? Her love for Naomi spoke to her with the voice of command. So it is sometimes with love. To cleave to another means to risk hearing the commanding voice asking you to step forth on a path you would not even have considered otherwise.

But, you say, Naomi did not even ask Ruth to come with her. For Ruth to listen to the "commanding voice of love" would have meant for her to do as Orpah did, to return to her mother's home. It is true that these are the words Naomi used in instructing her daughters-in-law. But here we see another dimension of love. Naomi, who had lost so much already, stood ready to sacrifice even more for love. She did not ask her daughters-in-law to return with her to the land of Judah. She knew that they would come with her if she asked. But she wished to spare them further grief.

And yet Ruth heard another voice urging her not to abandon her grief-stricken mother-in-law.

"She took me into her home as a daughter when I was a stranger. We have shared more than many mothers and daughters, more than I shared with my own mother or sister. Is this a woman I can simply walk away from? Especially now? I love her. And I love the ways of her people, the ways of her God. If she returns to the land of Judah I will go with her."

So Ruth responded to the quiet commanding voice of love. But this was not the only voice toward which she now turned.

"Your people shall be my people, and your God shall be my God," Ruth told Naomi (1:16). Ruth wanted her life to remain bound up with Naomi's. She also wanted to live her life, as did Naomi, in response to the God of Israel. She did not want to be an outsider anymore. Ruth was ready to come under the wings of the *Shekhina*[1];

returning to the land of Judah with Naomi was the next step. As Boaz would later say: **"May Adonai repay your efforts; may your reward be complete from Adonai the God of Israel under whose wings you have come to take refuge"** (2:12).

Ruth 2:13 **You have spoken to the heart of your handmaid.**

Touched by Boaz's compassion, Ruth's own heart stirs. Here in the time of the barley harvest, the seed of new love is planted.

Ruth 2:23–3:6 **Then she stayed at home with her mother-in-law. . . . She went down to the threshing floor and did just as her mother-in-law had instructed her.**

"This Boaz," Naomi said to herself one morning as she stood over the pot of soup that would serve as the main meal that day. Ruth had gone with the other young women to wash laundry at the spring but she would be back to join her mother-in-law for dinner. "What is he waiting for? He has been so kind to Ruth. From that first day when he singled her out, I thought maybe this will go somewhere—he's our kinsman after all. And it's clear to me that as far as Ruth is concerned, he's not just another man. At the mention of his name she blushes.

"Boaz has been very kind, very generous, I am not complaining. But no action. And now the barley harvest has ended, and the wheat harvest too. Could it not have occurred to him that Ruth needs a husband, that she has yet to have a child? How long must she wait? How long must I wait? I, who have lost everything—no, almost everything," she corrected herself. "*Almost* everything. I still have Ruth, my friends—and Boaz. Boaz could make all the difference—he could come forward as our redeeming kinsman. But how long must we wait? I'm not getting any younger. Ruth is not getting any younger. And Boaz," Naomi chuckled softly. "He's no youngster either." Naomi gave a stir impatiently. "No one lives forever." Naomi was startled to hear her own voice and realized she'd spoken the last words out loud.

"I, who have had to learn through so much pain that the flow of time does not stop for any of us. What am I waiting for?" she continued with a new sense of urgency. "It's not *all* in our hands," Naomi said to herself, "but maybe we don't have to just sit and wait either. Maybe

Ruth can take the first step and at least approach Boaz. Then if he
wishes, he can come forward as our redeeming kinsman. And if not,"
Naomi shrugged, "if not, he can turn her away. At least we will know
where we stand. Now, didn't Rebecca tell me the men would be winnowing barley tonight?" As Naomi adjusted the seasoning of the soup,
her thoughts raced ahead.

Later, when Naomi was putting the bowls on the table, expecting
Ruth to come in at any minute, her heart was pounding. The more she
thought about it the more strongly she felt it was the right thing to do.
But still there were lingering doubts. She did not, God forbid, want to
put Ruth in a position where she might be shamed.

"Dear God, may it be pleasing in Your sight that I do this thing. I do
it for Ruth's sake, for my sake, for the sake of my beloved Elimelech,
may his memory be for blessing, and also for Your sake, dear God. Don't
let me die, God, an old woman, the last link in a long chain, with no
one to follow. Don't let Ruth, such a golden gift of a person, so eager to
be a part of our people, remain with no husband, no child. Please God,
may our actions only be pleasing in your sight and may they, with Your
help, bear good fruit."

After Ruth returned home and they finished eating, Naomi outlined
her plan. **"Boaz will be winnowing barley on the threshing floor
tonight. So bathe, anoint yourself, dress up, and go down to the
threshing floor. But do not disclose yourself to the man until he
has finished eating and drinking. When he lies down, note the
place where he lies down, and go over and uncover his feet and
lie down. He will tell you what you are to do." She replied, "I
will do everything you tell me." She went down to the threshing
floor and did just as her mother-in-law had instructed her** (Ruth
3:2–6).

Ruth 3:9 **Spread your robe over your handmaid, for you are a redeeming kinsman.**

For a man to spread his robe over a woman was a formal act expressing his intention to marry her. As it is said, *You were naked and bare
when I passed you by and saw that your time for love had arrived. So I
spread My robe over you and covered your nakedness, and I entered into
a covenant with you by oath—declares the Lord God; thus you became
Mine* (Ezekiel 16:7–8).

In Ezekiel, while the image is that of a man speaking to the woman he betroths, the words are actually spoken between God and Israel, and it is this relationship which is the true matter at hand. *Spread My robe* in the Hebrew reads "spread My wings" and suggests the image of the *Shekhina* spreading Her wings to shelter Israel as part of the establishment of the covenant between God and Israel, likened here to the commitment of marriage.

In a similar way, when Ruth asks Boaz to spread his *robe* over her and thereby state his intention to marry her, the words have a second level of meaning. With these same words Ruth beseeches God, the ultimate Redeemer (*Goel*, the same word used to designate Boaz as the redeeming kinsman) to spread His protective *wings* over her and welcome her into the covenant between God and the Jewish people: **"I am Ruth your handmaid. Spread your wings over your handmaid for you are the redeemer"** (Ruth 3:9).

Ruth 4:14 **Blessed be Adonai, who has not withheld a redeemer from you today!**

The Book of Ruth begins with an emphasis on *teshuva*, "return," which can be understood as our turning or returning to God. This emphasis in chapter 1 is paralleled in the final chapter with an emphasis on *ge'ula*, "redemption." (The word "redeemer" appears fourteen times in the last chapter of the Book of Ruth; "return" appeared eleven times in the first chapter.) On the *pshat* level (plain-sense meaning of the text), **redeemer** refers to "redeeming kinsman." On a deeper level, the word refers to God, the ultimate *Goel*, Redeemer.

From the repeated use of the term **redeemer**, and from the birth of Obed, we learn here of the importance of trusting in God and building on hope even in the face of deep despair. In the darkest nights it is sometimes a struggle to remember that somewhere, sparks of hope remain even if we cannot see them. Naomi, upon her return to Judah, was blind to such sparks of hope. She could not even consider the possibility of a redeeming kinsman or of God acting toward her as a Redeemer. She had given up all hope.

But over time, with Ruth's devotion and Boaz's responsiveness to Ruth, Naomi's hopes are rekindled. She eventually instructs Ruth to approach Boaz directly and Ruth does so. Thus Ruth and Naomi participate in their own "redemption." They do not trust in God in the sense of passively waiting. Initially, Naomi and Ruth wait for Boaz to indicate his intentions. But after the barley and wheat harvest have ended, they take the initiative and approach Boaz directly.

While God is the true *Goel,* or Redeemer, God also calls upon us to play a significant role in bringing redemption to the world. We must always try to be open to hearing the still small voice within. What does God ask of us? There is much that only *we* can do; we must take responsibility for ourselves and the world around us. And yet we are not alone. God's redemptive power in the universe is available to us for these tasks. We can look to God as the Source of strength and empowerment as we struggle to take the steps necessary to make our lives and the lives of others more whole and complete.

So we say in the prayers of *Hallel* (praise) we recite on *Rosh Hodesh* and festivals:

> *Ana Adonai hoshia na,* Dear God, we beseech You to save us.
> *Ana Adonai hatzlichah na,* Dear God, we beseech You to make our own efforts fruitful.

That is to say, we look to You, God, to do what only You can do to bring us to a place of wholeness. We look to You, God, to strengthen and enable us to do what only we can do to bring wholeness and peace to the world.

Teshuva, "return," refers to our movement toward God. *Ge'ula,* "redemption," refers to God's movement toward us. The Book of Ruth teaches us that when we take steps toward God, God also moves toward us, although we may not always be aware of it. We do not always understand God's ways. There are times we feel our hesitating steps toward God are met only with silence and darkness. At such times we need to trust ourselves and God and, taking the next step forward, to listen and look more deeply.

Ruth 4:16–17 **Naomi took the child and held him to her bosom and she became his nurse. The women neighbors gave him a name, saying, "A son is born to Naomi!"**

Did Naomi, now in old age, really nurse her grandson? Was this really a son born to Naomi as her neighbors proclaimed?

The text teaches us that every child born is a special gift of life to the grandparents, who have entered the twilight of their own lives. The grandmother looks at the infant and sees that her life will not end with her physical death. The child will take some part of her into the distant future, extending her life beyond her own finite limits. In this way the infant is indeed her child, for he is her hope. So say the rabbis, *Grandchildren are like children* (Babylonian Talmud, Yevamot 62b). It is in this sense that Naomi's friends proclaimed to Naomi about her grandson, **"A son is born to Naomi!"**

And so we learn in the prayers of *Hallel,* in Psalm 115:17–18: *The dead cannot praise Adonai, nor any who go down into silence. But we will bless Adonai now and forever. Halleluyah!* Don't these verses contradict each other? If the dead cannot praise God, how can it be that we will praise God forever? Surely all of us are destined to die!

But our children and our children's children will continue to sing God's praises. In this way we indeed will praise Adonai now and forever! This is what Naomi's friends meant when they said of Obed, **"He will renew your life and sustain your old age"** (4:15). So may we all be blessed with grandchildren in our old age!

Ruth 4:17 **And the women neighbors named him Obed; he was the father of Jesse, the father of David.**

Son of Ruth and Boaz, father of Jesse, grandson of Naomi, grandfather of David. This infant would grow to be an important link in the chain of generations. With the name Obed, the women blessed him, saying, "May he grow to willingly embrace this land and this people and to *serve* God with the fullness of his being" (*oved* means "servant").

Why was it that Naomi's neighbors named Ruth's son? A name is a gift. It bestows a piece of a person's destiny. Obed's birth and the shape of his future owed much to Ruth's decision to join Naomi's circle of relations in the land of Judah. How fitting, therefore, that Ruth's son be named by a group of Naomi's neighbors, women defined both by their relation to the land of Judah and to Naomi.

The pulse that moves beneath the events in the Book of Ruth is the love between Ruth and Naomi. From beginning to end, the Book of Ruth is a celebration of the bonds between women that form the fabric of life. It is Naomi's women friends, therefore, who name the infant born to Ruth, new life and hope for both Ruth and Naomi.

May the bonds of love and friendship between women ever flourish and sustain us.

1

"But Ruth Clung to Her"

RUTH 1:14

$\mathcal{T}$HE WORD signifying Ruth's determination to stay with Naomi, "clung" (*davka*), astounds us in the biblical context because it suggests a permanent attachment. When we recognize that this verb, found elsewhere in the context of husband and wife or God and the people of Israel, here delineates a relationship between two women, we immediately wonder how the biblical author is conceiving of their attachment. In this section we bring together four authors who explore Ruth's "clinging" to Naomi and reflect on its rarity. Three of the writers conceive of the relationship as first and foremost a friendship, while one, Avivah Zornberg, uses the very implausibility, the lack of apparent benefit in the relationship, to uncover deeper significance in Ruth's choice to "cling" to her mother-in-law.

Gloria Goldreich reimagines the story through a fictional rendering that probes the inner lives of Naomi, Ruth, and Orpah. By granting Orpah a voice in this circle of friendship, Goldreich adds new meaning to her decision to return to Moab, while highlighting the poignancy of Ruth's determination to cling to Naomi. This idyllic retelling weaves a richly colored new thread into the texture of friendship in Ruth.

Ruth Anna Putnam, a philosopher, compares the friendship of Ruth and Naomi to the more usually noted friendship of David and Jonathan. She contrasts Ruth's clinging to Naomi with the description of David and Jonathan, whose souls are "knit together." Her philosophical learning leads her to reflect upon giving and receiving, taking risks, and the danger of conflicting loyalties in deep friendships.

Roberta Apfel and Lise Grondahl see this unusual, long-lasting attachment in light of both their experience as psychotherapists working with women in long-term therapies and their relationship to each other as supervisor and supervisee. What intrigues them most in the friendship between Ruth and Naomi is their persistent commitment to each other through shifting circumstances. Interpreting the story with what they have learned as psychotherapists, they in turn reflect on what Ruth teaches them about crucial patterns in therapeutic relationships between women.

This section closes with an edited transcript of a *shiur*, an oral reflection on classical Jewish texts, which Avivah Zornberg presented in one of the many classes for Jewish women she teaches in Jerusalem. Works from the Western philosophical and literary tradition as well as traditional Jewish commentaries figure prominently as Zornberg explores the meaning of Ruth's improbable choice of Naomi as the central figure in her life. Following clues suggested by close readings in rabbinic midrash and medieval commentaries, she opens up the Bible's language to startling possibilities. She rejects the clichéd literary view of Ruth as a charming idyll and instead unveils a stark existential drama of suffering countered by the determined, even willful lovingkindness of Ruth. By taking seriously Naomi's praise of her daughters-in-law for their kindness "to the living *and the dead*," Zornberg reveals a "concealed alternative," a level of passion and life-affirming courage in defiance of death, in Ruth's gesture of "clinging."

Ruth, Naomi, and Orpah

A Parable of Friendship

GLORIA GOLDREICH

They walk across the desert, a trio so light of step that their sandaled feet leave no impression on the shifting ocher sands. Their gait is measured and graceful. They are used to walking together, to accommodating their steps, each to the others. The two younger women keep a few paces ahead; their long gray desert cloaks cast a gossamer veil of shadow onto which the older woman glides.

They speak softly, in the lilting tones of intimacy. Often, they speak in half sentences. They understand each other so well that a cryptic code of dangling phrases suffices. Now and again, they drift into a dreamy, companionable silence. This has long been their habit—an exchange of words and then a retreat into separate fortresses of thoughts and memories. They are careful, at such times, not to invade each other's privacy with unbidden question or intrusive statement.

A rare, salt-scented breeze stirs the heavy air and they turn their eyes skyward. A snow-white egret scissors its wide-winged way toward the salt marshes of the Dead Sea.

"How beautiful. Do you see it, Ruth?" The older woman's eyes follow the bird in its flight.

"Yes, I see it, Naomi. Orpah?"

"I see it, Ruth."

The author used *Ruth* in *The Five Megilloth* (London, Jerusalem, New York: Soncino Press, 1st printing, 1946).

The names are small jewels upon their tongues, glittering, audible fragments of affection, each syllable finely polished by their love. *Ruth. Orpah. Naomi.* They know the meanings of those names and it bemuses them that they were so well chosen, as though their parents, holding the infant females, could predict the women they would become. Naomi means pleasant. Ruth signifies friendship. And Orpah, Naomi has told them, is derived from the Arabic and means "rich with hair."

It is true that calm and pleasantness are Naomi's mantle. That calm, that pleasantness, settles in a patina of beauty across the life-worn skin of her aging face. It translates into the wisdom, the persuasive reasonableness of her words. It has made her—the mother of their husbands, gentle youths who died so young—their teacher and their friend. Their friendly teacher, their teaching friend. Saddened by her own widowhood, Naomi did not surrender to bitterness. She mourned Elimelech, her husband, yet her ways remained as her name, the ways of pleasantness.

And yes, Orpah's curling chestnut-colored hair falls in heavy thickness to her waist. Her brows are soft furry slashes above her deepset violet eyes, the color of the hills of her native Moab at the twilight hour. Long silken hairs shimmer upon the tawny skin of her arms and legs, tuft the secret places of her body. Ruth and Naomi love Orpah's hair. They have brushed it and plaited it into intricate coronets. They have fashioned it into curls piled high upon her head so that she staggered playfully beneath the weight of her coiffure. Their laughter spilled out then, as though they were small girls caught in paroxysms of merriment. That is how grown women laugh, in the fastness of their relationship—without embarrassment, unencumbered by fear of judgment, secure with each other and within themselves.

Ruth, too, is true to her name. Friendship is the essence of her being, loyalty burns in her dark eyes, caring tenderness ignites her touch. She is passionate in her friendships, fiercely protective of those she loves. She takes her friends into her heart. She would share with them her soul's yearnings, her imagination's flight. And Naomi and Orpah, sister-in-law and mother-in-law, have been the dearest of her friends, her companions in laughter and melancholy. They have comforted her and she, in turn, has held them in her arms, felt the hot tears of their sorrow upon her skin.

She recognizes that her feelings for each of them are different. She

and Orpah are young. They are widowed and childless, yet each month
the flow of their blood reminds them that the potential for creating
new life dwells within their bodies. Their menstrual surge reassures
them. Their husbands, Mahlon and Chilion, are dead, but their own
lives stretch before them. They speak softly of this to each other, fearful
that their words might wound Naomi, discomfited by their own desires.
But when they speak, that discomfort is abated. Shared confidences re-
lieve their anxiety, anneal their sadness.

They are both daughters of Moab and they sing the songs of their
girlhood, dance toward each other in graceful partnership, exchange
reminiscences. Theirs is a friendship of mutuality, of easy rapport and
spontaneous affection.

But of Naomi, Ruth asks questions, probes for answers and insights.
She will learn from Naomi, her mother-in-law turned friend. In all
things Naomi has gone before her, and she offers the lessons of her life
with gentle generosity. Orpah too, listens to Naomi, but it is Ruth who
is the diligent student, the earnest observer. Naomi is her mentor; she
guides her into womanhood. Naomi taught her that even in mourning,
according to the beliefs of her people Israel, there is dignity and
purpose—a set plan in death as there is in life. It is from Naomi that
she learns the small secrets of survival, the intricacies of relationships.
These are things that an older woman teaches her young friends—the
wisdom that one generation wills to another.

Friendship was Ruth's talent. Naomi honed it into genius.

The egret alights upon the low-hanging branch of a terebinth tree
and the three women watch it from the distance. Soon it will soar
again, shearing its way through the cobalt sky, shadowing the pale sand
on its journey home.

"We draw near to the Sea of Salt," Naomi says, and her daughters-
in-law nod but do not speak. They know Naomi is reminding them
that they stand between Moab and Judah, equidistant between their
homeland and her own. They avert their eyes because they do not want
to see the sadness in Naomi's face as she remembers that ten years
earlier she had passed this way. She was wife and mother then, accompanied by her strong, proud husband and two young sons. They were
on a journey of hope, fleeing the famine in Judah to find sustenance in
the fields of Moab.

That famine has ended. Travelers to Moab brought them that news only days ago, and Naomi decided at once to retrace her steps. But now she is widowed and bereft of her sons, with only the friendship of Orpah and Ruth to sustain her.

Ruth reaches out to Orpah, touches her hand, but Orpah's gaze is fixed on the egret, now in swift flight, fast becoming a slash of white in the distance. Orpah has never seen the Sea of Salt, where the white bird will nest. She is a daughter of the flat fields of Moab. She loves the low hills of her homeland. Caves and mountains frighten her. And Judah is a land of caves and mountains, of rock-bound fields and thistled paths. Chilion spoke of them as he played with her hair, as he ringed his fingers with the red-gold tendrils, his voice like his mother's, dreamy and pleasant.

Naomi smiles at them.

"My brides," she begins. Always she has called them that, recalling their beauty on their wedding days, their courage in taking the young men from Judah as husbands. "I want you to return to the homes of your mothers." She speaks with quiet authority yet they all recognize that her only power over them is her affection.

Ruth, ever the querying student, wonders why Naomi speaks of her mother's dwelling place rather than the tent of her father. The answer comes to her when Naomi takes Orpah's hand in her own and places her arm about Ruth's shoulders. Of course, Naomi would have them make their home among women, because they have grown used to soft voices and gentle hands. They have lived, the three widows, as a family of women, sharing friends who understand the pangs of loss, the fear of loneliness, the solace of silence. They need the comfort of their mothers' soft breasts, their sisters' sweet voices. Later, when the wounds of grief are healed, they will find rest in the homes of the men who, one day, will become their husbands.

Of this Naomi assures them, in her pleasant musical voice, and then, drawing them close, she kisses them. Her lips taste the saline streaks of their sorrow. They are both weeping, and she knows that they will not be comforted.

Ruth and Orpah speak in unison, their words grief-strangled but their meaning clear.

"No. We will return with you to your people."

She laughs, a wounding, mocking sound that startles them, and when she speaks there is a hint of anger in her tone. They are aware, for the first time, of a strain of envy, a muted wrath. But because they know her so well, they realize that she does not begrudge them their youth but mourns the loss of her own. They recognize that her anger is directed not at them but at an arbitrary God who has left her widowed and childless, an aging woman who will never again love a husband or bear children.

She confirms this as she speaks to them with love and concern. They must return to their own land and build new lives. There is generosity in her plea, the generosity of her long affection for them. It does not matter that if they leave her, she will have to continue the long and arduous journey alone. Such is her devotion to them that their future takes precedence over her present. Such is her friendship for them.

They are silent. Always they have been obedient to her, relying on her wisdom, according her the deference of their love. Slowly, reluctantly, Orpah moves forward. She who watched the soaring egret with awe, submits to that wisdom.

She kisses Naomi; her lips flutter like a butterfly across her mother-in-law's sun-parched skin. But she does not kiss Ruth. She does not look at her. She fears that Ruth sees her departure as betrayal. She fears that if she meets Ruth's eyes (the dark eyes that burn with friendship), that if Ruth touches her hand with that caring tenderness she knows so well, she will not have the courage to turn and make her way alone, back to Moab and her mother's tent. And she knows too, that Ruth will not leave Naomi. Ruth is wedded to Naomi's friendship and her wisdom. Orpah has often had the sense that a single soul inhabits the bodies of both Ruth and Naomi.

Naomi's hand touches Orpah's face, her fingers trace her features. A blessing, a gesture of farewell. Ruth stands very still. She will not intrude upon Orpah's decision. She will not burden her with her grief. Slowly, slowly, Orpah retraces her steps, never once looking back.

Naomi watches until Orpah's slight form can no longer be seen and turns again to Ruth. She has obligations to Mahlon's widow. She wants to advise her well, even if that advice tears at her heart. The long years of her life have taught her that true love, true friendship, means setting the other before one's self. And so, again, she urges Ruth to follow after Orpah, to return to the familiar landscape of her life, the religion of her birth.

Ruth listens patiently. In all things Naomi has been right, but in this entreaty Ruth knows her to be wrong. She cannot and will not obey. She has crossed a new threshold of friendship and speaks to Naomi with a new confidence, an absolute certainty. The words fall from her tongue with silver fluency, each phrase heart-forged.

"Do not ask me to leave you. Always I will follow you. Where you go, I will go. Your home will be my home. Your people will be my people and your God, my God. Where you die, I will die, and there I will be buried. Only death will part you from me."

Certainty burnishes Ruth's strong voice. Her words defy further argument. And now it is Naomi who submits, who accepts the younger woman's decision. Hand in hand they continue on their journey, two continuing where three had begun. They feel Orpah's absence but they do not speak of her.

They arrive at last in the town of Bethlehem, where Naomi is remembered, but the misfortunes of her life have so altered her that the friends of her young womanhood are briefly bewildered.

"Naomi? Is it really you, Naomi?" they call to her. It is the time of the barley harvest and their arms are laden with sheaves of grain.

The ways of pleasantness desert her. She is surrounded by reminders of her vanished happiness, when Elimelech walked by her side and Mahlon and Chilion played in the garden of her large house. Her very name offends her.

"Do not call me Naomi," she says harshly and her fingers cut into Ruth's palm. "Call me Mara—'bitterness'—because my life has been bitter. When I left here I was full of love but I return empty-hearted and alone."

Her words wound Ruth. Naomi is not alone; Ruth is with her. And how can Naomi's heart be empty when Ruth's own heart brims with love for her? But with the wounding comes the balm of forgiveness. Ruth knows (because Naomi has taught her) that in friendship, one must look away, accept small hurts and probe the source of pain. The source of Naomi's pain is her terrible bereavement, her fear of a solitary and poverty-haunted old age. She has, for the moment, forgotten Ruth, but then she is not infallible. Ruth accepts her as she is, as, indeed, Naomi has always accepted Ruth. Naomi relaxes her grip; she holds Ruth's hand gently, as though in apology.

It strikes Ruth that their positions have been reversed. Naomi was a stranger in Moab; now Ruth is a stranger in Judah. There is a new balance to their friendship. Ruth feels a sense of excitement, of anticipation. Sadness leaves her. Naomi will teach her the customs of this land. Naomi will advise her.

And Naomi does advise her. It is Naomi who assents to Ruth's decision to go into the fields and glean after the reapers. Perhaps Naomi speaks vaguely of a particular field owned by Boaz, a close relation of Elimelech. In any case, it is to that field that Ruth goes, her skin honey-colored by the sun-drenched days of her travels, her slender body enfolded in the loose blue shift favored by the women of Moab.

The day is hot but Naomi has pulled Ruth's dark hair back and twisted it into a knot that settles moistly at the nape of her neck. They thought of Orpah then, with her richness of hair, but they had not spoken of her, so careful are they of each other's feelings.

At midday Boaz comes to the field and, as he greets his workers, he sees Ruth. He asks about the beautiful stranger and is told she is the Moabite maiden, the widow of his near kinsman Mahlon, who returned to Judah with Naomi.

Her story is familiar to him. All of Bethlehem has heard of the wondrous companionship of Ruth and Naomi. The townspeople have pondered its mystery, bemused by a friendship that spans the generations, that unites the woman of one land with the woman of another. Its rarity intrigues.

When Ruth approaches him, Boaz is moved by her dignity and beauty.

"Please stay and glean in my field," he pleads, as though it is she who grants him the favor. "My men will protect and serve you."

His kindness overwhelms Ruth, even bewilders her. But Boaz is swift to explain that he has heard of Ruth's fidelity to Naomi, her tenderness toward the older woman. He would emulate her kindness. The friendship between the two women, the pedagogy of their simple actions, has served as an example to him, has taught him to behave with similar generosity, similar caring. As Ruth and Naomi care for each other, so he will care for Ruth. He offers her the freedom of the field, the bounty of his reaper's table.

Ruth carries her gleanings to Naomi. She tells her of Boaz's words and Naomi nods. She is not surprised.

"This man is close kin to us," she says.

Ruth thrills at the words. *To us.* Not to Naomi alone. With this simple phrase, Naomi acknowledges that she and Ruth are truly one—melded—mutually caring, mutually responsible.

Naomi advises Ruth to continue gleaning in the fields of Boaz. Possessed of the foresight of her age, she perceives possibilities which do not occur to the young Ruth.

The corn is harvested and the days of the barley harvest pass. The gentle winds of spring welcome the wheat harvest. The community is energized by the joy of the season, aglow with the fecundity of the land. Young girls in white garments dance, cradling the first fruits of the harvest, and slender youths watch them with shining eyes. And each day, Ruth goes to glean in the fields of Boaz while Naomi watches and waits. At last she learns that on a particular evening, Boaz will winnow his barley on the threshing floor. She smiles. Her patience has been rewarded. She calls Ruth to her side.

"My daughter." She no longer calls Ruth her "bride." Ruth is truly daughter to her even as she feels herself mother to Ruth—unblooded but linked by heart and mind. "I want your life to be more restful." She speaks in the cryptic language of women who ease harsh reality with euphemism. It will not do to say that she wants Ruth to be free of worries about food and clothing and shelter, that she does not want her to stoop to glean in the corner of the field reserved for the poor.

And Ruth understands that Naomi is sharing ancient secrets with her, inviting her into a womanly intrigue, a delicious and delicate complicity. She listens as Naomi tells her to bathe, to anoint herself with fragrant oils, to dress in her most beautiful robe, and then to make her way to the threshing floor. Naomi is specific in her instructions. She is, after all, an older woman, with knowledge of the desires of men, experienced in subtlety and nuance. She is a wise and loving conspirator.

She tells Ruth that she must conceal herself until Boaz's work is done and he is sated with food and drink and lies down to rest. And Ruth agrees, accepting the authority of her teaching friend, the soft-voiced woman who calls her "daughter."

Beautifully dressed and sweetly perfumed, she waits in a shadowed corner of the threshing floor and watches as Boaz eats and drinks, as laughter lights his eyes and merriment ripples at his lips, as at last he falls into the sleep of exhaustion amid the fragrant husks.

And then, as Naomi has directed her, she moves quietly toward him, uncovers his feet, and lies down against them. He wakes at midnight, conscious of her scent, her touch.

"Who are you?" Hope triggers his question.

"Ruth. Your kinswoman." She whispers into the velvet darkness. "Spread your cloak over me." As birds shelter their mates beneath their wings, so would she have him shelter her.

He smiles, and his voice in reply quivers with pleasure. He blesses her and praises her.

"You have shown as much kindness in the end as in the beginning."

He speaks of the kindness she has shown to Naomi, the loyalty and affection that caused her to accompany Naomi to Bethlehem and to sustain her with her gleanings. It is that kindness, that compassion, that fire him with love for Ruth, who sits at his feet, her lovely face silvered by the drifting harvest moon. He recognizes that she is not a woman of shallow perception. Even as she made the aging Naomi the friend of her heart, so she has chosen the mature Boaz over the younger men of the community. Her choices are intermingled—friendship taught her the ways of love.

Boaz spreads his garment over her in pledge of his protection. He promises that he will seek out the man whose relationship to the family of Elimelech gives him rights over Ruth and he will ask him to release her into Boaz's care.

They pass the night together, speaking softly as the darkness recedes. At their parting, in the milky light of dawn, he places portions of barley within her mantle, enough grain for both her and Naomi. Boaz recognizes that as he sustains the one, so must he sustain the other.

Ruth dashes across the fields, jeweled with the dew of daybreak, to Naomi, who asks the same question that Boaz asked at the midnight hour: "Who are you?" They would both pierce Ruth's innermost self, have her reveal herself to them, gift them with her honesty and love.

Ruth tells Naomi of her exchange with Boaz and Naomi is satisfied. Her plan has succeeded. Her womanly wisdom has triumphed. Surely, Ruth and Boaz will marry. He is a man of action and will allow no impediment to their love. Of this she assures Ruth, as the bright sun of spring bathes Bethlehem in its golden light.

And, indeed, Boaz arranges a release from the other kinsman, in keeping with the customs of Israel. He proclaims then that he will marry Ruth, and the people of the town cheer his decision. Ruth and Naomi, hand in hand, wearing the hooded gray cloaks of their journey, listen to the acclaim that greets the words of Boaz.

"Let your bride be like Rachel and Leah, those who built the house of Israel," an elderly woman calls and Ruth and Naomi drift into reverie.

They remember a starlit evening early in their shared widowhood, when caring companionship soothed their sorrow. Languidly, Ruth wove Orpah's hair into braids and ringlets while Naomi told them the story of Rachel and Leah, the wives of her ancestor Jacob, the two sisters who bravely left the house of their father to follow their husband to his homeland.

"They were sisters," Naomi had said, her eyes resting on the upturned faces of the young women who had married her sons, "as you are, my daughters, my brides."

Do Ruth and Naomi feel Orpah's absence at this moment of sweet triumph? Perhaps. But they imagine her at peace in the fields of Moab and they wish her well. They are as generous in their hopes for her as they are generous in their hopes for each other. They do not blame her because she lacked Ruth's tenacity. The scope of their friendship is both accepting and forgiving, allowing for loss and disappointment, as all true friendships must.

Boaz and Ruth marry, and when Ruth bears Boaz a son the entire community rejoices. The women circle Naomi and exult over the birth of the child. Ruth's infant son will protect Naomi during the days of her old age. He will ensure her posterity. His name will be famous in Israel.

"He is the child of Ruth, who is better to you than seven sons," a woman calls to Naomi. Naomi nods in agreement. The woman has not exaggerated the magnitude of Ruth's friendship.

She kneels beside Ruth, who is still weak from the ordeal of childbirth, gently takes the infant from her and holds him to her own bosom. With this gesture she claims the child as her own. Ruth is his mother but she will be his nurse, her final act of friendship.

The assembled women recognize that Ruth and Naomi will share in the raising of the child, whom they call Obed.

"A son has been born to Naomi," they sing laughingly.

Ruth and Naomi smile, recalling the words she spoke when she entreated Ruth to return to Moab. "Do I have sons in my womb that may be your husbands?" she had asked.

Yet, Obed is indeed Naomi's son. As surely as he was conceived within Ruth's womb, so was he conceived within the womb of Naomi's wisdom. It was the bond between the two women, as much as the love of the man for his wife, that gave him life. He is son to them both, the bereft and childless women whose long shadows curtained the desert floor, now become joyous mothers at home in the heart of a loving family. He is the reward of their friendship, the inheritor of their talent for love.

Travelers to Moab, the same travelers who brought Naomi news of the end of the famine in Judah, bring Orpah the news of Obed's birth. They recognize her because of the beauty and thickness of the chestnut hair that falls to her waist. They remark upon the wistful sadness of her eyes, although she too has remarried and is the mother of an infant son.

She hugs the news of Obed's birth to her heart and remembers the touch of Naomi's life-worn skin upon her lips. Always, she will be haunted by melancholy because she parted from Ruth without kiss or embrace; always she will feel the loss of the gentle friendship that sustained her in the days of her sorrow.

"Naomi. Ruth." The names of her friends soothe her. Their joy is her joy, their delight, her delight, their lives entwined forever with her own.

Friendship

Ruth Anna Putnam

Friendship is the greatest human good; yet loyalty to a friend may conflict with loyalty to one's country or with the demands of morality. Thus the potential for tragedy appears to lie at the very core of friendship. As we examine one of the great stories of friendship in the Bible, the Book of Ruth, we need to ask whether Ruth's decision to go with Naomi to the land of Judah reveals that problematic core.

Consider, first, how amazing it is that these two women—Ruth and Naomi—were friends at all. If there had been no famine in Judah, Elimelech would not have taken his family to Moab. Even given the famine, he might not have done so. Others remained in Bethlehem, including relatives of Elimelech. But Elimelech left with his wife and sons and "sojourned" in the plains of Moab. They sojourned; that is, they did not intend to settle there permanently. Nevertheless, during their prolonged stay, Elimelech died and his sons married local girls. Had they not done so, Naomi might never have known a Moabite woman well enough to develop a deep and lasting friendship.

Or, again, Naomi might have reacted with anger to these marriages, might have refused to acknowledge these strangers as daughters-in-law. Instead, Ruth's and Orpah's behavior suggests that Naomi not only accepted these Moabite brides but befriended them. It is important to realize that Ruth would never have loved Naomi if Naomi had not acted in ways that ran counter to her tradition. It would be a mistake

---

The author used *Ruth* in *The Five Megilloth* (London, Jerusalem, New York: Soncino Press, 1st printing, 1946).

to see Naomi as a woman who was forced (by fear or by the prevailing morality) to follow her husband into Moab and to accept her sons' marriages, but who regretted and resented being forced to act in ways that she, as a pious Jew, regarded as sinful. That conception fails to explain the love Ruth felt for Naomi. A young Moabite woman might be expected to be polite, obedient, considerate, even kind toward her mother-in-law, but one would not expect a deep attachment. Had Naomi been rich and Ruth destitute, we could attribute Ruth's choice to economic necessity, but the facts were otherwise. Ruth chose Naomi out of a deep love, a love kindled by Naomi's character. Ruth was an extraordinary human being, but Naomi was her model.

Naomi accompanied Elimelech to the fields of Moab as a loving wife, not merely an obedient wife or one who feared starvation were she to remain behind. She chose to leave her home as Ruth would later choose to leave hers. Again, when her sons married Moabite women, she accepted her daughters-in-law not because she was dependent on the goodwill of her sons but because her relationships with her sons mattered to her; she knew that those relationships could be maintained and would continue to grow only if they included the new daughters-in-law. So she suppressed whatever misgivings she had. She welcomed Orpah and Ruth, and together they established relationships based on respect and trust. Finally, slowly and carefully, always mindful of their feelings, Naomi began to introduce these young women to Judaism. And then tragedy struck: both sons died.

Only then did Naomi hear that the famine in Judah had ended. Did the famine really last more than ten years? Would we not read more of a disaster of such proportions? Is it not more plausible that Naomi was able to hear this news only when ties of loyalty no longer held her in Moab? To be sure, she still had two daughters-in-law, but she knew very well that these young women would be better off without her. Once their old mother-in-law had returned to Judah, the young widows could return to their parents and, being young, childless, and, presumably, of good families, would probably find new husbands among the Moabites. Naomi's decision to return to her homeland now that she could do so without betraying any trust, without abandoning husband or sons, reinforced the model she provided for Ruth, the model of someone who put love for a human being over love for her country, not because she did not love her country, but because she put personal loyalty first.

So the three women left their home and the daughters-in-law accompanied Naomi. After a while she suggested gently, lovingly, that it was time for them to return to their mothers' houses. She knew that, in returning, they would return to Moabite ways, worship the Moabite deity, yet she did not believe that this would be, for them, a sin; "The Lord deal kindly with you," she said. Surely, she would not have blessed them had she thought their behavior would offend the Lord. The daughters-in-law demurred, but she urged them on. She painted for them a picture of the lonely life they would lead with her in Judah; there, as destitute strangers without family, their chances of finding husbands would be almost nil. And so, with tears and kisses, Orpah turned back; but Ruth clung to Naomi. And now Naomi made the choice very clear to Ruth; Orpah, she said, has "returned to her people and to her god"; she has, that is, returned to the circle of her family, to people with whom she will find it easy to establish lasting relationships, to a way of life that is second nature to her, to the morality in which she was raised, and to forms of worship that are, for her, rich with meaning. All this, and all the emotional attachments that go with it, from familiar surroundings ("where you lodge, there will I lodge") to burial in one's native land ("where you die, will I die, and there will I be buried"), Ruth was prepared to give up for Naomi.

While Ruth's sacrifice has been read as motivated by the desire to embrace a higher morality and the One God, this reading fails to reveal the moral ambiguities of the situation. The text does not describe the Moabites as idolaters nor does it suggest that Moabite morality was inferior to that of the Jews during the time of the Judges. The Moabites treated the family of Elimelech well; they allowed these Jews to live among them and even to marry their daughters. Neither justice nor mercy require more. Neither justice nor mercy required Ruth to accompany Naomi.

Reading the text in this way enables us to understand Ruth as a person who chooses her friend over her country. Nevertheless, while the book presents a model of the lengths to which a loyal friend will go, it does not reveal the potential for tragedy hidden within every deep friendship. No doubt Ruth grieved to leave her people, no doubt her parents grieved to see her leave, but this kind of grief is not the stuff of tragedy. To find tragedy we must turn to the other great friendship in the Bible, that between Ruth's great-grandson David and King Saul's son Jonathan.

This too was an unlikely friendship, this friendship between the son of a king and the shepherd who would be the next king. The events leading up to the moment when Jonathan's "soul was knit with the soul of David" and he "loved him as his own soul" are strangely tangled. David had been called to the king's palace to soothe him with his lyre playing, but he had not met Jonathan on any of these occasions. Later, after David defeated the Philistine champion, Goliath, he was once again brought before the king. Oddly, Saul seemed not to recognize that the young warrior was also the sweet singer who had comforted him in his distress. This was the moment when Jonathan and David met and became friends, when Jonathan shared his clothes with the shepherd, who no doubt had nothing suitable to wear at court, and when "they made a covenant because he loved him as his own soul" (1 Samuel 18:3). Is it not odd that they "made a covenant"? There was nothing like that in the case of Ruth and Naomi. Why did these young men need a covenant? Did they already understand that the situation was fraught with the potential for misunderstanding and mistrust? What was the content of this covenant? We are never told.

Things went badly almost immediately. David became a successful leader of Saul's army, and the people acclaimed him as more valiant than Saul. Although Saul and Jonathan did not know that the aging prophet Samuel had actually anointed David—that ceremony had been carried out in privacy, with only David's family present—Saul seems to have suspected that David was destined to be his successor. For Saul began to hate David, tried to kill him, and failing that schemed to bring about his death indirectly. Jonathan, in contrast, far from being jealous when the people praised David, rejoiced in his friend's triumphs. Whatever good happened to David delighted Jonathan, and he watched with growing concern his father's alienation from the young hero. When Saul suggested that Jonathan kill David, Jonathan not only warned David but remonstrated with his father and brought about a reconciliation. However, David excelled in yet another battle, and Saul once again could see him only as a rival; far from being soothed by his lyre playing, Saul because so enraged that he threw his spear at David. Although

Jonathan could not believe that his father really meant to kill David—surely, he thought, this episode was due to a temporary derangement—he agreed to test Saul's intentions and to warn David if the latter's fears were justified, as they turned out to be.

Now Jonathan had to choose. He had to choose not merely between his father and his friend, not merely between his king and his friend, but between his country and his friend. For Jonathan must have known that David would not simply go into exile. He must have anticipated that "every one that was in distress, and every one that was in debt, and every one that was discontented" would join David (1 Samuel 22:2), that David would become, in effect, the leader of a guerrilla band. Jonathan must have foreseen that Saul would pursue David and that there would be a civil war. Jonathan might even have worried that David would join the enemies of Israel and fight his own people. Might it not be better if this potential troublemaker were to die quickly and quietly? Yet Jonathan knew that David had served his king and country well and had made no moves to exploit his popularity. Under the terms of their agreement, not to warn David would be to lure him back to the court, where death awaited him. Jonathan had to choose between certain death for his friend and a high probability of civil war, a war in which many would die. When one adds to this the fact that the king was Jonathan's father, that by warning David he would disobey, would fail to honor, his father, one begins to understand the agony that Jonathan must have experienced during the long and lonely night before he went to warn David.

And yet, have I not exaggerated the problem? To be sure, one is supposed to honor one's parents, but this duty is overridden by the obligation to save an innocent life. Moreover, does one not honor one's father more by preventing him from sinning? Still, these considerations do not resolve everything. There is the real possibility of civil war and the question of what Jonathan ought to do after delivering the warning. Since it does not seem to have been in Jonathan's power both to warn David and to avert civil war, he had two alternatives: If he returned to the court, he would risk Saul's anger and might be killed. If he remained with David, he would not only save a life but would declare himself an enemy of the king. As we know, Jonathan warned David, then they wept together, fearing they would never see each other again; finally David went on his lonely way, and Jonathan returned to the court. The very fact that Jonathan returned to his father, that he did not at any time join David's little army is evidence that he was aware of the moral complexities of his situation. We know that at some time after the events just recounted it became clear to Jonathan, if it had not been clear before, that David would be the next king of Israel. Jonathan sought out David, the guerrilla leader, and told him, "You shall be king over Israel, and I shall be next to you, and my father Saul knows this also" (1 Samuel 23:17). Did Jonathan hope that by renouncing the throne, he might make peace between David and Saul? If so, he still did not understand what motivated Saul's fierce anger. Once again David and Jonathan made a covenant, and once again Jonathan went home.

Aristotle, the classical philosopher who wrote most adequately about friendship, claimed that true friendship is possible only between equals. These biblical stories force us to examine that claim. So far the friendship between Ruth and Naomi as well as that between Jonathan and David have seemed rather one-sided. Ruth and Jonathan acted, David and Naomi appeared to be the passive recipients of their overflowing love. These appearances are misleading, as the completed stories will show. David was prepared to risk as much or more for the sake of Jonathan as Jonathan had risked for him. David was twice given the opportunity to kill Saul with impunity, yet he refused both times. He would not, he said, raise his hand against the Lord's anointed (1 Samuel 24:4–6, and 26:8–9). But David knew that he, David, was also the Lord's anointed, that Saul was relentlessly seeking to kill him. He might well have thought, as his friends did, that God had delivered Saul into his hand. What prompted David's refusal was the following reflection. If Jonathan had not warned David, David would not now be leading an outlaw band, and Saul would not be making war on him and finding himself suddenly weaponless in David's power. If David were to kill Saul, Jonathan might consider himself responsible for his father's death. David could not impose this burden on Jonathan, not even to save his own life. No doubt, David took as great a risk in refraining from killing Saul as Jonathan took in warning David and, later, meeting him in the forest. Each friend, we may say, risked his life twice for the sake of the other; in love and in courage they were equals. Indeed, David shared both Jonathan's love for Saul and his agony, lamenting their joint death in these words, "Saul and Jonathan were lovely and pleasant in their lives, and in death they were not divided. . . . I am distressed for you, my brother Jonathan" (2 Samuel 1:23, 25).

It is a little more complicated to show that the friendship of Ruth and Naomi also involved equal giving and receiving. Ruth had been gleaning in Boaz's fields throughout the months of the harvest; she had stayed close to Boaz's female servants, thus protecting herself from unwanted male attention. As we find out later, this behavior was understood by Boaz as a further kindness. By not attracting the attention of a young man, by not getting married to a stranger, Ruth had made certain that she would continue to be in a position to provide for Naomi. A husband without family ties to Naomi might well have said, "What is this old woman to me?"

Slowly Naomi's feelings, which seem to have been numbed by grief, returned; she became concerned for Ruth's welfare, sensing that the younger woman needed a husband for comfort, for security, and for the sake of reputation. We do not know why Naomi did not go to consult with Boaz. Perhaps the very fact that she considered Boaz the most suitable, perhaps the only suitable, husband for Ruth, made it impossible to consult him as an older male relative. We do not know whether Boaz was married or a widower; we do not know whether he had any children. We do know that Boaz was a relative and that he had shown much kindness to Ruth. Naomi may have wondered why this man did not propose marriage to the young Moabitess; did he fail to see the beautiful woman under the dust and grime of the gleaner? Perhaps, if he were to meet her in different circumstances, he might think she would make a lovely wife. And Ruth would be able to trust him to provide for Naomi, so she would have no reason to reject his proposal.

So, Naomi, the old woman, wanting to show kindness to Ruth, proposed a scheme fraught with risk. Ruth was to go to the harvest party, dressed in her best clothes, washed and perfumed, yet she was not to make herself known to Boaz until after he had laid himself down for the night; she was to come to him as if she were a seductress. The risks in such behavior were clearly enormous; if she were seen by anyone, her reputation would be stained forever. Even if she were to escape premature detection, Boaz might react with anger and contempt, or he might avail himself of the sexual favors she seemed to offer. One wonders how Naomi could have been so certain that Boaz would not harm Ruth or ruin her reputation; one wonders how she persuaded Ruth to carry out this dangerous scheme. Perhaps what prompted Ruth to accept the plan was the realization that she would not be able, in the long run, to provide adequately for Naomi and herself. Perhaps she persuaded herself that, since Naomi would not ask her to do anything wrong, Naomi must be certain that Boaz would deal kindly and honorably with her. Still, how sure could Naomi be? What thoughts went through her mind during the long night while Ruth was away at the threshing floor? Was Ruth wily enough to remain undetected until she chose to reveal herself? Was Boaz indeed as upright as Naomi believed him to be? Might he misjudge Ruth's intentions or be offended by the sheer presumption of these women? Fortunately, both Ruth and Boaz followed the script perfectly, and soon thereafter they were married. Ruth gave birth to a son, and even Naomi learned to smile again. Who can argue with success?

But success does not prove that the relationship between Ruth and Naomi was based on equality. To be sure, both women were widows and of the same social class, but because Ruth was young and healthy while Naomi was old, broken perhaps in body as well as in spirit, Ruth made all the hard choices, did all the hard work, and took all the risks. Are we to infer that true friendship does not require equality or that this is, after all, not a case of true friendship?

The friendship of Jonathan and David enables us to avoid the conclusion that friendship does not require equality. David and Jonathan were unequal in just the ways Ruth and Naomi were equal, and vice versa. Jonathan was a king's son, heir presumptive to the throne; David was a poor shepherd, later a brilliant young general, and finally an outlaw. Yet the biblical text asserts explicitly that theirs was a deep and true friendship, in spite of the social inequality. What mattered was that each made hard choices and took risks for the other. But that seems to be exactly what Naomi and Ruth did not do. Must we conclude then that they were not friends? To lay this doubt to rest, one needs to recall that the very first friendships mentioned in the Bible are those between God and a human being. Abraham is referred to as God's friend, and God is said to speak to Moses "as a man speaks to his friend" (Exodus 33:11). Of course, there is no equality between God and human beings; all the giving appears to come from Him and all the receiving to be ours. Yet human beings have always given to God, whether in sacrifice or in prayer or in good deeds, and have taken it for granted that God receives these gifts. How can we say, then, that Naomi gave nothing to Ruth or that Ruth did not accept what was given to her? Naomi, by accepting Ruth and Orpah as daughters-in-law, by treating them with respect and love rather than disdain and resentment, taught Ruth to be the kind of friend she was to become. Again, when Naomi warned Ruth against accompanying her to the land of Judah, when she was prepared to give up her last tenuous connection to her dead son for the sake of an easier life for Ruth, was she not offering up everything she had? Finally, though the risk in going to the threshing floor appeared to be all Ruth's, must we not recognize that if the plan had failed Ruth might have had no choice but to return to Moab, that is, to leave Naomi utterly alone? What we learn, I think, is that friendship indeed involves an equal giving and receiving, but that the equality need not be apparent at first glance.

What more concerning friendship can we learn from these biblical texts? I ask this question as a Jewish woman but also as a philosopher. As a Jewish woman I am pleased that the Bible teaches us that true friendship is possible between women, thereby denying Aristotle's claim that it is possible only between men. Yet I am also struck by the fact that we are forced to infer the feelings of Ruth and Naomi from what they do and say; we are never told that their souls "are knit together" as were the souls of David and Jonathan. It is almost as if the modesty required of women forbids the narrator from revealing a woman's deepest self.

Finally, as a philosopher, I want to return to the theme with which I began this essay. Does friendship put one at risk of moral conflict or of tragedy? What one notices in reading these two accounts is the centrality of leaving and returning home. Naomi must leave home to make her friendship with Ruth possible, and she must return home for that friendship to develop fully. Jonathan must leave home to perform his most spectacular acts of friendship but must return home to resolve the moral ambiguity implicit in his actions. Ruth must leave home and not return—must find a new home—to be the friend she is. Even David must leave home to meet Jonathan, though his leaving home, unlike that of the others, is not morally ambiguous.

I am using "home" to represent the moral ways in which one has been taught to walk. Of course, the biblical narrator did not use "leav-

ing home" as a metaphor; I am using it as a metaphor for stepping outside one's moral tradition, in particular for being forced to do that by
loyalty to a specific human being. Such a step is always fraught with
moral danger. We learn to be moral by learning the standards and ideals
of the community in which we are raised; leaving it, we are liable to
flounder. Yet we recognize the existence of moral requirements that
transcend and sometimes transgress particular communal standards.
The Bible recognizes the communal nature of morality as well as the
moral inadequacy of most communities, and it recognizes that a human
being can step outside her or his tradition and make a radical choice.
The communal nature of morality is acknowledged when Ruth, in the
very act of choosing Naomi, also chooses Naomi's people and Naomi's
God. She does not become a person without a country, without a way
in which to walk; on the contrary, she chooses: "Where [how] you go,
there [so] will I go." Because Ruth is never a woman without a country
her story fails to reveal the difficulties of making a radical moral choice;
once again we must turn to the story of David and Jonathan.

David's original leaving home, to join Saul's court, is not morally
problematic; he does not leave the moral ways of his people. He does
just what a valiant young warrior would do and what a future king
ought to do. How else could he learn how to be a king? Nor did Jonathan transgress his people's law when he warned David of Saul's mur-
derous intentions or, later, when he renounced his claims to the throne.
Yet after he had delivered his warning, Jonathan, unlike Ruth, stood for
a moment alone, outside any tradition, for he had to decide whether to
remain with David or to return home. Unlike Ruth, Jonathan did not
have the opportunity to choose a new home. Had he chosen David, he
would have become an outlaw, a person without a country, without a
people, and without a law. Jonathan never betrayed David, but neither
did he leave his people.

Jonathan returned to Saul, and in the end they died together fighting
the enemies of Israel. What are we to make of this? I take my clue from
David's lament: "And in death they were not divided." Returning and
remaining at Saul's side was Jonathan's way of choosing his people and
his God. He could not give them up for David's people and God, as
Ruth had given up her people and god for Naomi's, for David had no
people and God other than Saul's, other than those to which Jonathan
returned. Though we are never told by the narrator that Jonathan loved

Saul, surely this too is acknowledged in David's lament. So we come to understand that Jonathan's death was a tragedy for David but that, for Jonathan, it might have been a greater tragedy to outlive Saul.

I have used the friendship of Jonathan and David to throw light upon the story of Ruth and Naomi. I have used both stories to reflect upon friendship, upon giving and receiving and taking risks, and in particular upon the danger of conflicting loyalties and the potential for tragedy. I was inspired to do this by the chapter on betrayal in Judith Shklar's book *Ordinary Vices.* There she responded to E. M. Forster's saying that if he had to choose between his friend and his country, he hoped he would have the courage to choose his friend. Forster realizes the anguish he would experience; the courage he thinks would be required is the moral courage to brave the condemnation of his countrymen. Shklar rejects Forster's thoughtless assumption that one should always choose the friend, but she agrees that the potential tragedy at the heart of friendship is the moral anguish suffered by one who must choose between loyalty to a friend and another equally stringent moral obligation. Jonathan suffered such anguish in choosing between David and Saul, and found, in the end, a way to choose both. His choice was wiser, more complicated, and, therefore, more morally adequate than simply choosing his friend or simply choosing his country. Though he chose between good and evil, he did not choose between David and Saul.

In contrast, Ruth does not choose between good and evil; she does not suffer moral anguish. The courage required for her choice is not the moral courage envisaged by Forster; it is the simple courage to share the hardships of her friend's life. One is tempted to say that Ruth's story reveals the potential for joy at the heart of friendship, as Jonathan's story reveals the potential for tragedy. Yet, in the end, I do not think that joy and tragedy wait at the core; rather they come into friendship from the outside. Just as tragedy is introduced into the friendship of Jonathan and David by Saul, so joy is introduced into the lives of Ruth and Naomi not by them but by Boaz. Friendships, we learn, do not exist in a social vacuum. Ruth chose Naomi but chose also a people, a moral way. Because Boaz, too, walked in that way, "joy comes in the morning" (Psalm 30).

Feminine Plurals

ROBERTA APFEL AND LISE GRONDAHL

The Book of Ruth is unique as a place in which to study a special category of relationship. It provides us with an example of two women who, though they might have reasons to fear one another, instead choose to share each other's plight. The improbable relationship of Ruth and Naomi permits each of them to forge a new life and to transcend famine, death, and loss. Our joint interest in these two women and their unusual relationship has led us along three paths. We begin this essay where our conversations about the book began—in our supervisory relationship—and outline the ways in which the story of Ruth and Naomi informed our discussions of psychotherapy, supervision, and psychiatry. Next we look at the story as psychiatrists, using our professional experience to better understand the two women at its center and the dynamics of their relationship. Finally, we return to our own interactions, with patients in particular, and suggest how the story of Ruth and Naomi has inspired and contributed to our rethinking of certain long-term therapeutic relationships.

I.

We are two women psychiatrists who met as supervisor (RJA) and supervisee (LMG) and realized early on our many differences—in age and experience, religious background, spiritual practice, and nationality. As

---

The authors used the Anchor Bible translation of the Book of Ruth (Garden City, N.Y.: Doubleday, 1975) and the Serendipity Bible for Groups (Littleton, CO: Serendipity House, 1988). They also used Ruth in *The Pentateuch*, Samson Raphael Hirsch edition (New York: Judaica Press, 1990).

our conversations evolved, we realized we also had a great deal in common—as women, in our approach to patients, in our relationships with our mothers, and in our views of God. We have come to see the enduring friendship that began as a routine supervisory relationship as a blessing.

Supervision, the basic mode of teaching in psychiatric training, consists of weekly one-on-one meetings of a faculty member with a trainee, focusing on individual psychotherapeutic work the trainee is doing with her patient(s). Routinely, supervision is a cordial, yearlong relationship that ends with the academic year and is limited to the discussion of patients, and sometimes of personal matters that are elicited during therapy. Our conversations, however, also included talk of personal, as well as professional, matters elicited by the story of Ruth.

At first Lise experienced Roberta (Robbie) as hostile. With the encouragement of a woman friend who had previously been supervised by Robbie, she decided to explore her feelings rather than yield to her discouraging impression. Lise, a Christian, realized that her first experience with a Jewish mother was with the mother of a man she had loved, a Holocaust survivor who had treated Lise aggressively and judgmentally. That experience was influencing her perception of Robbie's supervision. Robbie, in turn, recognizing Lise's needs, asked herself, "What would my mother have done?" and "What would Naomi have done?" The process of using the Book of Ruth as a touchstone had begun. We were able to talk about how threatening the prospect of losing a son to an outsider had probably been to that Jewish mother, and to distinguish Robbie the supervisor from Robbie as an incarnation of the menacing Jewish mother. Impressed by Lise's honesty, Robbie also shared her shame about the exclusionary views of some Jews who could prematurely judge and cast out a lovely young woman solely because she was not Jewish. Robbie determined to include Lise, who was open and curious about Judaism, in some of her family's Jewish rituals, to be a good Jewish mother to her, a "Naomi" to her "Ruth."

In supervision, we realized that our relationship had some similarity to the Ruth-Naomi relationship we had both admired for many years. The Book of Ruth became the place from which we launched our conversations. This moving biblical story provoked us to examine some rarely addressed aspects of supervision and therapy, to ask questions such as "How can therapeutic relationships be mutually rewarding and growth promoting without violating the essential differences and boundaries between the two individuals?" Gradually we came to appreciate that if we looked at the characters in the story through the prism with which we as psychiatrists look at people, we might add to our understanding of the relationships developed in the Book of Ruth.

II.

The Ruth-Naomi relationship is more than just a model of two people relating across culture, age, and status. It is a model of a mutual, nonjudgmental, accepting, caring, devoted relationship between people who might be expected to quarrel, compete, and find conflict. This type of relationship is found nowhere else in the Bible, and indeed is rare in the world's literature.

It is sometimes difficult to remember who is Ruth and who is Naomi, who the younger, who the older, because of the mutuality in the relationship. From a psychological perspective, each of these women is truly remarkable in her capacity to overcome differences and to act cooperatively and supportively toward the other. This is remarkable in any relationship, all the more so in a relationship between mother-in-law and daughter-in-law. In our culture, and in many others, this relationship is fraught with tension and jealousy. We tend to explain this by saying it is human nature for two women who love the same man to have trouble loving each other. How is it then, that Ruth and Naomi could overcome these differences and become attached, not constrained, by their common love?

The bond between Ruth and Naomi represents the fantasy of an ideal relationship: what mothers often wish to have with their daughters-in-law, and newly marrying women with their mothers-in-law. Ruth and Naomi have a cross-generational merging. Significantly, this merging is most vividly articulated when Ruth gives birth to Obed and the women proclaim, "A son is born to Naomi." Women's relationships often show blurred boundaries around the issue of childbearing. For instance, the mother may see herself in both the daughter and the grandchild. Childbirth thus provides especially powerful linkages for women.

Naomi needs Ruth to bear her a child, now that she has lost her

sons. Ruth needs the love and example of good mothering to become
a mother herself. Each looks to the other to fill an emptiness. Naomi
was a widow in a foreign land when her sons Mahlon and Chilion married the Moabite women Ruth and Orpah. Some women in Naomi's
position would have been bitter and lonely. They might have objected
to these marriages, which further tied them to the new country and
made the possibility of returning home more remote. When both of
these unions proved childless, Naomi suffered further disappointment
and grief.

We think that Naomi must have been unusually understanding and
nonblaming toward her daughters-in-law about their infertility. Having
spent many hours talking with contemporary childless women, we
know that infertility can be personally devastating, as well as profoundly
isolating and stigmatizing. Family members and in-laws can be insensi-
tive and blaming of the childless woman, even though infertility can
have many causes. In Ruth we could ask whether the sons were sick
during the ten years? Were they perhaps infertile or impotent? We don't
know. We do know that Naomi endured, along with her children, the
disappointment of childlessness, and then, with her daughters-in-law,
the loss of her sons, their husbands.

Loss is probably the central theme in psychiatry. Experiences of loss
bond or divide people. After her many losses Naomi renames herself,
changing her original name, which means "pleasant," to Mara, or "bitterness." She feels bitterly treated by God, but she does not act bitterly
toward those close to her. On the contrary, she considers their needs
and the realities of their situation, and offers to leave the young women
and return alone to her homeland. There is a dignity and a pride in this
selfless woman, even at her loneliest, most God-forsaken time; these are
qualities that both touch and engage another person.

Ruth seems to have many of the same qualities—serenity, poise, resolve, determination, devotion, and the willingness to leave her land
and sacrifice a great deal for a relationship (as Naomi did when she
went to Moab with Elimelech in the first place). What is the nature of
her attachment to Naomi? She appears to be perfectly humble and uncomplaining, never protesting the years of deprivation, recognizing that
Naomi needs her. Her deliberate choice to stay with Naomi, to cast her
lot with this older woman, bespeaks a relationship that combines mind
and heart. Ruth perhaps suspects or hopes that Naomi will look out for
her better than her own mother had.

In psychotherapy we often see that the lack of a "good enough mother" leads people to seek out alternative mother figures, the female psychotherapist being one of them. Women whose mothers have not adequately met their needs for nurturance and emotional validation inevitably bring wounds from the mother-daughter relationship into the relationship with the mother-in-law (and into a psychotherapeutic relationship). The quest for a healing maternal experience is powerfully motivated, and the possibilities for enormous disappointment exist. As clinicians, we might interpret Ruth's choice to be with Naomi as an indicator of her need for a caretaking mother figure to serve as a guide for future relationships with men and children. Naomi had already proved the strength of her love by her acceptance of Ruth throughout Ruth's barrenness, her desire for grandchildren and descendants notwithstanding. Their relationship had nurtured both of them; in spite of hunger and loss, Naomi did not engulf Ruth, who must have experienced some freedom to grow and be herself in their relationship.

We know that when people make major life decisions they are guided by multiple determinants, conscious and unconscious. What may seem to be a whim of the moment, with no apparent rationale even to the one making the decision, may in fact reflect a variety of experiences accumulated over many years. We can only speculate about the experiences that led to Ruth's decision to follow Naomi. Ruth had experienced Naomi's special relationship to her God and to her people, which she must have found compelling. Ruth may have sensed that Naomi knew the God of Israel in a way that she, as a Moabite woman, did not. Ruth may have come to know over the years of observing Naomi (and her own husband) that Naomi's life was based on faith in God and God's provision, even when the bounty was not apparent. The wisdom and beauty of a life based on the guidelines of the Bible, on prayer even in the absence of a Hebrew congregation, may have given beauty to her character and life that Ruth hoped to emulate.

When Ruth decides to emigrate with Naomi, we are told that "Ruth clung to her" (1:14). The word "cling" is not pejorative in the biblical usage, although nowadays it might suggest a dependent relationship that does not permit separation and growth. In our current culturally biased view, love relationships are only genuine when they permit separation and individuation. Clinging is seen as pathological or symbiotic and is derisively dismissed as unhealthy.

The special bond between Ruth and Naomi, characterized by attachment, identification, indebtedness, need, and altruism, provides a counter to the current model of relationships, with its emphasis on separation. In fact, it is an example of a relationship that overcomes the odds, that transcends what might be expected in human connections. Though Naomi and Ruth were mother-in-law and daughter-in-law, we see similarities to some other relationships between women that go beyond the usual limitations to a true, lifelong love relationship.

III.

Sometimes therapy relationships form under quite trying circumstances—for example, in a psychiatric hospitalization following a suicide attempt or during a psychotic episode. In such extreme situations a human bond is created. The patient feels that this therapist understands something about her and has shared something so painful and shameful that the attachment lasts for a lifetime. Almost every therapist, male or female, has one such patient, or several. These bonds can cross gender lines, but it is our impression that they most frequently form when both therapist and patient are women.

Often such special bonds develop with patients the therapist meets in the first stages of residency, when her vulnerability and therapeutic zeal combine with the helplessness and neediness of the patient to create a mutually satisfying and useful relationship. The patient may continue to see the therapist for many years, sometimes infrequently, sometimes regularly. She continues to progress in life, to have success in personal relationships, to fulfill her career ambitions. But whenever there is discussion of separation, the patient loses some ground, has difficulty contemplating being without the therapist. Furthermore, the therapist finds herself somewhat dependent on the patient, not just for the steady income or company, but for the opportunity to connect deeply with another human being over a lifetime—to feel gratified by whatever the patient achieves, to bask in her successes, and to cry with her over the sorrows and disappointments of life. While one person continues to be therapist and the other patient, there is an abiding friendship.

Therapists acknowledge these lifelong connections with patients hesitantly. They may feel they have failed to separate from these patients. Separation is a value and virtue in modern psychiatry, which is well

known for aiding and abetting independence. While recent psychoanalytic literature has increasingly recognized the mutuality of therapeutic
relationships, so that even the most classical psychoanalytic treatment is
understood to be a two-person event, there is little open discussion, or
even admission, of the reality of lifelong therapeutic relationships.
There almost seems to be a moral imperative to bring a therapeutic relationship to closure. When this does not happen readily, the therapist
may have a sense of shame for holding on to the patient too long.

This jaundiced view of the continuing connectedness that worked so
well for Ruth and Naomi, and works well (albeit quietly) for many patients and therapists, is decried in Ann Roiphe's popular novel *Lovingkindness*. Roiphe asks,

> Why do psychiatrists believe so firmly in separation? Why do they insist
> that each of us must stand free of the background, never cleaving or
> clinging or God forbid merging with another? Is it not excessive puritan-
> ism, this hellfire and brimstone preaching, this vision of the moral life
> as one in which one works through memories, parents, childhood, fan-
> tasies, and emerges from the past, single and singular? This is a cruel vi-
> sion that goes against the grain of human effort. Is it some ill will of
> Freud's that has broken across our time and causes this absence of love
> we call maturity?

In contrast, the following case history illustrates the bonding and mutually beneficial continuing relationship between one woman therapist
and her patient.

Mrs. Q was a depressed, suicidal stepmother of four and mother of
two small children who was overwhelmed and in a loveless marriage
when we first met. Relieved of her home duties by a psychiatric hospitalization, she quickly attached to members of the staff and to other patients, who liked her for her genuine interest in them, her wit, and her
willingness to help out with ward activities. She revealed her feelings of
shame regarding her marriage to an alcoholic widower, who at first had
seemed to rescue her from poverty and had made her an instant mother
at thirty-five; she, in turn, had tried to rescue him and his motherless,
unhappy children. This echoed her attempts to rescue her own depressed mother and alcoholic father. After her own babies were born,
she suffered severe physical illnesses. When a beloved housekeeper left
the family, Mrs. Q felt unable to cope and was referred for psychiatric

care by her obstetrician. Soon after Mrs. Q's psychiatric hospitalization, the obstetrician died suddenly; the loss was shared by psychiatrist and patient.

The patient came from an ethnic and religious background different from that of the psychiatrist; they were from the same city and had grown up at about the same time, each curious about, but fearful of, the other's group. This probably provided a background for mutual recognition and interest. The therapy continued over many years— through the patient's divorce, more serious illness, the growth of her children, the death of her parents. The therapist experienced similar life challenges and changes during this time and realized that she had learned from the patient about what to anticipate. The therapist had admired the patient's creativity in coping with stress and her ability to network with friends and to learn better self-care, and she was able to apply these lessons to her own life transitions. The patient grew enormously in her friendships and relationships with her children. She returned to graduate school, which she completed successfully, and became financially independent. She was always generous in expressing her gratitude, which made the therapist feel appreciated. Feelings of disappointment or anger were more difficult for the therapist to elicit and the patient to express.

Termination was considered with Mrs. Q several times between the fifth and tenth years of therapy, always at the initiative of the therapist. Each time the idea of termination had to be rethought because of the extreme desolation of the patient and, often, another life crisis. Each crisis clearly reestablished the doctor-patient relationship, which served to make the therapist feel legitimated and needed as a doctor. There typically was a need for explicit medical intervention, e. g., medication or specialty referral. The therapist got the renewed message that her relationship with the patient was stabilizing and therapeutic to the patient, but she worried that she had induced the crisis by suggesting the therapy come to a close. The therapist decided that it was alright to allow Mrs. Q to continue, even if it meant feeling she did not have to work too hard for this patient. The medical crises continued, though at decreasing intervals. The patient suggested meeting less frequently (twice a month instead of weekly) and augmented the sessions with phone calls and extra appointments as needed. When the psychiatrist left the country on sabbatical for a year, Mrs. Q saw a colleague, someone she had also first met during her hospitalization, and was able to use that therapy to her advantage and to expand her considerable network of friends and family. (While the patient always wants to know where she can find her original therapist, it is usually to place the therapist in space, rather than for direct contact. The therapist also likes to know where this patient goes, and carries Mrs. Q in her fantasies and dreams more than other patients who have not shared as much of a worldview, as many interests, and so long a time.) That sabbatical year, while the therapist was in Jerusalem, the patient moved to Jerusalem Road in her hometown; she wrote letters and even arranged to attend a conference in Israel on a topic close to her own area of professional interest. Like Ruth, she literally followed the therapist to Israel, where the two met as colleagues. After the sabbatical, the therapy resumed.

The process of psychotherapy has many parallels to the journey that Naomi and Ruth make. Ruth makes a decision to go with Naomi to a foreign land; Naomi had made the journey when she traveled to Moab with her husband many years before. Naomi knows the road, the best way to travel, how long the journey will take, and the destination. Naomi is the guide; she knows the difficulties and fears to be expected, and she has shared them with someone else before. Ruth embarks on the journey trusting in Naomi and in her own strength to reach the destination with Naomi's help.

In therapy, and in learning to be a therapist in supervision, the process of looking at yourself, your pain, fears, and woundedness, is terrifying. Both past and present fears loom larger than life along the way. How you should travel, who will accompany you, and where you will arrive are all unknowns. The journey often starts, as it did for Ruth and Naomi, at a time of utter darkness, a time of despair, pain, and loss. The supervisor and the therapist offer to walk beside you all along the way, holding the light and providing the hope which makes the journey possible. Ruth and Naomi embarked on a journey with the hope that, as difficult as it might be, they would arrive at a better place. Similarly, a patient embarks on the difficult process of therapy and needs hope from someone who can illuminate the way. And new therapists come for supervision to experienced ones who have traversed the path before.

By seeing her own wounds, deficiencies, and battles reflected in another woman who trusts her, the therapist can find herself more capable and merciful. Oddly enough, we therapists continually experience healing within the work we do. As long as there is integrity on both sides, and the therapist maintains some separate stance, she frequently finds herself being healed in the course of healing her patient.

Reading Ruth has added an unusual and very special quality to our supervisory and therapeutic relationships. We have used this story and its characters to guide us professionally as well as personally. By using our professional experience to fill out the story, we hope we have returned to Ruth a small fraction of what we have received from its continually sustaining tale.

The Concealed Alternative

Avivah Zornberg

The following piece, an edited transcript of a presentation on Ruth, offers an opportunity to enter into a form of traditional Jewish discourse, the shiur—*oral reflections on a classical Jewish text. Avivah Zornberg, who teaches in Jerusalem, gave this* shiur *in 1988 during an intensive day of study shortly before Shavuot sponsored by Lindenbaum Women's College. The structure of the piece reflects its oral character and we are invited into it primarily as auditors in a classroom, participants in an ancient tradition of oral interpretation now being extended by learned women such as Zornberg. Drawing upon a thorough knowledge of the biblical text and a variety of related sources—midrashim, medieval commentaries and works of philosophy, and* halacha *(Jewish law)—Zornberg immerses us in a sea of quotations and interpretations as she moves from one point to the next. She often makes connections (as the sources themselves usually do) through an associative process, based on complex connections among words shared and explored within the texts. At the same time she creates her own unique mode of interpretation, bringing the world of modern literature and philosophy into dialogue with traditional Jewish sources.*

—JAK AND GTR

Megillat Ruth: If one looks at literary criticism, the kinds of comments made on *Megillat Ruth*, until the last few years, all share a certain tone. Everyone thinks of *Megillat Ruth* as the perfect short story. The kinds of words you find are "charming," "picturesque," "idyllic," "attractive." On the whole one gets the impression that this is rather a bland work. And in fact, from a certain point of view, the book has no dramatic ten-

---

The author used her own translation of the Book of Ruth.

sion. There's no evil. There's no conflict, essentially. There doesn't seem to be a moment of crisis in the course of the book.

What makes it a good short story? Why has it charmed so many generations of readers? Is it simply the happy ending? It's understood that happy endings must emerge in counterpoint to some kind of tension before: release only becomes important and effective after tension. Where is the tension in *Megillat Ruth*?

I want to start with the passage that seems most diametrically opposed to the charming, idyllic, picturesque, attractive version of *Megillat Ruth*. It's the point at which Naomi returns to Bethlehem (*bet lechem*, literally, "house of bread"). She returns—she, and her daughter-in-law—the walking dead. When I say that, I have in mind what *Chazal* (the sages) say on the word *va-tishaer* (1:5). *Va-tishaer Naomi*, and Naomi was left over. Naomi was the residue after her husband died. And then, after her two sons died, the word is repeated. *Va-tishaer* one could translate blandly, "she survived." But it's really not that. *Va-tishaer*, the Midrash (Ruth Rabba) says, *Keshearei Menachot*, like the leftovers of a meal offering. When you have a *Korban*, a sacrifice, the main part of it has been sacrificed, has gone up in incense. What is left is the inessential. What is left feels like a husk. *Va-tishaer: Keshearei Menachot.* After Elimelech and the two sons have gone, the women feel themselves to be like nothing, like husks. The walking dead. They come back to Bethlehem because they hear there is bread in *bet lechem*. But there is a sense that they are going to sustain life only on a minimal level. They are ghosts walking along the road.

And then you look at chapter 1, verse 19: *Vayehi kevoana bet lechem, va-tehom kol ha-ir alehen*, and when they came to Bethlehem, all the city *tehom*, was in a turmoil, in a frisson. *Va-tehom* is a very strong word. It's a word for panic. To be *mehumam* (*hamama, mehumam*) means to be stunned. It means not being able to understand the beginning, the middle, or the end of what's going on. Everyone is in a panic when they see Naomi walking along the road. They don't give any physical description of what Naomi looks like, but one can imagine. When they see Naomi walking along the road, they ask, *Hazot Naomi?* Is this Naomi? (1:19). And that speaks worlds: it's existential wonder. How could this happen to the woman we knew? It was only a few years. She looks like *shearei menachot*, like the husk that has been left over after the core of life has been removed. It's not just that she doesn't have her husband with her. She doesn't have her children; she doesn't have her property; and that seems to have affected her very selfhood. It's not that she comes back alone, in her full selfhood; her selfhood is eroded.

Hazot Naomi?—Is this Naomi? Is this the same person?

Va-tomer alehen, al tikrena li Naomi—And she said to them, don't call me Naomi;

Kerena li mara—call me the bitter one.

Naomi is the sweet one, but call me the bitter one.

Ki hemar Shaddai li meod—because the Almighty has been very bitter to me, has dealt very bitterly with me. (1:20)

Ani, melea halakhti, ve-reikam heshivani Hashem—I was full when I left, and empty, God brought me back.

Lama tikrena li Naomi, veHashem ana vi, veShaddai hera li—so why should you call me Naomi, pleasant one, sweet one, when God has *ana vi*. (1:21)

I want to look at that.

What has God done to me? I suppose the simplest translation would be "God has afflicted me." God has afflicted me, and the Almighty has dealt evilly with me: *Hera li*. It feels bad, what God has done to me. She speaks from her subjective point of view. It's bitter and it's bad, what God has done to me. As she says elsewhere: *Yad Hashem yatza vi*, God's hand has gone out against me (1:13). God has it in for me. I feel there is a plot, a destiny against me.

Now this is not charming or idyllic or picturesque. This suggests a different mode. And what it suggests, if we take these verses as far as they'll take us, is exactly Kafka's world of existential guilt and despair. Take for instance that phrase: *Ani melea halakhti*, I was full when I went out, and I'm empty coming back, I return empty. What is *melea*? The classic commentator Rashi understands *melea*, full, as *beosher u-vanim*, (with wealth and children).

It seems that to be full means to have within oneself the best that the world can offer. Naomi is not talking about spiritual values here. She's talking about the things that fill one up in the world: To have a child, or even to have wealth or property—these are not extraneous things, something out there, apart from the self. Indeed, there is a surprising emphasis in the Megillah on the role property played in a person's sense of destiny, of selfhood. We see this when the Midrash (Ruth Rabba) comments that, in punishing Naomi's husband and children, God didn't strike them down right away but first killed their camels and their sheep. This isn't simply an early warning; it begins to erode the richness of their selfhood. When they lose their sheep and camels, that is the beginning. At this they should sit up and take notice; they should notice that something is being said to them, that there is a message. Wealth and property are not extraneous to the self; they're part of one's sense of oneself. As are children, even more so.

Then Naomi uses this strange expression: *Hashem ana vi*, God afflicted me. What exactly does "afflict" mean? Rashi says, "He testified against me, that I had been guilty in his presence." I had been guilty of something. He testified against me, that I am incriminated of some unknown crime. Then Rashi quotes another reading. *Ana vi: midat hadin*, God's faculty of judgment has afflicted me. God in his role as judge, as punisher, has come out and afflicted me. So *ana vi* can mean to afflict, to produce pain, to impose pain on me, or it can mean to testify against me.

What is the testimony that proves my guilt? The punishment itself. Although Naomi says that she must have been guilty, it's as if she doesn't really know what she is guilty of. It's only when things happen to her that she says, I assume, in a world that has meaning, in a world in which there is God, that these things that have happened to me serve the role of punishment. I must have done something to deserve it. But what am I guilty of?

Does Naomi know what she is guilty of? The verse expresses a double bitterness—not only do I have to suffer these losses, but I have to suffer the pain of knowing that these losses are an indication that I am guilty. Her losses are also her shame, her humiliation. This is what I want to stress here: the sense of humiliation with which Naomi, and Ruth by association, returns to Bethlehem. And it's not only that she suffers an actual diminution of self, but that she senses that everyone is looking at her, that everyone witnesses her humiliation, that everyone knows that if she suffers then she must be guilty of something.

Now that sense of enormous, of boundless, guilt is exactly what I mean by the Kafka situation. Take for instance, *The Trial*, where K. is constantly shifted from pillar to post as he tries to find out what he's being tried for. He knows that he's guilty of something. He tries to argue for his innocence, tries every means of escape from the situation.

Of course, his guilt remains nightmarishly unspecified. In the gruesome last paragraph of the book, as K. observes "with failing eyes" the two strange figures who take him to his death, the shame of his death seems to affect him more than the pain, more than anything else. The shame is aroused by these two witnesses, these two observers who know that he must be guilty and seem to know more than he does.

Now, the sense of the public nature of Naomi's destiny (she is constantly in the public eye) is with us throughout the Megillah. First the neighbors comment on her return. Then, when Ruth comes into the field, she has to run the gauntlet of the boys and the comments they make about her as they explain to Boaz who she is. I hear a certain note of contempt, of criticism—they don't seem to be very admiring. Only Boaz will find something to admire in what Ruth has done. Later, in chapter 4, when Boaz comes to the city, everyone discusses Naomi and Ruth, and finally, the neighbors come to congratulate Naomi and Ruth on the birth of the baby. Most of what happens in the Megillah happens in the public eye. People have all kinds of opinions about what has happened to Naomi.

Naomi assumes that all who witness her suffering know she must be guilty. In interpreting *Hashem ana vi*—God has borne witness against me—Ibn Ezra supports this translation by reference to a verse in Job. (Traditional commentaries often quote other biblical verses which use a cognate word in a context that can help us understand the fuller meaning of the verse being interpreted.) So, concerning *ana vi*, Ibn Ezra refers us to Job 10:17: *techadesh edekha negdi*—you are constantly sending new witnesses against me. The chapter of bitter complaint in which Job says this begins with his saying, *adabra bemar nafshi*, let me speak in the bitterness (*mar*) of my spirit. The word *mar*, of course, echoes one of the words Naomi uses regarding herself several times. What does Job say in the bitterness of his spirit? "I say to my God, don't condemn me. Let me know why You quarrel with me" (Job 10:2). Let me know why You have it in for me. I feel there is a mystery in the destiny You have imposed upon me. I must be guilty—I assume I must be guilty—but I am not clear why. At least tell me exactly what it is that justifies this terrible suffering. "If I am wicked, woe to me. But if I am righteous, yet I still can't lift up my head" (Job 10:15). In the next phrase, listen carefully to the Hebrew: *Seva kalon u-reeh onyi*—because I am filled with shame, and look on my affliction. *Onyi*—from the same root as *ana* in Naomi's *ana vi.* I'm filled with shame as I look on my affliction knowing that the affliction must mean guilt. But at the same time I have this absurd feeling (in an existential sense) that, whether I am guilty or innocent, I can't lift up my head. I experience shame or guilt regardless of what I think I have been doing. It doesn't seem to make sense.

Job is quite an extreme expression of this Kafkaesque vision of the human condition. But Ibn Ezra points to Job, and specifically to his complaint *techadesh edekha negdi*—you are constantly sending new witnesses against me—to give us the sense of what Naomi means here when she says, *Hashem ana vi*, God is constantly bearing witness against me. It isn't one time, it's much more than one time, it has been a whole process. This must mean something, but I don't quite understand what it means. According to the Midrash (Ruth Rabba), *Naomi matzdika aleha et ha-din*, Naomi justifies what has happened to her. In spite of the Kafkaesque aspect—what seems to be an absurd, incommensurate fate, quite out of proportion to anything she may have done—she tries to justify God's action against her.

We do find, in the Midrash, various views that attach meaning to Naomi's guilt. All dwell on her leaving the land of Israel in a time of famine. But I want to focus on Rashi, because I think he makes the moral point clearest. At the beginning of the story, he introduces the theme of the real guilt of Elimelech and his family. What did they do wrong? What justifies the suffering that's brought on them? Rashi comments on the words *va-yelekh ish*, a man went (1:1). *Asher gadol haya u-parnas ha-dor* (this is Rashi)—he was a very rich man, and he was a *parnas ha-dor*. *Parnas* is the benefactor, the one whom everyone comes to and takes from when in need. But *parnas* literally means feeder. He is the one who gives food to the generations. Rashi continues: *Veyatza me'eretz yisrael lechutz la'aretz, mipnei tzarut ha'ayin*—And he left the land of Israel to go abroad because of narrowness of vision, *tzarut ha'ayin*, literally narrowness of the eye, which really means stinginess. He didn't want to open his eyes wide enough to include the needs of other people in a time of famine. *Shehayta eino tzara ba-aniyim*—because his eye was narrow, was resentful, was grudging with the poor. *Habaim ledofko*—who came to pressure him, to press up against him. And that's why he was punished, Rashi says. The reason for the terrible punishment and the fall of his family was the narrowness of the eye, the closing of the apertures, the not wanting to open up because people were pressing against him, pressing against the openings.

These metaphors of pressure against openings, of closing up or narrowing of openings against that pressure, are more explicit in a midrash in Ruth Rabba: Why was Elimelech punished? Because when the famine came he said, *akhshav kol yisrael mesovevin petachai*—Now all Israel will surround my openings, my entrances. He imagines he will be besieged. In a panic, he imagines it as a kind of lynching: *Mesovevin petachai, ze bekupato, veze bekupato*—each one with his little box. Each with his bowl. Suddenly everyone will be there with enormous needs. Each person will become an expression of need. And when my *petachim*, my openings, that out of which I have to give, are so besieged by need—then where am I? The sense of terror at being besieged is very vivid. *Amad, u'varach lo mipnehem*—He stood up and fled before them. It's not just that he was guarding his capital, that he was afraid he wouldn't have any wealth left. It is the existential sense that he is going to be eaten alive by all these people. And that's why it says, *ish mi bet lechem*, a man from *bet lechem*, from the house of bread. The house of bread through the doorways of which he could have fed others. But he was afraid that bread—his own resources, his own being—would eventually be exhausted by all the demands being made through his openings, through his doorways. People coming to pressure him.

So he gets up by himself, whole, intact: *va-yelekh ish*, and a man went. The verb is singular; he went by himself. Not even his wife or his children are included. The family is added at the end of the verse as a kind of afterthought. What we have here is sterile individualism. He goes to protect his own interests; he doesn't want to have to provide for anyone. He doesn't want to have to give out of the bounty of himself to anybody. So that is the sin for which he and his family are punished. Through complicity, Naomi, as his wife, also suffers from this stinginess—the refusal to open up, to make contact with people outside.

On the other hand, Ruth is the opposing modality. The central expression used of her is *Ruth davka ba*, Ruth clung to her (1:14). You will remember that, after much persuasion, Orpah kissed her mother-in-law. (To kiss means to say good-bye.) Orpah kissed and Ruth hugged—actions with different meanings. Orpah's kiss is a kiss of parting, while Ruth's embrace is a refusal to separate. She attaches herself to Naomi, *Ruth davka ba*.

What is it that Ruth wants? Why does she cling to Naomi? One could say in very broad terms that she wants to return with Naomi.

The word "to return," *lashuv*, is used twelve times in the first chapter alone, and it's used in a highly paradoxical sense. What's the paradox? Ruth and Orpah say, *ki itakh nashuv*, we will return with you (1:10), and Ruth is described as *ha-shava misdei Moav*—the one who returns [to Bethlehem] from the fields of Moab (2:6). But she's never been to Bethlehem! She wants to return to a place where she's never been. She attaches herself almost leechlike to Naomi, because there is something that Naomi has that Ruth wants. This is against all logic, because Naomi, in returning there, isn't going to get much out of it. This is not a return to a place where she can become fruitful again. It's not a return to the days of her youth. It's a return in old age. She's going to have a very macabre vision of things now, seeing them from the point of view of emptiness, when before she saw them from the point of view of fullness. And this emptiness is what Ruth wants to attach herself to. She wants to attach herself to a past that's not hers.

The key terms of the book—words like *geula*, redemption, and *hakara*, knowledge—suggest a meaning for Ruth's "return." These are the things that Ruth is seeking. In the end she is recognized: she is known by Boaz, she is redeemed by him. All these words—to return, to redeem, to be recognized—imply going back, a connotation present even in the English prefix "re-."

What is Ruth returning to? She seems to be going into the unknown. *Vatelakhna*—and they went (1:7). That seems to be the more appropriate verb. Like Abraham, who is told *lekh lekha*, go forth (Genesis 12:1), Ruth goes off into the unknown, to a country and a people she doesn't know. As Boaz says to her, "You went to a people you have never known" (2:11).

Moreover, Naomi doesn't seem to want her all that much. Now this is very subtle, of course, and it's arguable. It seems to me, however, that if Naomi is capable of calling herself "the bitter one" who has "returned empty," she isn't much comforted by having Ruth with her. We can't simply say (as a friend of mine did on Shavuot when we were discussing this) that the love of Naomi for Ruth is the same as the love of Ruth for Naomi, a tremendous mutual love. *Ki mar li mikem*, she says to her daughters-in-law. Go back, because it is bitter for me because of you (1:13). Now what does that mean? I feel bad about you; I feel bad about your abandoned condition; I feel bad about your widowhood. Or perhaps it has a different nuance: You have caused me much bitterness.

The fact that my sons married you didn't make my life sweeter. That may be why they died—for marrying you Moabite girls.

Once we sense Naomi's initial lack of rapture, Ruth's attachment becomes even more puzzling. Naomi, of course, also praises Ruth in the beginning. She says, May God deal kindly with both you and Orpah as you have done *chesed im hametim veimadi*—kindness with the dead and with me (1:8). *Chesed* is normally translated "lovingkindness." But there's a very challenging midrash which suggests that perhaps we should translate *chesed* differently, and thereby understand better what is moving Ruth.

The Midrash (Vayikra Rabba 34:8) defines four situations involving *chesed*. One involves the person who does *chesed* with people who don't need it, the prime example being Abraham's feeding the angels who came to visit him (Genesis 18).

In the second situation we find people who don't do *chesed* with those who don't need it. The example here is the Ammonite and Moabite, the people of the two nations who didn't come out to greet the Israelites with bread and water. They didn't do the normal hospitable thing of offering bread and water to a traveling people (Deuteronomy 23:5). And they are terribly punished for it. Even in this case where there was no need for what they didn't give.

The third case is that of one who does *chesed* with someone to whom he really owes a great deal, as Jethro did with Moses (Exodus 2:20). Jethro's feeding of Moses is considered *chesed*, although he was clearly indebted to Moses for rescuing his daughters.

The fourth, and for us most significant, situation, is that of one who does *chesed* with someone who needs it. That is Boaz with Ruth, when in chapter 2 he invites her to partake of the meal. As in the other situations, the *chesed* of Boaz to Ruth is connected with food. But clearly it's not the food that Ruth needs at this point so much as the human acknowledgment that Boaz gives her. What does all this suggest? What is the Midrash saying, through the various permutations of the relation between giver and taker, about the meaning of *chesed*?

The last permutation is the most comprehensible form of *chesed*, the one we all understand, but the other ones fill out the picture. They cut away the normal associations of *chesed* and bring it down to something very pure—to a question of inspiration, of the spreading of life, the movement outward of life and goodness. I give because I want life to be more, because I want more life, because I want what may not be sufficiently alive to be more alive. Or, I want what may be already sufficiently alive to be more alive, because I have an abundance, because I have plenty within me, because I want to give out to the world, regardless of the particular need at the particular moment. It's the opposite of Elimelech, who closes up his entrances, entrenches himself within himself.

What do we have with Ruth here? The ending of the story shows her being redeemed. And Boaz acts out of *chesed*, in this fourth sense, when he redeems Ruth together with her fields. The obvious redeemer, the person closest to her husband's family, doesn't want to take her on. He's willing to take the field, but he won't take her. But Boaz does redeem her, not because the law demands it, but out of *chesed*. Though there is a law alluded to with the phrase *l'hakim shem ha-met*, to raise up the name of the dead (4:5), this law of *yibbum* (levirate marriage) applies only to the husband's brother and not to other relatives. In that sense Boaz, in marrying Ruth, is not fulfilling a law. What we are dealing with here is a metaphor.

To clarify the true meaning of *yibbum*, I want to draw your attention to two sources. One is Rambam (Maimonides) at the beginning of Hilchot Yibbum (laws of levirate marriage). According to Rambam, when the brother comes to marry the widow he doesn't need a formal marriage ceremony; he is automatically married to her. Why? Here we find a startling section in Sefer Hachinukh (the Book of Education), a medieval text which usually gives us lists of the commandments in each particular portion of the Torah with a detailed explanation of the laws derived from each commandment. But when the author deals with this law of *yibbum*, of the marrying of the brother-in-law and the widow, he shifts to another mode. He says that a man's wife is like one of his limbs—*ke'echad me'everav*—then quotes Genesis 2:23, where Adam describes Eve as "bone of my bones and flesh of my flesh." For him this represents a natural concept. By nature, a wife shares her identity with her husband; they're not two separate identities. When the husband dies, she remains in the world as an expression of something of him. If he dies childless, she remains as his one possibility for having children in his name. She is still married to him. She still remains, as it were, connected—"bone of my bones."

And with whom can she have a child? With his brother, who also is *chatzi mibesaro*, half of his flesh. This is very interesting stuff: half of his flesh. Where do we find the idea of brothers sharing the same flesh? In the Joseph story, where Judah, pleading for Joseph's life before his brothers, says, *achinu besarenu hu*—he is our brother, our flesh (Genesis 37:27). The Sefer Hachinukh is taking the concept of shared flesh very radically. The author invokes it to fulfill the unsatisfied need of the dead man who hasn't done the one thing a person wants to do in the world: to leave life behind him which bears his name. Not literally— *Lehakim shem hamet* doesn't mean to name him after the father—but there should be a continuance of the identity, of the memory of the dead in the world. How can that be done? Only through those who in some real sense belong to the dead.

Now there's a concept here of the relationship within a family, the relationship of husband and wife, the relationship between brothers, that goes very far. On this physical infrastructure a metaphysical notion is being built up, of individuality as being a very blurred matter. *Etzem meatzamai*, bone of my bones—there is something within Ruth's bones now that is unsatisfied. And there is even the suggestion that the child who is born in the end is a movement backward through her of the soul of Mahlon. As the neighbors say to Naomi, *yulad ben leNaomi*, a child is born to Naomi (4:17); *Vehaya lemeshiv nefesh*, and it will be a returner of the soul (4:15). In other words, the child has come back to Naomi.

The name Mahlon is generally connected with sickness, but it also suggests *mechilah*, entreaty. The expression appears when Moses prays for the people after the sin of the golden calf. *Vayichal Moshe*—and Moses entreated (Exodus 32:11). As every term for prayer has a different nuance, the rabbis ask what kind of prayer this is. In the Talmud (Berachot 32a) Rabbi Elazar says (it always sticks in my mind) that *vayichal* incorporates the notion of *esh shel atzamot*, the fire in the bones, a kind of fever. Moses prays with a kind of fever because he can't detach himself from his people as God has asked him to do. They are part of him, *etzem meatzamai*, bone of my bones. So they are a fever in his bones that he has to redeem, to give life to.

My suggestion is that Ruth loves her husband Mahlon with a fever in her bones. There can be no other reason for her attaching herself in this way to Mahlon's mother. Of course, I am not discounting all the other levels of the attachment. There is a personal level, obviously, and a sense in which Naomi represents the Jewish religion and the Jewish people.

At the level that I am suggesting here, I can't help hearing in the word *davek*, to cling, the word used about Ruth more than once, the sense of "dybbuk." She is a clinger, one who holds on desperately for the necessities of life. Because she has life to give and won't let go until she finds her opportunity for giving life, she is also, in a sense, possessed; she has *esh shel atzamot*, fire in the bones. She has that fire of Mahlon, who will find his life in the world through her.

Ruth is not only *davek*—one who clings—but, as Boaz says, she is one who "left her father and mother" (2:11). The two phrases recall the terms used in Genesis 2:24 regarding marriage: a man will leave his father and his mother, and cling to his wife. In the case of Adam, it's clear that by clinging to Eve, who has been taken out of him, he is restoring a prior unity. But Ruth's aim in abandoning her father and mother is to restore a larger unity, which means to produce a child, the possibility for which apparently has been lost. But she refuses to acknowledge that it has been eternally lost. She sets up a kind of counterfactuality which I want to explore here.

Naomi tries every way she knows to put her off. And if Naomi's words in the text aren't enough of a deterrent, the Midrash on the text (Ruth Rabba) puts even harsher warnings into Naomi's mouth. In the text, Naomi concentrates on the implications of her age: I am too old; even if I were to marry tonight would you wait for me to produce sons for you to marry? Would you constrict yourself? Naomi is offering Ruth (actually, both Ruth and Orpah at this point) a prospect that constitutes the opposite of life. She is saying, "That's all I can offer you." There is nowhere you can move if you come with me. You won't find any way of doing what you want to do if you cling to me.

The Midrash, by reading Ruth's poetic statements as literal responses to questions from Naomi, imagines Naomi presenting Ruth with even more constricted possibilities. Naomi has asked her, "Do you know that Jewish people don't go to circuses and theaters? That there are certain kinds of things Jewish people don't do?" Ruth responds, "Wherever you go, I shall go." Naomi says to her, "Do you know about the four kinds of death penalty with which the court punishes certain extreme crimes?" She raises the prospect of death as not only part of the inevitable human condition but part of the legal structure of the community, emphasizing its inviolable boundaries. Ruth responds, "Wherever you die, there will I be buried." Naomi tells her, "We are forbidden to walk beyond a certain distance on the Sabbath. We can go so far and no further. We have to stop walking." Again, a prospect of constriction, of lack of freedom. "Do you really want to get stuck with me?" Ruth answers, "Wherever you go, I shall go."

Note that Ruth characteristically uses the future tense. This suggests a tremendous concern with the relation between past and future. According to Naomi, things are closed, defined, decided; there is no exit from the situation; on every level, Ruth would be entering into constriction. This *teshuva*, this return, doesn't offer you a way of life. It's a dead end. But Ruth insists on using the future tense, with all that implies.

In the Midrash Naomi also tries to put Ruth off by explaining all the laws about conversion. She wants to show her how tightly she's going to be painted into a corner if she goes in for this. It's a no-exit situation. But Ruth, by talking in the future tense, sets up a kind of *alterité*, a kind of counterfactuality. Although I accept everything you say, I see a possibility. And even where I too must acknowledge finality, *ki yafrid*— that death does divide (1:17)—still I will find a way of saying no to death. I will find a way of affirming that life force, that fever in the bones that, in this particular case, is Mahlon, the unsatisfied, unconcluded story of Mahlon, the dybbuk by whom I am possessed.

Nietzsche said we invent for ourselves the major part of our experience. To use the future tense is to invent, to create possibility counter to the facts. The rabbis see this creativity as defining Ruth's character. Why, they ask, is she called Ruth? *Shera'ata divrei chamata*—she saw (*ra'ata*) the point of the words of her mother-in-law (Ruth Rabba). She didn't sweep them aside lightly or cavalierly. She saw exactly what her mother-in-law was saying to her about the anxiety of nonbeing (in Tillich's terms), about the fact that nonbeing, not to be, is the ultimate fate. And she accepts, *ra'ata*, that Naomi has nothing beyond that to offer her—not choirs of angels or transcendence or even a baby. Ruth accepts, and has, in Tillich's terms, "the courage to be," which is self-affirmation in spite of nonbeing.

As she uses the future tense, she absorbs the threat of nonbeing and acts. And this is what inspires Boaz to call her *eshet chayil*, woman of valor (3:11). This is a familiar expression, but let's look at the context here. In 3:9 Boaz suddenly feels Ruth at his feet. He thinks it's a demon (according to Rashi) and calls out, Who are you? A suggestive question given what we have been saying. Who is she? She has *esh ba'atzamot*, fire in the bones; she has Mahlon with her. So there is something demonic in this force. Plato says eros is a demon, and eros is this desire to increase life. There's a demon here; who are you?

She answers, "I am Ruth your handmaid, and you will spread your skirt over your maidservant because you are the redeemer" (3:9). Notice that it's not an imperative. She doesn't say, Do it; she says, You will do it. Why? Because I am Ruth—*Anokhi Ruth*. There is confidence here, but also modesty: "I am Ruth your maidservant." But to say *anokhi* and to follow it with the future tense reminds me of a way of hearing God's voice speaking the Ten Commandments in Exodus 20. A kabbalistic source interprets *Anokhi Hashem Elokekha*, I am Hashem your God; *Lo yiyeh lekha elohim acherim*, you shall have no other gods before me, (Exodus 20:2–3), as saying that if the "I" (*Anokhi*) is of a certain quality, then there can be no other gods before me. And you *shall* honor your father and mother. What follows is not a question of commandment but of an inevitable projection of the *anokhi*. Once the *anokhi* is understood, everything else follows—the future follows. So Ruth can say with magnificent confidence, *ufarasta*, you shall spread, because *anokhi Ruth amatekha*—I am Ruth your handmaiden.

Why does Boaz respond to this by calling Ruth an *eshet chayil*, a woman of valor? What might he mean by this term? We find a related phrase in Exodus 18:21, where Jethro, instructing Moses on how to organize the camp, tells him to appoint *anshei chayil*—men of valor. Various commentaries say that people of *chayil*, valor, are those who are "worthy to lead a great nation," people with leadership qualities. This doesn't necessarily mean military skills, Ramban (Nachmanides) stresses; it could mean wisdom; in the case of women, it could mean knowing how to manage a household.

Several of the commentaries also stress one particular quality: fearlessness. People of valor should not be afraid of anybody. Ramban calls it *zrizut*, a very extraordinary expression meaning a kind of energy, or alertness. It is again, in Tillich's terms, the courage to be, in spite of fears, hazards, and dangers such as surround Ruth even on a physical level. Notice how often Boaz has to say to his boys, don't touch her, don't hurt her, don't shame her. It's a world full of the possibility of shame, of pain, as we saw at the beginning.

Nevertheless, Ruth is an *eshet chayil* who can use the future tense, who can go through what is closed, what seems to be determined, and not admit that "death divides." There is a telling ambiguity in Ruth's statement to Naomi, usually translated as "Thus and more may God do to me if anything but death will divide between you and me." But the Hebrew can also be read as ". . . if even death will divide . . ." Is Ruth saying that *only* death can divide? Or does the linguistic form of the oath suggest that death will *not* divide? She both acknowledges the power of death, which is very obvious on every level of her experience, and she denies it, says no to the power of death. She will find a way of giving life to the dead.

In *The Prophetic Faith* Martin Buber writes, "Behind every prediction of disaster there stands a concealed alternative." Naomi presents Ruth with predictions of disaster. She tells Ruth that nothing good can come of Ruth's following her. Yet there is a concealed alternative, whether Naomi consciously intends it or not. The concealed alternative that Ruth articulates in her answer is based on the future tense. There is a narrow opening which the person of *chayil*, the person of strength, vitality, and courage, can find if she feels strongly enough both the closure of and the necessity for life.

One final point connects back to our discussion of *chesed*. In the first verse where *chesed* is mentioned, Naomi says to her daughters-in-law, "May God deal kindly with you as you have done with the dead and with me" (1:8). To do *chesed* with the dead, the Midrash (Ruth Rabba) says, is to prepare their shrouds. And what Naomi means by doing *chesed* "with me," with the living, is giving up their marriage contracts and not demanding money from her after their husbands' deaths. In other words, to do *chesed* means both to acknowledge that the dead are dead (to prepare a shroud is one way of doing this) and to refuse to admit that the marriage is over (to take advantage of the rights of the marriage document would indicate that it had ended). That is the *chesed* that Ruth does here. May God give you *chesed*, as you have done *chesed* with the living, this complex form of *chesed* which involves confrontation with nonbeing.

That is, God in *Megillat Ruth*, unlike God in *Megillat Esther*, does as humans do. Humans set the tone. If humans do *chesed*, then God mirrors them. God sometimes does the irrational, the unexpected. But humans set up what Peter Berger, in his book *Rumour of Angels*, calls "signals of transcendence." The phrase refers to certain ordinary human gestures which suggest transcendent order if one pays attention to them. We start with the anthropological and move to the theological. What are the gestures here? We have a woman carrying a load of grain. We have the spreading of a robe over a woman. We have a pinch of corn given to a woman. We have bread dipped in vinegar to stimulate a flagging appetite. We have extremely human gestures that have to do with feeding and sleeping and clothing: the basic human modes that suggest transcendent redemptions. The characters make these movements of *chesed* against the Kafkaesque universe which stares them in the face. When people find the *chayil*, the courage, to do this, then "God will do *chesed*" with them; God will come and break through the patterns that He Himself, apparently, has structured the world on.

A passage in the Midrash on what Adam says when he sees Eve speaks to the vision of *Megillat Ruth*. On Adam's statement "This time it's bone of my bones and flesh of my flesh" (Genesis 2:23), the Midrash (Avot DeRabbi Natan) comments that this one time, the first time, Eve was taken from Adam, and he recognized her as bone of his bones. From then on, however, a person has to marry the friend of his friend. That is, after the first marriage, a man doesn't marry someone who is literally bone of his bones.

He has to go to a stranger, to the daughter of his friend, and find a way of perceiving her as the "bone of his bones," find a way of recovering the lost part of himself through someone who seems to be anything but part of himself. Similarly, one time, the first time, God was the matchmaker for man. He brought Eve to Adam. God set the tone for the *chesed*, for this act of extension of life, increase of life. But from then on, a person must acquire a matchmaker for himself. A person must find within a given, empirical situation the will, the energy, the fire, the courage to find a matchmaker—a way of connecting or relating to something in the world that will allow him to give birth, to create life in the world.

And it is only as a result of this connecting that Adam becomes *ish*, man. He exists as *ish* only in relation to *isha*, woman. Adam recognizes this situation when he names Eve *isha* because she was taken from *ish*. Up to that point he was called *Adam*, human. The words *ish* and *isha* are used in just this sense about Boaz and Ruth. Toward the end, as Boaz is forming his association with Ruth, he is called *haish*, the man (3:16; 3:18). He becomes a man in relation to *ha-isha*, who is Ruth

(4:11). *Ish* and *Isha*, joined together, are now *anashim*, people. And *anashim*, according to the Ibn Ezra commentary (on Exodus 18:21), is the term Moses uses when he repeats Jethro's instructions about leadership in Deuteronomy. Jethro had said, appoint *anshei chayil*—people of courage, people of leadership, fearless people. When Moses passes on the instructions, he doesn't say, appoint *anshei chayil*, he simply says *anashim*, people. According to Ibn Ezra, *anashim* is Moses's translation of *anshei chayil.* So too, Boaz and Ruth reveal their character as *anshei chayil* in the act of becoming *anashim.* They now fully affirm the earlier characterizations of them as *anshei chayil*, people of power, people of courage, in the face of a reality that I find far from idyllic, far from charming, far from picturesque. But it is a reality that offers possibilities of extended life, which people themselves can choose to realize.

2

"For Wherever You Go,
I Will Go"

RUTH 1:16

*R*UTH'S PLEDGE to Naomi has been celebrated by generations of readers. But few discussions of Ruth hear it as a declaration of the love between women. The first two pieces in this section reflect on the woman-centered and erotic nature of the bond between Ruth and Naomi. Alicia Ostriker, in a lyrical prose poem, seeks to "connect scriptural time with our own moment," so as to "embody" a sense that biblical characters are our ancestors and therefore part of us. For her, this account, which focuses on Ruth's love of Naomi, provides a "countertext" to the male-centered design of most of the Bible.

Rebecca Alpert recounts the ways that Jewish lesbians have interpreted the "bond between Ruth and Naomi in the light of the emotional, sexual, and spiritual experiences of Jewish women who love women." She too seeks to see biblical characters as ancestors, providing "role models" that can lend validity to lesbian relationships. Placing herself in the tradition of midrash, she "reads between the lines" of the biblical text to unveil an erotic relationship whose continuity the male hero, Boaz, secures, but to which he is peripheral. By reading this way, she wishes to lend her voice to women who have loved women throughout Jewish history but whose story has been ignored.

Gail Reimer finds in Ruth an altogether different role model. While recognizing Ruth's devotion to Naomi, Reimer sees it as part of Ruth's extraordinary effort to create an autonomous self, a self defined "in relation neither to children nor to men." To go with Naomi, Ruth must abandon any hope of marriage and motherhood. Reimer pushes the idea of Ruth's self-definition in radical directions. Challenging a frequently heard feminist claim that the Bible excludes even the possibility of women reluctant to give birth or take on the maternal role, Reimer focuses on traces in the text that suggest Ruth's resistance to maternity, as well as a recognition and acceptance of that resistance by the women of Bethlehem. By acknowledging these women's interpretation of events, Reimer suggests that the tradition of women "reading Ruth" has its beginnings in the text itself.

The Redeeming
of Ruth

ALICIA OSTRIKER

*"The Redeeming of Ruth" combines biblical commentary with fantasy and autobi-
ography. Though the text reads like prose, I have composed it as I do poetry, seeking
a lyric truth in the text—a truth that will connect scriptural time with our own
moment, and will embody my sense that the men and women of the Bible are my
mothers and fathers: they a portion of me and I of them. Hence the apparent an-
achronisms in my "Ruth" and the gliding of my voice into hers. My writing also
reflects my belief that biblical texts are endlessly complex and subtle and that they
both resist and invite transgressive, antiauthoritarian readings. The story of Ruth
is for me an exemplary countertext within the overwhelmingly patriarchal design
of the Bible, for several reasons: It is a pastoral, where the dominant narrative
mode is epic; it is erotic and woman-centered rather than heroic or legalistic and
male-centered—a perfect counterweight to the appalling war stories of the Book of
Judges; and it stretches our notion of community, quietly endorsing the acceptance
of the Other.*

*Is it significant that love between women is what brings the outsider, the "strang-
er," into the covenant? Does the Naomi-Ruth bond repair the Sarah-Hagar split? To
me it seems a model of potential repair. It delights me as well that Ruth will be the
grandmother of Jesse, who will be the father of King David, since as a Moabitess
Ruth descends from one of Lot's daughters, who lay with her father incestuously
("Moab" means "from the father"). Indeed, Ruth's seduction of the paternal Boaz,
who calls her "daughter," is like an idyllic replay of the story of Lot's daughters. All
of this happens beneath the "wings" of a God whose kindness seems diffused
throughout the text: not a jealous God, not a warrior or punisher, but a being as
naturally benign as nature in a year of good harvest. Next to the Song of Songs, the
Book of Ruth is the biblical text most friendly to the woman reader.*

The author used the King James Version of the Book of Ruth.

And Naomi said, Turn again, my daughters . . .
And Ruth said, Entreat me not to leave thee,
or to return from following after thee: for
whither thou goest I will go; and where thou
lodgest I will lodge; thy people shall be my
people and thy God my God.
                              —RUTH 1:11–16

Some say a host of cavalry or infantry
is the most beautiful sight
on the black earth, and some say
long ships; but I say
whomever one loves, is.

                      —SAPPHO

Sometimes there is no war. It is like the promise. Mere normality is
born, grows up like an awkward country girl whom nobody notices
much until she comes home from dancing at the roadhouse, maybe, or
a backseat at the drive-in movie, and she's pregnant. Now she seems a
new person. Gradually she swells. The stringy hair begins to shine, so
she combs it. The skin clarifies, so she washes. Her stride tells you she
possesses futurity in her round belly, a mischievous miracle, she's been
eating the bread of boundlessness. Between wars, peace—shalom,
greeting—a lump sum, a pregnant young woman, her slender feet upon
the mountains, joy doubles and redoubles itself like cells in mitosis,
tumbles like the fluff of cottonwoods, there is a permanently startled in-
telligence in every seed. You almost forget that all of life is war. History
blurs a little, you can't remember your uncles' combat stories. You forget where the borders used to be. A cornfield on our side looks exactly
like a cornfield on their side, the wind rustles the foliage of the woods,
the guards at the checkpoints go home, their machine guns rust, they
beget numerous children, and on holidays they enjoy getting up early
to make coffee and slice oranges for the wife. Let her sleep in, they

think, rubbing their palms against their chests in morning satisfaction. They practice the clarinet, tend sunflowers in the front yard, coach the little league, polish the car until she gleams like a jewel.

Now in the drops of this most balmy time, with its unfulfillable promise and its eternal reality going hand in hand down the road, two barefoot women walk. They too are holding hands, an old widow and a young one.

Was it a trance I fell into, or what was it. My heart, that has no proper language, appeared to be giving me wordless instructions. Leave the country of your fathers, go with your mother-in-law Naomi. She is a kind woman and comes of decent people. Let her people be your people and her god your god. You are at a border. Walk across it. You will arrive under the wings of the Lord.

So I went. It was very strange. Naomi complaining, yet I love her. A bitter old woman, yet I cling to her. Greeted with joy on her return by her townspeople, she announces that she is empty. It is I then who must fill her.

Poppies between cornrows. Birdsong. The mastery of how that throbbing fills the air from its tiny source, invisible—oh stop, I ache—what, anyway, is music, why so fierce, so much greater than consolation, it tears your breast open like a shirt, takes your throbbing heart out, lets the heart feel fresh air bathe it—your heart the size of a bird. And the sunball scorches it, then the song quietly returns my heart to my body, sutures the wound, and in a moment there's no scar.

Heat—to take my shirt off, like the men—gleaning behind them, thinking of the generosity of him whose land this is. He who tells the men: let her glean, in fact be careless in your reaping so that the stranger will not go hungry. And I am still that stranger, wishing I might take my shirt off as I glean, to sweat like them, I don't mind the backache, bending and rising.

Words all stiff and wrong, if I could dance for you my body would explain. Every moment a threshold. No, an opening. The dirt road. The shack. The dome over one's head flaring, incredible, as one stands bare-foot in a cornfield, an armload of sheaves, dust tickling one's nose. Rich and poor scattered over the fields. The high hot cobwebby summer morning rolling by, the afternoon a cauldron. The reapers singing at work, the Hebrew rolling like a wheel. The sky turning pale, sighing, freshness of night through which like a sickle the moon rises.

(Naomi in a narrow room in the city, to whom I bring my skirtful of barley. Wide fields all around. He who blesses his workers and also his handmaiden: he is our kinsman, he is unmarried, what a coincidence; Naomi and I discuss this. What she tells me to do, I say I will do.)

Plentiful, plentiful, the drummers drum in unison, the pipes flying alongside like a flock of sparrows accompanying an eagle. The young men and women dance tirelessly, they stamp the ground, kick, reel, spin, arms around each other's shoulders, circling and shouting. Sparks fly upward from the bonfires. I am at the edges of the circles, walking swiftly. I uncover the landowner's body in the threshing house. He wakes, bewildered. Straw in his hair. A large thick body one must admire for its lingering strength, through which sadness courses like brine. Kindly eyes in their network of wrinkles. Rich, honest, gentle, childless man. I am like the sheaves, filled with nourishment, lying at his feet. Do I know that I am beautiful? Yes, naturally, my beauty is my language; with it I converse with Boaz. Generous middle-aged Boaz will possess my youth. Will protect me. I am a foreigner, am a bridge, am the erasure of borders. I am ready to be redeemed. My name is Ruth, daughter-in-law of your kinswoman the Hebrew Naomi who loves me and whom I love. I am Ruth the Moabitess. I shall be Ruth the root. Women shall call me better than seven sons. I bring joy to your house.

Finding Our Past

A Lesbian Interpretation of the Book of Ruth

REBECCA ALPERT

To the memory of Judy Mintier, friend and colleague

A lesbian is ready to convert to Judaism. She has lived a Jewish life for several years and wants to make her status official. She requests that the ceremony take place around the time of Shavuot, for she feels deeply connected to Ruth, a convert whom she understands to be like herself, a lover of women.

Two Jewish lesbians plan a ceremony of commitment. They know they cannot say the traditional wedding vows, which speak of being joined according to Jewish law. They choose instead to say Ruth's words to Naomi to each other: "Wherever you go, I shall go. And wherever you find rest, so shall I."

Another Jewish lesbian couple plans to celebrate the tenth anniversary of their relationship. To honor them in the ceremony, a friend writes and sings a musical setting for Ruth 1:16.

A book about lesbian ceremonies of commitment is published, called *Ceremonies of the Heart: Celebrating Lesbian Unions*. In it, Ruth 1:16 is referred to as the traditional Jewish wedding vow.[1]

The author used her own translation of the Book of Ruth; she also consulted the Anchor Bible (Garden City, N.Y.: Doubleday, 1975).

A major motion picture, *Fried Green Tomatoes,* uses Ruth 1:16 as the secret message sent by a woman to let her "friend" know that she wishes to leave an abusive marriage and come live with her.[2]

A gay and lesbian synagogue sponsors a conference on the theme, "Ruth and the Meaning of Female Friendship in the Jewish Tradition." At the keynote, a lesbian rabbi interprets the story of Ruth and Naomi as a model for the powerful love that is possible between women.

A book on gay and lesbian Jews includes an article by a gay Jewish scholar entitled "In Search of Role Models." He, too, refers to the story of Ruth and Naomi as a positive example of a primary relationship between women in the Bible. He suggests that the story hinges not on Ruth's devotion to the Jewish God, but rather on her devotion to Naomi. He suggests that Ruth marries Boaz to ensure the two women will have a source of financial support and be able to remain together.[3]

A friend of mine, a closeted lesbian minister, tells me she has been preaching about Ruth for years. "The people who are really listening," she tells me, "know what I mean."

During the past decade, Jewish lesbians have begun to grapple with the way these two primary identities interact. We have brought our identities as Jewish women into the lesbian community and have come out as lesbians in the Jewish community. Finding our home in the lesbian community has meant challenging anti-Semitism, sharing our culture, and demanding inclusion as Jews. Claiming our place in the Jewish community has meant taking leadership roles, challenging stereotypes, and defining uniquely Jewish lesbian customs and traditions.

An important part of that process has been the search for a Jewish past that includes us, an effort to locate ourselves in the context of Jewish history. We look carefully for women in the Jewish past who might have been, like ourselves, lovers of women. The search is a difficult one. For centuries in Western cultures, lesbian love has not been spoken of in public. Lesbian historiography is indeed a challenge, as there are no written records. Lesbianism is mentioned in Jewish legal texts only as a sexual behavior that husbands should vigilantly prohibit their wives from engaging in.[4] If there are to be lesbian role models, they must be found between the lines through imaginative reconstruction of the texts. Because the story of Ruth describes a loving relationship between women, it is a logical place to look in searching for our past.

Rarely do relationships between women receive prominence in Jewish texts. There are some stories about sisters and a few about mothers and daughters. When women do appear in relation to one another, they are most often competitors and antagonists, as in the cases of Sarah and Hagar or Rachel and Leah. The story of Ruth and Naomi is an exception. Ruth clearly loves Naomi and pledges a lifelong commitment to her:

> Do not press me to abandon you,
> To turn back from following you.
> Wherever you go, I shall go.
> And wherever you find rest, so shall I.
> Your people shall be my people,
> And your God shall be my God.
> Where you die, I shall die,
> And there I shall be buried.
> Thus may YHWH do to me,
> And thus may YHWH add
> If even death will separate me from you.
> —RUTH 1:16–17

When these words are read through the lens of lesbian feminist experience, they point toward something greater than a relationship of loyalty and obligation between these two women. This story of female friendship resonates powerfully with Jewish lesbians in search of role models. Ruth and Naomi have a committed relationship that crosses the boundaries of age, nationality, and religion.

Ruth makes a commitment to Naomi to stay with her, even to their deaths. Lesbians hear in Ruth's vow a foreshadowing of the commitment they may now, in contemporary Western societies, make to one another to be life partners. Among Jewish lesbians today, there is a high incidence of committed relationships that involve public ceremonies. It is not surprising that the vow Ruth makes to Naomi has been incorporated into lesbian rituals. Taken out of context, Ruth's declaration indeed sounds like a statement of primary commitment. Had the speakers been of opposite sexes, Ruth 1:16–17 would certainly have been read as a poetic statement of love. The frequency with which this vow is used in lesbian circles makes quite understandable the mistake made by the editor of *Ceremonies of the Heart* when she assumed that the line actually was part of the standard Jewish wedding vow.

In addition, Ruth and Naomi are making a commitment to maintain familial connections. More and more Jewish lesbians today are forming alternative families, relying on friendship networks to supplement or replace families that may have rejected them. They are also raising children together as couples, not unlike heterosexuals.

Ruth and Naomi's relationship has meaning for Jewish lesbians in another dimension as well. Many Jewish lesbians find themselves in relationships with women that cross boundaries of age, race, nationality, and religion. Perhaps, because we are the same gender, other factors must bring difference into our lives as couples. Ruth and Naomi certainly have a relationship across differences. Jew and Moabite, they come from different cultures and worship different deities. Given the fact that Naomi is the mother of Ruth's deceased husband, they are clearly from different generations. Yet they overcome these differences and make a permanent connection. Ruth's vow to share Naomi's faith in YHWH is one important model of a way for lesbian couples to deal with difference.

Finally, Ruth and Naomi are friends. They exemplify a caring relationship between women. Lesbian relationships incorporate the connections of female friendship and affection celebrated by lesbian and heterosexual women alike. That Ruth is willing to leave her homeland, marry a man of Naomi's choosing, and cast her fate entirely with Naomi speaks worlds about how deep the connection between these two women is. This bond is celebrated when lesbians examine the story of Ruth.

The connection between these two women is a fertile field for midrash. The Hebrew Bible tends not to focus on the motivation of its human characters, and it is up to later commentators to add explanations. Why is Samson persuaded to cut off his hair? Why doesn't Abraham protest the command to sacrifice his son? What convinces Moses to listen to the voice in the bush? Why does Joseph trick his brothers? What made Ruth want to follow Naomi? Lesbian midrash can answer this last question in ways that may fill in the blanks about Ruth and Naomi's relationship. Did they bond in common love for Ruth's dead husband? Was Ruth really persuaded to follow Naomi because of her love for YHWH? Or did Ruth and Naomi become special friends, companions, or even lovers when they lived together in Moab?

Only through this sort of midrashic suggestion do Naomi and Ruth become true models for contemporary Jewish lesbians. While public vows of commitment, familial connections, female friendship, and cross-cultural and intergenerational relationships are important aspects of lesbian culture, sexuality is central to lesbian identity. Many heterosexuals mistakenly assume that all that is different about lesbian women is that they have sex with other women. Jewish lesbians have sought to establish that lesbian culture includes other elements, including those described above. Yet without romantic love and sexuality, the story of Ruth and Naomi loses much of its power as a model for Jewish lesbian relationships.

A Jewish lesbian midrash on Ruth requires that we read between the lines of the text and imagine Ruth and Naomi to be lovers. To lesbians, this is not implausible. Throughout the centuries, sexual love between women was hidden from public view. That the Hebrew Bible prohibits male homosexuality but does not mention lesbian sex may be because women's private behavior did not matter or went unnoticed, rather than because lesbian sexuality was not practiced. The fact that Ruth was married does not detract from the plausibility of this suggestion. The only references to lesbianism in Jewish legal texts are those prohibiting married women from engaging in this practice. It is possible to argue that Ruth had to marry Boaz to protect herself and Naomi, since it was not possible for women to survive in biblical times without the protection and financial support of men.[5] The suggestion that the story of Ruth comes from an oral tradition of women storytellers further supports the plausibility of this interpretation.[6]

When other scholars and commentators look at the Book of Ruth, they fail to see what we see. They are sure that Ruth means only to dedicate herself to Naomi's God. They are convinced that the important love relationship is the one between Ruth and Boaz. They can't imagine that there is a theme of love between women written between the lines.

Establishing literary, historical, and logical possibilities that the story of Ruth and Naomi could be read as a lesbian love story will certainly distress some readers. Yet less plausible midrashim have been accepted throughout the ages. The explanation that Isaac did not return from Mount Moriah after the Binding because he was sent to yeshiva is one such example. It is not the goal of midrash to prove that the story actually happened this way, but to make room for change within tradition while providing historical antecedent for the change. Making room for lesbian interpretations of the Book of Ruth is a way of welcoming lesbians into the contemporary Jewish community.

To find what is written between the lines has been the essence of midrashic interpretation throughout the ages. What makes biblical narrative so powerful is that it can be reinterpreted in every generation. A midrash works when it enables people to see the story in a new light or with an added dimension. Midrash gives us an opportunity to embellish the stories of the Bible and Jewish history, and to look at our heroes from new angles. It is not surprising that now, as women have taken a more active role in Jewish life, midrashim are being written about Sarah, Miriam, and Deborah. When martyrdom was an important theme in the Middle Ages, many midrashim were written to reinterpret the Binding of Isaac. And when the Zionists were interested in proclaiming Jewish military abilities, new emphasis was placed on the heroism of the Maccabees.

Lesbian midrash on Ruth plays the same role. Lesbians have had to read between the lines for centuries in Western cultures, looking for role models where all traces were hidden. To those of us whose love of women has had no public acknowledgment, writing midrash has given an opportunity to make our presence known and to lend validity to our relationships. We must insist on our right to find hints of the existence of women like ourselves in the past where we can. Reading Ruth this way should be considered an obligation to our nameless ancestors, to give them, too, an opportunity to speak. It is our hope that our midrash will find an honored place in Jewish tradition.

Her Mother's House

GAIL TWERSKY REIMER

Midway through the opening chapter of the Book of Ruth, Ruth stands at a crossroads with her sister-in-law Orpah deciding whether or not to continue toward Bethlehem with her mother-in-law Naomi. For a moment, three grieving widows stand together, bound by their shared pain. But because the husbands that Ruth and Orpah had lost are Naomi's sons, the tenor of the scene quickly shifts to one in which two young women face an embittered and depressed older woman who feels her life has neither purpose nor value because she is no longer the mother of sons. Both young women understand Naomi's pain, but only Ruth resists the definition of women's destiny that it implies.

Naomi's view of women's destiny is evident in her first spoken words, addressed to her daughters-in-law: "Go, return each of you to her mother's house" (1:8). It is at once startling and fitting that, at the crossroads, when Naomi attempts to part from her daughters-in-law, she directs them to return to their "mother's house." Startling because the typical formulation in biblical narratives is "the father's house"; this narrative too, began by defining fathers as the heads of households— "and a man of Bethlehem in Judah, with his wife and two sons, went ..." (1:1). And fitting because the "mother's house" to which Ruth refuses to return represents the culture of conventional expectations that Ruth rejects.

The passion with which Ruth articulates this rejection forestalls our

---

The author used her own translation of the Book of Ruth; she also consulted *Tanakh: A New Translation of the Holy Scriptures* (Philadelphia, New York, and Jerusalem: Jewish Publication Society, 1985).

recognizing her "disobedience." Swept away by the poignant simplicity of her words—"for wherever you go, I will go" (1:16)—we fail to notice a crucial irony: that the pledge to follow Naomi is itself a refusal to follow, not just Naomi's advice, but her kind of life.

Motherhood is at the core of Naomi's identity. To emulate Naomi, Ruth would have to become a mother and, indeed, this is what Naomi asks of her childless daughters-in-law when she beseeches them to return "each of you to her mother's house." Whatever else one encounters in the mother's house, maternity or motherhood is at its core and a return to that house, be it for comfort, guidance, or security, is inevitably a return to the site of our mothers' maternity.

As Naomi continues to plead with Ruth and Orpah, she seems to emphasize their finding husbands. Yet the character of her plea indicates her overwhelming concern with childbearing and childrearing:

> Turn back, my daughters! Why should you go with me? Have I any more sons in my body, who might be husbands for you? Turn back, my daughters, for I am too old to be married. Even if I thought there was hope for me, even if I were married tonight and I also bore sons, should you wait for them to grow up? Should you on their account debar yourselves from marriage? Oh no my daughters! My lot is far more bitter than yours, for the hand of the Lord has struck out against me. (1:11–13)

Here, Naomi not only tells us much about her own desires, she also reveals her assumptions about the maternal inclinations of her daughters-in-law. As she mourns her own childlessness and momentarily indulges in the fantasy of yet being able to have children, she reminds her daughters-in-law that she neither has nor is likely to have any more sons for them to marry. She thus alludes to levirate marriage, the law which obliges the brother of a dead man to marry the widow if she has no children. The purpose of this law is not to provide the widow with a husband, but rather to allow her to have a child who will "raise up the name of the dead upon his inheritance" (Deuteronomy 25:6). Implicit in her argument that it is foolish for her daughters-in-law to follow her, is the assumption that they would customarily wait for her to provide them with sons to marry in order to have children by them.

At the conclusion of this argument, Orpah kisses Naomi and departs. Ruth, on the other hand, remains steadfast in her determination to stay with Naomi. In response, Naomi shifts her argument from motherhood to people and God, losing some of her eloquence in the process: "See, your sister-in-law has returned to her people and her gods. Go follow your sister-in-law" (1:15).

Ruth is more willing to accept these terms, and she declares her commitment to Naomi and to Naomi's people and God. Her lengthy and eloquent response stands in sharp contrast to her silence following Naomi's earlier plea. Her pledge to follow Naomi—"wherever you go . . . where you lodge . . . where you die . . ."—refers to a future in which Naomi has made clear Ruth is not likely to be wife or mother. Ruth thus pledges her commitment without agreeing to follow Naomi into her former roles as wife and mother.

It is now Naomi's turn to be silent. The narrator claims that Ruth's determination renders Naomi speechless. The simple words that conclude the episode—"and the two went on" (1:19)—suggest, however, that Naomi's silence is not one of acceptance or even of resignation, but rather a silence born of frustration and separation. In a narrative replete with allusions to the Abraham story, the phrase "the two went on" recalls a similar phrase in the *Akedah* story—the narrative of Abraham's attempted sacrifice of Isaac. There the phrase reads "the two of them went on together." The rabbis, sensitive to the redundant character of the phrase, explain the seemingly unnecessary "together" as an indicator of the unity of mind and heart with which both Abraham and Isaac approached Mount Moriah. In Ruth, however, there is no redundancy. Though the rabbis gloss the phrase by claiming that Naomi and Ruth in their approach to Bethlehem were "of one heart," the absence of the word "together," which elsewhere signified "of one heart," suggests just the opposite. The two women continue their journey to Bethlehem apart, not together.

When Naomi next speaks, upon arriving in Bethlehem, she makes clear how inextricably her identity is bound up with motherhood. "Do not call me Naomi," she says to the women who greet her. "Call me Mara, for Shaddai has made my lot very bitter. I went away full, and the Lord has brought me back empty" (1:20–21). With the rejection of her own name, Naomi suggests that without a conventional family, without sons to mother, she has ceased to exist. Her words also underscore the distance between her and Ruth, the disappointment and anger that inspired her earlier silence.

Readers impressed by Ruth's devotion to Naomi cannot help but be shocked by Naomi's statement. Her pain notwithstanding, how can Naomi fail to recognize Ruth's presence, let alone her singular devotion? Naomi's bitterness makes better sense once we recognize that in joining Naomi, Ruth simultaneously defines her own sense of self over and against Naomi's. Naomi cannot acknowledge or accept the sense of self Ruth has articulated—a self defined in relation to neither men nor children. As she indicates in her statement to the women of Bethlehem, in her mind the childless woman is an empty self, one to whom she may be likened, but not one with whom she identifies.

Naomi's emphasis on her emptiness places her with other biblical heroines—Sarah, Rebekah, Rachel, Hannah—who despair of their barrenness. And she, like them, eventually achieves fullness with the birth of a son. Though it is Ruth who actually gives birth, the women neighbors declare that this "son is born to Naomi" (4:17). This women's chorus intuits something about both Ruth and Naomi that eludes the elders of Bethlehem as well as the tale's narrator. The former, in offering their blessing to Boaz upon his "purchase" of Ruth, seek to align Ruth with the matriarchs: "May the Lord make the woman who is coming into your house like Rachel and Leah, who built up the House of Israel" (4:11). The elders, not unlike Naomi, assume that a woman's strongest desire is for children. Their formulations of this desire indicate how thoroughly this assumption is intertwined with patrilineage. The elders of Bethlehem make this clear as they associate the blessing of fertility already offered with the continuity of name: "Prosper in Ephrathah and perpetuate your name in Bethlehem" (4:11).

The narrator, who makes the same assumption, concludes Ruth's story with the words "And she bore a son" (4:13). The Book of Ruth, however, ends not with these words but with a lengthy genealogy through which the narrator celebrates the birth of the son. The continuity of the patrilineal line that begins with Perez and ends with David, is thus established.

Inserted between the conclusion of Ruth's story and the conclusion of the book is an alternative ending offered by the women of Bethlehem. They recognize that it is Naomi and not Ruth who is fulfilled by the child's birth, hence their insistence that the child born "of" Ruth is born "to" Naomi. For the women, it is not simply a matter of the child carrying on the name of Naomi's deceased husband, though they also acknowledge the child's role in that scheme: "Blessed be the Lord who has not withheld a redeemer from you today! May his name be perpetuated in Israel" (4:14). But the women know that the child will "renew [Naomi's] life and sustain [her] old age," enabling her to recover the name she abjured upon her return to Bethlehem. The same women who once asked, "Can this be Naomi?" now intuit the significance of this child in restoring Naomi to her former "maternal" self by emphatically stating, "A son is born to Naomi!"

It is not surprising that Naomi's former neighbors are engaged primarily with her story and not Ruth's. But in casting the birth of the son as the conclusion to Naomi's story they also demonstrate some understanding of Ruth, betrayed by the single comment they make about her: at this moment of childbirth, they speak not of Ruth's maternal love but of her love for Naomi, not of Ruth as mother but of Ruth as daughter-in-law. While acknowledging no disinterest in children on Ruth's part, neither do they acknowledge any interest. And with their concluding statement about Ruth—"She is better to you than seven sons" (4:15)—they not only underscore Ruth's devotion to Naomi but also suggest the degree to which Ruth undermines the patriarchal premise that structures the whole of this narrative: that women are fulfilled by sons.

But who is Ruth? According to the women in the town she is a loving and devoted daughter-in-law. According to Boaz, who also comments on her loyalty (2:11; 3:10), she is "a woman of valor." And according to the servant in charge of the reapers she is a Moabite and a tireless gleaner (2:7).

Curiously, other than characterizing Ruth as a Moabite, the narrator remains neutral, reporting what Ruth does and says and what other characters say about her, but never himself characterizing or ascribing motivation to Ruth. With other characters he doesn't hesitate to ascribe motivation. Elimelech leaves Bethlehem because there is a famine in the land. Naomi returns because she hears that "the Lord has taken note of His people and given them food" (1:6). Naomi ceases to argue with Ruth because she sees "how determined [Ruth] was to go with her." And Boaz is startled in the middle of the night because there is a woman lying at his feet.

With Ruth, however, we get almost pure description. She first appears onstage as one of the Moabite women Naomi's sons marry.

Though she lives with her husband for "about ten years" before he dies, his identity remains unclear until the final chapter, when Boaz refers to Ruth as Mahlon's wife. The narration in chapter 1, which mentions Mahlon before Chilion, then names the women they married, mentioning Orpah first, frequently leads readers to assume that Ruth is Chilion's wife. A significant confusion, I believe, for it suggests, at the start, that Ruth's identity is not defined by her husband.

An even more important fact is that this ten-year marriage, like that of Orpah and Chilion, is childless. Yet we hear no mention of either Ruth or Orpah suffering from their barrenness. Given the frequency with which such suffering defines biblical heroines, the silence here is pointed. Is the author/narrator being unusually reticent? Or do Ruth and Orpah feel differently about childbearing than Sarah (to whom the ten-year marriage figure alludes), Rachel, Hannah, and the others.

Since Orpah drops out of the story early, it is difficult to determine how she feels about anything. What we do learn about Orpah is that while she resists Naomi's plea about marriage (1:11), she responds to a plea about motherhood. Ruth, on the other hand, resists both, further reinforcing our sense that marriage and motherhood may not be central for her.

That Ruth is not averse to marriage is clear from her willing participation in Naomi's scheme for manipulating Boaz into marrying Ruth. Nor does she merely follow Naomi's instructions, but instead directs Boaz toward matrimony. Rather than waiting for Boaz to tell her what to do as Naomi had instructed, Ruth actively solicits him.

Though initially shocked by Ruth's forwardness—"the man gave a start and pulled back" (3:8)—Boaz immediately assimilates her actions. Ruth, he suggests, is motivated by lovingkindness *(chesed)* toward her dead husband Mahlon, a *chesed*, he claims, of greater value than the earlier *chesed* she had shown to her mother-in-law. Had she simply been seeking the sexual pleasure of marriage she would have surely turned to "younger men." But Boaz takes her seeking him out, in spite of his age, as a sign that Ruth wants to have a child by a relative of her deceased husband, a child who will "raise up the name of the dead."

Only when Ruth returns to Naomi do we hear her speak again. But those words, her last in the narrative, reverse Boaz's understanding of her acts and reaffirm her dedication to Naomi. By telling Naomi that the six measures of barley given to her by Boaz were given out of concern for her mother-in-law, Ruth assimilates Boaz's action into her worldview, insisting that the *chesed* that matters most to her has to do with personal devotion to a live woman, not to a dead male.

Ruth's transformation of Boaz's concern for her into a concern for Naomi suggests that her participation in Naomi's scheme is at least partially, and perhaps wholly, motivated by her desire to care for Naomi. During the barley and wheat harvest Ruth felt able to do this on her own and, as the servant in charge of the reapers reported to Boaz, she was a tireless gleaner (2:7). But with the harvest over, she could not help but see the limits of her power to provide for Naomi. She needed to turn elsewhere. Once Naomi clarifies to whom she may turn, Ruth pursues Boaz with the same intensity with which she gleaned. Just as she did not rest when gleaning, she does not wait for Boaz to tell her what to do, lest he once again suggest that she "have a full recompense from the Lord, the God of Israel, under whose wings [she has] sought refuge" (2:12). Ruth's clever and calculated use of the terms Boaz had used to introduce the subject of marriage and the obligations of human protection ("spread your wings over your handmaid for you are the redeeming kinsman"; 3:9) underscore the pragmatic, as opposed to romantic, interests that motivate Ruth's solicitation of Boaz.

For the better part of chapter 4 Ruth appears only as an object of exchange, rejected by one kinsman lest she "impair" his estate, and "acquired" by another, Boaz, "so as to perpetuate the name" of her deceased husband Mahlon. She momentarily reappears as a subject when the narrator reports the marriage and subsequent birth of a son: "So Boaz married Ruth; she became his wife and he cohabited with her. The Lord *gave* her conception, and she bore a son" (4:13).

Not surprisingly, given her earlier initiative, Ruth willingly becomes a wife. Becoming a mother, however, requires divine intervention. While commentators have interpreted this intervention as an indication of Ruth's infertility, which might explain the barrenness of her earlier marriage, it is worth noticing the marked difference from the standard description of divine response to infertile matriarchs; God is usually said to "remember" the woman or to "open her womb." The phrase "and the Lord gave her conception" refers neither to a biological problem that must be corrected nor to prayers for a child that must be answered. Here God intervenes not to facilitate a longed-for conception but almost, it seems, to force one. The absence of any description of Ruth's joy over birth or her maternal responsibilities—she neither names her child nor nurses him—reinforces the possibility that divine intervention was necessitated by Ruth's reluctance to become a mother.

Though the celebration of the birth of the son is described as a women's celebration, Ruth is not mentioned as a participant. The celebratory ritual begins with a blessing offered by the women neighbors, a blessing addressed to Naomi: "Blessed be the Lord, who has not withheld a redeemer from you today! May his name be perpetuated in Israel! He will renew your old age; for he is born of your daughter-in-law, who loves you and is better to you than seven sons" (4:14–15). The blessing concludes with praise for Ruth, but with words that celebrate Ruth in her role as child rather than as mother. The ritual continues with a symbolic act of bonding, not as we might expect between mother and child, but between Naomi and child. "And Naomi took the child and laid it in her bosom. She became its foster mother" (4:16). Naomi's action sets the stage for the conclusion of the ritual. "And the women neighbors gave him a name, saying, 'A son is born to Naomi!' " (4:17).

Even if we assume that Ruth is present in this scene, as some commentators have, and that the celebration is taking place at her bedside, Ruth's silence is puzzling. There is a pointed allusion to Hannah when the women say, "who is better to you than seven sons" (cf. 1 Samuel 1:8: "Am I not better to you than ten children"). Hannah, pained by her barrenness, prayed to God for a son, promising that if her prayers were answered she would dedicate the child to God "for all the days of his life." When she finally bore a son, however, she was reluctant to part with him and pleaded with her husband to allow her to wait "until the boy is weaned." Ruth, on the other hand, allows the child to be taken from her, both symbolically and literally, without a word.

But then Ruth never prayed for a child. Nor is there any indication that she suffered because of her childlessness. On the contrary, clues throughout the text suggest that Ruth had no desire for children and no interest in maternity. To be sure, Ruth is not the only biblical heroine who did not want children. But her story, unlike Deborah's or Huldah's, for example, includes particular references to childlessness and the birth of a son. These references and the allusions to other biblical stories (e.g., those of Sarah, Rachel, and Hannah) draw the reader's attention to Ruth's relationship to motherhood.

But rather than attending to that relationship, commentators past and present, male and female, have assimilated it into a single model of woman's relationship to motherhood. Even critics aware of the patriarchal nature of a model premised on women's "natural" desire to mother have failed to appreciate the challenge Ruth presents to this premise.[1]

As women seek to break the monopoly on biblical interpretation that men have held for centuries, are we still constrained by patriarchal biases that limit the questions we ask? Are feminist critics, as Ann Snitow has suggested in another context, unable "to imagine a full and deeply meaningful life without motherhood" and therefore reluctant to pose questions that interrogate women's desire for children? It is certainly possible that if we speak and question Ruth's desire for children from our position as mothers, our own children might read our analyses autobiographically. Similarly if we speak from the position of the childless, our interpretations may be dismissed, in Snitow's words, "as a species of sour grapes."[2]

Ruth risked a great deal when she lay down by Boaz and challenged him to "spread his wings over her." As we claim a place for ourselves in the interpretive tradition, we too must take risks and be as willing to break taboos within feminist discourse as those within patriarchal discourse on the Bible.

3

"I Went Away Full, and the Lord Has Brought Me Back Empty"

RUTH 1:21

*T*HE DEPTH of Naomi's pain at the loss of her husband and sons is reflected in her cry to the women of Bethlehem: "I went away full, and the Lord has brought me back empty." The first three pieces in this section reveal different dimensions of Naomi's anguish and the process through which she, with Ruth, eventually moves from emptiness toward fullness. The authors assign Ruth a critical role in moving Naomi beyond despair, while also exploring Ruth's own movement from "death and mourning back to life."

This group of essays, in particular, resembles Mikraot Gedolot, the traditional rabbinic Bible, in which a line of text is surrounded on the page by many different commentaries, each interpreting the phrase or verse from its own perspective and implicitly responding to the other commentaries and the tradition of commentary. Each author explores in detail the language of Ruth, weaving a fabric of meaning out of crucial phrases and images from the text. While each piece stands on its own, the reader who approaches these essays as a unit will hear an implied conversation.

Nehama Aschkenasy, for example, sees Naomi's lament over her losses as saturated with the tragedy of her experience. But she also recognizes that through the boldness of her statement and its implied comparison to Job, Naomi "places her[self] in the biblical tradition of men challenging God for great, undeserved suffering." Aschkenasy carefully situates the characters within biblical culture, identifying the linguistic creativity women can martial to challenge their fate and create new possibilities within their patriarchal context. She reveals language as a source of female power that often counteracts and even outweighs women's legal and economic powerlessness within biblical civilization. Ruth and Naomi, Aschkenasy demonstrates, are consummate practitioners of the verbal strategies used by women in the Bible. Once we appreciate this, we can see, within the language of seeming desperation, assertions of self-worth and daring revisions of reality.

Lois Dubin and Patricia Karlin-Neumann, on the other hand, see Naomi as "Everywoman," her story offering an understanding of the pain and loneliness experienced in loss—loss of loved ones, loss of fertility, and even loss of pregnancy—and the centrality of community to recovery from loss. For Dubin, Naomi's cry invites the women to whom she speaks, as well as readers of the text, to "plumb the depths of Naomi's emptiness." There Dubin hears the "classic cry of a woman who has suffered the loss of a pregnancy." Simultaneously a cry of pain and a cry for help, Naomi's lament, in this interpretation, is the first step in her gradual recovery. Her outcry against God, with its Jobian echoes, reflects the psychological necessity of publicly acknowledging private grief.

For Karlin-Neumann, Naomi's "Jobian railing" underscores the degree to which she resembles Job, not only in her accumulated losses "but in the utter isolation that she knows as a consequence." Naomi's self-description ("empty") begins the book's delineation of the emotional terrain that may accompany an overwhelming experience of loss. As a rabbi who has helped mourners in their grief, Karlin-Neumann is especially attentive to the story's capacity to serve as a "guide" to understanding the mourner's movement through and out of isolation in the world of death back to life and involvement in living.

The fourth essay in this section also traces a path from fullness to "emptiness" and back to a new kind of wholeness and promise. Here, however, the path is that of the reader rather than the characters. The memories Sylvia Rothchild invokes in her autobiographical reflections cluster around the meanings Ruth has held for her at three different moments in her life. Each moment also echoes a different stage in the life of the American Jewish community, as the essay moves from the richly textured Jewish lives of Rothchild's observant immigrant family, through a time of estrangement and fragmentation in her Jewish life, to a rekindled interest and hope in a Jewish future.

Language as Female Empowerment in Ruth

Nehama Aschkenasy

Verbal dexterity and linguistic creativity characterize many female protagonists in biblical literature. It is true that silence and anonymity sum up the existence of the multitudes of mothers, wives, and concubines of those men whose deeds are chronicled in the Bible. Yet the women who periodically take center stage and briefly capture the readers' attention often exhibit great linguistic talents, using rhetoric as a means of establishing their names and deeds within the recorded history of their people. The ability to articulate and communicate is a source of female power that often counteracts and even outweighs women's legal and economic powerlessness within biblical civilization.

Biblical style is male-intonated, written by men and addressing the community through its males. When women talk, it is not always clear whether the narrator makes an effort to emulate the nuances of female speech and to differentiate it from the male voice. But in a number of episodes, it seems that the woman's oratory is more inventive, elegant, and metaphoric, loftier in style, than that of the male protagonists. The earliest example is Eve's response to God when both she and Adam are confronted by Him after their act of disobedience (Genesis 3:12–14). Eve tries to explain herself by using an unusual, richly connotative verb: "The serpent *beguiled* me." By contrast, Adam claims that he ate from

---

The author used her own translation of the Book of Ruth; she also consulted the Anchor Bible (Garden City, N.Y.: Doubleday, 1975), the King James Version, and the Revised Standard Version.

the forbidden tree because Eve "gave" him the fruit, using the most elementary, ordinary verb to describe his experience. Eve has thus lifted her experience to the level of a complex emotional and intellectual process, while Adam has degraded his to a mere mechanical, unthinking act.

Another telling example of female verbal strategy is the episode involving the daughters of Tzelofchad. These five daring women leave Moses virtually speechless with the power of their rhetoric when they ask to inherit the land that Moses would have allocated to their father (Numbers 27:1–5). God himself is impressed, not only with their argument, but with their carefully worded speech: "The daughters of Tzelofchad speak right." These five courageous women actually challenge the divinely ordained Mosaic law, according to which only men may inherit their father's estate. But they so cleverly couch their questioning in the language of patriarchy, declaring their wish to perpetuate the patriarch's name rather than asserting any rights for women, that Moses and the elders of Israel actually believe their request is meant to reinforce patriarchy rather than challenge it. And the childless Hannah, beseeching God to give her a son, practically wills her child into being, mapping out an entire life for him (1 Samuel 1:11). In her language the child comes into being and is given a purpose and a destiny. It seems that Hannah leaves God no choice but to make her vision of a son who serves Him faithfully a reality.

These three forms of female rhetoric—declamation that endows the woman's experience with distinction and grandeur, cunning use of language to challenge and modify patriarchal rules while ostensibly submitting to them, and the creation of a seemingly unattainable reality through the power of the word—are just a few of the verbal techniques employed by women in biblical literature. In the addresses and discourses of the female protagonists of Ruth, it seems that these strategies are practiced to perfection.

Unlike the typical biblical episode in which women appear and speak briefly in a narrative focusing on men, the tale of Ruth provides numerous examples of female speech. It is structured as a series of dramatic scenes revolving around two women, animated by spirited and dynamic dialogues. Except for Boaz's exchange at the gate with the other, unnamed kinsman, each dialogue takes place either between Naomi and Ruth or between one of them and others.

•   •   •

Naomi and Ruth first appear together in the memorable scene in which the older woman pleads with her daughters-in-law to return to their mothers' homes, and Ruth remains determined to accompany Naomi to her homeland. Each woman has reached the nadir of existence within her world. They are destitute, homeless, and deprived of male protection, the only guarantee for female survival in the male-dominant society. Yet while both cry profusely, dwelling on those who have died and on their own misery, neither woman strikes the reader as weak, helpless, or lost. In two quite elaborate speeches (1:8–9, 10–13) Naomi thanks her daughters-in-law for their past kindness, urges them to turn back and leave her, and wishes them well. Her explicit argument is that she is past her childbearing years, that therefore the young women cannot expect to be "redeemed" by a brother-in-law. But Naomi's language, describing hypothetically the improbable event of her marrying a man that very night and eventually bearing sons, is so outrageously exaggerated that it points to a subtext quite different from the point that is ostensibly being made. Naomi describes at length what cannot happen, but merely elaborating on the impossible—that she will remarry and give birth to sons, that her daughters-in-law will wait for those sons to redeem them—points to hidden desires and hopes. While on the face of it Naomi rules out any possibility of her daughters-in-law remarrying within her family, her protestations create an imaginary world in which the unlikely might indeed come true; behind the language of seeming desperation lurks the vision of a potential miracle. Naomi's absurd scenario plants the idea and the hope of its being realized.

While dismissing the possibility of a levirate marriage for the two young women, Naomi in fact introduces the concept into both the tale and the consciousness of the reader. Moreover, to further build up her vision of the possible, to enhance her subliminal message, and to create a world out of the word, Naomi names the relationship between the two women using a term that technically does not denote the link between women whose husbands are brothers. Naomi tells Ruth to follow her sister-in-law, Orpah, who has finally taken Naomi's advice and headed back to Moab. But in the Hebrew Naomi does not use the term sister or sister-in-law; rather, she calls Orpah *yebimtekh,* using the term *yebamah* to describe the familial relationship between the two women. In biblical Hebrew the noun *yebamah* designates the childless widow in relation to her dead husband's brother. He is the *yabam,* or "redeemer" as it is usually translated, and she is the *yebamah,* the feminine form of the same noun. But nowhere in the Bible is it suggested that sisters-in-law are each other's *yebamah*. This should not be taken as a slip of the tongue, a careless mistake on the part of a wretched woman. Naomi has taken a liberty with the language, but in the process she has created a new frame of reference within the tale by filling the dialogue with intimations of *yibbum*, levirate marriage, thus mitigating the language of the unattainable. Like the desperate Hannah, Naomi creates a world with the force of her tongue, and the reader is left to wonder how the misnomer will force itself on reality and whether one of these two young women will indeed be rightfully called *yebamah*.

Furthermore, even as she pronounces her wretchedness, Naomi proclaims her self-worth by framing her present misery as part of an ongoing dialogue between herself and God: "The hand of the Lord is gone out against me" (1:13). At first we might consider these words a common utterance in a God-fearing culture, a cliché probably used universally by Naomi's contemporaries to describe their misery. But we come to see that this is not just a case of resorting to popular language. Rather, it is a well-thought-out argument on the part of Naomi, who repeats and elaborates upon the same idea later: "The Lord has testified against me, and the Almighty has afflicted me" (1:21). Naomi's rhythmic lament reverberates with Jobian echoes, and her plight is endowed with a colossal significance. Her polemical, philosophical language evokes the vision of a divine courtroom, where God is both witness for the prosecution and the judge determining the verdict. And in this heavenly courtroom, Naomi sees herself playing a major role, that of the accused.

This woman's personal complaint against a wrathful God places her in the biblical tradition of men challenging God for great, undeserved suffering. By couching her grievances in the language of the Jobian predicament, Naomi powerfully suggests that she calls God to task, that she sees herself as having been singled out by God for persecution. Behind the image of the woman punished by God is the image of the woman recognized by God, not of a woman swept away by accidental, meaningless catastrophe. What is more, the dialogue of retribution and suffering also implies deliverance and salvation; Job suffers by the hand of God but is ultimately rewarded by Him. Thus, Naomi's vision of the heavenly courtroom both asserts her importance within the divine scheme of things and suggests the possibility of the reversal of her divinely ordained fortune.

The dialectic of powerlessness suggesting hidden power is reinforced by Naomi's creation of a "community of women'" characterized by solidarity and affirmation of life. Naomi is not a modern feminist; she realizes that a woman's economic survival hinges upon her ability to find a husband and protector. She therefore suggests that each of her daughters-in-law return first to her "mother's house," and from there eventually to the security of a husband's home. We remember that the widowed Tamar, another enterprising woman who is related to this tale as an ancestress of Boaz, returns to her father's house after losing her second husband (Genesis 38:11). In our present tale, the image of the "mother's home" as a refuge for the grown daughter, together with the actual scene of three women, fiercely loyal to one another, huddled to discuss plans for the future, creates a vision of strong, independent women who unite to protect themselves and who believe in their ability to rise out of misery and devastation and rehabilitate themselves. In line with the basic tenets of patriarchy, this community of females is meant to exist only temporarily, until each woman departs to her husband's home; but it exists as a haven and an option, reaffirming the women's self-reliance and sense of hidden power.

Naomi's faith in the power of the word as mirror as well as creator of reality is further expressed in the small speech that she gives to the women of Bethlehem: "Call me not Naomi, call me Mara: for the Lord has dealt bitterly with me. I went out full, and the Lord brought me back empty: why then do you call me Naomi?" (1:20–21). The lamenting tenor of these words does not conceal the strength of their message: a person's name conveys the essence and the fortunes of the individual. Naomi claims that her name, which means pleasure, contrasts with her sorry reality, that therefore it should be changed to communicate the bitterness of her lot. Naomi is here in line with biblical tradition, which attributes great importance to names; children, cities, and memorial sites are given meaningful names that denote the emotions and often the hopes of the name givers. What Naomi means is, of course, not that her name should be changed, but that her *reality* should be mended and altered to conform to her original name. Naomi's elaborate polemics about her name are meant as a challenge to her own fate, a call to God to adjust her life so that it will once again reflect the true meaning of her name.

Ruth's rhetoric in chapter 1 is as overwhelming as that of her mother-in-law; we can understand the special relationship between these two strong, articulate women. The dialogue between them seems as much a clarification of positions as a hidden contest of the power of the tongue. To match Naomi's persuasive plea that she and Orpah return home, Ruth comes up with an even more effective pronouncement, that seems to leave Naomi speechless. Ruth's famous oath of loyalty to Naomi herself, as well as to Naomi's people and God, has become in Western tradition the ultimate declaration of devotion, effective in its simplicity and in the sense of determination that it transmits. Only death will separate her from her mother-in-law, she claims. The finality of death gives Ruth's speech the stamp of finality, too, convincing Naomi that any more words would be wasted: "Then she [Naomi] left off speaking to her"(1:18).

What is quite surprising is that, while in Naomi's language God is a stern judge who pronounces harsh verdicts, Ruth nevertheless includes God in her proclamation of loyalty: "Your God is my God" (1:16). Ruth seems to understand that the implication of Naomi's words goes beyond the explicit meaning of her complaint: that while God is the one who punishes, He can also be addressed with one's grievances, complained to, and beseeched—that the same God who sits in judgment is the one who metes out reward and redemption. Moreover, Ruth makes it clear that in choosing to return with Naomi she has not only made a decision about the person she wants to stay with but also about the faith that she wishes to adopt. In her dialogue with Naomi, Ruth also starts a dialogue with Naomi's God. Both women are daring in their religiosity, since matters of faith and intimations of the divine are seen in the Bible as mostly within the male domain; it is to Abraham that God reveals Himself, and it is with him that He makes the covenant.

The scene of the women's arrival in Bethlehem is structured as a dialogue between Naomi and the women of Bethlehem, who play the part of the chorus, spectators who participate actively in the dramatic events. The two words (in Hebrew) that they speak—"Is this Naomi?"—convey a wide spectrum of responses: initial surprise at seeing their old townswoman, shock at the obvious change in Naomi's appearance, and the wish to know much more. But the women also set up a little ceremony of welcome which allows Naomi to release her anger; they provide the audience for Naomi's grievance against God and serve a therapeutic purpose by allowing Naomi to express herself and vent her emotions of sorrow and bereavement.

Naomi's language in chapter 1 sets the tone for the whole tale and establishes the leitmotif of fullness and emptiness. Again, Naomi, in her use of language, bows to the standards of a patriarchal society. She claims that she was "full" when she left Bethlehem but that she is "empty" now. In a male-dominant socioeconomic order, a woman bereft of husband and sons is indeed "empty"; but we already know that Naomi does not consider herself insignificant, small, or unimportant. Moreover, Naomi's present emptiness is set against her former "fullness," thus implying anticipation of a return to the earlier state; it also reverberates loudly against the scene of seasonal abundance that the women encounter on their return.

The close and intimate understanding that exists between Naomi and Ruth is fully displayed in Ruth's quick adoption of Naomi's linguistic imagery of emptiness and fullness. Later, when Boaz promises to help Ruth, after discovering that she has slept at his feet all night, he ceremoniously measures out a significant portion of barley, and tells Ruth to hold up her apron so that he can fill it (3:15). Ruth returns "full," both symbolically and physically: she has received a definite pledge of redemption, and her bulging apron serves as evidence and promise of things to come. When Ruth comes home she quotes Boaz, but adds words that he did not say to her that would comfort a woman who complained about her "emptiness": "For he said, 'You shall not go empty / To your mother-in-law' " (3:17). Since we witnessed the actual dialogue between Ruth and Boaz, in which Boaz did not address the question of Naomi's emptiness, we can conclude that Ruth has put these words in Boaz's mouth. We see here another linguistic tactic used by women: Ruth does not exactly lie, but while ostensibly quoting Boaz, she attributes to him the use of an image, especially meaningful to Naomi, that he probably never used.

In spite of the great emotional and spiritual bonds that exist between Naomi and Ruth, the two women come from different backgrounds, and Ruth has to become acquainted not only with the religious laws and social customs, but also with the prevailing code of conduct in this society. It is clear that Naomi has explained to Ruth the meaning of the levirate custom, as well as the tradition of kin responsibility that prevails among the Israelites. She also directs Ruth toward a conduct more in line with a society bound by the laws and customs prescribed by their God. It is in the nuances of language that the differences in culture and class between these two women are displayed. Ruth the Moabite comes from a morally loose, corrupt society, and in order to learn the customs of her adopted people, she has to shed many of her old ways. For instance, when Boaz meets Ruth for the first time, he requests that she cling to his girls, or "maidens" (2:8); yet when Ruth repeats his words to her mother-in-law, she says that Boaz instructed her to stay close to his "young men" (2:21). Ruth may still be struggling with the language, making the mistake of using the masculine plural instead of the feminine plural. But it is more likely that she uses the masculine plural to mean "young people," in other words, all the hired hands who are working in the field. She may not have understood that Boaz was making the specific point that she should stay with the women, and probably thought he was telling her to stay close to his workers, male or female. Naomi redirects the young Moabitess by suggesting that she go out to the field with Boaz's "young women"; she thus teaches her not only what proper conduct is, but also that language should not be used loosely and freely, since it is a mirror of culture, signifying the ethics of the speaker and of the civilization in which it arose.

In Bethlehem, Ruth's language is markedly different from Naomi's in other ways, too. Ruth uses the vocabulary of deference and humility, which is nevertheless invigorated by a youthful spirit of adventure, curiosity, and questioning. It seems that Naomi has exhausted her own storehouse of words after arguing with God, and it is Ruth who, respectfully but also somewhat impatiently, suggests to her mother-in-law that she venture out to the fields to glean after the reapers. Ruth's vigorous words are contrasted with Naomi's terse, perhaps tired "Go, my daughter" (2:2). In her dialogue with Boaz, Ruth adopts the language and posture of respect and self-effacement, calling herself a "stranger" and his "handmaid" and bowing down before him, a gesture of subservience. At the same time, Ruth elicits from Boaz perhaps more than he initially means to say: she asks him why he has singled her out for special treatment by his servants in the field, and he has to admit that he has heard about her meritorious qualities and actions. It even seems that Boaz gets carried away when describing Ruth's kindness toward her mother-in-law, and he invokes God's name in wishing that Ruth be rewarded by Him under whose "wings" she has come to take refuge.

Ruth has thus achieved two purposes: she has established herself as a relative of Boaz, one who deserves preferential treatment in the field, and she has made Boaz acknowledge the fact that he knows much more about Naomi and Ruth than his actions so far have shown. After all, if Boaz has indeed heard about the women's tragedies and their present destitution, why hasn't he approached them and offered his help before? Why is it that Naomi and Ruth have to sit home, obviously desolate and near hunger, until Ruth the foreigner decides to set out to the field and test the kindness of their townspeople? Ruth's question to Boaz, while seemingly rhetorical and meant to emphasize her great surprise at his unusual magnanimity, achieves almost the opposite effect: perhaps by having to articulate Ruth's admirable actions and needy situation, Boaz is led to ask himself if he has done enough for his female relatives. Both the women's actions and their language are meant to stir in the man, their distant kin, a sense of responsibility, and perhaps even guilt, that would drive him to do more for them than he has so far or than he ever meant to do.

Within the structure of this tale, silences are as meaningful as the dialogues themselves, and the movement of a set of dialogues punctuated by speechless intervals invigorates the dramatic tension and reflects transitions in moods and states of mind. Chapter 1, containing the most provocative and memorable dialogues in the tale, ends with silence: the women's stunned, hushed reaction to the abundance that they encounter in Bethlehem, which contrasts sharply with their own destitution. Chapter 2 starts with the statement that Naomi has a relative in town, a man of position and capacities; but the text does not disclose why this information is given at this point, and the women make no comment concerning Boaz. The opening to this chapter chronicles a painful period in which the women expect help from neighbors and relatives (such as Boaz) but are offered nothing. Naomi's uncharacteristic reticence regarding her situation signifies a dispirited, disappointed state of mind, revitalized only when Ruth takes the initiative and in impatient but animated language suggests that she go out to glean in the fields. This triggers the set of events narrated in chapter 2, including an unexpected encounter with Boaz and a lively series of dialogues. But this chapter, too, ends with silence; the season of harvest is over, nothing came of Boaz's kindness and interest in Ruth, and the women find themselves alone at home, probably too discouraged to talk: "And [Ruth] dwelt [stayed at home] with her mother-in-law" (2:23).

It is Ruth's turn to feel dejected and wordless, and therefore it is Naomi who starts the dialogue in chapter 3. Naomi describes an elaborate and cunning scheme to which Ruth responds tersely, and perhaps also somewhat mechanically and unenthusiastically, "All that thou sayest to me I will do" (3:5). But soon Ruth's buoyant and daring spirits as well as her eloquence are revived, and she expands on her mother-in-law's initial plan. Naomi had instructed Ruth to wait for the man to speak when he discovers her, but Ruth says more than the man's question warrants. In response to Boaz's startled inquiry as to who she is, Ruth not only identifies herself but makes a courageous, almost audacious suggestion: "I am Ruth thy handmaid: spread therefore thy skirt [or wing] over thy handmaid; for thou art a near kinsman [or, a redeemer]" (3:9).

Naomi's intention is probably to arouse sexual feelings and fantasies in Boaz, and thus instill in him a sense of sexual guilt that will lead to his undertaking to solve Ruth's problem. But Naomi does not indicate that she means for Boaz himself to redeem Ruth. We know that in the technical sense, Boaz is not a redeemer, since he is not Ruth's brother-in-law. For Ruth to suggest, openly and unequivocally, that Boaz marry her is a bold move, in which her ability to combine the language of deference with that of implied challenge is illustrated once more. While again describing herself as Boaz's "handmaid," Ruth does not refrain from using the imperative "spread," in effect commanding the man to redeem her. She also gives him a clear reason why the responsibility falls on him: "You are a redeemer."

In this nocturnal encounter, the tale's climax, Ruth reveals in both her words and the manner in which she delivers them that she has completed her education in Israelite customs and traditions, that she is spiritually ready to become one of them and therefore worthy of being assimilated and accepted by them. She is not only acquainted with the law of *yibbum*, the redemption of the childless widow by her brother-in-law, but she uses the appropriate language when offering herself to Boaz. First, she designates him as a "redeemer," not simply as a potential husband. Ruth thus proves to Boaz that she now moves within the patriarchal legal system. At the same time, Ruth, like the daughters of Tzelofchad before her, succeeds in shaping this system to her advantage. By calling Boaz a "redeemer," whose responsibility it would be to marry her, Ruth is technically wrong. But she makes Boaz understand the spirit of the law, rather than simply its narrow meaning. She makes him realize that the law itself does not always cover all the cases confronted in real life. With Ruth's subtle help, Boaz broadens his conception of the levirate custom to include not only the widow's brother-in-law but also her more distant relatives. Ruth teaches Boaz a lesson in the humanitarian interpretation of the law, which he readily accepts. She also creates a new reality with the aid of language; by naming Boaz a "redeemer," Ruth makes him one.

Ruth's linguistic wisdom is further manifested in that she refrains from pleading with Boaz to "marry" her and thus rescue her from destitution. Instead, she uses the ceremonious phrase that Boaz himself employed in 2:12, "under [God's] wings," thus playfully linking God's wings and the corners of Boaz's garment. The play on words carries a serious message: Boaz will be fulfilling his God's law, as well as his own earlier good wishes, if he marries her.

Elsewhere I have discussed the link between the Ruth tale and two previous biblical tales that also revolve around the seduction of a man by a woman who finds herself in a hopeless situation: the Genesis episodes of Lot and his daughters (chapter 19) and of Judah and Tamar (chapter 38).[1] The tales are linked not only stylistically, through the motif of the seduction of a man, but genealogically. The product of the incestuous relationship between Lot and his daughter is Moab, Ruth's ancestor, and the product of the sexual encounter between Judah and his daughter-in-law is Perez, Boaz's ancestor. It is therefore possible to view the three tales as a chain of narratives that exemplify stages in an evolution in attitudes toward sexual taboos and mores. It starts with the barbaric, cave-people tale in which Lot's daughters get their father drunk and then lie with him, moves to the somewhat more civilized ambience of the tale in which Judah's widowed daughter-in-law uses guile in order to conceive from Judah, and climaxes in the cleaned-up tale of Ruth's successful efforts to make Boaz recognize his familial responsibilities and "redeem" her.

The tale of Ruth is purged of the many unseemly elements of the two previous tales. It offers no graphic description of the sexual act during Boaz's encounter with Ruth on the threshing floor. The narrator uses the euphemistic, suggestive phrase, the uncovering of the man's feet (or legs) (3:7), which is laden with sexual connotations, but does not explicitly indicate that Boaz was actually seduced by Ruth. More important, Ruth herself, in her use of language, "redeems" her female precursors by converting the crass, vulgar, and unabashedly explicit vocabulary that prevails in their tales to the dignified language of redemption and moral responsibility. Lot's daughters are very blunt when they connive to "lie" with their own father, and Tamar, dressed as a harlot, is forced also to talk like one. She is, therefore, no less graphic when she asks Judah, "What wilt thou give me, that thou mayest come in to me" (Genesis 38:16). By contrast, the nocturnal dialogue between Ruth and Boaz is laced with the honorable concepts of covenantal law, familial obligations, and divine blessing and approval.

While both Ruth and Boaz resort to the same lofty rhetoric, it seems that Ruth is the one who sets the tone. Instead of dwelling on the sexual indiscretion, feigning innocence and demanding restitution, or hinting at the potential embarrassment for the old man, the quick-witted Ruth repeats the image that Boaz himself used earlier, the spreading of the wings. And by naming him a "redeemer," she places him within the respectable tradition of a man who fulfills his familial obligations as prescribed by Mosaic law. Boaz, who at first sounds alarmed and angry, calms down and picks up the tone, as well as the thrust, of Ruth's speech. He continues in the same vein by repeating the verb "to redeem" a number of times. And being an old man who, as we have seen before, can become emotional and effusive, he proceeds to bless Ruth and commend her profusely.

A cynical view of Ruth might regard her grand, metaphoric language as a strategy to win Boaz, a respectable elder and pillar of the Israelite community who is himself given to flowery speech. In this interpretation, Ruth's cunning rhetoric complements her ruse of surprising Boaz in the middle of the night after he has eaten and drunk perhaps more than usual. But Boaz himself discards this notion, when he reminds us that some of the young men, both poor and rich, have shown an interest in Ruth, which she did not reciprocate.

Boaz understands that Ruth has not been waiting merely for material salvation, ample food and comfortable shelter, nor for the appeasement of her maternal yearnings. She could have satisfied these needs by marrying one of the younger men in town. Ruth is looking to find a niche for herself within the Israelites' religious and ethical structure and therefore wishes to enter the Israelite family through the institution of the levirate marriage. This custom, intended to perpetuate a dead man's name and at the same time rescue his widow from poverty, is a new framework within which Ruth finds fulfillment and a sense of completeness. The earlier women, Lot's daughters and Tamar, are seen as terrorized by their fear of remaining "empty" in the biological sense. Driven by material concerns as well as their feminine instincts to become mothers, they act in a manner that recognizes no morality or civilized custom. In the Ruth tale, the theme of emptiness and fullness is first related to nature and to women's physical needs, but is then converted into a spiritual, religious, and historical concept. Ruth's reward is that she becomes an important link in the Israelites' historic journey toward redemption, by becoming the ancestress of the glorious David, and thus she "fills" and completes the generational chain.

It is through the language of honor and respectability that Ruth has converted her tale from the familiar pattern of a poor woman's rise to riches and prominence through a man, to a religious *bildungsroman* in which the foreign woman espouses a people and a faith, learns their legal code and customs, which are anchored in patriarchy, and proceeds to educate the patriarch and direct him toward a more humane interpretation of his God's law.

Significantly, the last episodes of the tale, narrated in chapter 4, are characterized by Naomi and Ruth's untypical silence. There are no exclamations of joy on the part of either woman, and, surprisingly, it is the women of the town, rather than the mother herself, who name Ruth's newborn. Again playing the role of the chorus, they sum up the protagonists' miraculous journey from bereavement to redemption. Naomi and Ruth's great respect for language and their faith in its power is revealed precisely in their reticence. They have exercised their linguistic ingenuity with the best possible results, but they are not wasteful of their eloquence. Their initial harsh fate has yielded to the power of their language. Naomi's lexicon of the unattainable—*yibbum*, redemption, matrimony—has forced itself on reality and materialized, and the nonexistent "redeemer" has come to life on Ruth's tongue, with Boaz persuaded to play the role. Naomi's grand vision of herself being tried by the heavenly court and her discourse with God, and Ruth's lofty style of sacred responsibility and covenantal redemption, have proven to be more than shallow ornamentation or calculated tactics. The women's colloquy of grandeur and religious ardor is genuine, corresponding to the greatness of their minds and hearts. Their verbal ability is testimony to their inner powers and indestructible nature. But mainly, it empowers them to continue their struggle for status and recognition and to carve out a magnificent destiny in a community, a system, and, indeed, a divinely mandated order that were not ready to yield easily to them.

The Journey Toward Life

Patricia Karlin-Neumann

The experience of moving from death and mourning back to life and vitality is one that most of us will repeat several times in our lives. The Book of Ruth, which we read annually at Shavuot, is a phenomenology of that journey. While Judaism has developed clear and helpful rituals to move us through that experience and inform our understanding of mourning, the Book of Ruth offers a different kind of guidance. Naomi, the primary mourner, experiences most of her mourning outside of a communal context. She begins her mourning as an individual, and her path back to the community—to hope and to life—charts the emotional terrain that may accompany an overwhelming experience of loss.

In the first five verses of the Book of Ruth, death and desolation reign:

> There was a famine in the land; and a man of Bethlehem in Judah, with his wife and two sons, went to reside in the country of Moab . . . and remained there. Elimelech, Naomi's husband died; and she was left with her two sons. They married Moabite women . . . and they lived there about ten years. Then [her sons] also died; so the woman was left without her two sons and without her husband.

Famine, exile, displacement, death, raising children alone in a foreign land, intermarriage, surviving one's children. Just as, in the Pesach story, the ten plagues of Egypt suggest the overturning of creation,[1] the seven "plagues" here suggest complete and utter loss. If the seven of Shabbat

---

The author used *Tanakh: A New Translation of the Holy Scriptures* (Philadelphia, New York, and Jerusalem: Jewish Publication Society, 1985).

is the seven of ultimate *shelemut* (wholeness and rest), the seven of Naomi's losses suggests its opposite. Naomi knows the death of the land,
the death of her husband, the death of her children, the death of her
family name. She is in exile with her roots and branches cut.

Twice the Torah tells us, "The woman was left" (*vatishaer hi*, 1:3;
vatishaer haisha, 1:5), reinforcing her sense of aloneness. The Midrash,
playing on the root letters *sh, a,* and *r,* which are found in *vatishaer* and
form the root of *she'erit* (remnant), teaches: "R. Chanina, the son of
R. Abbahu said: She became like the remnants of the meal offerings"
(Ruth Rabba 2:8). Since the meal offerings were made not of animals
but of fine flour and oil, they were the offerings of the poor. The image
thus reinforces the sense of Naomi's poverty, uselessness, and despair.

The Midrash also recognizes a parallel between Naomi and Job: both
lose property, then family (Ruth Rabba 2:10). Naomi is like Job not only
in experiencing loss, but in knowing utter isolation as a consequence of
her losses. Job has friends who try to console him but reinforce the distance between their understanding and his plight; Naomi has foreign
daughters-in-law who accentuate her distance from her land and her people. Naomi's first words in the Book of Ruth, repeated on two occasions,
are attempts to dissuade her daughters-in-law from following her: "Turn
back, each of you to her mother's house" (1:8; cf. 1:11, 12).

Like Job, Naomi attributes her losses to God. "My lot is far more
bitter than yours, for the hand of the Lord has struck out against me!"
she tells her daughters-in-law (1:13). When she enters Bethlehem and
the city women greet her, she responds, "Do not call me Naomi. . . .
Call me Mara, for Shaddai has made my lot very bitter. I went away
full and the Lord has brought me back empty. How can you call me
Naomi, when the Lord has dealt harshly with me, when Shaddai has
brought misfortune upon me!" (1:20–21). Five times Naomi insists that
it is God who is responsible for her suffering. Her refusal to be identified with pleasantness, the root of the name Naomi, and her renaming
herself "bitterness," communicate how completely Naomi is suffused
with the tragedy of her experience. Even when she is back in Bethlehem, back in her country, back with her people, she is railing at and in
exile from God.

There are hints of her sense of distance from God earlier in the text
when Naomi makes the decision to leave Moab, "for in the country of
Moab, she had heard that the Lord had taken note of His people and

given them food" (1:6). The word used to describe God's "taking note" *(pakad)* is used in the story of Sarah to report God's making the barren woman fruitful (Genesis 21:1). Here *pakad* emphasizes the distance between Naomi and her people and Naomi and God. She is not "of her people" at this moment; while they, like Sarah, are being remembered, Naomi is the remnant of the remnant. She tries to persuade Ruth and Orpah to leave her by bemoaning her own barrenness: "Have I any more sons in my body, who might be husbands for you? Turn back, my daughters, for I am too old to be married" (1:11).

In traditional Jewish mourning practices, the mourners are offered the consolation, "May God comfort you among all the mourners of Zion and Jerusalem." The recognition that there is a community of mourners, that others can know the emptiness following loss, is implicit in this greeting. Naomi is unable to be part of that community of mourners. In her home are two other mourners, yet Naomi wants to turn them away. Instead of representing comfort, Ruth and Orpah are bitter reminders of her loss. She cannot provide for them or protect them, and she has lost those who could have done so. Naomi's mourning is made more painful by her exile. She has no community, no comforters, and only fury at God.

But Ruth will not be pushed away. She insists on being with Naomi. Although she frames her declaration as a following of Naomi— "Wherever you go, I will go" (1:16)—it is actually Ruth who leads Naomi out of the darkness. In this context, two aspects of Ruth's words are astounding. She states that "your God [shall be] my God." The God Naomi repeatedly names as the source of her desolation and bitterness is the God Ruth is prepared to embrace. Although she too is a mourner, Ruth is able to turn to Naomi's God. The feminist theologian Rachel Adler once commented that the power of the mourner standing up to say Kaddish Yatom, the prayer of the mourner, in the midst of a community at prayer is that the very person who has a right to be the angriest at God is the one uttering God's praises. And by doing so, the mourner affirms the praise of God for others in the community. Ruth by declaring, "Your God my God," makes God, once again, Naomi's God.

Moreover, Ruth says, "Where you die, I will die, and there will I be buried" (1:17). For two who have experienced so much death together, this affirmation is not surprising. They are bound by the deaths of the men in the family. The men are presumably buried together, and Ruth vows that the women in the family will also be buried together. Yet, one can also see in this line another way in which Ruth helps to move Naomi out of her despair. They have been surrounded by death. For the mourner, to leave death requires an act of extraordinary energy and courage. Naomi, pummeled by so many losses, filled with so much bitterness, epitomizes death. And yet, she lives. Ruth is reminding, perhaps cajoling, Naomi to see that she is not dead yet. "Where you die, I will die." I will be there, Ruth promises, but it is not here, not yet. Ruth has taken the initiative in moving from death back to life, and she intends to bring Naomi with her on that journey.

For Naomi, the way back to life, vitality, and restoration cannot be directly through faith because her estrangement from God is so critical to her understanding of herself as Mara. Instead, it is through human acts that she is ultimately restored, and the language of the Book of Ruth reflects that. Words that are usually associated with God are, in the Book of Ruth, associated with people. In Ruth 1:14, Ruth clings to Naomi *(V'Rut davka bah)*. In 2:8, Boaz tells Ruth to cling to his girls *(devekut)*. The root *dvk*, meaning "to be close to" or "to cling" in Ruth, is used throughout Deuteronomy to refer to the experience of cleaving to God: "But you that cleave unto the Lord your God this day . . ." (Deuteronomy 4:4). The concept of *devekut* (cleaving to God) became central in Kabbalah, Jewish mysticism. Those familiar with the mystical tradition hear in the verb *(davak)* the implied object God, even as they recognize that the clinging here is to people.

Similarly, in Ruth 2:12, Boaz, praising Ruth for what she has done for Naomi says, "May you have a full recompense from the Lord, the God of Israel, under whose wings you have sought refuge." The phrase "under the wings" is used in rabbinic literature with reference to those who have joined the Jewish people, as Ruth did. Indeed here, Boaz is asking for God's shelter. The wings are divine wings. But when, in Ruth 3:9, Ruth uses the phrase "Spread your wings over your handmaid," she is addressing Boaz.[2] In choosing this image to seek the protection of a human being, Ruth symbolically seeks a promise of commitment not only from Boaz, but from God through Boaz.

The action of the last chapter of the Book of Ruth revolves around Boaz facilitating the redemption of, or himself redeeming, the field of Elimelech. The Hebrew root *gal* (redeem) occurs in this book twenty-one times. While the story itself addresses the question of redemption in a specific way, the resonance for those who are familiar with Jewish liturgy and rabbinic thought, where God is continually spoken of as *Goel Yisrael,* the redeemer of Israel, is strong.

By redeeming this field, Boaz becomes the means by which Naomi is finally able to embrace God once again as the Redeemer. Naomi's first praise of God occurs when she learns that Ruth has been gleaning in Boaz's field: "Blessed be he of the Lord, who has not failed in His kindness to the living or to the dead!" For, Naomi explains to her daughter-in-law, "the man is related to us, he is one of our redeeming kinsmen." The mention of the word *goel* (redeemer) directly after Naomi's words of praise, suggests a larger understanding of redemption operating in the text.

Indeed, Naomi seems to come back to life when, in chapter 3, she instructs Ruth to visit the threshing floor. It is Naomi who initiates the plan that will enable Boaz to act as the agent of redemption. The chapter begins with Naomi expressing concern for Ruth: "Daughter, I must seek a home for you, where you may be happy" (3:1). This is the first time Naomi becomes active as a caregiver and willingly takes responsibility for Ruth's welfare. In recovering her concern for her daughter-in-law, she creates a strategy that will ultimately provide her with a home as well.

Initially through Ruth, and then through Ruth and Boaz, Naomi's bitterness, and ultimately even her barrenness, fades. Despite her earlier predictions, Naomi, like Job, has a second family after the loss of her first family: "And the women said to Naomi, 'Blessed be the Lord, who has not withheld a redeemer from you today! May his name be perpetuated in Israel! He will renew your life and sustain your old age; for he is born of your daughter-in-law who loves you and is better to you than seven sons'" (4:13). Once again, the city women reflect Naomi's state. Here, she is unequivocally Naomi (pleasantness), and on her behalf, the women are blessing God, acknowledging the process of redemption through which Naomi has reentered the world of life and continuity. When Naomi takes the child, the women once again speak, this time declaring, "A child is born to Naomi."

The narrator links redemption in this specific case with redemption for Israel by providing the reader with the child's genealogy. Just as Naomi begins with seven experiences of loss, so Boaz, the redeemer, is the seventh generation in that genealogy, which culminates in David. And if Boaz, the father of the child, is the seventh son in the line of Perez, Ruth, the child's mother, is "better than seven sons."[3]

Although the child is regarded as Naomi's child, Obed, whose name means "the server," is very much Ruth's son. It is through Ruth's waiting, her service both to Naomi and to God, that the movement from death to life takes place. In those moments when the distance from God is so great that it cannot be traversed by the mourner, it is an Obed, one in service to God, who can take the mourner by the hand. This was Ruth's contribution to Naomi's mourning. In moments when death seems intractable and the only reality, it is sometimes another human soul, perhaps suffering, perhaps journeying, who can move a mourner slowly toward life, toward hope, toward redemption.

Fullness and Emptiness, Fertility and Loss

Meditations on Naomi's Tale in the Book of Ruth

Lois C. Dubin

To the memory of Robert Cohen,
friend and colleague

I went out full, but empty has God returned me.
—Ruth 1:21

Naomi is Everywoman. Everywoman who struggles with the problems of life and death, of perpetuating life and losing life. Everywoman who has lost her mate. Everywoman who worries about fertility and its loss or absence. Everywoman who has lost her children, the fruits of fertility. Death and loss—of varying kinds, and in different phases of the life cycle—are all too familiar to Naomi. Her tale in the Book of Ruth speaks directly to women who have lost a husband or children or fer-

---

The author used her own translation of the Book of Ruth; she also consulted *Torah Neviim Ketuvim: The Holy Scriptures* (Jerusalem: Koren, 1989), *Tanakh: A New Translation of the Holy Scriptures* (Philadelphia, New York, and Jerusalem: Jewish Publication Society, 1985), the Revised Standard Version, the Anchor Bible (Garden City, N.Y.: Doubleday, 1975), and Jack M. Sasson, *Ruth: A New Translation with a Philological Commentary and a Formalist-Folklorist Interpretation*, 2nd ed. (Sheffield: Sheffield Academic Press, 1989).

tility, or indeed a pregnancy.[1] A sufferer of some of the most painful losses a woman can know, Naomi is a female Job.[2]

The Book of Ruth opens with misfortune. Famine had driven a small family—husband Elimelech, wife Naomi, and two sons—to seek food and plenty in Moab. The family was successful in its quest for food, but not in its quest for posterity. "Elimelech, Naomi's husband, died, and she was left alone with her two sons" (1:4). Naomi went to Moab as wife and mother. Now she has become a widow. The family has lost its head and security, she has lost her husband and companion. In Ruth 1:1 the sons are described as "his sons." Now they are *hers*, all she has left.

Naomi is a survivor. She manages because she has to. In a strange land, who else will take care of her young sons? She raises them to adulthood. They marry. Then disaster strikes again. Both sons die, "and *the woman* [my emphasis] was left alone without her two boys and without her husband" (1:5). The woman survives both her husband and her children. Her proper name, Naomi, which means pleasant and sweet, is missing here, for it cannot be placed within this sad verse.[3] She is nameless, faceless, universal in her loss.

A woman who loses her husband is called a widow. A person who loses parents is called an orphan. But so against the order of nature is it for parents to survive their children that in English we have no word for a mother whose children die. A childless mother? So Naomi the wife and mother has become Naomi the widow and childless mother.[4] Though her two sons grew to manhood and married, she feels that she has lost her "boys" (1:5).[5] Her offspring, the fruits of her womb, are still somehow her babies, and especially so in their deaths. The childless mother has no more babies, the family no future.

Yet one facet of Naomi's identity remains: she is still a mother-in-law. Naomi has two daughters-in-law, two people who care about her, one of whom ultimately will mean "more to her than seven sons" (4:15). But she cannot know now what this daughter-in-law will provide in the future. In the present, the daughters-in-law are of little comfort. They are not the loved ones Naomi has chosen or given birth to. Whatever her regard for them, they are now extra and burdensome, still essentially outsiders or strangers, so she wishes them away. But one, Ruth, chooses her, and neither Ruth nor Naomi knows just how fateful, how binding, how fruitful that choosing will prove to be.

Naomi is mired in distress and grief. Not only has she lost her children; with husband gone, she has no socially acceptable means of conceiving more children. Moreover, because of her advancing age, she may no longer be physically capable of doing so. She tells her daughters-in-law that she is past childbearing age. "Have I yet more sons in my womb?" (1:11). "I am too old [*zakanti*] to be with a man and conceive" (1:12). The harsh truth renders the question merely rhetorical. For Naomi is indeed too old to menstruate. She is like Sarah who, "after it had ceased to be with her after the manner of women" mockingly said, "I have stopped having my monthly periods. . . . Shall I indeed bear a child though I am already old [*zakanti*]?" (Genesis 18:12–13).

Naomi is a menopausal widow: first she lost the living fruit of her womb, then the very capacity to bear children, fertility itself.

For some women, menopause may come as a blessing, perhaps as a kind of liberation. The death of fertility brings the promise of a new stage of life for a mature woman. But not so for Naomi. Death of husband. Death of sons. Death of fertility. Loss and death have become her lot in life. Loss of the living and loss of the potential for future life. These are the facts; Ruth 1:12 speaks in the indicative mood: "I am too old." But Naomi does not want to accept these facts. How do we know? By the use of the interrogative in Ruth 1:11: "Do I still have children in my womb?" And the subjunctive in the second part of 1:12: "If I were to say, 'I have hope,' if I were to be with a man tonight, and if I were to bear sons . . ." The shifts in grammatical mood are revealing of Naomi's complex psychological moods. Can I, could I? No! But perhaps . . . Wistful, impossible hope?

Even a woman who welcomes menopause may feel ambivalent about the great change. Even she may oscillate between the indicative and the subjunctive, between acceptance and rejection of her new facts of life.

Naomi was a fertile woman. She had known plenitude and plenty. But now it is as if she never had. It seems all was for nought. She had children, but they are gone. The childless widow has become, in effect, an infertile or barren woman.

Ruth wanted her life to be intertwined intimately with Naomi's. And so it was. When Naomi turned back toward Bethlehem, she urged Ruth to remain in Moab, but her injunctions against movement—go, turn back, don't come (1:6–15)—failed to persuade. Ruth insisted on joining Naomi on her journey.

There is no security for Naomi either in Moab or in Judah, but Bethlehem in Judah had been her home. So she returns home, retreats, perhaps to heal and build herself anew. She must find her own self, forge a new identity. Perhaps it will be easier to do that in her homeland. Her former home may yet offer her some strength, security, and comfort.

For Ruth, Judah is completely new, not home at all. Bearing a son will also be completely new for her, for Ruth was barren or infertile. The ancients called a woman barren who bore no children in ten years; today a woman who fails to conceive or to carry a fetus to term is called infertile. The end to barrenness, the blessings of fertility, will belong to Ruth's new home, to her new self. Becoming a mother is indeed an uncharted journey for a woman. One must journey, one must grow to be ready. A woman must depart from her old self to prepare a new self ready for this deep and demanding responsibility and commitment.[6]

Naomi and Ruth set out together. They leave Moab, the erstwhile land of plenty, and head for Bethlehem, literally "house of bread." The two companions have come to resemble each other: both are childless widows, one an aged childless mother, the other a young barren woman. Each seeks to forge a new self, one by returning home, the other by journeying to a new home. Though one returns, both venture forth to something new.

> As they arrived in Bethlehem, all the city stirred with excitement because of them. "Could this be Naomi?" asked the women. She answered:
> "Don't call me Naomi, sweet one, call me Mara, bitter one.
> For Shaddai (God) has made me bitter indeed.
> I went out full, but empty has God returned me.
> Why call me Naomi, sweet one?
> For God has testified against me
> And Shaddai had brought misfortune upon me."
> —RUTH 1:19–21

Naomi the widowed, childless, menopausal mother-in-law returns. Her old friends and neighbors see her as she approaches Bethlehem. So changed is her appearance, so downcast is she, that they hardly recognize her. As the Midrash puts it, in the old days she was carried by servants on litters, wore cloaks of fine wool, looked hearty and well fed. Now she appears barefoot, dressed in rags, pale and emaciated. "And the women said: 'Is this Naomi?' " (1:19). "Is this the one whose actions were fitting and pleasant [*ne' imim*]?" (Ruth Rabba 3:6).[7] Can this be the Naomi they knew, Naomi the pleasing one?

Naomi wants the women to recognize her, to know her as she now is. She needs a listener other than Ruth. And she wants sympathy from a new yet familiar quarter, her old friends and neighbors.[8] They knew her in better days, they see how reduced she now is. They know the beginning and see the end of her journey; she has to supply only the details. They see her empty, but they remember her full.

"I went out full, but empty has God returned me" (1:21). Commentators have interpreted the simple, powerful words to mean full of husband, children, riches, goods, pleasantness. How then is Naomi empty? Obviously widowed and childless, she is depicted further as poor, bereft of all good, sad and afflicted, alone.[9]

We must try to plumb the depths of Naomi's emptiness. Feeling completely empty, she is bitter, devoid even of hope, utterly alone. She pays no attention to her devoted daughter-in-law, Ruth, standing at her side; she does not even introduce her to the women of Bethlehem. At this moment Ruth is irrelevant for Naomi, for Naomi feels cut off from all, absorbed in her sorrow. And yet she is alienated even from her own self. Only two relations exist for her now: she must bring forth her cry of pain for her old acquaintances to hear, and she must blame God for her state, place responsibility where it belongs.

It is Shaddai whom Naomi blames for her bitterness and misfortune. The name El Shaddai is obscure; it is variously understood to mean God Almighty, God the self-sufficient, God of the mountain, God of overpowering strength, God the destroyer.[10] It was El Shaddai whom the patriarchs Abraham, Isaac, and Jacob associated with "being fruitful and multiplying," with the promise of numerous descendants and many nations issuing from them (Genesis 17:1, 28:3, 35:11). It was El Shaddai whom Jacob invoked when he blessed "fruitful Joseph" (Genesis 49:22): "By the God of your father who shall help you, and by Shaddai who shall bless you with blessings of heaven above, blessings of the deep that couches beneath, blessings of the breasts [*shadayim*] and of the womb" (Genesis 49:26). No wonder Naomi spoke the name of this God—the God responsible for fruitfulness, for progeny, the God whose very name *Shaddai* sounds so much like *shad*, the female breast. Thus as God of the mountain, God of the breast, El Shaddai is a symbol of fullness, of generativity, of fertility.[11] But Shaddai is perhaps no less a destroyer, from the root *shadad*, to pillage or destroy, as in "destruction [*shod*] from Shaddai" (Isaiah 12:6). For God, creating and destroying belong to the same primal power: "I deal death and give life" (Deuteronomy 32:39). Naomi has known God in both aspects: as creator of fertility and as its destroyer. So she lodges her complaint specifically against Shaddai, the very God who has betrayed her.

Naomi's pain-filled cry is absolutely necessary for the story to proceed: she must vent her sorrow and bitterness, her anger and sense of betrayal, to a group of women who might understand her pain; the women's listening and acknowledgment is a first step in Naomi's gradual recovery, in her eventual return to satisfaction and wholeness. Public acknowledgment of private grief is essential.

Naomi's inner core has been shaken, her identity shattered. She cannot bear to hear her name, Naomi, which means "pleasant" and "sweet." Now it mocks and reproaches, since the sweetness of life no longer fills her cup and the dregs leave but a bitter aftertaste. Empty, stricken, alienated—she feels singled out by God for misfortune. In phrases unique for the Bible, she says, "God's hand has come out against me" (1:13), "God has testified against me" (1:21).[12]

Naomi wants her name to accord with her present inner reality, so she tells the women to call her Mara, the bitter one. Her instruction is both a cry of pain and a cry for help. If they address her properly, then they will know who she really is and how to respond to her. Only then can she begin to be healed. Only if they call her "the bitter one" can the suffering Naomi begin to suffer less.

Be fruitful and multiply, and fill up the earth.
—GENESIS 9:1

Don't come before the Lord empty-handed.
—DEUTERONOMY 16:16

I went out full, and empty has God returned me.
—RUTH 1:21

Midrash Rabba (Ruth Rabba 3:7), echoed by Rashi, offers another explanation of Naomi's fullness: "I was pregnant." This is to say that she was pregnant when she left Judah years earlier. But perhaps we can expand our understanding of Naomi's fullness by developing the possibility offered by the Midrash. We can imagine Naomi knowing pregnancy, fullness, and emptiness within a much shorter and compressed time span, the events following one upon the other in rapid succession. Her words bespeak a situation other than the one in which we find her now. "I went out full, and empty has God returned me" (1:21). Naomi's lament sounds like the classic cry of a woman who has suffered the loss of a pregnancy: the loss of potential new life through miscarriage or stillbirth.

Hearing the verse thus, let us explore fullness and emptiness further, and meditate upon them from a variety of perspectives: Naomi, Everywoman, and even Jerusalem.

"I went out full, and empty has God returned me" (1:21). So too does the well-known opening verse of Lamentations, the Jewish cry of national grief, speak of emptiness and fullness: "How does the city sit solitary, that was full of people!" (Lamentations 1:1). Alas! How does she sit lonely, she once great with people, once full of life.

"Bursting with joy," "full of hope," "I could hardly contain myself," "I feel empty inside"—our language reflects our knowledge of the deep connection between our emotional and physical states. But our bodies can contain feelings, the emotional self, both figuratively and literally, and at no time more so than when a woman is pregnant, possessed of an intimate fullness, filled with seed, with fetus, with present and future life, with hopes and dreams. Fullness of spirit is reflected in expanding body and radiant face—life growing, reaching outward, spreading and shining. She comes to feel her every step heavy with child; *ani mele'ah halakhti* (1:21) means literally "I walked full." The natural ending to this process is birth, the life within breaking forth to begin life independently, in physical fullness, as a separate human being. As a mother's womb empties, she is filled emotionally. But when the growing of pregnancy comes to an untimely end, the womb is left empty and its issue develops no fullness. No new life stirs within or without. The potential mother is no more. She who bore life now carries death inside her. "The opposites of life and death are present within one person."[13]

A pregnant woman goes forth full, and she is brought back empty.

She has known new life so tiny and tender: "For he grew up before him as a young plant, as a root out of a dry ground. He had no form, no beauty that we should look at him, and no countenance" (Isaiah 53:2). No form, no shape, not yet visible to the human eye. But already life, hopes, dreams, and the images of a smiling child, loved and growing, and of oneself as mother, loving and nurturing. Potentiality seems real, all implicit in the beginning.

And she has known how sudden and brutal is the loss of that almost imperceptible life:

> Scarcely are they planted;
> scarcely are they sown;
> scarcely has their stem taken root in the earth.
> He merely blows upon them and they wither;
> and the storm wind takes them away as straw.
> —Isaiah 40:24

So she knows how fragile is early life and how fleeting its promise:

> A flower and not a flower;
> Of mist yet not of mist;
> At midnight she was there;
> She went as daylight shone.
> She came, and for a little while
> Was like a dream of spring.
> And then,
> As morning clouds that vanish traceless,
> She was gone.[14]

A pregnant woman goes forth full, and she is brought back empty. The fetus dies. The dream vanishes. The extraordinary is gone. The almost everything is suddenly nothing. A pregnant woman, filled with an awakening growing self, is now empty both of new life and of hope.

That hope, that prospect of a new living being, had really filled her, and its loss is real. From growing home, she becomes a truly empty vessel. "They didn't find water, they returned their vessels empty" (Jeremiah 14:3).

A woman and her mate may have planned to have a child at this moment, or they may not have, but they had a sense of human initiative and action. Intercourse between man and woman leads to conception, humans beget new life. She can say: we made me pregnant, from our action I am pregnant. But the sudden, unplanned ending of pregnancy through miscarriage comes from beyond, from an unknown mysterious cause, from God, or Shaddai in Naomi's terms. Humans act, but do not control completely matters of life and death.

> Just as we do not know how the lifebreath passes into the limbs within the full womb of her that is with child, so we cannot foresee the actions of God, who causes all things to happen.
>
> —Ecclesiastes 11:5

> There are three keys which the Holy One, blessed be He, entrusts to no creature . . . but are kept in His own hand: the key of rain . . . the key of resurrection . . . and the key of the womb.
>
> —Pesikta Rabbati 42:7[15]

Naomi must blame Shaddai. She must hold God responsible for her fate. There is no other. It is Shaddai who bestows the "blessings of the womb" and Shaddai who denies or withdraws them.

"*I* went out full, and empty has God returned *me*" (1:21; my emphases). At the end, we, God, you—all disappear. Only the I remains. The woman alone feels the great emptiness, the life within her departed. The Hebrew places unusual emphasis on the I by starting the verse with *ani*, a word superfluous in terms of Hebrew grammar.[16] The woman's solitary, pain-filled self is stressed.

> Alas! How does she sit lonely . . .
> She that was great among nations
> Is become like a widow . . .
> Bitterly she weeps in the night,
> Her cheek wet with tears.
> There is none to comfort her
> Of all her friends.
>
> —Lamentations 1:1–2

A woman who suffers an early miscarriage is often plagued by her own choice of privacy. The pain of loss is often intensified by discretion and secrecy. For the pregnant woman who has not told friends or family of her pregnancy, the privacy deprives her of comfort and sympathy afterward in time of loss. Early pregnancy is not public, nor is grieving after miscarriage. But if very early tender life be real, then its loss is real, and so is the need to mourn. But who even knows that one has been full, and is now empty and struggling in pain?

Friends may not know a woman is in need of comforting. She tries to manage with the comfort and solace offered by her mate, or perhaps by medical helpers. But that often does not suffice. A partner, hard as he tries, sometimes simply cannot comprehend the pain of the once-filling, now empty womb. It is a story for women:

> The wombs of women form a secret, silent network of communication all over the world. . . . Every time a woman tells a story "from her womb," other women hearing the story feel it in their depths as well.[17]

The solitude of the woman who has miscarried is deep and silent. So many women know this pain, so many have sat lonely, so many have wept in the night. . . .

Naomi needed the women of Bethlehem to greet her, to comment on her sad state, to listen and share. So Naomi wept not only by night, but also by day. She was wise: she cried out in bitterness so that she could seek comfort.

A woman whose pregnancy has suddenly ended wants desperately to communicate with the little one who is lost. But she must learn to communicate with those who are living. They were not part of this intimate union, but if they learn of it and listen, they may offer some understanding, comfort, and hope.

Moods constantly shift, one becoming intertwined with another. Interrogative: Do I still have children in my womb? Indicative: No, not at this moment. Subjunctive: "If I were to say, 'I have hope,' . . . if I were to bear children . . ." A woman who is infertile or who has suffered loss of pregnancy is suspended somewhere between indicative, interrogative, and subjunctive, somewhere between the sadness and pain of the past and hope for the future. Could I? Until now I cannot. Perhaps . . . ?

A commentary on Midrash Ruth Rabba (2:17) says that Naomi was praying with hope and trust that God would perform a miracle to enable her to conceive despite her advanced age.[18] There are so many goings and comings in the Book of Ruth, so many journeys. The journey from emptiness to the very beginnings of allowing hope to enter and start filling one can be long and tortuous. But complete emptiness is very heavy, and very difficult to contain. The subjunctive of hope is necessary.

> For my thoughts are not your thoughts
> Nor are your ways my ways, says the Lord.
> For as the heavens are higher than the earth
> So are my ways higher than your ways
> and my thoughts higher than your thoughts.
> For as the rain comes down, and the snow from heaven,
> and returns not there,
> but waters the earth, and makes it bring forth and bud,
> that it may give seed to the sower, and bread to the eater,
> So is the word that goes forth from my mouth:
> It shall not return to me fruitless [*rekam*, literally empty],
> but it shall accomplish my purpose
> and succeed in the task I gave it.
>
> —ISAIAH 55:8–11

> A son is born to Naomi!
> —RUTH 4:17

To Naomi?

Naomi and Ruth become strangely conflated in the story. Ruth wants their fates to be intertwined intimately, and they are. Journeying to Bethlehem, the two widows share lack of husband, and lack of children, one through death, one through apparent barrenness. The daughter-in-law, now fertile in Bethlehem, the "house of bread," conceives directly after intercourse with her second husband, Boaz. When the daughter-in-law gives birth to a son, the female neighbors exclaim that a son is born to the mother-in-law!

Are Naomi and Ruth one? Who is the infant's mother? Whose son is he? Leaving aside the intricacies of levirate marriage (hinted at in

1:11–13), redeemer and redemption (2:20, 3:12–13, 4:1–6, 4:14), and the raising of a dead man's name upon his inheritance (4:5, 4:10),[19] how can we understand this?

The child was born to Ruth and Boaz. It happened quickly: told in a rush of verbs in 4:13, Boaz took Ruth, she became his wife, he had intercourse with her, God made her conceive, and she bore a son. "God gave her conception" (4:13)—it is an expression unique in the Bible.[20] The Midrash says that something unnatural was at work, that God had to intervene: Ruth "lacked the main portion of the womb, but the Holy One, blessed be He, shaped a womb for her" (Ruth Rabba 7:14). So Ruth, like matriarch Sarah as portrayed in the Midrash (Genesis Rabba 47:2, 53:5),[21] had a physical problem that required God's direct, miraculous intervention for conception to occur.

When God remembered Sarah, he remembered all barren women with her (Pesikta Rabbati 42:4; Genesis Rabba 53:8). Any birth after difficulties of infertility or pregnancy loss is experienced as a miracle. For every woman who has had trouble conceiving or carrying to term or giving birth to a healthy child, the successful bearing and birth of a healthy child is a miracle—a miracle as great as the birth of a baby to ninety-year-old Sarah, or to menopausal Naomi. . . .

So is every healthy pregnancy and birth a miracle.

After the child is born in Bethlehem, female friends and neighbors crowd round to congratulate the happy family. These are the women who greeted Naomi upon her return to the town, who invited her to pour out her heart to them. Now they express their good wishes specifically to Naomi: "Blessed be God who has not denied you a redeemer, who has brought you a restorer of life [*meshiv nefesh*, literally returner of the soul] and a sustainer of your old age, one whose name will be celebrated in Israel." Naomi takes the child and places him on her bosom. The excited women name the child, exclaiming with joy, "A son is born to Naomi!" (4:14–17).

The child is at Naomi's breast, Naomi holding him in a maternal embrace. Ruth 4:16 describes Naomi as *omenet*. The exact meaning of the Hebrew word is uncertain. What is she? wet-nurse? adoptive or foster mother? guardian? caregiver?[22] Did Naomi the experienced mother immediately take the child to caress and suckle, lending both hand and breast? Could her breasts have miraculously given forth milk as did Sarah's at the age of ninety? (Genesis Rabba 53:9, 53:5)

The child is called "restorer of life," *meshiv nefesh*, returner of the soul, but in the image of Naomi holding close the infant, we see *her* nurturing, giving suck, sustenance, and comfort. By giving Naomi the opportunity to give the basics of life, this little *meshiv nefesh* helps return Naomi to herself. At the opening of the story, she lost her boys (*yeladeha*; 1:5), but at the end a boy is born (*yulad*; 4:17) to her. Repetition of the Hebrew root *y,l,d* signals that he replaces the boys she has lost.[23] It doesn't matter whether he belongs to Ruth and Boaz, whether he is son or grandson to Naomi. He is a child of her family who will carry on the family's name, who provides again the possibility of posterity. He gives Naomi the chance to cast off her bitterness and return to her sweet self, to her true identity, to be a nurturing mother and sustainer of life. She can once again experience satisfaction and fulfillment, fullness and wholeness. "The woman of emptiness has become the woman of plenty."[24] Earlier she complained that God had returned her (*heshivani*; 1:21) empty. Now—we are told by means of the same Hebrew verb *sh,u,v*—the child returns her soul, restores her to life (*meshiv nefesh*; 4:15).[25] So identity and name change again. The women no longer need listen to Naomi's instructions to call her Mara. Mara can depart and Naomi return. It is time for the women to name the child (4:17)[26] and in effect to rename Naomi publicly too.

During their first meeting, Boaz had blessed Ruth: "May the Lord repay your good deed. May your full [*shalem*] reward come from the Lord, God of Israel, under whose wings you have sought shelter" (2:12). Now this blessing upon Ruth has been fulfilled for Naomi too. Naomi, like Ruth and through Ruth, has been blessed with the joy of new life and the responsibility of helping to care for it. Now, indeed, Naomi is *shelemah*—whole and at peace [*shalom*] with herself. She is also at peace with her God: the child at her bosom, she need no longer rail against Shaddai. The "blessings of the breasts and of the womb" (Genesis 49:25) are hers again. Naomi, Ruth, Boaz, the baby—a new family has been created. The boy belongs to them all. For two women, this child brings life and reverses infertility and loss. The new offspring returns fruitfulness to the womb, hope, and posterity.

A child, born naturally or adopted, transforms an infertile woman or a woman who has known loss of life from her womb. After the great loneliness of loss, the cries of pain and mourning and anger, a child brings calm and comfort, soothing balm, a link to the future. The Bible always states, a son was born to such-and-such a man. Except in this one case (4:17), it never states that a child was born to a particular woman.[27] But here, the phrase "a son is born to Naomi!" emphasizes the importance of birth to the mother, and perhaps especially to a woman who has suffered infertility or loss.

Both Ruth and Naomi learned the way from emptiness to fullness. In leaving Moab and going with Naomi to Bethlehem, Ruth made the journey from infertility to motherhood, from her own emptiness to fullness. She joined the matriarchs Sarah, Rebecca, Rachel, and of course Hannah, all infertile, or in biblical language barren, all ultimately remembered by God, blessed finally with fertility and children. Naomi crossed back and forth between plenty and famine, emptiness and fullness. At the end of the book, with food and progeny restored, the family knows abundance again.

From the pain and suffering of her great emptiness, Naomi had cried out. That lament and that cry—from her heart and her womb—marked the beginning of healing. Naomi needed to blame God and to seek redress in the company of other women. From her great emptiness, her deep loneliness, she managed somehow to seek human contact. Though she tried initially to push her daughter-in-law away, she gradually came to recognize her need for public sharing of private grief. Through human solidarity—with the women of Bethlehem, with Ruth and Boaz—and through her patient faith and hope in God, she was able to achieve wholeness of self, family, community, and people.

Shaddai did restore fruitfulness to the family of Naomi and Ruth. In showing concern for these particular people, Shaddai was yet working toward a larger purpose. In making Ruth the ancestor of King David, El Shaddai fulfilled his promise to Jacob, spoken at the fateful moment when Jacob's name was changed to Israel, the future name of the entire people: "I am El Shaddai, be fruitful and multiply as a nation, a host of nations shall come from you, and kings from your loins shall go forth" (Genesis 35:11). From the renewed family of Naomi and Ruth the Davidic dynasty of kings did go forth.[28] Naomi went out full, and is finally returned full. She is no longer empty.

Growing Up and Older
with Ruth

Sylvia Rothchild

ﮯ

We called it "Shveeis" before it became "Shavuot." It was the most benign and cheerful of the holidays celebrated in my family. Memories of it are stored for me in smells, tastes, textures of fabric and leaf, in the special light of early summer and in some mysterious promise that I don't understand but that lightens my heart. The story of Ruth and Naomi was woven into those memories, a theme with variations that played themselves out in unexpected ways for more than half a century.

I thought of Shveeis as a woman's festival because my father had no visible role in it. It was a holiday my mother made by filling the house with the smell of caramelized sugar, the juice of huckleberries bursting out of her sweet yeast dough, the pungent smell of onions and farmer cheese in mouth-watering little rolls called *platshintis* and platters of kreplach and blintzes dripping with butter she herself churned. (She didn't trust the grocer's vat of butter, which might have been touched by a knife contaminated by sausage or some forbidden cheese.)

Then there were the long, narrow boxes of greenery and flowers, an annual present from Spitz's florist, bringing aromas from places I'd never seen. My older sister and I would decorate the house. I adorned the places I could reach—the sewing machine, the brass samovar, the bottom of the oak buffet and the china closet. My sister, eight years older, filled the heavy crystal vase and pitcher. She climbed up on a

---

The author used *Tanakh: A New Translation of the Holy Scriptures* (Philadelphia, New York, and Jerusalem: Jewish Publication Society, 1985).

kitchen chair and I handed her the leafy branches one by one, for her to rest on the tops of pictures and mirrors and hang from the Dutch shelves and door lintels. Our walls were covered with pictures. There were the large photographs of grandparents: my father's father who had not come to America, a well-dressed, prosperous-looking burgher with a neatly trimmed beard, wearing a top hat; my mother's father in a skull cap with a beard that fanned out like butterfly wings, a younger version of the grandfather I saw every Sabbath; my gentle-faced grandmother in a wig that made her look older than she was. There were also the pictures my grandfather painted. He was an unusual pious Jew who spent part of his days in prayer and study and the rest painting pictures of the world he left behind. He looked out of his fifth-story tenement on the teeming streets below and painted meadows, orchards in bloom, ducks in a pond, deer in the forest. His pictures filled me with longing for calm, spacious, sweet-smelling rural places, far from the noisy, ugly streets of Williamsburg and the Lower East Side.

My grandfather paid us his annual visit on the afternoon before the holiday began. It was a formal visit to honor his favorite daughter and to enjoy the decorated house and the first fruits from my mother's oven, artfully arranged and presented to him as if he were our surrogate for a Temple priest. I would be dressed up for the occasion in a dress so stiffly starched it hurt to sit down and unbending patent leather shoes that pinched my toes.

When my grandfather had blessed, tasted, and praised everything offered to him, he sat down in the rocking chair next to the piano, filled his pipe, and listened to me play all my pieces. If he asked me to I would sing a few Yiddish songs as well. I wasn't shy. Hungry for praise and attention, it pleased me to entertain him.

On Shveeis, the three small rooms our family of five called home became a magical place, a stage, a bower redolent with the smell of fresh green leaves, roses, and peonies. My pleasure was not only in the transformation we brought about but, even more, in the seasonal discovery that it was possible to alter what was familiar and prosaic, that escape could come not only in daydreams but through physically changing things.

One of my earliest fears was that our lives in those cramped rooms were fixed, that our living arrangements, like our observances, were unalterable. Too young to understand that my parents, in coming to

America from villages in Bukovina, had already experienced more change than they could absorb in a lifetime, I knew only that they were content with what they called their "portion" and had no wish for anything new. Even at the age of eight or nine I thought them too easily satisfied, too quick to thank the Almighty for what seemed to me small favors. Spasms of impatience and anger made me feel like a bad daughter. I escaped my bad conscience by losing myself in daydreams in which I was free to be anyone and anywhere I wanted.

In reality, however, I was bound by the restrictions of an observant Jewish home and my parents' fear that I might be led astray by children from families that did not share their sense of what was forbidden and what permitted, what was "edel" (noble) and what "prost" (common). These categories existed not because of what people might say, but because of the "Law" and the "One Above," who was all knowing and all seeing.

I couldn't tell where the law-inspired prohibitions ended and those created by custom and propriety began. Life seemed a minefield of inexplicable "shalt nots" to be negotiated with extreme caution. From the tone of the *mi tur nisht* (one mustn't), I would try to grasp the seriousness of the matter. There seemed, however, to be no hierarchy of prohibitions. I would lie awake at night on the narrow cot I shared with my sister, puzzling over the forbidden things. The dietary rules were no problem. Everything forbidden seemed loathsome and inedible by that time. Sabbath taboos, however, troubled me. Reading was permitted, writing forbidden. Walking was permitted, taking the trolley forbidden, visiting permitted, going to movies forbidden. I knew I must not touch a pencil, a scissors, or a penny. I could not play a note on the piano from sundown to sundown or turn on a light until I had seen three stars, which could be hard to find on a rainy, cloudy Sabbath. I wondered why I, unlike the children of our neighbors, was permitted, even encouraged, to play the piano during the week and not permitted to play in the street where the other children were running, jumping, and shouting. And there were other restrictions: "Have you no one else to befriend?" I heard when I chose Marcella, the Polish janitor's daughter.

Friends my parents approved of were hard to come by. Opportunities for being led astray were minimal. I was enrolled in the Talmud Torah of Williamsburg when I was five, the year I started kindergarten, the year my younger sister was born and I was told that my childhood was over and the time for "acting like a mensch" had arrived. My doll and tea set were packed away in the closet for the baby to play with when she was old enough. From then on I was to devote myself to learning, the opportunity my mother had missed.

I quickly became a small adult with worries, responsibilities, and questions I didn't know how to ask. I watched the adults around me, eavesdropped on their conversations hoping to pick up clues to the mystifying phrases I kept hearing and trying to decode. *Dos redele dreit zich* (the wheel turns) was one. An *ehrlich leben iz* a *shverlich leben* (an honest life is a hard life) was another, and *shver tzu zein* a *Yid* (hard to be a Jew) was a kind of refrain that followed the others.

It was at this time that I found the story of Ruth in *The Yiddishe Geshichte*, my Talmud Torah textbook, a collection of legends and stories about events from the time of the Judges till the destruction of the Kingdom of Israel. The stories about Deborah, Samson, and Samuel were interesting but had nothing to do with me. Ruth, however, found a place in my imagination. The illustration that came with the story showed a sweet-faced girl of uncertain age who looked a little like Marcella, the janitor's daughter I was forbidden to play with. Her hair hung to her shoulders and her arms were full of the grain she had gleaned. She was standing in a field my grandfather might have painted.

Reading of the time "when a famine broke out," I imagined it as a variation of the Depression years we were living in. There were no fields to glean in Williamsburg, but it was a time of grave money worries, of pitiful beggars in the streets, of pawning a ring or watch to "make a holiday." One might find a once-prosperous relative selling apples from a little box on the street corner. Reading about Elimelech taking his family to Moab in search of better opportunities, I wondered whether my uncomplaining father, if besieged by famine, would take his family to another place.

That shortened Yiddish version of Ruth's story suggested possibilities I hadn't thought of. For example, the words *shviger* (mother-in-law) and *shneer* (daughter-in-law) sounded ugly to me because I associated them with gossip and family strife. It pleased me to discover a mother- and daughter-in-law who were not each other's enemies. Watching my older sister and her friends searching for husbands made me worry whether anyone would choose me when I grew old enough. In that frame of mind I noted that Ruth didn't wait to be chosen but offered herself.

The circumstances of her offer weren't clear in my children's version of the story, nor did it mention that Boaz was an old man, soon to die. It read only as a romance with a happy ending for Ruth, who was "redeemed," for Naomi, who had a grandchild, and for the Jewish people, who would a few generations later have King David, evidence that there was a Father in Heaven looking out for His children, something I desperately wanted to believe.

What amazed me the most was that Ruth and Orpah were Moabites, who were supposed to be forbidden to Jews, just as Marcella the janitor's daughter was forbidden to me. If that were not enough, Ruth's wish to join the Jewish people added another dimension of astonishment.

I had learned early that I had been born into Jewishness and that it couldn't be rejected even if it came with sorrow, difficulties, and disappointments. I was told that our Father in Heaven, who was supposed to be looking out for us, worked in mysterious ways, beyond our understanding. I was expected to live with two contradictory messages. One was *Got iz mit dir* (God is with you), the other, *Vos iz mit dir? Me farlozt zich nisht aufen Rebonoshelolem?* (What's wrong with you? Are you expecting God to come down to help you?).

Ruth's choice and Naomi's gratitude made it seem that He might. Their story made the life I was born into seem more worthy and desirable. It was the perfect story to read on Shveeis, when the house smelled of greenery and caramelized sugar.

Almost *twenty years* would pass before I had reason to think of the Book of Ruth again. During that time everything that seemed fixed and unchangeable to me as a child gave way. The structure of our lives had depended on my grandparents' presence. With their deaths the structure collapsed. We moved from Williamsburg to East Flatbush, where Jewish life was more American. English, not Yiddish, was the language of the street. My parents no longer went to an orthodox shul where my grandfather sat in a place of honor on the *bimeh* and my grandmother, surrounded by her daughters, sat in the women's balcony praying loudly, to help the women around her who couldn't read. In the new neighborhood my father joined a large conservative temple and my mother sat beside him.

Studying Hebrew as a modern language in high school, I discovered that "Shveeis" was to be called "Shavuot." I joined a Hebrew Culture Club where we sang about pioneers building "Eretz Yisroel." For Shavuot we danced gestures of gleaning and skipped barefoot on the gym floor with imaginary baskets of *bikurim* on our heads. The Shveeis of my childhood would not be forgotten, but it was relegated to the past. It became my grandfather's holiday, my mother's culinary celebration, not mine.

World War II soon wreaked havoc on all holidays and Sabbaths. They were left to parents to attend to while the children went out to do the work of the world. At eighteen I worked in a defense plant making quartz crystals for the Signal Corps while attending Brooklyn College at night. The administration at that time was trying to free its students from immigrant gestures, accents, and loyalties to prepare us for joining the mainstream without debilitating "defects." Supplying the Signal Corps had a high priority and permitted no time off for holidays. Visible and invisible forces pulled me away from the traditions and prohibitions that had shaped my childhood. It all happened very quickly. At the age of twelve I had expected the Williamsburg Bridge to collapse the first time I took a trolley across it on the Sabbath. At eighteen I rode a nearly empty subway to work on Yom Kippur with impunity, even with some feelings of exhilaration at my liberation.

At twenty-one I married a fellow student, an Air Corps lieutenant, just before he went overseas. It was when he returned and I followed him as an army wife, and later, when I was working while he went to graduate school, that the liberation began to pall, even to feel like a kind of deprivation.

I missed Jewish life and began trying to read myself back into it. In the years of planning my escape from Brooklyn, I read Emerson and Thoreau and imagined myself a writer in a small New England town. Now, in libraries in Texas and Colorado, I read Martin Buber, Maurice Samuel, and Sachar's *History of the Jews*. My search for a way back or forward began with reading.

Two years of teaching elementary Hebrew to rambunctious seven-year-olds in a conservative congregational school added to my confusion. The temple was large and affluent, the rabbi formal and pompous, and the cantor, an opera singer. Services were performances attended as if they were concerts. I could not go back to the world of my parents or grandparents, but I also knew I could find no place for myself in such a congregation.

A few years later, we settled in a small New England town close to Boston, where my husband found work. I was still searching, but less concerned about myself than about how to raise our three young children as Jews. I should have been content in a spacious house of our own, finally surrounded by woods and meadows, the landscape of my grandfather's pictures. I had begun writing and publishing stories. Caring for our two daughters and infant son kept me very busy but didn't assuage a kind of anxiety I couldn't shake off. I suddenly needed to try to bridge the chasm that had developed between my mother's life and my own. I began making Sabbaths and paying attention to holidays. My husband, raised in a secular, nonobservant family, would have been content without my efforts but didn't try to stop me.

I resented having to create holidays without any help but had no choice. The holidays I didn't make, wouldn't happen. Without parents or grandparents close by we were free to live as we pleased and just beginning to understand the weight of that responsibility. The small Jewish community in the town was too new to be of help. It was organized in response to the fact that there were seven churches in the town of four thousand people, each with its Sunday school. Jews, whether or not they'd been members of synagogues before, were expected to create their own "church" and school.

Soon after we arrived, I was recruited to teach a class of twelve-year-old girls. Classes for seven-year-olds were already underway, but there was concern about the older girls, girls going to church dances with their classmates who might be lost to the Jewish community without some special efforts on their behalf.

The parents had modest expectations. They were not interested in studying with their daughters or in observing traditions they had discarded. They were, after all, American-born and trying to live like their American neighbors. Eastern European Jewish life had no claim on them. It was 1951, only six years after the liberation of Auschwitz, too close to that dreaded time even to speak of it. The state of Israel was only three years old, but of interest only to Zionists—and they were not Zionists. They hoped for what they called "a little bit of Jewishness," for the girls to be able to follow the Hebrew in the prayer book and to learn a little history—"not the sad parts," but enough so they would "know who they are." It was agreed that the girls would be more amenable to a year of intense study if it could conclude with a celebration, a kind of bat mitzvah on Shavuot.

When I began looking for books and making lesson plans, I realized that what I wanted to offer my students would not be found in the books available. I wanted nothing less than to convince them that Judaism was a gift they should not refuse and that they would not want to part with it if they knew what it offered. I wanted to lure them away from what I thought to be trivial American temptations and get them to choose to be Jewish. I decided that the story of Ruth and Naomi and the holiday of Shavuot could provide the focus for our discussions. We could talk about Sinai, about what it meant to "receive" the Torah. We could think about commitment and loyalty, and I could tell them about growing up in a Jewish world.

I would encourage them to write poems and stories, possibly a play based on the Book of Ruth, and see if they could imagine themselves in another time and place. I was excited about leaving my toddlers at home with a baby-sitter three afternoons a week while I spent time with older children. I looked forward to the questions they would ask and planned answers.

I wasn't prepared for the magnitude of their resistance. One or two had come willingly. The others, bribed or nagged, made it clear that they would rather be somewhere else. They learned the Hebrew alphabet in spite of themselves, could read haltingly within a few weeks. We made time lines, played games with history, talked about holidays they didn't celebrate and Sabbaths they didn't keep, but I always felt their distrust and skepticism. They did not want to hear what I had to say.

The questions they asked about the Book of Ruth were not the questions I wanted to answer. That Naomi and Elimelech permitted their sons to marry Moabite women interested them more than Ruth's affection for Naomi. They wondered whether Ruth chose not to return to her people because she was afraid they wouldn't take her back. They fell into fits of giggles about Ruth's coming at night to lie at Boaz's feet and wanted to know what exactly was meant by her being "covered by his blanket." They saw no happy ending in Ruth's marriage to Boaz, who was old enough to be her father, and were outraged to discover that Ruth came with a parcel of land that seemed more valuable than she.

They argued that it wasn't fair for the Jews at Sinai to make a covenant for future generations to keep. They were sure that every generation should be free to choose for itself. I then told them about the rabbi in a little Polish town long ago who on Shavuot absolved his congregation of their Jewishness so that year after year they could choose to accept the Torah and continue to live as Jews.

The girls assured me that would never work in America. Given a choice, they were sure everyone would prefer to be born Christian. Two of the students announced that they'd already decided to marry out of Judaism. The others confessed that they were not yet sure what they wanted or believed, except that they wanted to look, behave, and be accepted as Americans. To be Jewish was to be different and separate, out rather than in. They did not want to be outsiders. Ruth's choice meant nothing to them. The Ruth who had given me a vision of freedom and affection seemed bound, dependent, and manipulated to them.

The year of struggle passed quickly. The celebration at Shavuot took place as planned. There was a brief service led by the cantor, and certificates and prayer books were given out. They read their stories and poems and did the dances I had taught them. The parents were pleased to see how much their daughters had learned. I worried about what they had not learned and wondered how much they'd remember.

Years later one of the students came to see me to tell me what she had done with her life. She confessed that from that year she remembered only the Hebrew letters and the sense of urgency I had created. "What I couldn't forget," she said, "was that you cared so much. Why," she asked, "was it so important to you that we be Jewish and choose Jewish husbands?"

By then I knew that the jousting with my bat mitzvah girls was a preview of and preparation for the struggles I would have with my own children. For a while I had believed that I'd assured their Jewish future. Unlike the girls in my class, they'd grown up with Sabbaths and holidays, with Jewish books and stories and visits to grandparents. They were enrolled in the congregation school when they were seven, had proper bar and bat mitzvot, even visits to Israel.

Saved from the restrictions that had made me rebellious, they were raised to be independent and iconoclastic, Jews who could accept their differences from their peers as we, their parents, accepted ours. They were serious and intelligent. I had trusted them to find their way and believed it would be a Jewish way, not necessarily mine, but Jewish.

I was not prepared to hear "Judaism means nothing to me," as one by one, my young adult children let me know that my "prejudices" were not theirs. My loyalties and compulsions, they said, were not transferable. They were members of a new generation, free to choose their own interests and values, free to live as they pleased, marry as they pleased, and someday raise children as they saw fit. Hadn't I done the same?

An anxious, unsettling time! My husband and I told each other it was a stage that would pass, a trial we would live through as others had before us. We should not have been so sure of ourselves, so arrogantly confident of our power over our children. We should have known it was impossible to impose our loyalties. Why then did we feel so rejected?

We mourned when our children chose non-Jewish mates. In the old days, when intermarriages were rare, the mourning was dramatic and public. In the new time, when intermarriages were common, there was only private, unspoken anguish. "Welcome to the club," whispered friends who had traveled that uncomfortable road before us. No child was cast out, no mirrors were covered, but the feeling of tearing was there. My husband, in spite of the casualness of his Jewish upbringing, had been affected by our years together and felt as keenly as I about the lost Jewish future of our family. We brooded together about what we had done wrong. I began for the first time to wonder how my parents felt when I made choices so different from theirs.

It was in this mood one Shavuot that I read the Book of Ruth again. This time I found myself thinking about Naomi in Moab, wondering if she had feared for her sons in a place where there were no Jewish girls to marry. Had she wept or danced at their weddings? Did she and Elimelech quarrel about the wisdom of living so far from their own people?

There were no clues in the text. I found a midrash that suggested that the misfortunes that befell the family were punishments for choosing Moabite women. In another, however, Elimelech, a man of wealth and power, was himself seen as the cause of the calamities. The marriages to the Moabite women were effects, not causes. His flight from Bethlehem, where he should have accepted responsibility for the poor, was seen as a mark of poor character that deserved punishment.

We hear about Ruth and Orpah only after ten years have gone by. We don't know whether they are typical or unusual Moabite women. We are told nothing about their problems and adjustments when their husbands were alive or how long it took before they were resolved. I thought, of course, of myself and wondered how long it would take before I reconciled myself to what had for so long seemed unacceptable to me. My protracted quarrel with myself was especially painful because I was genuinely fond of the mates my children had chosen. They were not abstract non-Jewish adversaries but good people who had done what I wished my children to do, namely, chosen Jewish mates. Wasn't it unreasonable to hold against them the fact that they hadn't chosen their parents more carefully?

I was, at first, most conscious of what I thought were their un-Jewish qualities. With the passing of time, however, I began to look for aspects of Ruth in each of them. I took comfort from their willingness to share the holiday celebrations I organized. I was grateful for the questions they asked and the respectful way they listened when I tried to answer them. The bonds grew stronger after the births of grandchildren, which gave me and my husband the magical power of grandparents, power we were prepared to exploit and enjoy to the fullest. Unspoken was the hope that our grandchildren would choose the commitments their parents rejected.

Our tension and anxiety began to diminish when we found our children worrying about what to teach their children, asking the same question we had asked at their stage of life. They didn't ask for our advice or help, but watching them begin to search for meaning and structure, it began to seem likely that my people would be theirs after all. The Jewish future of their children would be no more predictable than theirs had been, but they were behaving as if Jewishness was a gift they were finding hard to refuse. I don't know what they would make of the story of Ruth and Naomi or whether they are ready to read it with empathy. I treasure it for the memories and perspectives it brings to life for me and still find in it a promise of hope for the unknowable future—what it has offered since it was first told.

Poetic Movements

The Book of Ruth and Naomi

MARGE PIERCY

∾

When you pick up the Tanakh and read
the Book of Ruth, it is a shock
how little it resembles memory.
It's concerned with inheritance,
lands, men's names, how women
must wiggle and wobble to live.

Yet women have kept it dear
for the beloved elder who
cherished Ruth, more friend than
daughter. Daughters leave. Ruth
brought even the baby she made
with Boaz home as a gift.

Where you go, I will go too,
your people shall be my people,
I will be a Jew for you,
for what is yours I will love
as I love you, oh Naomi
my mother, my sister, my heart.

Show me a woman who does not dream
a double, heart's twin, a sister
of the mind in whose ear she can whisper,
whose hair she can braid as her life
twists its pleasure and pain and shame.
Show me a woman who does not hide

in the locket of bone that deep
eye beam of fiercely gentle love
she had once from mother, daughter,
sister; once like a warm moon
that radiance aligned the tides
of her blood into potent order.

At the season of first fruits we recall
those travellers, co-conspirators, scavengers
making do with leftovers and mill ends,
whose friendship was stronger than fear,
stronger than hunger, who walked together
the road of shards, hands joined.

Ruth's Journey

RUTH WHITMAN

1.

I hated being a Moabite.

I thought the villagers
greedy, vulgar, noisy,

worshippers of Chemosh,
the god who devoured
human flesh.

My father wanted me
to marry our neighbor's son,
a stupid shepherd.

I was fifteen, trapped,
smothering in those
prison mountains.

Somewhere, I knew, there was
a different, larger world
waiting for me.

But how to find it?
A girl was expected
to stay at home forever.

The author used the Holy Scriptures (Philadelphia: Jewish Publication Society, 1955).

2.

Naomi, a Hebrew woman from
starving Bethlehem
came to Moab with her family.

My people despised me
for admiring these foreigners,
but I was dazzled.

Their son, Machlon, was a man
I had dreamed of—
tall, wise, kind.

His gray eyes always
smiled at me when I came
to visit Naomi.

He learned to speak
our Moabite dialect,
But I had no Hebrew yet.

When Machlon asked me
to marry, my father
cursed me out of the house.

I ran away, to Naomi,
who welcomed me
as the daughter she never had.

She taught me
all the womanly arts
she knew:

how to cook tasty dishes,
how to sew and weave,
to sing.

She became my mother.

3.

After ten years,
Naomi's husband died.
Both sons grew sick and

soon followed—my gentle Machlon
and his brother, husband
of my friend Orpah.

We three women
were left alone
to live with our grief.

In those arid mountains
the shadows every twilight
made us tremble.

In the crevices of
the limestone gullies,
lions lurked at night.

Naomi said, *Let us go back
to Bethlehem.* But Orpah
wanted to stay.

Naomi said to me, *Go,
I have no more sons
for you.*

But I said, *No,
you are my mother,
my family, my future.*

4.

Naomi and I packed
our clothes, our pots,
a little food,

and left the valley.
Down through the mountains,
across gaping sudden canyons,

hot, dusty, our dresses torn
from catching on thorns
and sharp boulders,

we came finally to the
rocky Dead Sea road.
It smelled of sulphur.

Judaea was on the other side.
But how to get across
the terrifying green expanse?

Naomi remembered the route south
to the Vale of Salt,
the marsh she had crossed

ten years earlier.
Our legs stinging with salt,
covered with mud and scratches,

we crossed into Judaea—
as desolate and barren
as the land we left behind.

The sea was turquoise,
a sea of death
where nothing could live.

Never mind, said Naomi,
we have come this far
and we are almost home.

We came to a hut
shaded by a thorn tree,
where we found fresh water.

But we still had miles to go,
across the Judaean hills
to Hebron. Finally,

5.

we came to Bethlehem.
It was barely harvest.
We were exhausted, starving.

Naomi said *Go to my cousin's field*
and find what the farmers
have left behind.

Her cousin, a kindly man,
invited me to help myself, saying
You will be safe in my field.

I brought all the sheaves I could
back to Naomi,
who told me her plan:

that night, bathed and dressed
in my cleanest gown,
I found my way back

to the field of tents
where the farmers
were celebrating.

A full moon was shining.
I crept into the tent
where Naomi's cousin

lay sleeping.
I uncovered his naked feet
and curled up beside them.

He woke, startled.
Then smiled, recognizing
the woman from Moab.

My mouth tasted
his Hebrew name, round as a fruit:
Boaz.

At the Crossroads

MERLE FELD

❧

An awful lot happens in the first five verses of the Book of Ruth: a famine descends on Judah, a family sets out in search of sustenance, the husband dies, the two sons marry, ten years pass, both sons die, the woman and her daughters-in-law must carry on alone. But the men and the marriages seem less than real to me; we don't even know until the end of the story who was married to whom—Orpah and Mahlon? Chilion and Ruth? Ruth and Mahlon? The ultimate irony of the story, and one that should arouse our suspicion, is that while the motor driving the action is ostensibly the finding of a second husband for Ruth in order to perpetuate the name of the dead first husband, in the end number one is lost in the shuffle and it is Boaz who is remembered in the lineage.

In a mere five verses Naomi has lost a husband, acquired two daughters-in-law, lost two sons. It seems as though, by dispensing with all of this so quickly, the author intended to set the stage for the real drama, to fashion a story in which to explore a series of questions: What happens when people, when women, stand at a crossroads? How do you find your true path in this world? What role does love play in charting the course? How do unforeseen consequences unfold from the choices we make and the relationships we enter into, and how are our characters forged by the ways in which we improvise responses to what fate throws our way? Does the decision to commit our lives to an "other" represent the abdication of personal responsibility or the strong-

---

The author used Ruth in *The Five Megilloth* (London, Jerusalem, New York: Soncino Press, 1st printing, 1946).

est expression of personal courage? How do we mediate the boundaries between ourselves and those we choose to care for? Those we are obligated to care for? How do we emerge from loss and mourning? How do our experiences with death, with the loss of those we have loved, force us to re-create ourselves? And what is the interplay between human devotion, the love one feels for another person, and the covenant one makes to live as a Jew with a circumcised heart?

Three women embark on an almost predictable journey. Naomi is heading back to Judah and instructs Orpah and Ruth to return to their mothers' houses. "Then she kissed them and they lifted up their voices and wept." Here we have the first outward signs of emotion in the story; so much loss, so much pain, but only now do we hear them cry. Sometimes it hurts too much to cry. Sometimes you are hit but you steel yourself to absorb the next blow, and the next, and the next. Finally your strength, your will, is gone. So she kisses them and they lift up their voices and weep. And then something unexpected, something genuinely extraordinary, happens. Ruth steps off the edge of the world and follows her heart:

> Entreat me not to leave you, or to return from following after you. For wherever you go, I will go. Wherever you lodge, I will lodge. Your people shall be my people, and your God my God. Where you die, I will die; and there will I be buried.

So much is contained in this moment at the crossroads. First, it seems like such a gift that Ruth recognizes this as a crossroads, that she sees it as a moment of choice, that she sees she has some power to exercise over her future. So much of the time we can't see that about our lives— that in a given moment lies the possibility for change, for taking control, for claiming one's life as one's own. And then, Ruth is blessed with further vision: she discovers an organizing principle on which to base her choice. Until this moment on the road, we know nothing of the life she came from, nothing of her life with her husband and his family. We can only imagine what it is she has chosen. Her words are so full of love, animated by a tender yet powerful passion. She doesn't know what's in store for her if she returns to her mother's house, what's in store for her if she veers from that course to walk with Naomi. What she does know is that she cannot ignore the strength of her instinct.

I. At the crossroads

April 1969. I am sitting in a seedy all-night cafeteria in Inman Square, Cambridge, with my fiancé Eddie and his roommate David. It's 1 A.M., maybe 2. We are beyond knowing what time it is, or caring. We have just finished cleaning their apartment for Passover. My fingers are red and cracked from hours of scrubbing. The muscles in my legs shake from bending, kneeling, crouching. My back is utterly destroyed. I want a shower, a hot bath, I want to feel shampoo and warm water in my hair. I want my bed, my bed with clean sheets. I want scrambled eggs and french fries and a toasted English muffin with strawberry jam and a black-and-white ice cream soda, not only because I'm hungry and exhausted and for me this is comfort food, but also because I know I won't be able to eat any of it for the next eight days: this will be my first Passover as an observant Jew. I'm working hard to make sense of it all. I've never kashered a home for Pesach before. "The symbolism is wrong to me," I tell Eddie and David. "When the Israelites were leaving Egypt they didn't clean out the muck behind the toilet bowl, they didn't dismantle the stove and scrub it with a toothbrush. Even if we were desperately poor and needed every penny of the rent deposit back, we wouldn't have cleaned the way we did tonight." I'm not challenging the system. I am the wise son—I want to know all the laws and customs, but I also want to know why. I'm struggling to understand the system. From the inside. I love the system, I love being inside it. In a strange way I even love being this tired.

From the time I was ten years old I was in the dark, groping, seeking something central around which to shape my identity, some organizing principle for my life. For a long time I thought it was being a writer, and that did satisfy some of the hunger, but then I found Judaism and it was bigger and better, bigger than me and my sadness and my cleverness and my talent and my hunger. It did something else too—it released me from my loneliness. In the years of my childhood and adolescence I was profoundly alone, different. Choosing an observant way of life, I felt buoyed, supported by a gentle, invisible strength, which I think was less a faith in God than a rejoicing in the intrigue and shape of ritual and the nurture of community. Raised in an assimilated home, I came to Judaism as a young adult. I was the stranger, I was the outsider. Before I fell in love with a man, I fell in love with a way of life.

July 1968. Many months before the all-night cafeteria. In the early hours of the morning, up and down the streets of Cambridge, of Somerville, we walk and talk. Walking, standing, sitting on the banks of the Charles. He wants to get married. I am afraid, much more than afraid. I go over it again and again in my mind: I want to be with him, I am physically pained to be separated from him, I enjoy him, I trust him, I like him, I love him. (This is the man who, more than twenty years and two children later, still makes my heart leap when I unexpectedly catch sight of him on the streets of our town.) So what is the problem? Being at the crossroads, making a decision. I am rooted to the spot where I stand, surveying a limitless horizon, limitless paths opening onto more limitless paths opening onto more limitless paths. I am twenty years old, it's all ahead of me. Making a decision (I don't see then that not making a decision is also making a decision) will set me on a course, a particular path. I don't want to. I've resisted for a long time now. He's been waiting, persistently waiting. I am tired of resisting. This night on a dark street corner somewhere in Cambridge or maybe in Somerville, I stop resisting. I stop walking, I turn to face him. Yes, I say, yes. Making a choice, I begin my life.

June 1968

The first time we made Shabbos together

The first time we made Shabbos together
in our own home
(It wasn't really "our home"
it was your third-floor walk-up
and we weren't even engaged yet)
I had cooked chicken
my first chicken
with a whole bulb of garlic
(my mother never used garlic)
and we sat down at that secondhand chrome table
in the kitchen.
It was all so ugly that we turned out the lights.
Only the Shabbos candles flickered.

And then you made kiddush.

I sat there and wept—
Oh God, you have been so good to me!
Finally, for the first time in my life,
you gave me something I wanted.
This man, whose soul is the soul of Ein Gedi.
We will be silent together
We will open our flowers in each other's presence.

And indeed we have bloomed through the years.

I didn't know it and you didn't know it, but this was the moment I really decided. Sometimes you make a decision and it lies inside you dormant, waiting. Then, when the right moment comes, the choice unfolds, opens, like a flower. When was the moment, really, when Ruth chose Naomi? That moment on the dusty road, when she declared herself? Or earlier, when they put Mahlon in the ground? Or before that even, on a day in the fields when Naomi's face was flushed and sweaty and she turned unexpectedly to smile? The moment my heart chose was at that kitchen table, the first time we made Shabbos together. When you made kiddush.

II. *"Do not call me Naomi, call me Mara"*

Mara. Bitterness. Only in reentering her old reality does Naomi need to rename herself. She needs to tell her kinsmen, her old neighbors, "I am someone new. Grief has taken away that other woman, Naomi, the one you knew. She doesn't exist anymore." What does grief so deep and wide look like, a grief large enough to prevent you from recognizing your face in the mirror when the days of shiva[1] are over and looking in mirrors is permitted once again?

December 1976. I am in mourning for my mother. I quit my job, unable to concentrate on my duties. I feel dislodged from my community, separated from my friends. Each morning as I awaken there is the unbearable moment of remembering—my mother is dead. And then the daily struggle to do the hardest thing of all, get out of bed. If I were a mother I suppose I would not have the luxury of debating whether to get up, I would have responsibilities to draw me back into life, but I'm not and I don't. Four weeks after my mother died, I miscarried my first child. So really, there seems to be no reason to get out of bed.

Healing after a miscarriage

Nothing helps. I taste ashes
in my mouth. My eyes are flat,
dead. I want no platitudes,
no stupid shallow comfort.
I hate all pregnant women,
all new mothers, all soft babies.

The space I'd made inside myself
where I'd moved over
to give my beloved room to grow—
now there's a tight angry
bitter knot of hatred there instead.

What is my supplication?
Stupid people and new mothers,
leave me alone.
Deliver me, Lord,
of this bitter afterbirth.
Open my heart
to my husband-lover-friend
that we may comfort each other.
Open my womb
that it may yet bear
living fruit.

January 1977. I begin to connect with a new neighbor. I say little about my mother—it hurts too much. I don't say anything at first about the miscarriage. I notice that when people become aware of the full burden I'm carrying, they back away, as if all that bad luck is contagious. No doubt the aura about me is foul. I don't know how the days pass, they just do, without purpose, without difference. Sometimes when I go to synagogue I say the kaddish out loud; often I just stand, silent, tears streaming down my face. I want to hide. I want to disappear.

February 1977. The new neighbor and I begin a ritual of early-morning running together. The first time, when Laura reaches the "finish line" she holds out her hand for me to "give her five." I misunderstand—I'm neither a participant in nor even a spectator of any sport. When I cross the finish line, I shake her extended hand. She can't stop laughing. Her laughter is contagious. She reminds me how to laugh. Now when I wake up in the morning, I lie there thinking, "I have to get up, I promised Laura I would run," and then, after my shower, "I might as well get dressed, I'm already up."

March 1977. I take the train down to Washington to see an old friend, a therapist, to ask if she thinks I should "see someone professionally," to ask if she thinks it seems feasible for me to undertake a significant weekly commute to see her professionally. Esther deems the commute unrealistic and unnecessary, but says it could be a propitious time to begin therapy because loss opens special opportunities for self-understanding and growth.

Loss as an opportunity. I come to understand this. Slowly, I am delivered of my bitter afterbirth. Eventually, I am even blessed to bear living fruit. And ultimately, I am reconciled to the loss of my mother, or, perhaps more accurately, ultimately I come to understand how to find her in the world.

Spring 1990

The warmth of the sun

My fingers were cold this morning
hanging out the wash
but the warmth of the sun
reminded me of how I had planned
to sit in the sun with my mother

I was going to take off
from teaching in the spring
because she had leukemia
and I had just learned
I was pregnant

I thought in the spring
I would go down to Florida
and we would sit together
in the sun

But in November
on Thanksgiving Day
she died
before the spring
before the sun

Then I sat on a hard
cardboard box sent over
by the Jewish undertaker
and I consoled myself
with many cigarettes
under the disapproving
eye of my sister-in-law

In the twelfth week
I lost that baby

All this happened so long ago
but still, even today
the warmth of the sun
reminds me of my mother.

After all, they don't call her Mara. She loses herself in caring for the
younger widow, the one who came along to care for her. Seasons pass,
new life, she is drawn back into sunshine, into harvest, into the rhythm
of new life. And the time comes again when she feels comfortable as
Naomi.

III. I didn't see that you were Naomi

Mother-in-law, a bizarre nomenclature. Almost an oxymoron. What has
formalism to do with that body, that being which embraced you
loverlike, with her insides. Mother-in-law, she who comes along with
the one you chose. In my day, we were expected to call her "Mom."
Smile and call her Mom and don't think what the sounds mean.

August 1990. I am sitting on the edge of a bed in the room where my
husband spent his boyhood. We will each speak, both sons, both
daughters-in-law. Forty-four hours ago I was in an apartment in Jerusalem, packing to return to the States after a year's sabbatical, when the

phone rang. "Let me speak to Eddie." I knew then. He wanted to tell his brother first that their mother was dead. . . . I don't know what to say. I am exhausted from packing, from the transatlantic flight, from the bizarre coincidence that this is Tisha B'Av,[2] and so out of respect for a houseful of Orthodox mourners, I too am fasting. I am surrounded on all sides by loss—loss of the joy and intensity of the year in Israel, my husband's loss of his mother, my children's loss of their only grand-mother. All year we had stored away memories to share with her, images and experiences she would have relished. I was proudly bearing back to her my treasures—the grandchildren—each a head taller, the boy proud of his *tzitzit*[3] and *ivrit*,[4] the girl who had become a young woman. Waiting to be kissed, to be loved, to be reclaimed. Now robbed. I feel inadequate, powerless. I have no other grandmother for them. I don't know what to say. And she and I, apart from the grandchildren, what was our relationship?

Wednesday, Thanksgiving weekend 1971. They are visiting us in our own home for the first time. She walks through the house, past the bur-lap living-room curtains I have made myself, the bed with a colorful throw which serves as our couch, the bricks-and-board coffee table, the tiny wood-paneled dining room with its burled oak table, through to the cheerful yellow kitchen with its ruffled yellow curtains. "The land-lord couldn't give you a new sink?"

She didn't mean to be unkind. She could see how hard I'd worked to make this a home. She just couldn't see that what I needed was a compliment. She was uncomfortable with compliments. She had been raised to recoil from them; she had been raised to be modest, proper. Careful about her appearance, with pretty hats and suits for synagogue, careful with her words, careful with her feelings. Once, early on, after an unpleasant exchange, I try to "talk" with her. Honestly. About our feelings. She will have none of it. "I'm not supposed to get upset," she says.

Shabbos, Thanksgiving weekend. The air is filled with tension. I try hard to be halakhically correct, up to snuff. I don't turn the lights on and off, no Judy Collins singing "City of New Orleans" on Friday night, no incense candles burning in the living room. It doesn't feel like our Shabbos. But it doesn't feel to them like their Shabbos either.

Meeting in the middle it has somehow become a less-than-Shabbos, a no-exit Shabbos.

She never spent another Shabbos in my home. Over the years I learned to have a relationship with her on her terms, first cordial, then friendly, then caring, then loving. Loving without touching, a first for me. We built a relationship on the things we shared—our respect for hard work, our frugal natures, our love of things Jewish, our love of her son, our love of my children. Most often, when we met, we met in her Shabbos.

August 1990. Sitting there on the edge of a bed in the room where my husband spent his boyhood, on the morning of my mother-in-law's funeral, I began to write her eulogy.

By the light of the Shabbos candles

Friday afternoon
we spill out of the car
our arms laden
with luggage and toys
two golden children
race down the narrow hallway
your arms their destination

The table set
licht bensching[5]
the men come home from shul
kiddush
then soup, chicken, fricassee
each a celebration
each seasoned with your love
what my children will not eat at home
at your table they devour
sated, they are put to bed

By the light of the Shabbos candles
we sit, we talk, we read
a new novel, an old newspaper
the pistachio nuts dwindle
in the crystal bowl

At your Shabbos table
I learned how sacred time

could be a home
I came to understand
why the rabbis say
on Shabbat we have
a second soul.

IV. "And the two went on until they reached Bethlehem"

Back to Judah, to Bethlehem. Two women, women from different tribes
who insist on their bond, their love, who insist that the world see them
as connected to each other. Two women from different tribes—Israelite,
Moabite—each one thinking, how can I sustain the other, nourish the
other. Two women, women from different tribes, and "the whole city
buzzed with excitement over them."

August 1989. I am sitting crammed into the backseat of a small old
Renault with a checkered *kefiyah* prominently displayed on the dash-
board, driving through the West Bank at high speed along winding narrow roads on the way to the village of Wadi Fukin. The inexpressible
beauty of the landscape distracts me only slightly from the conversation
inside the car: Abed, a Palestinian journalist, Fatme, a psychiatric nurse,
Yael, an Israeli social worker, and Veronika, a peace activist and long-
time friend of mine, catch up on the latest political developments, the
health of husbands, wives, and children, and the current situation in
this village, well known to all of them, where they will be meeting a
European film crew eager to do a story on Israeli-Palestinian peace efforts. Having arrived in the country only a week earlier to begin a year's
sabbatical with my family, I accept their gracious invitation to join
them for the day. I bring to this year a resistance bordering on
hostility—I don't want to be away from home, I don't want to be in a
violent country whose politics seem so unholy. We arrive at Wadi Fukin
and are greeted by a crowd of friendly children, about a dozen men,
and half a dozen women in traditional dress who seat us on a simple
patio and then come out bearing large copper trays with little glasses of
sweetened, hot spiced tea. Veronika, an observant Jew, politely declines
the drink; I alone realize that she is in fact fasting because today is
Tisha B'Av. In this intense desert heat she sits without even water, talk-

ing with ease and warmth about her work and her hopes for peace, listening to villagers who are culturally if not politically alien with a concentration which the pious reserve for prayer.

September 1989. I'm at a designated bus stop with my water bottle and a bag lunch waiting to be picked up to go to East Jerusalem to get an Arab taxi to go to a military base outside Nablus (which is under curfew) to be an observer at the Beita trial. I have no idea what to expect, but in the twilight of sleep this morning I dreamt there was an attempt on Veronika's life.

Beita was the village on the West Bank where a group of settler high school kids went on a Pesach hike and clashed with some local youths. When the dust settled, one Arab boy and one Jewish girl lay dead, both shot by the same Israeli guard. Twenty-three villagers were subsequently arrested and, over the course of the last year and a half, held in prison while waiting to be tried, mostly for stone throwing. A committee of Israelis formed, first to provide the accused with a lawyer, then to help rebuild the many homes in Beita demolished illegally by the army in the aftermath of the original tragedy. Now members of the Beita Committee travel here to sit as interested observers at the trials of these villagers they had come to know.

We arrive at the military base and join a large number of Arab men and women milling around outside the fence. They are waiting for sight of a brother, waiting for a word with a son's lawyer, waiting to find someone who might take the case of a newly arrested husband. They are waiting. I am incredulous when first a man and then a woman approach Veronika to ask for help. They talk quietly in turn, the man writing down some phone numbers Veronika offers. They know of her, they know to trust her; even more remarkable, she knows how to help them. We wait to be admitted to the base; finally, single-file, we show our passports, we are in. We, myself and a dozen or so Israelis from the Beita Committee, mostly sit together in the far back. In front of us in the small hot courtroom are the relatives and neighbors of the accused. The Arab men and women sit separately, the men on the benches to the left of the aisle, the women on the benches to the right. The women are wearing large, white head coverings. As I view this scene from a back bench I could almost feel myself in synagogue. Veronika, sitting up front with the village women, shares a bag of fruit she has brought.

The beautiful young wife of one of the accused, a girl with an open shining face, sits next to her, smiling, talking, her arm linked through Veronika's. I keep looking from one face to the other—younger/older, Palestinian/Jew—yet they could easily have passed for sisters.

March 1990. After months of meeting in a women's dialogue group that Veronika and I have organized, the Palestinian participants invite the Israelis to join them in a demonstration on International Women's Day. They warn that it may prove dangerous, but I have become a regular on the West Bank, a regular in this town overlooking Bethlehem, and I figure, as usual, if they're willing, I'm willing. A dozen of us arrive and join in the march—a hundred of them, two hundred of them—young girls in jeans, old women in traditional dress, many friends from the dialogue. Up and down the streets we wind, carrying banners, singing; a few of them hold aloft small pieces of fabric—red, green, black, and white—national colors, illegal colors. The march itself is illegal—the gathering, the banners, the songs. We turn a corner and there at the bottom of the hill is an Israeli patrol. Maybe they don't see that we are just women, that we are unarmed. First they fire tear gas. Everyone expected this, but still it is unpleasant. The crowd does not disperse. Then suddenly, plastic bullets, and we all start running. Into a courtyard, down a long flight of stone steps. My heart is beating very fast, but at the same time I am standing outside myself, calmly observing: "I'm capable of being more frightened than this." The tear gas, I am told, will linger in the air for the next few days, but within an hour we—the Israelis—are in a taxi driving back to Jerusalem. One of the women in our group is clutching a plastic bullet she picked up from the ground. She shows it to her husband when she gets home. She brings it to synagogue with her. She cannot seem to stop shaking. She doesn't come back to dialogue.

April 1990. Some of us go to the Russian Compound where a teenage Palestinian neighbor of Dahlia is having a preliminary hearing, held but not yet charged with setting a bomb in *Machane Yehuda*.[7] His elderly mother is beside herself under the strain of this first-time separation from her youngest child. When he is brought into the hallway, she falls upon him with kisses and tears. The prosecutor shouts angrily at her that this is not permitted, this is not a visit. To those who know him, the boy looks terrible. One Israeli runs next door to bring him hot coffee, also coffee for the guard. The guard urges him to drink the warm liquid, to drink the second cup as well. Veronika, seeing he is cold, goes off to a corner for a moment. She comes back with her pullover sweater in hand. Gratefully, he puts it on; had he noticed she was wearing it, he would not have accepted. My mind races—what do I have to contribute? Then suddenly I smile to myself, it is Friday. The two *challahs* I bought for Shabbat are still warm in the bag in my hand. To offer a whole loaf would shame him. I begin tearing off pieces, which he rapidly devours. His hunger abated a bit, he begins to enjoy the sweetness of the warm bread, the novelty of the plump raisins. The guards smile knowingly at my offering; they encourage him to eat. They are tired of being the enemy.

V. Again at the crossroads

May 1990. Our year in this land is drawing to a close. We are having Shabbos lunch with Naomi and Roni, their airy third-floor flat filled with the strong Jerusalem sun which pours through the sliding glass doors opening onto their balcony. "Your sabbatical is almost over," he says. "Rumor has it you are considering staying." I stare out the window, lost in my own thoughts. "I suppose that's more a fantasy than anything else," I tell him. He is a quiet man, very still, a good listener. He goes on. "You're not an innocent—all your peace work—you know the problems. Why would you want to stay here?" I am grateful he asked me this, grateful for the opportunity to try to put into words what I feel. "In part to continue the peace work. But that's not all. In America I'm always struggling to give my life meaning; I need to produce, to write, to feel I'm worthwhile. Here, breathing the air, just walking on the street . . . I feel the sun on my body, I'm jostled on the bus, I schlepp my packages from the market, I'm happy, I'm at peace." He sees that I am forcing back the tears. He responds quietly, "It's hard to make a living here." We say the blessings after the meal and end with a few Shabbos songs.

January 1992. Princeton. Days pass into days, months become years. My son loses a few teeth and grows some new ones. My daughter has begun to menstruate. And still I am here, here where chance placed me so long ago. Was I meant to stay so long? How do I know when it's time to go? How do I know when I am at a crossroads? I feel an unspeakable envy, an envy of Ruth, of Naomi, each standing alone at the crossroads. I wish I, like they, were free to make a choice, just for myself. I feel longings stirring within me, but perhaps it is a siren song. I don't want to be old, I want to have it all still in front of me, plenty of time to make mistakes, to take a wrong turn and go back to the starting line, still fresh for the race which is only now about to begin.

Jerusalem, I write your name

Jerusalem
I write your name
as long ago I wrote the names
of boys who made me flush
with inexplicable pleasure

I wrote their names
then linked my name to theirs—
Merle Pierce, Merle Spirn—
an old-fashioned Brooklyn way
for a twelve-year-old girl
to practice intimacy

In my notebooks
in calligraphies of infinite variety
I wrote Merle Pierce, Merle Spirn
and my breathing became irregular

as long ago I wrote the names
I write your name
Jerusalem

March 1992. A phone call from Israel. Veronika's mother, Adel Wolf, has died. A woman of extraordinary grace and moral integrity. Fascism, Nazism, Communism, Zionism propelled her from country to country, crisscrossing continents, and with each move she found within herself the strength to re-create home. Now she has been received in her final home, her journey completed. May her memory be for a blessing. Now she sits with Ruth and Naomi. They call to me, they try to reassure me, but I am afraid and I cannot hear what they are saying. I close the book, I am afraid. I try to lose myself in the everyday. I go to the supermarket, I buy lentils and barley and carrots and salmon. I come home and begin to cook for Shabbos. My task is ordinary, familiar. I set the table, the sun sets. It is time again for Shabbos.

On the other side of the world
FOR VERONIKA

I closed my eyes
to light the candles
and it was you I saw
on the other side of the world
you were lighting candles too.

I could see the tracks of the comb
through your wet hair
the part that shows
under your kerchief
I saw the blouse you were wearing
white with blue embroidery
I saw how it stuck to your back
not quite dry from the shower.

Your hands covered your face
but I could feel the concentration
with which you said your prayer
I imagined that as you paused
to bless the candles
you included me as I included you.

I write these words tonight
to reach out to you
as I reached out to you
when I lit the candles
as I reach out to you now
in all my best prayers.

4

*"Your Latest Act
of* Chesed*"*

RUTH 3:10

$\mathcal{A}$s JUDITH KATES notes in the opening essay in this section, Ruth has been called the Book of *Chesed* (lovingkindness). The essays in this section look at the text in light of central Jewish ideas, reflecting on the place of kindness in Jewish thought and society. For Kates, the spiritual (theological) significance of this thematic emphasis on kindness offers a compelling explanation for why the Book of Ruth is read on the holiday of Shavuot, the festival of the giving of Torah. In her reading, Ruth dramatizes "the essence of Torah," locating the idea of *chesed* at the "very heart of the Biblical vision of human society and of God." By highlighting how the *chesed* of women arouses the community to live up to its own ideals, Kates proposes the centrality of women to that vision.

Susanne Klingenstein focuses her attention on the daring acts of kindness—particularly the embrace of the outsider, the convert—that challenge the community and its understanding of Torah. She reveals the radical unconventionality of a narrative that attributes King David's ancestry to a complete outsider, to a peasant woman, to Ruth the Moabite. She then extends the argument to trace the Book of Ruth's transformation of kindness toward one's own kin into true *chesed*, which embraces the stranger.

In both essays Ruth emerges as a revisionary text reversing our usual understanding of periphery and center. As women and converts move from the margins of the Jewish story to its core, they come to embody what Klingenstein calls "the vision that constitutes the chosenness of the Jewish people."

Cynthia Ozick's meditation on Ruth, circling through personal memory and reflection on the text, finds in the "unearthly tongue of the visionary" precisely the source of this book's enduring significance. For her, the "kindness" reflected in Ruth's embrace of Naomi would remain within the realm of "normality" were it a kindness based simply on personal feeling or on "pragmatic" considerations arising from Ruth's sense of familiarity and comfort with Naomi. Ozick reverses the valuation of Ruth's choice celebrated by many writers in this volume. Love and loyalty directed to human beings are much, but not all, she claims. Rather, Ruth's choice is elevated spiritually at the "volcanic heart of the Book of Ruth" by the "majesty" of Ruth's declaration of loyalty to the God of Israel.

Women at the Center
Ruth and Shavuot

JUDITH A. KATES

❧

I knew nothing about Shavuot from childhood—at most a vague memory of flowers in the synagogue from the pious period of my adolescence, before religion and Jewish observance became the superheated (because the only possible) terrain of rebellion and dissent. The holiday had been muted in my youth even in the nominally Orthodox practice and teaching of my family's synagogue in the '40s and '50s. Its significance within the traditional Jewish year came to me with the force of revelation in my adult discovery of the unexpected emotional depth and intellectual complexity of the liturgical cycle, which I had pushed to the back shelves of my life during college. Passover and its seder, which for me had always been the central drama of both my Jewish family and of Jewish peoplehood, only begin the journey, I learned. Shavuot, the biblical agricultural holiday reinterpreted by the rabbis as *zman matan toratenu*—the time of the giving of Torah, of revelation—invests it with purpose.

The experience of exodus from Egypt culminates in the revelation at Sinai. For Jews were delivered from slavery not simply to become a free people, but to be transformed into a holy nation. The covenant between God and Israel, affirmed by God in Egypt, is clearly unveiled in all its details at Sinai, and the whole people of Israel accepts it: "Moses

---

The author used her own translation of the Book of Ruth; she also consulted *Tanakh: A New Translation of the Holy Scriptures* (Philadelphia, New York, and Jerusalem: Jewish Publication Society, 1985).

went and repeated to the people all the commands of the Lord and all the rules; and all the people answered with one voice, saying, 'all the things that the Lord has commanded we will do!' " (Exodus 24:3). Sinai is the answer to the question "For what purpose were we freed from Egypt?" Sinai—Torah—provides the goal to strive for and the obligations to fulfill. We were transformed from *ovdei pharaoh* (slaves of Pharaoh) to *ovdei hashem* (servants of God). From this perspective, Pesach without Shavuot is incomplete. To share in the identity of a free, distinctive people is only the beginning. The experience of Shavuot enables us to see the purpose of that identity.

A further revelation: the texts prescribed to be read out loud in the synagogue on this holiday include a book which, from my perspective as an adult woman, I could see as primarily a story of women. But why should this book, Ruth, be recited on the holiday celebrating revelation and covenant renewal? Is there, in fact, an implicit connection between this woman-centered text and the center of Jewish life—Torah?

The traditional explanations for the linkage of the Book of Ruth with Shavuot make sense but seem insufficient. In fact, that connection (like the reading of Song of Songs on Passover or Ecclesiastes on Succot) remains a bit mysterious and therefore invites suggestive midrashic explanations. The importance of the harvest, with its particular commandment to allow the poor and the widow to take freely of the leftover gleanings in the fields, plays a major role in the book's events and provides a general sense of seasonal appropriateness to reading Ruth on Shavuot, just as the springtime landscape of Song of Songs connects it to Pesach and the autumnal tone of Ecclesiastes seems to fit in with Succot. But vaguely impressionistic links of this kind have never really satisfied the Jewish imagination.

A series of other, more specific, explanations has been produced over the years. For instance, midrashic legend claims that Shavuot was both the birthday and the day of death of David. To honor King David on Shavuot we read the story of the courage and loyalty of his foremother Ruth and the generosity of his forefather Boaz. This explanation requires that we direct our entire reading of the book toward the last few verses, in which the genealogy of David is recorded. Another traditional explanation centers more on the history of Ruth herself. Just as the Jewish people accepted all the commandments of Torah on Shavuot, so Ruth willingly accepted the obligations of the covenant with the God of Israel. In this reading, she is understood to be a convert to Judaism, a concept important to rabbinic, though not yet existent in biblical, Judaism. By that very act, in choosing an irrevocable commitment, she also becomes a personification of the people of Israel at Sinai.

These and other traditional explanations for the connection between text and occasion make sense, but they don't invite us to enter into the fullness of the text. They make use of the end result—the child born to Ruth and Boaz who becomes the grandfather of King David—or an early moment in the plot: Ruth's declaration of loyalty to Naomi, or in the traditional interpretation, to Naomi's God. But they leave out the development of personal relationships and the dramatic unfolding of the story—features of the text that for most readers assume central importance. So I would like to offer a *davar acher*—another interpretation—of the relationship between the Book of Ruth and Shavuot. This interpretation arises from the way the story unfolds and the nature of the personal relationships developed in it, and its woman-centered focus connects to the core of the Torah first revealed at Sinai.

Ruth is a story of women struggling to survive in a man's world. The book begins in the male-centered mode we expect from biblical stories, identifying a "man from Bethlehem in Judah" (1:1) as the principal character and the woman as simply "his wife." The already familiar pattern of movement out of the land of Israel to a neighboring pagan territory in time of famine reinforces the sense that we know this story (compare Genesis 12 or 44). It seems to play on the irony that *bet lechem* (the house of bread) has ceased to sustain this family, fleeing famine and death and moving elsewhere to find life and sustenance. But the text shatters the familiar narrative, both its pattern and its human center. The place of refuge becomes a place of death. And in death Elimelech becomes simply "Naomi's husband" (1:3). Naomi begins to take center stage, so that by verse 5 she preempts our attention, ironically because she has been left alone: "so the woman was left without her two sons and without her husband." The text enters into her experience of loss, referring to the sons as *yiladeha* (her children) from the root meaning to "give birth," to "bear," rather than *baneha* (her sons). The word poignantly reminds us of the sons' essential meaning to her: they are *yiladeha*, the children she bore, in the very moment when death severs her connection to them.

The focus now shifts to the relationships between Naomi and her two daughters-in-law. Not only does the narrative pattern break, but we begin to get hints of something unexpected in the nature of those relationships. Although the narrator uses the proper technical term for them—Ruth and Orpah are repeatedly called *kaloteha*, or daughters-in-law (1:8)—Naomi, when she speaks directly, addresses them as *benotai*, my daughters (1:11). And her first words speak to their needs, despite the renewed separation and loss imposed on her by her concern for their welfare. She offers them all she has—a prayer that God should show them the same *chesed* that they have given to the dead and to her—that is, that God should respond in kind to the *chesed* already enacted by these women.

Ruth has traditionally been called the book of *chesed*, a word usually translated as lovingkindness or benevolence. It refers to acts of care and love that go beyond obligation and to a quality of generosity, of an abundance in giving. The Bible attributes this quality most particularly to God. When God reveals Godself to Moses (Exodus 34:6–7), God's self-description reiterates only one word beside the name itself: "The Lord! the Lord!—a God compassionate and gracious, slow to anger, abounding in kindness [*chesed*] and faithfulness, extending kindness [*chesed*] to the thousandth generation." In Ruth this quality is introduced as an attribute that human beings, especially women, demonstrate. The conversation between Naomi and her daughters-in-law itself embodies the quality of *chesed*. Naomi's concern for Ruth and Orpah reflects what she describes as their past *chesed* for her, and she hopes to arouse in turn that essential aspect of the divine.

The text endows Naomi with a language rich in religious resonances, created by echoes of and allusions to other parts of the Bible, like Exodus 34. It immediately connects her voice to the essential language of Jewish religious vision. This deepening of the speaking voices initiates a mode of narration that constantly invites us to perceive, in this apparently personal, mundane story of food and family connections, large realms of spiritual significance.

Even more closely tied to the Bible's language of religious commitment, Ruth's singular response partakes of the core vocabulary of Israel's covenant with God. Ruth, we are told, clung *(davka)* to Naomi. The root (DVK) echoes not only the language of the primordial bond between the first and therefore paradigmatic two human beings ("Hence a man leaves his father and mother and clings [*davak*] to his wife";

Genesis 2:24), but also the language of love and commitment to God and Torah: "If, then, you faithfully keep all this instruction that I command you, loving the Lord your God, walking in all His ways, and holding fast [*l'dovka*] to Him" (Deuteronomy 11:22); "Choose life—if you and your offspring would live—by loving the Lord your God, heeding His commands, and holding fast [*l'dovka*] to Him" (Deuteronomy 30:19–20); and many other examples.

Ruth's declaration of loyalty must also be heard in the context of the primary statements of commitment to human beings and to God that constitute the very foundation of distinctive Jewish peoplehood. When she says, "wherever you go, I will go," particularly in Hebrew *(el asher telkhi elekh)*, we hear echoes of God's first call to Abraham ("Go forth," *lekh likha*; Genesis 12:1) and Abraham's response ("Abram went forth [*vayelekh*] as the Lord had commanded him"; Genesis 12:4). Ruth speaks "Abraham language"; her words also precisely echo those of the central covenantal figure of the next founding generation, Rebekah. When Rebekah is asked, "Will you go with this man?" *(ha-telkhi im ha ish haze)*, she replies, "I will go" (*elekh*; Genesis 24:58), embracing the connection to an as yet unknown man, Isaac, and to the God of Israel. Ruth's language of commitment to Naomi and to her God declares her to be another Abraham, another Rebekah. Like them, Ruth willingly leaves the familiar, the comfortable, for a strenuous, risky journey into foreign territory, where she cannot be sure even of acceptance, let alone welcome. But unlike Abraham, she is not "going" with family, wealth, and servants, but as an unsupported widow tenuously connected to her widowed mother-in-law, who has described herself as being without resources. Unlike Rebekah, she knows full well that there is no protecting husband waiting for her. The singular power of her *chesed* springs from the contrast to the other characters whose "going" from their homes resonates in the background of Ruth's declaration. For Ruth, it seems, there is nothing to be gained from the journey, beyond the continuation of her bond to Naomi.

The women's return to Bethlehem, ironically, seems to mark the nadir of their experience, projected as it is through the despairing eyes of Naomi. The older woman can only see herself in contrast to the fullness of connection with which she had left this very place. Now she returns, she says, empty, bitter, totally alone. She does not even respond to Ruth's startling assertion of the bond between them. In a story told largely in dialogue, Naomi's silence following Ruth's speech in itself speaks her utter desolation. In addition, the new perils of Ruth's situation immediately manifest themselves. In the closing verse of chapter 1, the narrator, describing their return to Israel, refers to Ruth for the first time as she will be known in that community, as Ruth the Moabite woman—not only a poor widow, without any male relation to protect her, but a foreigner from a despised people. Only the apparently random "realistic" detail, that their return coincides with the barley harvest, sounds a note of hope.

Other such notes sound in the second chapter. We learn that Naomi does in fact have a kinsman, and a man of resources (*gibor chayil,* 2:1) at that. But he seems to require mobilizing for that passive fact to be turned into an active force for good in the lives of the two women. It is actually Ruth who takes the initiative, generating the sequence of events that will end in satisfaction and fruitfulness. With no preliminaries, she simply takes responsibility for providing sustenance. In response to this, Naomi acknowledges her as "my daughter" (2:2).

Ruth is here relying on one of the fundamental principles of Torah law—in fact, on a commandment given immediately after the commandments relating to the festival of first fruits which came to be called Shavuot: "And when you reap the harvest of your land, you shall not completely reap the corner of your field nor shall you gather the gleaning of your harvest, you shall leave them for the poor and the stranger: I the Lord am your God" (Leviticus 23:22). Leviticus makes it clear that we should understand this obligation as a mode of connection to God—through fulfilling a commandment and through *imitatio dei,* imitating the compassion of God and acknowledging that what we have is ultimately a gift and needs to be shared. Ruth stirs the covenantal community into realizing this ideal when she looks to the owner of fields to fulfill his obligations by allowing her to glean.

But the text subtly suggests that this would represent only a minimal response to the needs of the vulnerable and unprotected. Boaz goes beyond his obligation when he immediately speaks to the risks endured by a single woman alone in the fields: "I have ordered the men not to molest you" (2:9). Ruth's astonishment reflects her expectation of low status and danger and her recognition that he is offering her generosity beyond obligation—i.e., *chesed.* She asks him, "Why are you so kind as to single me out, when I am a foreigner?" (2:10). Boaz, on the other hand, presents his *chesed* as a response to hers. He also implicitly casts her commitment in the mode of Abraham: "You left your father and mother and the land of your birth and came to a people you had not known before" (2:11; his statement recalls Genesis 12:1—"The Lord said to Abram, 'Go forth from the land of your birth and from your father's house to the land that I will show you' "). In his prayer that she find not only refuge but reward "under the wings" of the God of Israel, he articulates further the spiritual territory her actions have opened to her. The image of finding refuge "under the wings" of God, which appears repeatedly in the Bible (Psalms 36 and 91, among many others), evokes God's attribute of *chesed.* Boaz, in using such language, invests Ruth's acts of lovingkindness with their full covenantal associations and enriches his own enactment of the idea of *chesed,* embodied in his offer of protection and abundant goodwill, beyond his obligation.

Ruth's courageous initiative arouses a response not only in Boaz, but also in Naomi. Her return with plenty of food gives concrete meaning to her commitment to her mother-in-law. Naomi, who had seen herself as empty and abandoned, unable to care for anyone, now recognizes that she is neither. Her daughter-in-law's gift of physical sustenance enables Naomi to perceive her simultaneous gift of emotional sustenance in the form of companionship (as the very name Ruth, which some scholars derive from *reut,* "friendship," may imply). Ruth ultimately provides spiritual nurturance as well. Naomi had come to see God as a bitter enemy ("The Lord has dealt harshly with me. . . . Shaddai has brought misfortune upon me"; 1:21). With excruciating irony she used the divine name, Shaddai, associated throughout Genesis with God's promises of fertility, progeny, prosperity, to refer to a God who has deprived her, turned her fullness into emptiness. Now, in response to Ruth, Naomi sees God as the God of *chesed*—"Blessed be he of the Lord, who has not failed in His kindness [*chasdo*] to the living or to the dead" (2:20). She begins to speak as a person of resources. Now she remembers that Boaz is a *goel,* a redeeming kinsman, and most significantly, includes Ruth in the family ("The man is related to us; he is one of our redeeming kinsmen"; 2:20). In ominous counterpoint, the chapter's end records the end of the harvest. Their sources of sustenance depleted, the two widows remain alone together.

In the third chapter Naomi moves from her position as victim of calamity and recipient of kindness to active shaper of destiny. It is crucial to recognize that her motivation for action is care for the younger woman. Up to this point, Ruth's courage and effort have not only provided for the two women, but also aroused kindness and generosity in their redeeming kinsman. The narrative suggests that this *chesed* from Boaz, a man of power and resources, is aroused only in response to Ruth's loyalty and commitment. After all, although the whole town knows of Naomi and Ruth's return to Bethlehem and their situation, he, the kinsman, has not acted prior to Ruth's appearance in his fields. In fact, we might hear an ironic note in his prayer that God take her under the sheltering wings of divine protection—"Let God take care of you, not me!" Now that both the barley and wheat harvests are finished, the women are again alone, and, with no possibility of supporting themselves through Ruth's gleaning, are bereft. At this moment of desperation, Naomi, strengthened, or, in the imagery of the text, filled up, by the lovingkindness of her daughter-in-law, and given hope by the *chesed* that Ruth's actions have engendered in Boaz, conceives a daring and risky plan.

It would be hard to overestimate just how daring and risky a scheme it is. Ruth is already vulnerable—a woman alone, a foreigner, with no man obligated to protect her. Naomi proposes to startle Boaz into remembering his connections to her family by placing Ruth in a situation of even greater vulnerability. She is to risk her reputation and the tolerance of the community by going to him secretly at night. Ruth is not just a foreigner, but a member of a people despised and considered dangerous because of their sexual depravity. Israel's contempt for Moabites is embodied most fully, after all, in the story inscribed in Genesis 19 of Moab's origins in the incestuous intercourse of Lot and his daughters. Naomi proposes that Ruth, the Moabite woman, deliberately cast herself in the role of seductress, making herself sexually attractive and hoping that Boaz's response will continue to be one of kindness and generosity. Perhaps to minimize the potential scandal, Naomi instructs Ruth to take initiative only to the point of attracting his attention. Then, she prescribes the conventional, submissive female role—waiting for him to tell her what to do.

The text heightens the drama and deepens our understanding of Ruth's character. We have to imagine Ruth waiting anxiously until midnight, when Boaz wakes up in a panic (*vayecherad*, 3:8), discovering an unidentified woman lying next to him. In this moment of great erotic suggestion (the phrases "uncover his feet" and "lying at his feet" are, in biblical Hebrew, deeply sexual in their associations), Ruth, with consummate control, identifies herself and proceeds to tell him just what he needs to do, reminding him of his relationship of obligation to Naomi's family. Boaz's reply partially relieves the tension, as he characterizes her action, not as intolerable chutzpa, but as an even greater *chesed* than she had shown before ("Your latest deed of loyalty [*chasdekh*] is greater than the first"; 3:10).

Ruth and Naomi have finally managed to get Boaz to work actively for their good. But the dramatic tension is not totally resolved. The vision of this text requires acts of *chesed* not only in the private, intimate realm of personal relationships which, so far, has been the sphere of action, but also in the public world of legal obligation, property rights, inheritance, and formal ritual. At the moment that Boaz begins to act in his role of redeemer, the narrative shifts to the public, man's world of the elders sitting at the village gate, acting as judges and witnesses to legal transactions that determine the social and economic relationships of their community. Boaz, like Ruth, shows initiative and daring in his brilliant use of legal obligations and public rhetoric. He outmaneuvers the anonymous kinsman, who thought he saw a good opportunity to acquire some extra land for his family estate. The kinsman's withdrawal signifies success for Boaz and a happy ending for Ruth and Naomi. As a result of his effective ploy, Boaz literally "acquires" the property rights which are suddenly described as belonging, not to Naomi, but to Elimelech and his sons, Chilion and Mahlon. But he also "acquires" Ruth the Moabite, who is now verbally reinstated as the wife of Mahlon, just as she is about to be given the even more desirable status of wife of Boaz (4:9–10). Boaz, in his role of public advocate, explains his purpose—"so as to perpetuate the name of the deceased upon his estate, that the name of the deceased may not disappear from among the kinsmen and from the gate of his home town" (4:10). His language subsumes the women's focus on sustenance and protection, their fear of loneliness and abandonment, under the male preoccupation with lineage, status, and property rights. He speaks a language of legal obligation.

But just at this moment, the narrative subtly reintroduces the women's concerns as well. When the elders of the town respond with a formal blessing of the couple, they wish for Boaz that his wife resemble the matriarchs of Israel, Rachel and Leah. But they continue with a further blessing through simile: "And may your house be like the house of Perez whom Tamar bore to Judah—through the offspring which the Lord will give you by this young woman" (4:12). On the surface it seems entirely appropriate that these men call attention to Perez, since he is a patrilineal ancestor of Boaz. The allusion meshes neatly with the men's emphasis on patriarchal rights and lineage. But when they identify Perez as the child whom Tamar bore to Judah, they evoke the story of Tamar in Genesis 38. Suddenly our field of vision expands to include another occasion, literally in the background of this one, when a non-Jewish woman, who had become part of Judah's family by marriage, had to provoke a man into fulfilling his obligations to her. Tamar, even more than Ruth, risked her very life by using sexual enticement when Judah, like Boaz an older man related to her through marriage, had reneged on his responsibility to provide her with the protection of marriage and an opportunity to bear children. At the climax of that story, Judah has to confess, "She is more righteous than I" (Genesis 38:26).

In a sense, Ruth is a redeemed version of the story of Judah and Tamar, for Ruth's sexually provocative, nighttime plot results in Boaz's immediate assumption of responsibility, providing an opportunity to display not only *tzedaka*, righteousness, i.e., fulfillment of one's legal and moral obligations, but also *chesed*—lovingkindness, generosity, abundant goodness—corresponding to what he perceives as Ruth's *chesed*.

The book's finale returns to this perspective on events. When Ruth bears a child, the chorus of women provides the commentary. They mention the legal role this child can play ("Blessed be the Lord, who has not withheld a redeeming kinsman [*goel*] from you today!" 4:14), but they celebrate most emphatically the overflowing generosity represented by this child, perceived as a gift from Ruth to Naomi. The same voices that had greeted Naomi when she first returned in bitter emptiness, feeling abandoned by God, now register her abundant fullness in old age: " 'He will renew your life and sustain your old age; for he is born of your daughter-in-law, who loves you and is better to you than seven sons.' Naomi took the child and held it to her bosom. She became its foster mother, and the women neighbors gave him a name, saying, 'A son is born to Naomi!' " (4:15–17). They rewrite (or respeak) the event as the emotional fulfillment of the personal relationship between the two central women. But the narrator returns us, at the end, to the public, dynastic significance of the child's birth. From him will descend David—and, if we add a rabbinic perspective, the ultimate redeemer, the messiah son of David.

The Book of Ruth fully enacts the ideals of Torah. Its characters fulfill their legal and moral obligations under Torah law. In fact, the law itself, by establishing the framework for Ruth's gleaning, the redemption of Naomi's land, and Ruth's marriage to a kinsman, provides the means through which personal desire and need can find response in a way consonant with life in the community. Without Torah law, mere impulses of kindness or pleasure would offer only ephemeral help. But the ideal of Torah encompasses more than a minimal response to the law's requirements. The rich development of the theme of *chesed* throughout the book embodies a vision of fulfillment of *mitzvot* (commandments) in a spirit of lovingkindness, of generosity, of actively reaching out to the most vulnerable and bereft. This ideal is finally enacted by means of the courage of two women, Ruth and Naomi.

But if the Book of Ruth means to dramatize the essence of Torah—a life in which the fulfillment of commandments both creates and is sustained by *chesed*, an essential attribute of the God of Torah—why does the book apparently present only human origins and motivations for action? Why should we hear of God's presence only indirectly, through people's prayers? We might find an explanation in an equally central theme in Torah—the relationship between God and the people of Israel as one of covenant, of mutuality. In the words of philosopher David Hartman, the God of Israel "relies on humans to embody [God's] designs and expectations in history because of [God's] uncompromising commitment to safeguard human freedom and integrity." The idea of covenant implies a sense of human "adequacy."[1] The Torah was revealed to enable human beings to exercise that freedom and integrity in a way consonant with the will of God. Throughout Judaism, we encounter this crucial notion of the necessity for human cooperation in fulfilling divine purposes in history.

If the text embodies these fundamental Jewish ideas, why should it choose women as its protagonists? Women, apparently the beings least likely to shape their own or others' destinies, here initiate the action and propel the story. Their centrality to the story most radically unveils a theology of human partnership with God. The human actors, since they are women, could have seemed to represent humanity as creatures acted upon, figures in someone else's design rather than designers themselves. Yet this story insists on their essential role. Without their active pursuit of their relationships, needs, and desires, the lifeline of Israel's history, stretching from Judah to David, would be cut off in the death and separation of the fields of Moab.

More than that, the text, by focusing on women, points to an interpretation of the essential content of Torah. Its central characters are literally the poor, the widow, the stranger, those whom Torah calls us to care for, continually reminding us that our care should arise from empathy. We need not only to provide bare necessities, but to enter into their condition by remembering that we too have been "strangers in the land of Egypt" ("The stranger who resides with you shall be to you as one of your citizens; you shall love him as yourself, for you were strangers in the land of Egypt: I am the Lord your God"; Leviticus 19:34).

As the most vulnerable members of a covenantal community, these women reveal the very heart of the biblical vision of human society and of God. They arouse the community to live up to its own ideals. The text presents them as acting out of *chesed* themselves and activating the *chesed* of those among whom they live. Even God's lovingkindness is invoked as if in response to theirs. Women, in this biblical book, inhabit the center, both of community and of religious vision. They represent Israel as it is meant to be, the *goi kadosh* (holy nation; Exodus 19:6).

If we understand the Book of Ruth as an interpretation of the essence and consequences of Torah, we can call it a midrash on *matan Torah*—the giving of Torah. It embodies in imagination the covenantal community initiated at Sinai. And reading Ruth in these terms, we can understand how it belongs to Shavuot—*zman matan toratenu*—the time of our renewed covenant with the God who gives Torah.

Circles of Kinship
Samuel's Family Romance

SUSANNE KLINGENSTEIN

∾

For Jerome Fishman z"l

Samuel's Bold Idea

One of the most fascinating aspects of the Book of Ruth is its unconventional view of lineage. Certain elements related to the issue of genealogy, such as the rights and duties of kinship, are taken very seriously
indeed, particularly the obligations of a kinsman toward the least powerful members of his extended family (older widows without sons). The
idea of noble lineage, however, is clearly debunked, and with it the uses
to which the fantasy of impeccable descent (social and racial) has been
put in Western history.

The author of the Book of Ruth and the family he tells about are of
the finest. The Talmud (Baba Batra 14b) ascribes the authorship to the
prophet Samuel, who anointed David as the king of the Jews. Other authors and times of composition have been proposed, but none is as sat-
isfactory and pleasing to readers with literary minds as the one the
Talmud suggests. In this essay, Samuel will be recognized as the author
of the Book of Samuel *(Shmuel)*, the Book of Judges *(Shoftim)*, and the

---

The author used the Revised Standard Version of the Book of Ruth (*The New Oxford
Annotated Bible with the Apocrypha*, ed. Herbert G. May and Bruce M. Metzger [New York:
Oxford University Press, 1977]).

Book of Ruth (*Megillat Ruth*). He is a man concerned with the political fate of Israel and the idea of just government. In *Megillat Ruth*, which the Christian tradition places cleverly between *Shoftim* and *Shmuel*, the prophet describes an ideal state. The genre of *Megillat Ruth* is the idyll. Nevertheless, it is a political book. What Samuel, who as prophet is a political writer, has to say about genealogy, and hence Israel's élite, is provocative for those with more conventional ideas about royalty.

In *Megillat Ruth* Samuel describes the courtship of David's paternal great-grandparents and reveals their pedigree. The fact that Boaz is a direct descendant of Abraham (through ten generations of fathers) is not mentioned until the very end of the narrative. It is clearly less important than the fact that David's great-grandmother Ruth is from Moab. The *megilla* is mainly interested in her story. She is not of noble descent; Ruth is plain folk from the countryside. There is not the least effort on Samuel's part to write what Sigmund Freud called a "family romance" (*Familienroman*). Most high cultures, Freud argued, have endowed their kings with powerful, sometimes exotic, but always noble, parents, so as to elevate them above the common people. The myth of the hero's mysterious but royal descent becomes a source of magic power that sets him apart from the people and makes him invulnerable and invincible. In pagan cultures, this founding myth was dominant; Freud himself succumbed to the genre when he suggested in *Moses and Monotheism* that Moses was really an Egyptian of noble descent.[1] As we know from David's battle with Goliath, however, Samuel locates the source of power elsewhere (cf. 1 Samuel 17:45).

Samuel has no such conventional fantasies. He was a man of grand vision and daring imagination. His notion of an ideal Jewish people (calling for an ideal governor) was unusual to the degree that it was unostentatious. On the one hand, Samuel acknowledged that a people is a social body. Its members will be well when they are governed lawfully. Under a just government, Samuel claims, even the least powerful members of society are treated with dignity and have rights that assure a minimal subsistence. This was not the case in the time of the Judges, during which the story of Ruth is set. In *Megillat Ruth* Samuel expressed this aspect of "peoplehood" through the rights and duties of kinship revolving around Boaz. The Boaz strand of the narrative represents what Samuel considered worth preserving about genealogy: biological descent that translates into social responsibility.

On the other hand, Samuel knew better than anyone that a people is not just an aggregate of extended families, of small caretaking units, but is held together by a set of ideals, a common vision, an Idea. Although we may "inherit" ideals from our parents in the form of cultural, political, or religious commitments, there is nothing physical or genetic about that inheritance. One may abandon it at any time, just as any stranger may take it up. In *Megillat Ruth*, Samuel took the daring step of entrusting the genealogy of Idea—the inheritance of the vision that constitutes the chosenness of the Jewish people—to a complete outsider, a young peasant woman from Moab.[2]

Megillat Ruth is an ingenious book that debunks conventional views of genealogy and their uses in the official historiography of the time. It proposes an alternative Jewish view. Thinking about King David's ancestry, Samuel counterpoints the lineage of Nature and the lineage of Idea and concludes that however important biological descent may be, what finally matters is one's commitment to a set of ideals. Ruth, who was born a Moabite, proves that she can overcome biological descent (the lineage of Nature) by committing herself to the ideals of the people of Judah. With the anointing of her descendant David as king of Israel a new notion of lineage (the lineage of Idea) emerges, in which purity of biological descent is no longer required. Simply put, Samuel argues that the ethical commitment and ideas of the king's family are more important than their genes. It is worth examining Samuel's vision in greater detail.

Naomi's Kin

Like a Shakespearean drama, *Megillat Ruth* has a double plot whose strands are finely intertwined. The same story of returning to Judah is told for two protagonists. The third protagonist, if we may say so, is Naomi's kin, the Jewish people in general and Boaz in particular, in whom Samuel as political writer is most interested. Samuel's double plot puts the Jewish people to the test. The Jews are accustomed to making the minutest distinctions in daily life between the holy and the profane, between what is and what is not Jewish. How far will they take such distinction-making, Samuel asks. Will they treat a stranger who comes into their midst differently from their own kin? Will Judah take back Naomi and reject Ruth? We would not be surprised if this were the case, because Ruth is not simply a stranger, but a native of Moab, whose people once refused to give vital assistance to the Israelites. The Torah admonishes: "No Ammonite or Moabite shall enter the assembly of the Lord; even to the tenth generation none belonging to them shall enter the assembly forever; because they did not meet you with bread and with water on the way, when you came forth out of Egypt" (Deuteronomy 23:3). Yet Ruth has given Naomi all assistance imaginable. How will the people of Israel react? The words of the Torah are challenged by the acts of a stranger. Can the memory of a former unkindness be blotted out by kindness rendered in the present? How long must one hold a grudge? Thus, for Samuel, the Jewish people are as much a player in the idyll as the kinswoman and the stranger.

Samuel's vision, however, reaches further than a simple quid pro quo, an easy moral that repays good deeds with good deeds. In Ruth he explores the nature of kindness and its place in Jewish thought and society. He is, after all, not just a political but also a moral and utopian writer. Samuel knows that there are two essentially different sorts of kindness: the kindness that comes naturally because it is extended to kin (Naomi's reintegration) and kindness to the stranger, which requires an effort (Ruth's acceptance). The latter, Samuel considers the crowning achievement of *chesed* (lovingkindness), Abraham's virtue. To be a man or a people of *chesed*, in Samuel's view, means to extend kindness beyond the limits of kin, that is, to transform kindness from a natural attitude toward one's own kind into an ideational principle that can reach out and embrace the stranger. That is why Abraham's tent is said to have been open on four sides: to welcome the stranger. We will see later how Samuel argues that kindness elevated from biology to idea (when it becomes *chesed*) forms the basis of just government.

As a writer Samuel is faced with a difficult problem: in its utopian conclusion his story runs counter to the Torah's admonition never to accept Moabites. But Samuel comes up with an ingenious solution. He arranges his narrative so that the story of Naomi's return and social reintegration traces her slow movement from margin to center and her progress from inherited kinship to the creation of new kinship bonds (through Ruth's marriage to Boaz); and still more important, the flow of Samuel's narrative reflects the Jewish people's compliance with increasingly specific obligations spelled out in the Torah *(mitzvot ha-*

Torah). Thus, Samuel's narrative strategy culminates in the paradoxical situation that a new, revised understanding of a Torah rule (a so-called *chidush be-halakha*), namely the acceptance of a Moabite, is actually derived from the meticulous fulfillment of a series of other *mitzvot.*[3] This sounds a bit complicated, but it is important that we see this paradox. Samuel's aim is to bring about the amendment of an arrogant, vengeful, exclusionary *halakha.* He achieves it by arranging his narrative in such a way that the fulfillment of specific *mitzvot ha-Torah* leaves no choice but to revise the old understanding of Deuteronomy 23:3. Moreover, Samuel bases the ancestry of Israel's beloved King David on the acceptance of a stranger into the Jewish people. It was wise of Samuel to couch such prophetic boldness in layers of halakhic observance. But let's see how Samuel designs Naomi's strand of the narrative.

After ten years of residence in Moab, Naomi wants to rejoin the Jewish people. Since neither of her sons has lived, she is looking for another way to continue to be an integral part of her folk. Naomi's reintegration, her return to Judah, can be described with the help of the four *mitzvot ha-Torah* (social and religious obligations derived from the Torah), which, according to the teachings of the modern rabbinical authority Rav Abraham Isaac Kook, are exemplified in *Megillat Ruth.*[4] We can imagine these *mitzvot* as concentric circles of kinship through which Naomi moves from the outskirts of society, from the rim of belonging to her people, into the very heart of familial bondage. These *mitzvot* are (1) *matanot ani'im,* agricultural gifts to the poor (such as permission to glean); (2) *geula,* the redemption of property from a kinsman; (3) *yibbum,* levirate marriage; and (4) acceptance of the *georet,* the woman convert, as part of Israel. In short, Naomi's plot line culminates in Ruth's election to be the wife of Boaz.

You may sense already that the fourth *mitzva* is out of keeping with the first three: the first three are meant for Jews; they address the social rights of specific groups of Jews (paupers and widows). The fourth *mitzva* does not cover Jews proper, but another disenfranchised group on Jewish territory, foreigners. Samuel's story ties the four *mitzvot* into an intricate knot, which is particularly tight between the third and the fourth *mitzva.* We hardly notice the jump from biology (the rights of kin) to idea (the extension of kinship to a stranger). We need to spell out Naomi's plot to arrive at Ruth's election.

When Naomi comes to Bethlehem in Judah at the beginning of the barley harvest, she reenters the realm of kinship. This is stated in the opening sentence of chapter 2: "Now Naomi had a kinsman of her husband's, a man of wealth, of the family of Elimelech, whose name was Boaz." This sentence signals two things: Naomi's marginality—she is the poor relative settled on the outskirts of the family circle—and her eligibility for certain social rights, specifically the receipt of Jewish welfare. She is eligible immediately upon reentry into Judah. In the second sentence of chapter 2 an appeal is made to *matanot ani'im.* Ruth says to Naomi, "Let me go to the field and glean among the ears of grain after him in whose sight I shall find favor." We notice here the beginning of the intertwining of the double plot: Ruth takes Naomi's place, so that Naomi need not do the hard work. Thus Ruth becomes Naomi's substitute, even though technically Jewish social law does not apply to Moabites. It is precisely Ruth's kind act of volunteering for Naomi that propels the action further, because in the field Ruth comes to Boaz's attention.

The Midrash is more specific than the *megilla* about the nature of Boaz's relationship to Naomi. The majority of the rabbis hold that Naomi's husband Elimelech, Boaz, and another inhabitant of Bethlehem, mentioned briefly in chapter 4 of the *megilla,* are brothers (Ruth Rabba 6:3). That opens up an interesting prospect for Naomi, namely her eligibility for a levirate marriage like the one Tamar claims from Judah (Genesis 38). The law of levirate marriage, defined in Deuteronomy 25:5–10, states that a woman who is left a widow without children can require that a brother of her dead husband be given to her in marriage, and that any children resulting from the union be regarded as the offspring of the deceased. Unfortunately, Naomi is not eligible for a levirate marriage, because Elimelech died *before* his sons; hence Naomi was left a widow with children. Although Naomi is thus prevented from reentering the innermost circle of kinship, she can claim another right, namely the *geula,* defined in Leviticus 25:25. It, at least, admits her into a more exclusive circle of kinship than the very general *matanot ani'im,* which applies to all Jewish poor. The law of *geula* states: "If your brother becomes poor, and sells part of his property, then the next of kin [*goel*] shall come and redeem what his brother sold."

At the beginning of chapter 4 we hear that Naomi has indeed put up for sale a parcel of land that belonged to Elimelech. This alerts Boaz, Elimelech's brother according to the Midrash, who accosts another, probably older kinsman, to remind him of his duty as *goel*. At first the dialogue at the city gate between Boaz and the other kinsman, whose name the Midrash infers to be Tob, is unexceptional; but then it takes a rather peculiar turn. Boaz says to Tob in the presence of ten witnesses: "Naomi, who has come back from the country of Moab, is selling the parcel of land which belonged to our kinsman Elimelech. So I thought I would tell you of it, and say, Buy it in the presence of those sitting here, and in the presence of the elders of my people. If you will redeem it, redeem it; but if you will not, tell me, that I may know, for there is no one besides you to redeem it, and I come after you." The kinsman replies, "I will redeem it." Here the matter could rest. Boaz has reminded Tob of his duty as *goel*, and Tob has agreed to discharge it. But then, as if afraid a great prize were slipping from his hands, Boaz adds an odd condition. We can almost see Boaz get up and reach out to hold back the kinsman who has turned to go. "The day you buy the field from the hand of Naomi," Boaz tells him, "you are also buying Ruth, the Moabitess, the widow of the dead, in order to restore the name of the dead to his inheritance." We don't know what gives Boaz the authority to attach such a condition. He clearly has the law of the levirate marriage in mind, but as we have seen, it is applicable neither to Naomi (who was left with children) nor to Ruth (who is from Moab). Or has Ruth by now succeeded to Naomi's rights? Is she Naomi's substitute only when it comes to the collecting of *matanot ani'im*? Or can she establish a claim to Naomi's other rights as well? If she can, it would mean that she is Jewish.

Boaz seems to think so. The fact that he articulates a condition, which amounts to a levirate marriage for Ruth, in public and in a formal setting, shows that he has accepted her into the innermost circle of kinship. For Boaz, Jewish law applies to Ruth. Tob, it seems, does not agree, as we see from his reply to Boaz: "I cannot redeem it for myself, lest I impair my own inheritance. Take my right of redemption yourself, for I cannot redeem it" (4:6). What Tob means, the Midrash tells us, is that if Ruth turns out not to be considered Jewish, his children would not be Jews. Tob does not want to run that risk. Like Orpah, who left Naomi, Tob shrinks from the unknown, the untested. He clings to the familiar; the law is on his side with its admonition that "no Ammonite or Moabite shall enter the assembly of the Lord" (Deuteronomy 23:3). Tob, like Orpah, chooses the ordinary path. Boaz, who embodies Samuel's ideal of a just governor, does not. He seems to know that laws based on human flaws, on hostility and misjudgment, can change as human beings amend their ways. No two members of one people are the same, and each case has to be examined for its individual merit. Boaz, we believe, has insight into Ruth's extraordinary qualities as a mensch and the foresight to recognize that a novel interpretation of the law *(chidush be-halakha)* is possible. In fact, when he accepts Ruth as his wife, Boaz himself implements the partial amendment of Deuteronomy 23:3.

Boaz's acceptance of Ruth as his wife is formulated in purely legal terms to demonstrate that Jewish law has now embraced Ruth officially: "Also Ruth the Moabitess, the widow of Mahlon, I have bought to be my wife, to perpetuate the name of the dead in his inheritance, that the name of the dead may not be cut off from among his brethren and from the gate of his native place" (4:10). Boaz's marriage vow—one of the least appealing marriage vows in Western literature, a stark articulation of the law of levirate marriage—stands in place of a formal conversion *(gerut)*. But it has a small redeeming element in the pity it takes on the dead who died in exile. It brings them home to Judah.

But what basis does Boaz have for his courageous step? How can he be so sure that Ruth is indeed a worthy successor, a daughter, rather than a daughter-in-law, to Naomi? That Ruth should be included in the innermost circle of kinship was in fact Naomi's idea. We remember that on the last day of the harvest, Naomi told Ruth to wash and dress up and to lie down at Boaz's feet, because "the man is a relative of ours, one of our nearest kin" (2:20). When Boaz discovers Ruth, she leaps gracefully over the embarrassing moment by reminding him of his duty as *goel*: "I am Ruth, your maidservant; spread your skirt over your maidservant, for you are next of kin" (3:9). Naomi is of course a generation closer to Boaz than is Ruth. But since the collecting of the *matanot ani'im*, the two women have become interchangeable. Naomi does not recognize any difference in status between herself and her daughter-in-law. She considers Ruth her equal as a potential progenitrix of Israel.

Naomi's view, eventually accepted by Boaz, is confirmed in the blessings showered on the newlyweds by the community: "May the Lord make the woman, who is coming into your house, like Rachel and Leah, who together built up the house of Israel . . . and may your house be like the house of Perez, whom Tamar bore to Judah, because of the children that the Lord will give you by this young woman" (4:11–12). The reference to Judah and Tamar (Genesis 38) is of course an allusion to the levirate marriage by which Naomi claimed Boaz for Ruth, just as Tamar had claimed Judah. Thus Obed, born to Ruth and Boaz, has two mothers (alluded to in the blessing's reference to Rachel and Leah as mothers of the house of Israel), just as Perez, born to Tamar and Judah, has two fathers (the deceased in name and Judah).

The *megilla* ends by celebrating not the acceptance of Ruth, but the homecoming of Naomi. Her reintegration is complete when Ruth bears a son, in whose mothering Naomi shares by becoming his nurse. Again, the people refer to the law that made her return possible: "Blessed be the Lord who has not left you this day without next of kin" (4:14). For Ruth, there could be no greater token of acceptance into Naomi's people than the exclamation of her neighbors: "A son has been born to Naomi." It may seem paradoxical, but for a *georet* the greatest blessing is not to stand out but to blend in smoothly, to be effaced as a stranger.

Ruth's Ur-Father

Naomi's reentry into the circles of kinship, first with and then via Ruth, would not have succeeded if Ruth had not had precisely the quality that Samuel considers central to the Jewish people: *chesed*. Boaz chooses Ruth as his mate after he finds himself an object of her kindness. Discovering her at his feet he exclaims, "May you be blessed by the Lord, my daughter; you have made this last kindness greater than the first, in that you have not gone after young men, whether poor or rich" (3:10). Boaz is not disturbed by Ruth's rather compromising position because he has learned of her impeccable reputation in the community: "All my fellow townsmen know that you are a woman of worth [*eshet chayil*]" (3:11), a reputation Ruth earned during the harvest season through her modest behavior in public and her steady support of Naomi.[5] Ruth's integration, her movement from margin to center, from a gleaner in Boaz's field to his wife, runs parallel to Naomi's; but it exemplifies a different set of laws, those pertaining to the stranger, or *georet*, who is willing to become a member of the Jewish people. The pace of Ruth's formal integration is set by Boaz; yet all his actions come in response to Ruth's initiatives. This is particularly clear in the end and at the beginning of their encounter, as Boaz indicates in his phrase "you have made this last kindness greater than the first" (*chasdekh ha-acharon min ha-rishon*; 3:10).

These acts of kindness function as signposts marking Ruth's progress. We know that Ruth's reminder that she and Naomi are childless is a kindness toward Naomi. But why does *Boaz* take Ruth's plea as the ultimate, crowning kindness (*chasdekh ha-acharon*)? The Midrash give us a hint: "R. Samuel b. R. Isaac said: A woman prefers a poor young man to a wealthy old man" (Ruth Rabba 6:2). Ruth's consenting to enact Naomi's plot by reminding Boaz of his obligations as a kinsman (and so to choose him as her husband) signals a complete denial of her own desires. Herein she acts out, in the most personal arena, Abraham's *lekh-lekha* (Genesis 12:1). She is willing to leave behind her old self for a new identity. We are not told when and how Ruth's commitment to Judaism began. Like all biblical writers, Samuel is too cautious to speculate about the stirrings inside people. The soul is a danger zone; emotions in flux are treacherous. While intentions are unreliable, deeds can be counted on. Ruth's decision to remain with Naomi is a reliable indicator of an event, perhaps a turn (conversion), inside Ruth.

Boaz refers to that first kindness (*chasdekh ha-rishon*) indirectly when he first speaks to Ruth. During this encounter Boaz does three things which mark Ruth's admission into the outer circle of his people: (1) He invites her to stay in his field and to keep close (*tidbakin*) to his women servants. The verb he uses (in 2:8) is the same as the one that describes Ruth's cleaving (*davka-ba*) unto Naomi (in 1:14). (2) He forbids his young male field workers to molest Ruth. Thus Boaz acts toward the young foreigner like a male family member (father, brother, or uncle) who protects his own kind. And (3) he invites her to drink from the water his men have drawn. This is as much an allusion to the gift the Moabites once refused to the Israelites as to the later courtship of Ruth and Boaz. Wells and the gift of water play an important role in biblical courtship. Eliezer, for instance, recognizes in Rebekah Isaac's future wife when she gives him and his animals water to drink from the well of her family (Genesis 24:15–21). When Ruth asks Boaz, a bit astonished, "Why have I found favor in your eyes, that you should take notice of me, when I am a foreigner?" (2:10), Boaz's answer is twofold: "All that you have done for your mother-in-law since the death of your husband has been fully told me, and how you left your father and mother and your native land and came to a people that you did not know before. The Lord recompense you for what you have done" (2:11–12).

Boaz recognizes that Ruth repeated the feat of his ancestor Abraham who left his kin to commit himself to a new life. Of course, God commanded Abraham to leave his home—"Go from your country and your kindred and your father's house to the land that I will show you"—and God promised him that in return He would make him "a great nation" (Genesis 12:1–2). Nothing is promised to Ruth and she is not "called." One might argue that Abraham's feat was more difficult because he had to set out alone, while Ruth simply followed Naomi. On the other hand Abraham has the voice of God for reassurance, whereas Naomi is "only" a human being. Although she can be turned to for comfort and knows her way around Judah, she is also a broken woman. Ruth's initial commitment is courageous and entirely her own, like Abraham's, and so is its daily repetition during the months of the harvest. Abraham's attribute is *chesed*, as is Ruth's. Abraham derived his *derekh eretz*, his kindliness, from an ideational commitment at the outset. Ruth, by contrast, arrived at her ideational commitment by way of *derekh eretz*, that is through her graciousness toward Naomi. We recognize Ruth's path into Judaism as psychologically more realistic than Abraham's. Ruth loves Naomi and wants to be close to her: "Where you go, I will go, and where you lodge I will lodge; your people shall be my people; and your God my God" (2:16).

Boaz, however, does not take the psychologically realistic for the ultimate explanation. He seems to know that Ruth's speech to her mother-in-law is a tremendous understatement, another kindness to Naomi, to keep her from worrying about the enormity of the step Ruth is about to take. Boaz's formulation of Ruth's feat—all that you have *done* for your mother-in-law; and how you *left* your father and mother and your native land—is based on the subtext of Abraham's calling (Genesis 12:1). Ruth enacts *chesed*, the essence of the law, before she knows the law. This reflects the response of all Israel to the revelation of the Torah at Mount Sinai: *na'ase ve-nishma*, let's do and (then) hear and understand (Exodus 24:7). Ruth is also like Abraham, who acts immediately when called, before he knows the particulars of the contract *(brit)* God will offer him. One might say then that Abraham's task was in fact easier because he had the divine promise; but Ruth had her love for Naomi. Sometimes, having someone to embrace makes life easier than having the most divine promise. Ruth's social conduct is selfless, like Abraham's commitment to God. Boaz sees that Ruth has earned her name, *Ruth bat Avraham avinu* (Ruth, daughter of Abraham our father). In the genealogy of Idea, Ruth is closer to the source, the father of *chesed*, than Abraham's physical scion, Boaz. As prophet and politician, Samuel recognized that there could be no better ancestry and political endowment for Israel's favorite king than the marriage of ideational commitment and just government.

Ruth

CYNTHIA OZICK

∾

For Muriel Dance, in Seattle;
Sarah Halevi, in Jerusalem;
Lee Gleichman, in Stockholm;
and Inge Mirsky in New York

I. Flowers

There were only two pictures on the walls of the house I grew up in. One was large, and hung from the molding on a golden cord with a full golden tassel. It was a painting taken from a photograph—all dark, a kind of grayish-brown; it was of my grandfather Hirshl, my father's father. My grandfather's coat had big foreign-looking buttons, and he wore a tall, stiff, square *yarmulke* that descended almost to the middle of his forehead. His eyes were severe, pale, concentrated. There was no way to escape those eyes; they came after you wherever you were. I had never known this grandfather: he died in Russia long ago. My father, a taciturn man, spoke of him only once, when I was already grown: as a boy, my father said, he had gone with his father on a teaching expedition to Kiev; he remembered how the mud was deep in the roads. From my mother I learned a little more. Zeyde Hirshl was frail. His wife, Bobe Sore-Libe, was the opposite: quick, energetic, hearty, a skilled *zogerke*—a women's prayer-leader in the synagogue—a whirlwind who kept a dry-goods store and had baby after baby, all on her own, while

---

The author used the Jewish Publication Society edition of the Book of Ruth.

211

Zeyde Hirshl spent his days in the study house. Sometimes he fainted
on his way there. He was pale, he was mild, he was delicate, unworldly;
a student, a melamed, a fainter. Why, then, those unforgiving stern eyes
that would not let you go?

My grandfather's portrait had its permanent place over the secondhand piano. To the right, farther down the wall, hung the other picture.
It was framed modestly in a thin black wooden rectangle, and was, in
those spare days, all I knew of "art." Was it torn from a magazine, cut
from a calendar? A barefoot young woman, her hair bound in a kerchief, grasping a sickle, stands alone and erect in a field. Behind her a
red sun is half swallowed by the horizon. She wears a loose white peasant's blouse and a long dark skirt, deeply blue; her head and shoulders
are isolated against a limitless sky. Her head is held poised: she gazes
past my gaze into some infinity of loneliness stiller than the sky.

Below the picture was its title: *The Song of the Lark.* There was no
lark. It did not come to me that the young woman, with her lifted face,
was straining after the note of a bird who might be in a place invisible
to the painter. What I saw and heard was something else: a scene older
than this French countryside, a woman lonelier even than the woman
alone in the calendar meadow. It was, my mother said, Ruth: Ruth
gleaning in the fields of Boaz.

For many years afterward—long after *The Song of the Lark* had disappeared from the living-room wall—I had the idea that this landscape
(a 1930s fixture, it emerged, in scores of American households and
Sunday-school classrooms) was the work of Jean-François Millet, the
French painter of farm life. "I try not to have things look as if chance
had brought them together," Millet wrote, "but as if they had a necessary bond between them. I want the people I represent to look as if
they really belonged to their station, so that imagination cannot conceive of their ever being anything else."

Here is my grandfather. Imagination cannot conceive of his ever being anything else: a melamed who once ventured with his young son
(my blue-eyed father) as far as Kiev, but mainly stayed at home in his
own town, sometimes fainting on the way to the study house. The
study house was his "station." In his portrait he looks as if he really belonged there; and he did. It was how he lived.

And here is Ruth, on the far side of the piano, in Boaz's field, gleaning. Her mouth is remote: it seems somehow damaged; there is a blur

behind her eyes. All the sadness of the earth is in her tender neck, all
the blur of loss, all the damage of rupture: remote, remote, rent. The
child who stands before the woman standing barefoot, sickle forgotten,
has fallen through the barrier of an old wooden frame into the picture
itself, into the field; into the smell of the field. There is no lark, no
birdcall: only the terrible silence of the living room when no one else
is there. The grandfather is always there; his eyes keep their vigil. The
silence of the field swims up from a time so profoundly lost that it annihilates time. There is the faint weedy smell of thistle: and masses of
meadow flowers. In my childhood I recognized violets, lilacs, roses, dai-
sies, dandelions, black-eyed Susans, tiger lilies, pansies (I planted, one
summer, a tiny square of pansies, one in each corner, one in the middle), and no more. The lilacs I knew because of the children who
brought them to school in springtime: children with German names,
Koechling, Behrens, Kuntz.

To annihilate time, to conjure up unfailingly the fragrance in Boaz's
field (his field in *The Song of the Lark*), I have the power now to sum-
mon what the child peering into the picture could not. "Tolstoy, come
to my aid," I could not call then: I had never heard of Tolstoy. My
child's Russia was the grandfather's portrait, and stories of fleeing across
borders at night, and wolves, and the baba yaga in the fairy tales. But
now: "Tolstoy, come to my aid," I can chant at this hour, with my hair
turned silver; and lo, the opening of *Hadji Murád* spills out all the
flowers in Boaz's field:

> It was midsummer, the hay harvest was over and they were just begin-
> ning to reap the rye. At that season of the year there is a delightful va-
> riety of flowers—red, white, and pink scented tufty clover; milk-white
> ox-eye daisies with their bright yellow centers and pleasant spicy smell;
> yellow honey-scented rape blossoms; tall campanulas with white and lilac
> bells, tulip-shaped; creeping vetch; yellow, red, and pink scabious; faintly
> scented, neatly arranged purple plantains with blossoms slightly tinged
> with pink; cornflowers, the newly opened blossoms bright blue in the
> sunshine but growing paler and redder towards evening or when growing
> old; and delicate almond-scented dodder flowers that withered quickly.

Dodder? Vetch? (Flash of Henry James's Fleda Vetch.) Scabious? Rape
and campanula? The names are unaccustomed; my grandfather in the
study house never sees the flowers. In the text itself—in the Book of

Ruth—not a single flower is mentioned. And the harvest is neither hay nor rye; in Boaz's field outside Bethlehem they are cutting down barley and wheat. The flowers are there all the same, even if the text doesn't show them, and we are obliged to take in their scents, the weaker with the keener, the grassier with the meatier: without the smell of flowers, we cannot pass through the frame of history into that long ago, ancientness behind ancientness, when Ruth the Moabite gleaned. It is as if the little spurts and shoots of fragrance form a rod, a rail of light, along which we are carried, drifting, into that time before time "when the judges ruled."

Two pictures, divided by an old piano—Ruth in *The Song of the Lark*, my grandfather in his *yarmulke*. He looks straight out; so does she. They sight each other across the breadth of the wall. I stare at both of them. Eventually I will learn that *The Song of the Lark* was not painted by Millet, not at all; the painter is Jules Breton—French like Millet, like Millet devoted to rural scenes. *The Song of the Lark* hangs in the Art Institute of Chicago; it is possible I will die without ever having visited there. Good: I never want to see the original, out of shock at what a reproduction now discloses: a mistake, everything is turned the other way! On our living room wall Ruth faced right. In the Art Institute of Chicago she faces left. A calendar reversal!—but of course it feels to me that the original is in sullen error. Breton, unlike Millet, lived into our century—he died in 1906, the year my nine-year-old mother came through Castle Garden on her way to framing *The Song of the Lark* two decades later. About my grandfather Hirshl there is no "eventually"; I will not learn anything new about him. He will not acquire a different maker. Nothing in his view will be reversed. He will remain a dusty indoor melamed with eyes that drill through bone.

Leaving aside the wall, leaving aside the child who haunts and is haunted by the grandfather and the woman with the sickle, what is the connection between this dusty indoor melamed and the nymph in the meadow, standing barefoot amid the tall campanula?

Everything, everything. If the woman had not been in the field, my grandfather, three thousand years afterward, would not have been in the study house. She, the Moabite, is why he, when hope is embittered, murmurs the Psalms of David. The track her naked toes make through spice and sweetness, through dodder, vetch, rape, and scabious, is the very track his forefinger follows across the letter-speckled sacred page.

II. Mercy

When my grandfather reads the Book of Ruth, it is on Shavuot, the Feast of Weeks, with its twin furrows: the text's straight furrow planted with the alphabet; the harvest's furrow, fuzzy with seedlings. The Feast of Weeks, which comes in May, is a reminder of the late-spring crops, but only as an aside. The soul of it is the acceptance of the Torah by the Children of Israel. If there is a garland crowning this festival of May, it is the arms of Israel embracing the Covenant. My grandfather will not dart among field flowers after Ruth and her sickle; the field is fenced round by the rabbis, and the rabbis—those insistent interpretive spirits of Commentary whose arguments and counterarguments, from generation to generation, comprise the Tradition—seem at first to be vexed with the Book of Ruth. If they are not actually or openly vexed, they are suspicious; and if they are not willing to be judged flatly suspicious, then surely they are cautious.

The Book of Ruth is, after all, about exogamy, and not simple exogamy—marriage with a stranger, a member of a foreign culture: Ruth's ancestry is hardly neutral in that sense. She is a Moabite. She belongs to an enemy people, callous, pitiless, a people who deal in lethal curses. The children of the wild hunter Esau—the Edomites, who will ultimately stand for the imperial oppressors of Rome—cannot be shut out of the family of Israel. Even the descendants of the enslaving Egyptians are welcome to marry and grow into intimacy. "You shall not abhor an Edomite, for he is your kinsman. You shall not abhor an Egyptian, for you were a stranger in his land. Children born to them may be admitted into the congregation of the Lord in the third generation" (Deuteronomy 23:8–9). But a Moabite, never: "none of their descendants, even in the tenth generation, shall ever be admitted into the congregation of the Lord, because they did not meet you with food and water on your journey after you left Egypt, and because they hired Balaam ... to curse you" (Deuteronomy 23:4–5). An abyss of memory and hurt in that: to have passed through the furnace of the desert famished, parched, and to be chased after by a wonder-worker on an ass hurling the king's maledictions, officially designed to wipe out the straggling mob of exhausted refugees! One might in time reconcile with Esau, one might in time reconcile with hard-hearted Egypt. All this was not merely conceivable—through acculturation, conversion, family ties,

and new babies, it could be implemented, it *would* be implemented.
But Moabite spite had a lasting sting.

What, then, are the sages to do with Ruth the Moabite as in-law?
How account for her presence and resonance in Israel's story? How is
it possible for a member of the congregation of the Lord to have vio-
lated the edict against marriage with a Moabite? The rabbis, reflecting
on the pertinent verses, deduce a rule: *Moabite, not Moabitess.* It was
customary for men, they conclude, not for women, to succor travelers
in the desert, so only the Moabite males were guilty of a failure of humanity. The women were blameless, hence are exempt from the ban on
conversion and marriage.

Even with the discovery of this mitigating loophole (with its odd
premise that women are descended only from women, and men from
men; or else that all the women, or all the men, in a family line are interchangeable with one another, up and down the ladder of the generations, and that guilt and innocence are collective, sex-linked, and
heritable), it is hard for the rabbis to swallow a Moabite bride. They are
discomfited by every particle of cause-and-effect that brought about
such an eventuality. Why should a family with a pair of marriageable
sons find itself in pagan Moab in the first place? The rabbis begin by
scolding the text—or, rather, the characters and events of the story as
they are straightforwardly set out.

Here is how the Book of Ruth begins:

In the days when the judges ruled, there was a famine in the land; and
a man of Bethlehem in Judah, with his wife and two sons, went to reside
in the country of Moab. The man's name was Elimelech, his wife's name
was Naomi, and his two sons were named Mahlon and Chilion—
Ephrathites of Bethlehem in Judah. They came to the country of Moab
and remained there.

Elimelech, Naomi's husband, died; and she was left with her two sons.
They married Moabite women, one named Orpah and the other Ruth,
and they lived there about ten years. Then those two—Mahlon and
Chilion—also died; so the woman was left without her two sons and
without her husband.

Famine; migration; three deaths in a single household; three widows.
Catastrophe after catastrophe, yet the text, plain and sparse, is only
matter-of-fact. There is no anger in it, no one is condemned. What

happened, happened—though not unaccoutered by echo and reverberation. Earlier biblical families and journeys-toward-sustenance cluster and chatter around Elimelech's decision: "There was a famine in the land, and Abram went down to Egypt to sojourn there, for the famine was severe in the land" (Genesis 12:10). "So ten of Joseph's brothers went down to get rations in Egypt. . . . Thus the sons of Israel were among those who came to procure rations, for the famine extended to the land of Canaan" (Genesis 42:3, 5). What Abraham did, what the sons of Jacob did, Elimelech also feels constrained to do: there is famine, he will go where the food is.

And the rabbis subject him to bitter censure for it. The famine, they say, is retribution for the times—"the days when the judges ruled"—and the times are coarse, cynical, lawless. "In those days there was no king in Israel; everyone did what he pleased" (Judges 17:6). Ironic that the leaders should be deemed "judges," and that under their aegis the rule of law is loosened, each one pursuing "what is right in his own eyes," without standard or conscience. Elimelech, according to the rabbis, is one of these unraveled and atomized souls: a leader who will not lead. They identify him as a man of substance, distinguished, well-off, an eminence; but arrogant and selfish. Even his name suggests self-aggrandizement: *to me shall kingship come.*[1] Elimelech turns his back on the destitute conditions of hungry Bethlehem, picks up his family, and, because he is rich enough to afford the journey, sets out for where the food is. He looks to his own skin and means to get his own grub. The rabbis charge Elimelech with desertion; they accuse him of running away from the importunings of the impoverished, of provoking discouragement and despair; he is miserly, there is no charitableness in him, he is ungenerous. They call him a "dead stump"—he attends only to his immediate kin and shrugs off the community at large. Worse yet, he is heading for Moab, vile Moab! The very man who might have heartened his generation in a period of upheaval and inspired its moral repair leaves his own country, a land sanctified by Divine Covenant, for a historically repugnant region inhabited by idolators—and only to fill his own belly, and his own wife's, and his own sons'.

Elimelech in Moab will die in his prime. His widow will suffer radical denigration—a drop in status commonly enough observed even among independent women of our era—and, more seriously, a loss of protection. The rabbis will compare Naomi in her widowhood with "the remnants of the meal offerings"—i.e., with detritus and ash. Elimelech's sons—children of a father whose example is abandonment of community and of conscience—will die too soon. Already grown men after the death of Elimelech, they have themselves earned retribution. Instead of returning with their unhappy mother to their own people in the land dedicated to monotheism, they settle down to stay, and marry Moabite women. "One transgression leads to another," chide the rabbis, and argue over whether the brides of Mahlon and Chilion were or were not ritually converted before their weddings. In any case, a decade after those weddings, nothing has flowered for these husbands and wives; fertility eludes them, there will be no blossoming branches: the two young husbands are dead—dead stumps—and the two young widows are childless.

This is the rabbis' view. They are symbolists and metaphor-seekers; it goes without saying that they are moralists. Punishment is truthful; punishment is the consequence of reality, it instructs in what happens. It is not that the rabbis are severe; they are just the opposite of severe. What they are after is simple mercy: where is the standard of mercy and humanity in a time when careless men and women follow the whim of their own greedy and expedient eyes? It is not merciful to abandon chaos and neediness; chaos and neediness call out for reclamation. It is not merciful to forsake one's devastated countrymen; opportunism is despicable; desertion is despicable; derogation of responsibility is despicable; it is not merciful to think solely of one's own family: if I am only for myself, what am I? And what of the hallowed land, that sacral ground consecrated to the unity of the Creator and the teaching of mercy, while the babble and garble of polymyth pullulate all around? The man who throws away the country of aspiration, especially in a lamentable hour when failure overruns it—the man who promotes egotism, elevates the material, and deprives his children of idealism—this fellow, this Elimelech, vexes the rabbis and afflicts them with shame.

Of course, there is not a grain of any of this in the text itself—not a word about Elimelech's character or motives or even his position in Bethlehem. The rabbis' commentary is all extrapolation, embroidery, plausible invention. What is plausible in it is firmly plausible: it stands to reason that only a wealthy family, traveling together *as* a family, would be able to contemplate emigration to another country with which they have no economic or kinship ties. And it follows also that

a wealthy householder is likely to be an established figure in his hometown. The rabbis' storytelling faculty is not capricious or fantastic: it is
rooted in the way the world actually works, then and now.

But the rabbis are even more interested in the way the world *ought*
to work. Their parallel text hardly emerges *ex nihilo*. They are not
oblivious to what-is: they can, in fact, construct a remarkably particularized social density from a handful of skeletal data. Yet, shrewd sociologists though they are, it is not sociology that stirs them. What stirs
them is the aura of judgment—or call it ethical interpretation—that
rises out of even the most comprehensively imagined social particularity.
The rabbis are driven by a struggle to uncover a moral immanence in
every human being. It signifies, such a struggle, hopefulness to the
point of pathos, and the texture and pliability of this deeply embedded
matrix of optimism is more pressing for the rabbis than any other kind
of speculation or cultural improvisation. Callousness and egotism are an
affront to their expectations. What are their expectations in the Book of
Ruth? That an established community figure has an obligation not to
demoralize his constituency by walking out on it. And that the Holy
Land is to be passionately embraced, clung to, blessed, and defended as
the ripening center and historic promise of the covenanted life. Like the
Covenant that engendered its sanctifying purpose, Israel cannot be
"marginalized." One place is not the same as another place. The rabbis
are not cultural relativists.

From the rabbis' vantage, it is not that their commentary is "implicit" in the plain text under their noses; what they see is not implicit
so much as it is fully intrinsic. It is there already, like invisible ink gradually made to appear. A system of values produces a story. A system of
values? Never mind such Aristotelian language. The rabbis said, and
meant, the quality of mercy: human feeling.

III. Normality

I have been diligent in opening the first five verses of the Book of Ruth
to the rabbis' voices, and though I am unwilling to leave their voices
behind—they painstakingly accompany the story inch by inch, breath
for breath—I mean for the rest of my sojourn in the text (perforce
spotty and selective, a point here, a point there) to go on more or less

without them. I say "more or less" because it is impossible, really, to go on without them. They are (to use an unsuitable image) the Muses of exegesis: not the current sort of exegesis that ushers insights out of a tale by scattering a thousand brilliant fragments, but, rather, the kind that ushers things *toward*: a guide toward principle. The Book of Ruth presents two principles. The first is what is normal. The second is what is singular.

Until Elimelech's death, Naomi has been an exemplum of the normal. She has followed her husband and made no decisions or choices of her own. What we nowadays call feminism is of course as old as the oldest society imaginable; there have always been feminists: women (including the unsung) who will allow no element of themselves—gift, capacity, natural authority—to go unexpressed, whatever the weight of the mores. Naomi has not been one of these. Until the death of her husband, we know nothing of her but her compliance, and it would be foolish to suppose that in Naomi's world a wife's obedience is not a fundamental social virtue. But once Naomi's husband and sons have been tragically cleared from the stage, Naomi moves from the merely passive virtue of an honorable dependent to risks and contingencies well beyond the reach of comfortable common virtue. Stripped of every social support,[2] isolated in a foreign land, pitifully unprotected, her anomalous position apparently wholly ignored by Moabite practices, responsible for the lives of a pair of foreign daughters-in-law (themselves isolated and unprotected under her roof), Naomi is transformed overnight. Under the crush of mourning and defenselessness, she becomes, without warning or preparation, a woman of valor.

She is only a village woman, after all. The Book of Ruth, from beginning to end, is played out in village scenes. The history of valor will not find in Naomi what it found in another village woman: she will not arm herself like a man or ride a horse or lead a military expedition. She will never cross over to another style of being. The new ways of her valor will not annul the old ways of her virtue.

And yet—overnight!—she will set out on a program of autonomy. Her first act is a decision: she will return to Bethlehem, "for in the country of Moab she had heard that the Lord had taken note of His people and given them food." After so many years, the famine in Bethlehem is spent—but since Naomi is cognizant of this as the work of the Lord, there is a hint that she would have gone back to Bethlehem in Judah in any event, even if that place were still troubled by hunger. It is no ordinary place for her: the Lord hovers over Judah and its people, and Naomi in returning makes restitution for Elimelech's abandonment. Simply in her determination to go back, she rights an old wrong.

But she does not go back alone. Now, willy-nilly, she is herself the head of a household bound to her by obedience. "Accompanied by her two daughters-in-law, she left the place where she had been living; and they set out on the road back to the land of Judah." On the road, Naomi reflects. What she reflects on—only connect! she is herself an exile—is the ache of exile and the consolations of normality.

> Naomi said to her two daughters-in-law, "Turn back, each of you to her mother's house. May the Lord deal kindly with you, as you have dealt with the dead and with me! May the Lord grant that each of you find security in the house of a husband!" And she kissed them farewell. They broke into weeping and said to her, "No, we will return with you to your people."
>
> But Naomi replied, "Turn back, my daughters! Why should you go with me? Have I any more sons in my body who might be husbands for you? Turn back, my daughters, for I am too old to be married. Even if I thought there was hope for me, even if I were married tonight and I also bore sons, should you wait for them to grow up? Should you on their account debar yourselves from marriage? Oh no, my daughters!"

In a moment or so we will hear Ruth's incandescent reply spiraling down to us through the ardors of three thousand years; but here let us check the tale, fashion a hiatus, and allow normality to flow in: let young, stricken Orpah not be overlooked. She is always overlooked; she is the daughter-in-law who, given the chance, chose not to follow Naomi. She is no one's heroine. Her mark is erased from history; there is no Book of Orpah. And yet Orpah *is* history. Or, rather, she is history's great backdrop. She is the majority of humankind living out its usualness on home ground. These young women—both of them—are cherished by Naomi; she cannot speak to them without flooding them in her fellow-feeling. She *knows* what it is to be Orpah and Ruth. They have all suffered and sorrowed together, and in ten years of living in one household much of the superficial cultural strangeness has worn off. She pities them because they are childless, and she honors them because they have "dealt kindly" with their husbands and with their mother-in-law. She calls them—the word as she releases it is accustomed, familiar, close, ripe with dearness—*b'notai*, "my daughters," whereas the voice of the narrative is careful to identify them precisely, though neutrally, as *khalotekha*, "her daughters-in-law."

Orpah is a loving young woman of clear goodness; she has kisses and tears for the loss of Naomi. "They broke into weeping again, and Orpah kissed her mother-in-law farewell." Her sensibility is ungrudging, and she is not in the least narrow-minded. Her upbringing may well have been liberal. Would a narrow-minded Moabite father have given over one of his daughters to the only foreign family in town? Such a surrender goes against the grain of the ordinary. Exogamy is never ordinary. So Orpah has already been stamped with the "abnormal"; she is already a little more daring than most, already somewhat offbeat—she is one of only two young Moabite women to marry Hebrews, and Hebrews have never been congenial to Moabites. If the Hebrews can remember how the Moabites treated them long ago, so can the Moabites: traditions of enmity work in both directions. The mean-spirited have a habit of resenting their victims quite as much as the other way around. Orpah has cut through all this bad blood to plain humanity; it would be unfair to consider her inferior to any other kind-hearted young woman who ever lived in the world before or since. She is in fact superior; she has thrown off prejudice, and she has had to endure more than most young women of her class, including the less spunky and the less amiable: an early widowhood and no babies. And what else is there for a good girl like Orpah, in her epoch, and often enough in ours, but family happiness?

Her prototype abounds. She has fine impulses, but she is not an iconoclast. She can push against convention to a generous degree, but it is out of the generosity of her temperament, not out of some large metaphysical idea. Who will demand of Orpah—think of the hugeness of the demand!—that she admit monotheism to the concentration and trials of her mind? Offer monotheism to almost anyone—offer it as something to take seriously—and ninety-nine times out of a hundred it will be declined, even by professing "monotheists." A Lord of History whose intent is felt, whose Commandments stand with immediacy, whose Covenant summons perpetual self-scrutiny and a continual Turning toward moral renewal, and yet *cannot, may not, be physically imagined*? A Creator neither remote and abstract like the God of the philosophers, nor palpable like the "normal" divinities, both ancient and contemporary, of both East and West? Give us (cries the nature of our race) our gods and goddesses; give us the little fertility icons with their welcoming breasts and elongated beckoning laps; give us the resplendent Virgin with her suffering brow and her arms outstretched in blessing; give us the Man on the Cross through whom to learn pity and love, and sometimes brutal exclusivity! Only give us what our eyes can see and our understanding understand: who can imagine the unimaginable? That may be for the philosophers; *they* can do it; but then they lack the imagination of the Covenant. The philosophers leave the world naked and blind and deaf and mute and relentlessly indifferent, and the village folk—who refuse a lonely cosmos without consolation—fill it and fill it and fill it with stone and wood and birds and mammals and miraculous potions and holy babes and animate carcasses and magically divine women and magically divine men: images, sights, and swallowings comprehensible to the hand, to the eye, to plain experience. For the nature of our race, God is one of the visual arts.

Is Orpah typical of these plain village folk? She is certainly not a philosopher, but neither is she, after ten years with Naomi, an ordinary Moabite. Not that she has altogether absorbed the Hebrew vision—if she had absorbed it, would she have been tempted to relinquish it so readily? She is somewhere in between, perhaps. In this we may suppose her to be one of us: a modern, no longer a full-fledged member of the pagan world, but always with one foot warming in the seductive bath of those colorful, comfortable, often beautiful old lies (they can console, but because they are lies they can also hurt and kill); not yet given over to the Covenant and its determination to train us away from lies, however warm, colorful, beautiful, and consoling.

Naomi, who is no metaphysician herself, who is, rather, heir to a tradition, imposes no monotheistic claim on either one of her daughters-in-law. She is right not to do this. In the first place, she is not a proselytizer or polemicist or preacher or even a teacher. She is none of those things: she is a bereaved woman far from home, and when she looks at her bereaved daughters-in-law, it is home she is thinking of, for herself and for them. Like the rabbis who will arrive two millennia after her, she is not a cultural relativist: God is God, and God is One. But in her own way, the way of empathy—three millennia before the concept of a democratic pluralist polity—she is a kind of pluralist. She does not require that Orpah accept what it is not natural for her, in the light of how she was reared, to accept. She speaks of Orpah's return not merely to her people but to her gods. Naomi is the opposite of coercive or punitive. One cannot dream of Inquisition or jihad emerging from her loins. She may not admire the usages of Orpah's people—they do not concern themselves with the widow and the destitute; no one in Moab comes forward to care for Naomi—but she knows that Orpah has a mother, and may yet have a new husband, and will be secure where she is. It will not occur to Naomi to initiate a metaphysical discussion with Orpah! She sends her as a lost child back to her mother's hearth. (Will there be idols on her mother's hearth? Well, yes. But this sour comment is mine, not Naomi's.)

So Orpah goes home; or, more to the point, she goes nowhere. She stays home. She is never, never, never to be blamed for it. If she is not extraordinary, she is also normal. The extraordinary is what is not normal, and it is no fault of the normal that it does not, or cannot, aspire to the extraordinary. What Orpah gains by staying home with her own people is what she always deserved: family happiness. She is young and fertile; soon she will marry a Moabite husband and have a Moabite child.

What Orpah loses is the last three thousand years of being present in history. Israel continues; Moab has not. Still, for Orpah, historic longevity—the longevity of an Idea to which a people attaches itself—may not be a loss at all. It is only an absence, and absence is not felt as loss. Orpah has her husband, her cradle, her little time. That her gods are false is of no moment to her; she believes they are true. That her social system does not provide for the widow and the destitute is of no moment to her; she is no longer a widow, and as a wife she will not be destitute; as for looking over her shoulder to see how others fare, there is nothing in Moab to require it of her. She once loved her oddly foreign mother-in-law. And why shouldn't open-hearted Orpah, in her little time, also love her Moabite mother-in-law, who is as like her as her own mother, and will also call her "my daughter"? Does it matter to Orpah that her great-great-great-grandchildren have tumbled out of history, and that there is no Book of Orpah, and that she slips from the Book of Ruth in only its fourteenth verse?

Normality is not visionary. Normality's appetite stops at satisfaction.

IV. Singularity

No, Naomi makes no metaphysical declaration to Orpah. It falls to Ruth, who has heard the same compassionate discourse as her sister-in-law, who has heard her mother-in-law three times call out "Daughter, turn back"—it falls to Ruth to throw out exactly such a declaration to Naomi.

Her words have set thirty centuries to trembling: "Your God shall be my God," uttered in what might be named visionary language. Does it merely "fall" to Ruth that she speaks possessed by the visionary? What is at work in her? Is it capacity, seizure, or the force of intent and the clarity of will? Set this inquiry aside for now, and—apart from what the story tells us she really did say—ask instead what Ruth might have replied in the more available language of pragmatism, answering Naomi's sensible "Turn back" exigency for exigency. What "natural" reasons might such a young woman have for leaving her birthplace? Surely there is nothing advantageous in Ruth's clinging to Naomi. Everything socially rational is on the side of Ruth's remaining in her own country: what is true for Orpah is equally true for Ruth. But even if Ruth happened to think beyond exigency—even if she were exceptional in reaching past common sense toward ideal conduct—she need not have thought in the framework of the largest cosmic questions. Are we to expect of Ruth that she be a prophet? Why should she, any more than any other village woman, think beyond personal relations?

In the language of personal relations, in the language of pragmatism and exigency, here is what Ruth might have replied:

> Mother-in-law, I am used to living in your household, and have become accustomed to the ways of your family. I would no longer feel at home if I resumed the ways of my own people. After all, during the ten years or so I was married to your son, haven't I flourished under your influence? I was so young when I came into your family that it was you who completed my upbringing. It isn't for nothing that you call me daughter. So let me go with you.

Or, higher on the spectrum of ideal conduct (rather, the conduct of idealism), but still within the range of reasonable altruism, she might have said:

Mother-in-law, you are heavier in years than I and alone in a strange place, whereas I am stalwart and not likely to be alone for long. Surely I will have a second chance, just as you predict, but you—how helpless you are, how unprotected! If I stayed home in Moab, I would be looking after my own interests, as you recommend, but do you think I can all of a sudden stop feeling for you, just like that? No, don't expect me to abandon you—who knows what can happen to a woman of your years all by herself on the road? And what prospects can there be for you, after all this long time away, in Bethlehem? It's true I'll seem a little odd in your country, but I'd much rather endure a little oddness in Bethlehem than lose you forever, not knowing what's to become of you. Let me go and watch over you.

There is no God in any of that. If these are thoughts Ruth did not speak out, they are all implicit in what has been recorded. Limited though they are by pragmatism, exigency, and personal relations, they are already anomalous. They address extraordinary alterations—of self, of worldly expectation. For Ruth to cling to Naomi as a daughter to her own mother is uncommon enough; a universe of folklore confirms that a daughter-in-law is not a daughter. But for Ruth to become the instrument of Naomi's restoration to safekeeping within her own community—and to prosperity and honor as well—is a thing of magnitude. And, in fact, all these praiseworthy circumstances do come to pass, though circumscribed by pragmatism, exigency, and personal relations. And without the visionary. Ideal conduct—or the conduct of idealism—is possible even in the absence of the language of the visionary. Observe:

They broke into weeping again, and Orpah kissed her mother-in-law farewell. But Ruth clung to her. So she said, "See, your sister-in-law has returned to her people. Go follow your sister-in-law." But Ruth replied: "Do not urge me to leave you, to turn back and not follow you. For wherever you go, I will go; wherever you lodge, I will lodge; your people shall be my people. Where you die, I will die, and there I will be buried. Only death will part me from you." When Naomi saw how determined she was to go with her, she ceased to argue with her, and the two went on until they reached Bethlehem.

Of course this lovely passage is not the story of the Book of Ruth (any more than my unpoetic made-up monologues are), though it might easily have been Ruth's story. In transcribing from the text, I have left out what Ruth passionately put in: God. And still Ruth's speech, even with God left out, and however particularized by the personal, is a stupendous expression of loyalty and love.

But now, in a sort of conflagration of seeing, the cosmic sweep of a single phrase transforms these spare syllables from the touching language of family feeling to the unearthly tongue of the visionary:

> "See, your sister-in-law has returned to her people and her gods. Go and follow your sister-in-law." But Ruth replied, "Do not urge me to leave you, to turn back and not follow you. For wherever you go, I will go; wherever you lodge, I will lodge; your people shall be my people, and your God my God. Where you die, I will die, and there I will be buried. Thus and more may the Lord do to me if anything but death parts me from you."

Your God shall be my God: Ruth's story is kindled into the Book of Ruth by the presence of God on Ruth's lips, and her act is far, far more than a ringing embrace of Naomi, and far, far more than the simple acculturation it resembles. Ruth leaves Moab because she intends to leave childish ideas behind. She is drawn to Israel because Israel is the inheritor of the One Universal Creator.

Has Ruth "learned" this insight from Naomi and from Naomi's son? It may be; the likelihood is almost as pressing as evidence: how, without assimilation into the life of an Israelite family, would Ruth ever have penetrated into the great monotheistic cognition? On the other hand: Orpah too encounters that cognition, and slips back into Moab to lose it again. Inculcation is not insight, and what Orpah owns is only that: inculcation without insight. Abraham—the first Hebrew to catch insight—caught it as genius does, autonomously, out of the blue, without any inculcating tradition. Ruth is in possession of both inculcation *and* insight.

And yet, so intense is her insight, one can almost imagine her as a kind of Abraham. Suppose Elimelech had never emigrated to Moab; suppose Ruth had never married a Hebrew. The fire of cognition might still have come upon her as it came upon Abraham—autonomously, out of the blue, without any inculcating tradition. Abraham's cognition turned into a civilization. Might Ruth have transmuted Moab? Ruth as a second Abraham! We see in her that clear power; that power of consummate clarity. But whether Moab might, through Ruth, have entered the history of monotheism, like Israel, is a question stalled by the more modest history of kinship entanglement. In Ruth's story, insight is inexorably accompanied by, fused with, inculcation; how can we sort out one from the other? If Ruth had not been married to one of Naomi's sons, perhaps we would have heard no more of her than we will hear henceforth of Orpah. Or: Moab might have ascended, like Abraham's seed, from the gods to God. Moab cleansed and reborn through Ruth! The story as it is given is perforce inflexible, not amenable to experiment. We cannot have Ruth without Naomi; nor would we welcome the loss of such lovingkindness. All the same, Ruth may not count as a second Abraham because her tale is enfolded in a way Abraham's is not: she has had her saturation in Abraham's seed. The ingredient of inculcation cannot be expunged: there it is.

Nevertheless it seems insufficient—it seems askew—to leave it at that. Ruth marries into Israel, yes; but her mind is vaster than the private or social facts of marriage and inculcation; vaster than the merely familial. Insight, cognition, intuition, religious genius—how to name it? It is not simply because of Ruth's love for Naomi—a love unarguably resplendent—that Naomi's God becomes Ruth's God. To stop at love and loyalty is to have arrived at much, but not all; to stop at love and loyalty is to stop too soon. Ruth claims the God of Israel out of her own ontological understanding. She knows—she knows directly, prophetically—that the Creator of the Universe is One.

V. Unfolding

The greater part of Ruth's tale is yet to occur—the greater, that is, in length and episode. The central setting of the Book of Ruth is hardly Moab; it is Bethlehem in Judah. But by the time the two destitute widows, the older and the younger, reach Bethlehem, the volcanic heart of the Book of Ruth—the majesty of Ruth's declaration—has already happened. All the rest is an unfolding.

Let it unfold, then, without us. We have witnessed normality and we have witnessed singularity. We will, if we linger, witness these again in Bethlehem; but let the next events flash by without our lingering. Let Naomi come with Ruth to Bethlehem; let Naomi in her distress name herself Mara, meaning "bitter," "for the Lord has made my lot very bitter"; let Ruth set out to feed them both by gleaning in the field of Elimelech's kinsman, Boaz—fortuitous, God-given, that she should blunder onto Boaz's property! He is an elderly landowner, an affluent farmer who, like Levin in *Anna Karenina*, works side by side with his laborers. He is at once aware that there is a stranger in his field, and is at once solicitous. He is the sort of man who, in the heat of the harvest, greets the reapers with courteous devoutness: "The Lord be with you!" A benign convention, perhaps, but when he addresses Ruth it is no ordinary invocation: "I have been told of all that you did for your mother-in-law after the death of her husband, how you left your father and mother and the land of your birth and came to a people you had not known before. May the Lord reward your deeds. May you have a full recompense from the Lord, the God of Israel, under whose wings you have sought refuge!" Like Naomi, he calls Ruth "daughter," and he speaks an old-fashioned Hebrew; he and Naomi are of the same generation.[3]

But remember that we are hurrying along now; so let Naomi, taking charge behind the scenes, send Ruth to sleep at Boaz's feet on the threshing floor in order to invite his special notice—a contrivance to make known to Boaz that he is eligible for Ruth's salvation within the frame of the levirate code. And let the humane and flexible system of the levirate code work itself out, so that Boaz can marry Ruth, who will become the mother of Obed, who is the father of Jesse, who is the father of King David, author of the Psalms.

The levirate law in Israel—like the rule for gleaners—is designed to redeem the destitute. The reapers may not sweep up every stalk in the meadow; some of the harvest must be left behind for bread for the needy. And if a woman is widowed, the circle of her husband's kin must open their homes to her; in a time when the sole protective provision for a woman is marriage, she must have a new husband from her dead husband's family—the relative closest to the husband, a brother if possible. Otherwise what will become of her? Dust and cinders. She will be like the remnants of the meal offerings.

Boaz in his tenderness (we have hurried past even this, which more than almost anything else merits our hanging back; but there it is on the page, enchanting the centuries—a tenderness sweetly discriminating, morally meticulous, wide-hearted, and ripe)—Boaz is touched by Ruth's appeal to become her husband-protector. It is a fatherly tenderness, not an erotic one—though such a scene might, in some other tale, burst with the erotic: a young woman, perfumed, lying at the feet of an old man at night in a barn. The old man is not indifferent to the pulsing of Eros in the young: "Be blessed of the Lord, daughter! Your latest deed of loyalty is greater than the first, in that you have not turned to younger men." The remark may carry a pang of wistfulness, but Boaz in undertaking to marry Ruth is not animated by the lubricious. He is no December panting after May. A forlorn young widow, homeless in every sense, has asked for his guardianship, and he responds under the merciful levirate proviso with all the dignity and responsibility of his character—including an ethical scruple: "While it is true that I am a redeeming kinsman, there is another redeemer closer than I"—someone more closely related to Elimelech than Boaz, and therefore first in line to assume the right—and burden—of kinship protection.

In this closer relative we have a sudden pale reminder of Orpah. Though she has long vanished from the story, normality has not. Who conforms more vividly to the type of Average Man than that practical head of a household we call John Doe? And now John Doe (the exact Hebrew equivalent is Ploni Almoni) briefly enters the narrative and quickly jumps out of it; averageness leaves no reputation, except for averageness. John Doe, a.k.a. Ploni Almoni, is the closer relative Boaz has in mind, and he appears at a meeting of town elders convened to sort out the levirate succession in Naomi's case. The hearing happens also to include some business about a piece of land that Elimelech owned; if sold, it will bring a little money for Naomi. Naomi may not have known of the existence of this property—or else why would she be reduced to living on Ruth's gleaning? But Boaz is informed of it, and immediately arranges for a transaction aimed at relieving both Naomi and Ruth. The sale of Elimelech's property, though secondary to the issue of marital guardianship for Naomi's young daughter-in-law, is legally attached to it: whoever acquires the land acquires Ruth. The closer relative, Ploni Almoni (curious how the text refuses him a real name of his own, as if it couldn't be bothered, as if it were all at once impatient with averageness), is willing enough to buy the land: John Doe always understands money and property. But he is not at all willing to accept Ruth. The moment he learns he is also being asked to take on the care of a widow—one young enough to bear children, when very likely he already has a family to support—he changes his mind. He worries, he explains, that he will impair his estate. An entirely reasonable, even a dutiful, worry, and who can blame him? If he has missed his chance to become the great-grandfather of the Psalmist, he is probably, like Ploni Almoni everywhere, a philistine scorner of poetry anyhow.

And we are glad to see him go. In this he is no reminder of Orpah; Orpah, a loving young woman, is regretted. But like Orpah he has only the usual order of courage. He avoids risk, the unexpected, the lightning move into imagination. He thinks of what he has, not of what he might do: he recoils from the conduct of idealism. He is perfectly conventional, and wants to stick with what is familiar. Then let him go in peace—he is too ordinary to be the husband of Ruth. We have not heard him make a single inquiry about her. He has not troubled over any gesture of interest or sympathy. Ruth is no more to him than an object of acquisition offered for sale. He declines to buy; he has his own life to get on with, and no intention of altering it, levirate code or no levirate code. "You do it," he tells Boaz.

Boaz does it. At every step he has given more than full measure, whether of barley or benevolence. We have watched him load Ruth's sack with extra grain to take back to Naomi. He has instructed the reapers to scatter extra stalks for her to scoop up. He has summoned her to his own table for lunch in the field. He is generous, he is kindly, he is old, and in spite of his years he opens his remaining strength to the imagination of the future: he enters on a new life inconceivable to him on the day a penniless young foreigner wandered over his field behind the harvest workers. *Mercy, pity, peace, and love:* these Blakean words lead, in our pastoral, to a beginning.

The beginning is of course a baby, and when Naomi cradles her grandchild in her bosom, the village women cry: "A son is born to Naomi!" And they cry: "Blessed be the Lord, who has not withheld a redeemer from you today! May his name be perpetuated in Israel! He will renew your life and sustain your old age; for he is born of your daughter-in-law, who loves you and is better to you than seven sons."

Only eighty-five verses tell Ruth's and Naomi's story. To talk of it takes much longer. Not that the greatest stories are the shortest—not at all. But a short story has a stalk—or shoot—through which its life rushes, and out of which the flowery head erupts. The Book of Ruth—wherein goodness grows out of goodness, and the extraordinary is found here, and here, and here—is sown in desertion, bereavement, barrenness, death, loss, displacement, destitution. What can sprout from such ash? Then Ruth sees into the nature of Covenant, and the life of the story streams in. Out of this stalk mercy and redemption unfold; flowers flood Ruth's feet; and my grandfather goes on following her track until the coming of Messiah from the shoot of David, in the line of Ruth and Naomi.

Poetic Movements

Words Not Said

Four Poems after the Book of Ruth

KATHRYN HELLERSTEIN

These four poems—dramatic monologues and dialogues—were conceived in the interstices of the Book of Ruth. They attempt to give voice to characters at the few moments when the narrator of the book falls silent, juxtaposing actions that do not follow directly one from the other, or to offer an interpretation of what might lie behind a character's words or deeds. Compared to other narratives in the Bible, Ruth is unified and coherent, with well-developed major characters, who speak their minds at crucial moments in the story, or, better yet, respond to one another forthrightly. For the most part, Ruth plays itself out in a well-lit foreground, rather than in the shadows of what Erich Auerbach calls a backgrounded narrative, like the Binding of Isaac. Unlike Genesis, Ruth gives us the most crucial exchanges, between Ruth and Naomi or Ruth and Boaz, that help us see the largesse of spirit inherent in these characters' gentle dealings with one another. Still, there are moments in which the characters' inner lives are not explicit, and my poems depart from four of these.

My models for these dramatizations of the biblical characters are the works of two Yiddish poets, Roza Yakubovitsh and Itzik Manger. Manger is famous for his Medresh Itzik, *first published in Warsaw in 1935, which recast the biblical stories in the clothes and countryside of Jewish Eastern Europe; Yakubovitsh's dramatic monologues, in which biblical women speak in voices at once modern and medieval, came out in Warsaw in 1924 and are virtually unknown today.*

The author used the Holy Scriptures (Philadelphia: Jewish Publication Society, 1955).

Naomi: Loss

—Ruth 1:1-5

And a certain man of Bethlehem in Judah went to sojourn in the
field of Moab, he, and his wife, and his two sons. . . . And Mahlon
and Chilion died both of them; and the woman was left of her two
children and of her husband.

Suddenly, they were not "his sons" but "my sons,"
and I sat at the edge of this field sprouting green,
far from the tawny hills, the thirsty stubble
we'd decided to leave just weeks before
for the sake of our hungry boys, wondering
why he had left me so soon. We thought the hunger
there would kill us. What made him die, here,
where we have more than enough? They saw me weeping
in the morning mist—drops bitter on my tongue,
on the grass blades. They sat by me on the stone wall,
one on each side, dear boys, and they cried, too.

We made a new home, anyway. We worked hard in the fields,
we made do without all the comforts of Bethlehem, without
their father, without my Elimelech. I came not to mind
sleeping alone. Years passed. The boys grew up.
They started looking at the neighbors' daughters.
I wasn't crazy about them marrying
local girls, but I couldn't afford even
a messenger to Elimelech's relatives back home.
They chose well, Chilion his Orpah and Mahlon his Ruth,
and their families made them sumptuous weddings, months ago.
I'm glad to have the young women around to help
with the planting and the cooking. But now,
just as suddenly as their father, both boys are gone!
How can such young brides be widows? They weep into their soup.
Their tears bleach the laundry and moisten the muddy paths.

Once again, seedlings come up, pushing aside the clods,
pale leaflets furled in the fog. The crop promises
to be good this year. But I will have no grandchildren.

Ruth and Orpah

—RUTH 1:6

Then she arose with her daughters-in-law, that she might return
from the field of Moab; for she had heard in the field of Moab that
the Lord had remembered His people in giving them bread.

"There's bread again in Bethlehem!"
breathes Orpah, through her own dull ache
toward where Ruth lies—sad, sleeping form.
Ruth stirs, then sits up, wide awake.

"Naomi certainly will go
when she is told." Ruth rubs her eyes.
"Should we go with her?" "Yes, we must!"
Bride-widows, both gasp in surprise

That yet another change will come.
Then Orpah gets up from her bed,
washes her face, begins to pack
her clothes and bracelets with bowed head.

Ruth stands up, stretches. Then she cries,
"Our families! We will never see
our fathers, mothers, sisters, friends!
The land of Judah is far away."

But Orpah rolls her blankets, sheets,
and pillow up for traveling,
then over her bright, braided hair,
she pulls a scarf, unraveling

black fringes where she'd torn the edge
in mourning, only weeks before.

Reluctantly, Ruth folds her skirts
and underclothes and says no more.

Naomi: "Call Me Bitter"
—Ruth 1:19-22

The path grows stonier, the hills are steep
and sheep and goats graze on the prickly brush.
On terraced plots cling olive trees, their leaves
sigh ashy melodies of my return.
I walked this path ten years ago, going up,
away from Bethlehem, whose walls now glisten
where the road dips and branches out, a maze
of what I've lost and what my God has gained.
Ten years ago, I had to leave behind
this starving puzzle of the ways of God.
I was young then. My husband, hungry for
a better life, trudged at my side, our sons
walked, dreaming of their suppers in Moab.
High noon. The sun is strong. It finds my face
although I want to hide how old I am,
how much I've lost. I'm not alone, there's Ruth,
but how can I without my husband, sons,
be coming home? The women peer out from
their market stalls, their courtyard gates, at Ruth
concealed beside me in her foreign veil,
and ask, "Naomi? Is that you?" I spit.
"Do not call me Naomi, pleasant name.
But call me bitter, Mara, for my God
dealt bitterly with me. He emptied me
of all my fullness. I have nothing now."

Ruth to Naomi:
After the Threshing

—RUTH 3:6-15

And she went down unto the threshing-floor, and did according to
all that her mother-in-law bade her.

Without understanding them, I followed your words,
hiding in shadows of the granary
while threshers—men and boys—ate well and drank.
They fell asleep on bales of hay, their sieves
scattered across the piles of winnowed grain

as careless as the bawdy jokes and songs
they left off, mid-verse, slipping into dreams.
Stone walls absorbed their even breathing and
fresh dust from beaten husks. I held my breath
as Boaz, laughing, a little drunk, yawned, belched,

then lay down by a heap of corn, and slept.
As you instructed, I came softly to
that spot, uncovered his feet—their calloused heels,
worn arches in repose—and curled up there.
At midnight, he turned over, brushed his foot

against my scarf, and suddenly sat up.
"Who are you?" his words probed into the dark.
To him, the rough-edged shadow, darkness on
pure dark, not knowing why, I answered, "Ruth,
your handmaid. Spread your skirt upon me—you

are a near kinsman." His reply blessed me
as "daughter." He praised me for kindness shown
to you, Naomi, and to him, old man
whose grace you ask through me. I never thought
to follow after young men, rich or poor,

or any man, since Mahlon, for when
I followed you, I found my way through grief.
He called me "daughter" again, and "virtuous." His beard
tickled my ear. I shivered in the warmth
of this man's breath, as he explained your laws

that let the nearer kinsman of the dead
be first to choose the widow and the land.
I started to stand up. He told me, "Sleep,"
and just before the dawn broke, helped me leave,
unnoticed, as the moon slipped from a sky—

indigo turned violet—and the sun
inched up to gild the rooftops brilliant as
the barley he poured in my heavy cape.
You ask me, "Daughter, who are you?" I'm filled
with dreams. The chaff of widow falls away.

Awakening Ruth

BARBARA HELFGOTT HYETT

❧

> And when Boaz had eaten and drunk
> and his heart was merry, he went to lie down
> at the end of the grain pile: and she came
> softly, and uncovered his feet, and lay down.
> —RUTH 3:7

Who can understand why a woman would
lie awake all night at the feet of a stranger?
She rests on her shoulder, all tide and riptide,
not floating, not drowning in dreams.

Boaz flexes his nostrils. He groans
like a thirsty orchard; his windpipe
opens for air. His old feet are barely
grazing the fields of her loosened hair.
Ruth studies the bony equipoise of arches,
his vulnerable heels. The half-moons
of his toenails gleam. In daylight, she will
meet the beast in the caves of his eyes.

She lifts her cheek from the pillow
of his hem, flexing her neck
like a scythe from side to side.
She rearranges shadows: each corn stalk
flattens into dark geometry; beetles
glean dust and silk from the sheaves.

The threshing floor grows warm. Her hunger
ripens. She draws the back of her hand
across her teeth. The story proceeds.
A kingdom begins at the delta of her thighs.
Behind the tongue of every language, she
is psalm and exaltation. She is the restless harp.

The author used the Holy Scriptures (Philadelphia: Jewish Publication Society, 1955).

Isa

NESSA RAPOPORT

∾

*I could not be a Jewish writer without being a Jewish reader first. Because of my
mother's passion for Hebrew, I am able to read the central Jewish book in its original, most beautiful language. And because of my own passion, I have written a
novel that asks to be read Jewishly: that is, a book in which story and commentary
are indivisible.*

Isa, the heroine and narrator of The Perfection of the World, *is a lawyer in
Washington, a young woman without history, orphaned, atomized, estranged from
her family's past and loath to know it. The novel is the story of her journey home,
her slow awakening from displacement to community, redeeming love, and her true
name.*

*At the same time, however, another story is taking place, between Isa's five-part
narrative and the five biblical texts that underlie it: Esther, Ecclesiastes, Lamentations, Ruth, and the Song of Songs.*

*These sacred texts and their differing Hebrew music, singing of exile, worldli-
ness, grief, devotion, and love, embody the novel's theme: a woman's return to an
authentic life through authentic language; the retrieval of meaning through the
shared tales of a family and a people.*

*Isa's story has its own integrity, but it joins a larger story unknown to her: the
tale of the Jews in our century, and of a people so intoxicated by one book that for
thousands of years the reading of it and writing about it has been saving.*

*For the reader who knows them, the texts inform Isa's life, comment on it, and
draw renewed meaning from it without ever being alluded to directly by the
heroine—or author. And for readers to whom they are unfamiliar, the texts will,
I hope, still exercise their mysterious potency, serving as the "hidden spring" of Sol-
omon's Song that nourishes all things.*

The two excerpts that follow are from the fourth section of the novel called "Isa,"

The author used her own translation of the Book of Ruth; she also consulted *Tanakh: A
New Translation of the Holy Scriptures* (Philadelphia, New York, and Jerusalem: Jewish
Publication Society, 1985).

beneath which lies the Book of Ruth. "Isa" represents the heroine's pastoral return from bereavement to sanctuary. In this section, the narrator travels with her cousin, Gali, to Gali's farm community in the north of Eretz Yisrael. Until now, Gali has refused her because of the estrangement between their fathers, but now she softens as she takes Isa to her home. Under Gali's dominion, Isa can face her uncle's final bequest, and her husband Ishai's inability to return from the seduction of America to the land of his birth. Now her devotion effects a turning; at last Isa is sovereign enough to choose.

It was the time in the land when the country was being judged, a time bereft of a leader, when Gali and I left Jerusalem to stay in the fields where her friends lived and worked. I was far from the land of my birth as we drove through brown grasses and through the laden air to the sea-coast. Nothing flourished or was fruitful as we traveled, gone from my uncle's home to a foreign place.

The sorrow of departure returned to me. So my uncle had left his native land and, with my aunt, built a new family, two sons—one ill, one vanished—and a daughter, next to me. The house impoverished, Gali had left, too, nourished herself in another house, not in the desert mountains but on green hills above the sea. My uncle's hope of a dynasty in the walled city had expired. But Gali sang as we wound our way alongside the thrashing water. Out of the stone city her heart lightened, away from her grieving mother, while I, leaving one place for another, was leaving everything: my father's grave, receding across this water, my mother tongue, and the husband not able to turn, to face me.

He would take another wife when I was gone, under a blue American sky, fed on alien corn. Soon a decade of his life would be spent in exile. He had forgotten: This was the land that sustained him, where he broke bread in his mother's house.

I could have cleaved to what was past, returning to my people and their gods, but Gali had said: "Come to me." Now the forbidding landscape, barren as I, was asking my loyalty.

"What God bequeathed this people," I said bitterly. And inwardly I was mocking our journey, for I had left America with a husband and abundant wealth to come to an empty house.

"My mother's alone," Gali said. "But she was not always so embittered. I have a picture of her in happier days. It was taken when she first arrived here, knowing my father loved her. Then she did not feel that the Lord had given her only suffering, affliction."

The transformation was astonishing. "Can this be she?" The picture showed a woman, young, whose face was sweet delight.

Outside the window, the sky was muddy as the ground. "Turn around," I said to Gali, desperately. "I cannot stay in a place where nothing grows."

"Foolish exile," she said. "What do you think lies beneath the earth?"

I answered her: "The dead."

"Seeds, in which you have no faith. The seeds we need to plant if we want food."

"I'm hungry, suddenly."

"We'll stop to eat. This is the season for sowing what we hope to reap. And if you stay until the spring, the first crop to ripen will be barley, and you can help us with the harvesting."

As we neared our destination, my sorrow eased. I was doing what I had set out to do, and so I would stop railing against the fates' allotment.

Gali, eager for homecoming, explained: "The farm is small, but the people are like kin to me. The fields support us, and the factory. The yield is rich if we work hard; the poorest can glean a living for her family."

"I need to walk after this long drive," I said.

"Go into the fields, to the vantage point past that far hill. Even in winter you cannot fail to see the bounty of the land."

"How romantic you've become."

"You cannot know the peace of a country evening in these hills, the troubled border not in sight, newspapers folded, the lights remote and random in the embracing darkness. No one can take this from us. Watch—"

As she spoke, a gold light of early dusk suffused the heavens, a slow, magnificent winter light. The red roofs of whitewashed houses appeared in the distance. And the road turned, turned again.

What would I find here? I had gone from my home, my country, the land of my birth to retrieve my portion.

We walked up the narrow path through the fields, and Gali greeted each person she met by name. A woman in her garden. One accompanying children.

"Peace be with you," Gali said.

"And with you," each replied.

A little girl whispered her question.

"She wants to know to whom you belong. I claimed you," Gali told me.

Even as we stood, night's quick descent overtook us. A harsh cold struck my tired flesh.

"In the morning you'll meet the others," my cousin said. "Now you must rest."

I thought I would lie in frigid terror beneath a stranger's sheets, but Gali lent me her own room, setting me beneath a heavy quilt. Neither the scratching branches at my window, the erratic wind, nor the foreign bird and animal sounds assailed me. I was surprised by shelter, under the protection of a kinswoman.

The smell of boiled coffee woke me. It was early, barely first light in the uncurtained window. When I went into the kitchen, the cold tile stinging my bare feet, Gali had already been to work.

"If you don't mind," she said, "perhaps you'll follow me. Go where I go and do as I do, for the only way to understand the rhythm of the day is by doing. I began in the factory, but today we start preparing the garden. When you're thirsty, you can share what we have, and when you're hungry, you can eat."

"Why have you taken me in?"

Gali stopped pouring. "When you go back, I want you to have, stamped in the flesh, the covenant of these fields. I know what you did, what you tried to do, for my father."

"This is quite a transformation," I had to point out.

"I needed to be home," she said simply. "For your successes, your past failings, I can offer this refuge, in praise of what you've undertaken."

On the threshhold of the house, I surveyed the empty fields, unfenced at my feet, to the edge of the hills. "Is it safe?" I asked my cousin.

"Try," she said, "to cast off the habit of American thought."

The sharp smell of the land, its badge of identity, was like a young man's touch. Beneath my padded body, the stuffing of my borrowed navy jacket, I felt Ishai near me, his skin's smell corresponding in unnatural recall to this revealed morning's. I saw his body made of this earth, arising limb by formed limb in naked splendor, stained from the soil's pigment, inhabited. I wanted to stake my claim to his nakedness, the one like no other, but here, not longed-for across a separating ocean, not in exile.

All morning I did as Gali directed. We were planting bulbs by hand, turning the furrows in symmetrical rows, bending and straightening for hours in the still, gray light. When I wanted to be with her, I worked beside her, and when I wanted to be alone, she let me be.

The clotted roots we sunk into the earth would turn into flowers, sold as luxuries in European markets.

And in my head, Ishai's body was flowering, his flesh, the substance of him, in my hands. At my side, Ishai was matching me motion for motion, and in bed, tonight, his back was bending and straightening over me. Within this reverie I was not angry. He had not failed me or himself as, joined skin to skin, we lay in Gali's house.

∾

On the high hills there was nothing to occlude the light. Despite the wintry chill, it was possible to believe that the fields would yield barley and wheat, the garden bud and flower as the days grew warm.

I felt, beneath my workman's gloves, the thin gold of the wedding band I'd retrieved.

"If he deserted you," Gali said, "why would you want him back? He's weak."

"Sometimes there is strength even in retreat. He didn't want to be a hero."

"Please," she said. "Shouldn't each of us be a hero in the only life we have?"

"Your father tried to make me one, and I fled."

"Then you and Ishai deserve each other," she said.

"Wait until you marry," I told her, "and see how humbling it is to pledge honorably and fail to keep your pledge."

"As you can see, I'd rather build with inanimate materials."

"You would not desert this land," I pointed out. "In marrying him, I wed unknowingly the place he came from, embodied in him." The texture of his skin, the hardness of muscle and bone forged here to protect this place. The home he was to have been.

We worked steadily. The sky over us was silent, large, the hills unfolding to the hidden sea. How simple it would be to despair of him, but displacement had stirred my curiosity. I wanted the completion of our story. Without concluding words there would be no solution to the puzzlement of our impetuous union.

And yet I did not know how to begin. I could not beseech again, nor lure him falsely.

"Don't misunderstand," Gali said suddenly. "It's true, I do despise him for not finishing what he began. But I want rest for you from turmoil. If he can repair what he severed, or if you can— Perhaps you can win him still."

I shook my head. "I don't want to seduce him into fulfilling a vow we made years ago, in partial knowledge."

"All vows are made in partial knowledge," Gali said.

I looked down ruefully at my muddy boots and unidentifiable body. "He'd have to want me truly."

She looked thoughtful.

"Even if he wanted me," I said, "he could not find me."

"Anyone can be found, as long as he or she's not dead."

Could Ishai cast off the dross we had become, bare himself to me as I'd first encountered him, the boy my uncle had sent on a mission? There was no knowing an abstract man, the one I'd married, then dismissed. But if I flew back to him, I would be lost.

I pictured my aunt, sitting alone, cut off from the imperfect flesh that had been her rescuer, my uncle, flawed. Only the earth was permanent, nothing else. No great love would transform Ishai and me. No myth could be invented now to save us. Even if all his life he toiled far from home, to this dust he would some day, as dust, return. When the harvest ended, months hence, my questioning would again begin: how to build a house, whether to be a temporary dweller or construct a life of fidelity to what I had uncovered, the hidden spring in the heart of my father, a romance my mother must have perceived beneath his forthright manner.

If Ishai did return, we'd hardly live under our fig and vine, not in a country at war with its neighbors and itself, riven by dispute. A day of work in the garden might augur paradise, but soon circumstance, headlines, would force their entry. This interlude, Gali's real life, was not my own. And even she would have to return sometimes to her aging mother in Jerusalem.

What would my parents have advised? I heard my mother urging me: "Believe." And my father's, "You must do what seems wise."

But I had acted to the extent I could. There was one weapon remaining in my arsenal: faith, that the choice I had made blindly then was also prophecy. Now neither impatience nor anxiety would hasten the resolution of this drama.

As I walked back to Gali's house in the deepening afternoon, I feared nothing. I washed myself in bracing water and prepared for dinner. Gali was at a meeting, and so I dawdled, shivering, elated, anointing myself with perfume, discarding the dull work clothes for something festive.

The air was brittle, and the early stars pierced the darkening sky, a new day being born within the dusk. Sitting beside Gali as we ate, I felt an unfamiliar peace. My cousin teased me about my changing face, my holiday clothes. "Will you be all right tonight?" she said. "I won't be back until very late."

I smiled at her.

"You're fine," she assessed.

"If I go along the road beyond this door, where will it take me?"

"There's a movie at the assembly house." Gali was reluctant. "But you don't know your way."

"Point me in the right direction. I can't be lost."

"Follow this road until it ends," Gali said, "and then turn right along the little path. If you keep walking straight, you'll reach the movie."

The air seared my chest as I cut through the dark. I was imagining another season, summer, when a woman might linger, inhaling the fragrant night. Instead of tightening her skin, she might stretch contentedly, taking everything in.

I strode with such vigor that those I passed were too startled to say goodnight. What was the hurry? Where could I be running when the day's work was done?

From the blackness loomed the outline of the assembly house. The lights already flickered for the beginning of the film. I stood at the door, not sure if I wanted to go in. The cold had banished my dreamy state, but as soon as I loosened my coat, languor resumed. I knew the movie, a love story in another tongue. But tonight— This night had moment, gravity, which I dared not dispel. I did not want to escape into an invented couple's predicament. I wanted to be home, to rest in the shelter of human arms. I wanted to be known, flesh on flesh.

Approaching Gali's house, I felt myself shaken. The door was open. The moon had risen above the hill, casting its brilliant light over the stillness. No sound came from the small house as I stood on the threshhold, listening.

A breath withdrawn filled and emptied me. I moved forward to my room, enchanted. The window was full of moon, the floor, the single chair, the bed. Heaps of bedclothes I'd disturbed when I woke formed an elaborate landscape. As I watched, they assumed charmed shapes, animals and figurines. And then the figure of a man.

He had laid himself down at the edge of the bed. I slipped off my shoes and quietly I came to him. I uncovered his legs. I lay down next to him.

At midnight he woke up, startled to find me there. "Who are you?" he said. He couldn't see.

"Isa." Your wife. Your friend.

He spread his covers over me. "Bless you for bringing me here," he said. "It is a good deed you've done. Now, whatever you ask—"

I was listening to him speak.

"You are the warrior," Ishai said. "You fought for me. Lie with me this night, and in the morning we will decide together what to do. And with God's help I will honor my pledge to you."

All through the night I lay beside him as he slept. My mind imagined many things, portraits of my mother and my father, phrases to my uncle, never uttered, my wedding ceremony, the words Ishai and I had once exchanged. Years of conversation, then silence, as I felt his blood beating its pulse through me.

5

*"Like Rachel and Leah, Both of Whom
Built Up the House of Israel"*

RUTH 4:11

$\mathcal{T}$HE INVOCATION of Rachel and Leah toward the end of the Book of Ruth gives rise to a series of meditations on the relationship between Ruth and these two matriarchs as well as other biblical mothers. In articulating the continuity between this story and narrative patterns and themes in the Bible as a whole, the writers in this section enable us to appreciate Ruth's importance within a larger biblical scheme. All three essays also push feminist analysis of the Bible one step further. Recognizing the Bible's patriarchal character, these writers nevertheless uncover surprising antipatriarchal, even feminist, perspectives in the most intractably male-centered dimensions of the text.

The invocation of the matriarchs comes in the form of a blessing spoken by the men of Bethlehem and literally represents patriarchal desire—"May the Lord make the woman coming into your house like Rachel and Leah." Francine Klagsbrun liberates this invocation from its narrow frame by exploring the actual relationship between Rachel and Leah. By juxtaposing the apparently ideal relationship between two women in Ruth to the seemingly competitive and unhappy relationship between two women in Genesis, Klagsbrun allows us to better appreciate the complexity of both the sister and the sisterly relationships. By the end of her essay, both pairs of women are liberated from the narrow frames to which they have often been constrained.

The desire for children, a prominent motif in the Rachel and Leah story, is, as Klagsbrun details, an underlying motif in all of Ruth and Naomi's actions. Granting the validity of a feminist critique which sees this narrative pattern as a representation of women's incorporation of patriarchal values, Klagsbrun nevertheless refuses to dismiss these women "simply as products of patriarchy." She imagines the possibility of women's experience of their children as an expression of intimacy with the divine and identification with national purposes.

The shaping of a nation, according to Adele Berlin, is the overarching theme of the Hebrew Bible, a theme which, she suggests, reaches a critical moment in the Book of Ruth. Berlin draws out the connections between this story and the rest of the history of Israel as a developing nation, showing that the Book of Ruth forms a "bridge between the era of Israel as a family or tribe and Israel as [a] nation" settled on its own land. Ruth and Naomi belong in the company of other biblical women, Rachel and Leah among them, who take responsibility for the continuity of the family (which represents the people here) and the guardianship of its lineage.

Sylvia Fishman writes about the courage and ingenuity of biblical women who overcome obstacles and achieve seemingly impossible goals. She resists a feminist analysis that criticizes the guile and trickery these women frequently rely upon and sees their manipulativeness as the patriarchal text's denigration of women. Fishman characterizes both men's and women's heroism in the Bible in terms of the goals being fought for rather than in terms of the means of fighting. She suggests that if we can conceive of plotting as an appropriate strategy for certain forms of struggle, we come closer to the biblical author's understanding of this behavior and the women who relied upon it.

Ruth and the
Continuity of Israel

ADELE BERLIN

The Book of Ruth is a short self-contained story, unconnected to the narrative sequence from Genesis through Kings. Its protagonists, Naomi, Ruth, and Boaz, are not mentioned elsewhere in the Bible (except for the listing of Boaz in a genealogy in Chronicles). And its various placements among the biblical books—in Christian Bibles after Judges and in Jewish Bibles among the five scrolls in the Writings—suggest that it does not fit intuitively into a specific slot. That is not to say that Ruth is an anomaly. On the contrary, I propose that its thematic connections with the rest of the Bible are much stronger than we generally perceive. The fact that the Book of Ruth is traditionally read on the festival of Shavuot, the time of the giving of the Torah, should alert us to possible connections with the Torah. But, alas, both the usual explanation (that Shavuot celebrates the grain harvest which forms the setting for Ruth) and various lesser-known explanations (that David, a descendant of Ruth, died on Shavuot or that Ruth's loyalty to Naomi symbolizes Israel's loyalty to the Torah) touch only upon superficial connections or are clearly midrashic attempts to find a connection. I will set forth a much more fundamental and far-reaching link between Ruth and the Torah—indeed, the entire Bible—a link which goes to the very heart of the overarching theme of the Bible.

The theme which gives continuity to the books from Genesis

The author used her own translation of the Book of Ruth.

through Kings, and informs much of the Prophets and the Writings, is *the land and the people*. This theme forms the covenant in which God tells Abraham, "Raise your eyes and look out from where you are, to the north and south, to the east and west, for I give all the land that you see to you and your offspring forever. I will make your offspring as the dust of the earth, so that if one can count the dust of the earth, then your offspring too can be counted" (Genesis 13:14–16). The early chapters of Genesis are a prologue to this covenant, describing the creation of all the land in the world and all of its peoples, until the narrative comes to focus on one particular family, the family of Abraham. The rest of Genesis concentrates on the growth of this family (the theme of people), flirting intermittently with the theme of the land, as the patriarchs move within it and outside of it. By the end of Genesis the family is extensive, but is settled in Egypt. At the beginning of Exodus the family is transformed into a people (*am bnei yisrael,* "the Israelite people," Exodus 1:9), and the narrative from Exodus to Deuteronomy is concerned with getting this people to the land which it has been promised. The Former Prophets continue the story of the vicissitudes of the people in its land, until the end of Kings when Judah is exiled from this land. Ezra and Nehemiah resume the story with the return to the land of Judah and the restoration of the community in it.

The Book of Ruth, too, speaks to the issue of exile and return. Like Abraham, and like the family of Jacob, the family of Elimelech was forced to leave its home in the land of Israel in time of famine and to seek to preserve itself in a foreign land. When the famine was over, Naomi returned to Bethlehem. This was far from a casual move, and indeed the theme of returning is emphasized in chapter 1 by the repetition of the root *shuv,* "return," twelve times, as Naomi bids her daughters-in-law return to their families and returns to her land, accompanied by Ruth. Technically Ruth cannot return to Bethlehem, since she has never been there before. Her return is really Naomi's return, with which she becomes joined. This is the characteristic by which Ruth is known in Bethlehem: "the one who returned with Naomi" (1:22; 2:6).

The theme of land is picked up later in the book in two ways. One is the physical connection that is established between Ruth and her newly adopted land as she gleans in the field of Boaz. The other, a more complicated matter, is the fact, sprung suddenly on the reader, that there exists a parcel of land that once belonged to Elimelech and that it is being offered for sale or redemption by Naomi. This transaction raises some legal questions, but the important point is that the *proper inheritance of land* is a concept of major importance in the Bible. Land was not to be alienated from its original owner or his descendants. This principle lies behind many of the Bible's laws and narratives, from the division of property between Lot and Abraham, to the claims of the daughters of Tzelofchad (Numbers 27), to the laws of the sabbatical and jubilee years (Leviticus 25), to the story of Nabot (1 Kings 21). Most germane to Ruth is the institution of the *goel*, the "redeemer," who, according to Leviticus 25:25, must redeem landholdings that his kinsman was forced to sell because of economic necessity. Seen against this background, the references to land in the Book of Ruth not only provide the setting for a pastoral romance, they link the story to the biblical theme of land, both private land and the land of Israel.

More prominent than the theme of land in the Book of Ruth is the theme of family and people. This is marked, first of all, by the ties that bind Naomi and Ruth. After the death of their husbands, Elimelech and Mahlon, the two women do not constitute a family in any legal or practical sense. They have no legal obligation to each other and can offer no mutual protection or support. More to the point, neither seems to have the ability to reconstitute the family by producing a child who will become the heir. It is therefore entirely appropriate that Naomi pleads with her widowed daughters-in-law to return to their original Moabite families, and it is entirely appropriate that Orpah accedes to Naomi's wish. Ruth's response is extraordinary, for she is under no obligation to care for Naomi, just as Naomi, with her own extraordinary response, is under no obligation to provide for Ruth. Ruth's poetic words, "Wherever you go I will go, wherever you lodge I will lodge," are rightly famous, both for the beauty of their expression and for their sentiment. The thought behind "Your people will be my people and your God my God" is radical, because it signals that Ruth is changing her identity in a world where it was inconceivable to do so. In the ancient world there was no mechanism for religious conversion or change of citizenship; the very notion was unthinkable. Religion and peoplehood defined one's ethnic identity, and this could no more be changed than could the color of one's skin. A Moabite was always a Moabite, wherever he or she lived. And, indeed, Ruth is referred to throughout the story as "the Moabitess." But from Ruth's point of view, she is becoming an Israelitess. She is joining herself to Naomi not only on the private family level, but also on the larger national level.

In this coming together of family and peoplehood we are again reminded of the stories of the patriarchs, in which the family represents the people. In these stories the main concern is the establishment of the family line—the quest for an heir who will be designated by God as the one through whom the people of Israel will be born. The amazing thing about these stories is that, although lineage is defined through the males, it is the women who take responsibility for the continuity of the family and the guardianship of its lineage. It is the women, often despite their husbands, who ensure the birth of the next generation and direct the proper line of inheritance. Sarah, at first barren, provides a "surrogate mother" for Abraham, and later, when she bears her own son, sees to it, with God's approval, that he is the designated heir. Rebekah, too, guides the line of descent away from Esau and toward Jacob, as God had wanted. In the stories of Leah and Rachel, the issue is no longer which son will be the heir, for they are all "the children of Israel." Rather, the emphasis is on progeny. Rachel, initially barren, is jealous of Leah's ability to bear children, and so supplies her maidservant to Jacob for this purpose (as Sarah had done to Abraham). Leah, during a hiatus in her childbearing, does the same. The episode of the mandrakes shows how eager both women are to bear children. And they are successful, providing for Jacob twelve sons (and one daughter) who will father the twelve tribes—the people of Israel.

Ruth is linked to Rachel and Leah in the blessing of the townspeople as they witness Boaz's acquisition of Ruth and of the land of Elimelech and Mahlon: "May the Lord make the woman who is coming into your house like Rachel and Leah, both of whom built up the House of Israel." They add a specific reference to Judah, the founder of Boaz's tribe: "May your house be like the house of Perez whom Tamar bore to Judah." The story of Tamar and Judah is also a story of family continuity achieved by a woman. The references to Rachel, Leah, and Tamar, then, not only serve to welcome Ruth into the Judean community by linking her with the mothers of that community; they also, and most especially, lead us to view her in the mold of the heroic women who preserved the people of Israel and ensured its continuity. It is through

Ruth that the family of Naomi (strangely, the text does not put it in terms of Elimelech or Mahlon) survives and continues. The child born to Ruth and Boaz is "a son ... born to Naomi"; he will "renew her life." Ruth is better for Naomi than seven sons, for she has produced what Naomi's sons failed to produce: an heir.

An heir implies an inheritance, and in the Bible that means land. At the end of the Book of Ruth the themes of land and family, which have been meandering separately through the story, come together. Whatever the legal confusion about the obligation of the *goel* ("redeemer"), which normally did not include marrying the widow, the double obligation of redeeming the land and marrying the wife of the deceased, as specified by Boaz, serves to reunite the family with its land—"to perpetuate the name of the deceased upon his estate" (cf. the levirate law in Deuteronomy 25:5–10). The story comes full circle: the family that left its land and lost its male line has returned to its homeland and restored its male line and its patrimony.

This would be uplifting enough even on the level of an individual family; but, like the patriarchal stories, the Book of Ruth speaks to the national level as well, for this is no anonymous family being restored, but the family into which King David will be born. Just as Ruth adopts Naomi's people and God, raising the return to Bethlehem from the personal to the national, so the genealogy at the end lifts the story to the national plane. There are actually two genealogies. One begins with Obed and culminates three generations later (notice the special number, three) in David; the second goes back to Perez (the son of Judah and Tamar) and, ten generations later (again, a special number), culminates in David. David, of course, is the king of Israel. Moreover, he is the first in the Davidic dynasty, the one to whom God promised an eternal dynasty. The figure of David represents the united monarchy at its height and the promise of its existence forever. The covenant to David, like the covenant to Abraham, is an emblem of God's promise to Israel. The story of Ruth provides for David the same pattern that produced the patriarchal line and the line of Judah—namely, the perpetuation of the family through the deeds of a woman—and it thereby joins the covenant with David to the covenant with Abraham. The promise to Abraham of progeny and land is relived, as it were, in the promise to David of the dynasty and the kingdom. The theme of family continuity becomes the theme of national continuity. The Book of Ruth is the bridge between the era of Israel as family or tribe and Israel as nation. Far from being peripheral to the main narrative sequence of the Bible, Ruth dramatizes the Bible's main theme—the continuity of the people and its land.

Ruth and Naomi, Rachel and Leah

Sisters under the Skin

FRANCINE KLAGSBRUN

There is an irony that runs throughout the Bible. Consistently, brother fights brother and sister competes with sister, but outside the sibling bond, the warmest and purest friendships are portrayed in idealized sibling terms. The brothers Jacob and Esau trick and provoke each other, speak words of rage and hatred, and even in reconciliation live with an uneasy peace that separates them through most of their lives. David and Jonathan, on the other hand—the one a pretender to the throne, the other the king's son—with every reason for jealousy and mistrust, become the finest exemplars of brotherly love. "I grieve for you my brother Jonathan / You were most dear to me" (1 Samuel 1:26), David exclaims in anguish at Jonathan's death, and the rabbis explain that theirs was a love devoid of even the slightest trace of selfishness.

Like David and Jonathan, Ruth and Naomi, not sisters but mother-in-law and daughter-in-law, enjoy the most idealized of sisterly relationships. More like a big sister than a mother-in-law, Naomi guides Ruth in the ways of a woman with a man, teaching her how to dress and speak, how to be coy and seductive, how to seek a husband, almost as if Ruth had never before been wed, let alone to Naomi's son. As a

---

The author used the Jewish Publication Society edition of the Book of Ruth (Philadelphia: Jewish Publication Society, 1969).

younger sister might, Ruth idolizes Naomi and willingly follows her from one land to the next and from one way of life to another, simply accepting as fact that her elder is wiser and more worldly than she. In contrast, like Jacob and Esau, the real sisters Leah and Rachel deceive each other, compete, grow angry, and exchange harsh words.

What does the Bible mean to convey with this topsy-turvy portrayal of siblings and friends? Perhaps that friends may achieve the heights of sisterhood or brotherhood, whereas the relationships between actual brothers and sisters are too complex to be idealized. Perhaps that there is an ideal toward which sisters and brothers might strive, even if they have not yet achieved it. Perhaps that nothing in the world can be taken for granted, that even the natural order is reversible: not only is true siblinghood realized only beyond the limits of the sibling bonds, but second children invariably win out over firsts in the biblical universe. Or perhaps the biblical narratives are telling us that people and events, in life as in religious lore, are not always as they appear. If we look closely enough, we will find that the battling brothers or sisters are far more connected and the loving, idealized siblings far more complex than they seem at first blush.

Certainly this last possibility applies to biblical sisters. When I was a child studying the Hebrew texts in day school, I accepted the idyllic friendship of Ruth and Naomi as fact—and found this pair of idealized women somewhat boring. Ruth always seemed too passive for my taste, Naomi too good. I much preferred the true sisters Rachel and Leah, full-blooded, complicated, picking at each other the way my brother and I picked at each other. Those distinctions have disappeared. Now, when I examine the lives of Naomi and Ruth, I am able to see in them reflections of the lives of Leah and Rachel, and when I trace the saga of Rachel and Leah, I am able to see foreshadowings of the story of Ruth and Naomi.

What I see in both the sisters and the sisterly friends are strong women interacting with each other directly, in a manner unlike that of any other biblical women. I see in both cases women journeying together through a world over which they have little control, and together managing to control and shape that world. Ultimately, what I see in Naomi and Ruth and Leah and Rachel are two pairs of women who lived at different times and in different places but who, through the force of their determination and the sweep of history, together created the core of Jewish nationhood.

The first association to be made between these two sets of women is simply in the nature of their being. With one exception, in no other biblical narrative do we hear the voices of women speaking directly to each other. We hear fathers blessing sons and sons arguing or reconciling with each other. We hear husbands speaking to wives and occasionally wives speaking to husbands or children. We sometimes hear an angel, and sometimes even God, address a woman. But never do we hear the words Sarah says to Hagar when she offers her maidservant to her husband. Never do we hear Hagar's response or the insolence of which Sarah complains or the harsh tones with which Sarah reprimands her. Never, in the book of Samuel, do we hear the words exchanged between Hannah and Penina as they vie for the attentions of their husband Elkanah.

In almost every instance, aside from those of Leah and Rachel and Naomi and Ruth, women communicate with each other only through men or have their thoughts conveyed to us by a narrator who summarizes only enough to move an episode along. The one exception, and it is significant to our subject, comes in a single incident early in the book of Genesis. The cities of Sodom and Gomorrah have been destroyed. Lot and his family have escaped, but Lot's wife has been turned into a pillar of salt. Lot responds to the cataclysm by crawling into a cave with his two daughters. Convinced that they are the last beings on earth, the daughters conspire to sleep with their father in order to perpetuate the human race. We know nothing about them, not even their names, although we do know that before the destruction, their father had offered to hand them over to be ravaged by a wild crowd of Sodomites in order to protect a male guest in his home.

Now the sisters whisper to each other, and the elder eggs on the younger. "Come, let us make our father drink wine, and let us lie with him, that we may maintain life through our father," she says (Genesis 19:32). Two nights in a row they ply their father with drink so that the elder can sleep with him the first night and the younger the second. Both daughters become pregnant as a result of their act and give birth to the progenitors of two great nations of the world: Moab and Ammon. It is from Moab, of course, that Ruth descends, and it is Moab that she rejects when she vows to follow Naomi until death parts them.

Because the sisters' incestuous acts made Lot the ancestor of Ruth, the later rabbis did not strongly condemn any of them for their behavior. One might speculate that it is precisely and only because their act led to the eventual birth of Ruth that the Bible presents the words of one sister to the other. Their plotting had momentous import for the future of the Jewish people, making it worthy of inclusion in the biblical narrative.

How much worthier, from this point of view, are the interchanges between Rachel and Leah, and between Naomi and Ruth, for from their differences and cooperations will arise the twelve tribes of Israel and the house of David. Their dialogues and direct exchanges were doubtless considered significant enough to be recorded primarily because of their role in establishing the nation. As in most other biblical narratives concerning women, these interchanges are presented from a male perspective and focus on perpetuating the male line. Nevertheless, the words these women speak to each other and the interactions between them offer the best opportunities we have to understand them and other biblical women in relation to each other, as sisters, competitors, and friends.

Competition is what comes through most clearly in the dialogue between Rachel and Leah. Barren and longing for children, Rachel asks Leah for some of her son's mandrakes, a plant long regarded in folklore as an aphrodisiac. Leah, knowing herself to be less loved by their mutual husband, Jacob, inquires sharply why she should share her son's mandrakes with the sister who stole her husband. Finally, Rachel obtains the mandrakes only in exchange for Jacob's conjugal services for the night (Genesis 30:14–15). Rachel's words are cool and straightforward; Leah's ungiving. There appears to be little love lost between the women.

But wait. These are two women who share a husband and are part of a culture that revolves around his interests. Their interchange is an expression of the life they lead and their adaptation to it. Each sister has something the other wants and needs: Leah, the blessing of fertility; Rachel, the husband's love. In their seemingly snappish dialogue, they bargain with each other so that both give and gain something. In an earlier, parallel, biblical scene, Esau sells his birthright to Jacob in return for some lentil stew, much as Rachel barters her night with Jacob in return for some mandrakes. But Jacob and Esau become enemies, moving off in different directions. Rachel and Leah remain together, members of the same household, competing but also bargaining, negotiating, cajoling, and ultimately cooperating with each other.

We see that cooperation most clearly later when Jacob decides to leave his father-in-law's home in Paddan-aram and return with his family to his parents' land of Canaan. When he consults his wives, they respond with one voice, assuring him together of their anger at their father and their readiness to depart. Whatever the differences between them, they are united in their loyalty to Jacob and each other and their knowledge that they must take their children away from their father's influence and make their lives elsewhere.

The cooperation that is hidden between the lines in the conversation of Rachel and Leah forms the essence of the relationship between Ruth and Naomi. As it is with the sisters, each of these women has something the other desires. Naomi offers Ruth strength and confidence and a vision of possibility. She is willing to risk returning to Bethlehem, alone, unprotected, with no apparent means of support. To the younger woman she seems guided by a faith—in herself, in her people, in a Being beyond both—and Ruth is drawn to that faith. "Wherever you go, I will go," she says, hitching her wagon to Naomi's star, drinking in Naomi's strength of purpose.

For Naomi, Ruth provides youth and a chance to undo the past. "Do not call me Naomi, call me Mara" (1:20), she tells the townspeople upon arriving in Bethlehem. Like Rachel, she is angry at her emptiness and the unfairness of her lot. But instead of directing that anger toward Ruth and envying the younger woman's potential to bear a child—as Rachel envies Leah—she makes Ruth her surrogate. Ruth will replace the sons Naomi has lost—indeed, she becomes more precious to Naomi than "seven sons" (4:15)—and will bear the children Naomi no longer can.

"I must seek a home for you" (3:1), Naomi tells her young charge, and proceeds to find one in which she herself becomes of central importance. There is no fighting over mandrakes or men here. Ruth and Naomi are interlocked, ideal sisters serving each other's needs and wishes.

And yet. This relationship, as evidenced from the dialogue between the pair, is not problem-free. I still see in these sisterly women what I sensed in them as a child: Ruth's passivity, Naomi's goodness, which takes the form of directing and controlling Ruth. Ruth serves Naomi—lovingly, willingly, generously, but serves her nevertheless. Naomi dominates Ruth—with concern, deep love, and an eye to Ruth's best interests, but dominates nevertheless. Naomi is the motherly older sister, guiding Ruth's every step, directing her, and encouraging her dependency. "Where did you glean today?" she asks (2:19); "Go out with his girls" (2:22), she advises, grooming and shaping Ruth to the image she wishes.

By the end of the book, the women are settled together in the household of kindly Boaz—almost like two wives, almost like Rachel and Leah. Naomi has become nurse to Ruth's baby, Obed, who is known around town as Naomi's baby. We hear no more dialogue between them. Perhaps if we did we might discover it to be less idyllic than before. We might discover that Ruth has grown to resent Naomi's dominance over her and her child, or has given up, pushed into total submission by the power of Naomi's personality. We might discover that in its own way even this perfect friendship includes some of the imperfections of all close sisterly relationships.

From the point of view of the biblical narrator, the words spoken by Leah and Rachel and Naomi and Ruth are important for their consequences in Israelite history. But those words and the undercurrents that surround them also offer us pictures of real women whose separate journeys through life reveal as many similarities as differences.

The journey of Ruth and Naomi makes up the heart of their story. In mythology and folklore, in the Bible itself, a hero—almost always a man—undertakes a journey that transforms him as it changes his life situation. "Go forth from your native land and from your father's house" (Genesis 12:1), the Lord commands Abraham, who gives up the world he knew to obey that command. Jacob journeys from Canaan to Paddan-aram and back again, and in the process wrestles with himself and an angel as he becomes Israel, forefather of a nation. Rarely are we privy to the exterior or interior journeys of women, and almost never do we meet women who journey alone, unaccompanied by a man.

Ruth and Naomi are such women. Destitute, bereaved of her husband and sons, Naomi musters her strength and decides to return by herself to her homeland. Paralleling Abraham, Ruth leaves her home and her family to follow Naomi into the unknown. Her passionate words and her fierce act of courage and faith have resounded through history. With utter trust in a future with Naomi, she discards her old gods and ways of life, never once looking back. Descended from a people conceived through an incestuous act, she rejects all that the act and the people stood for as she turns away from her native land.

For both women the journey marks the beginning of a new life together and in society. On a previous journey Naomi had left Bethlehem "full" with husband and sons. Now she returns "empty" (1:21). A new fullness will come from Ruth, who gathers grain for food and who ends years of barrenness by bearing a child. On their own, with no one to help them, Naomi and Ruth overcome all obstacles on a journey that begins with death and bitterness and leads to redemption and rebirth.

Rachel and Leah also undertake a journey, theirs the culmination rather than the beginning of their lives together. Their journey fits a more traditional mold. They will follow their husband as he heads back toward his homeland. Unlike Ruth and Naomi, they set out with the fullness of wealth, children, and much cattle. They don't have to make their way alone. They are cared for, established, settled in their traditional roles as wives and mothers.

Yet their decision to leave their father's home has the import of Ruth's decision to leave her homeland. Jacob doesn't force them to leave. He consults them, and they instantly respond. "Surely he regards us as outsiders," they say of their father Laban. "Now then, do just as God has told you," they advise their husband (Genesis 31:15–16). Like Ruth, they are prepared to turn their backs on the practices of their people and the gods of their father.

But not completely. Rachel steals and carries off some of Laban's idols, unable, it seems, to give them up altogether. Unlike Ruth, she appears not to have the moral fiber to truly renounce her father's way of life, to follow the invisible God of whom her husband speaks. Longing for more children since the birth of her only son Joseph, she believes, perhaps, that these idols will help her become fertile again. The rabbis, looking for ways to exonerate Rachel, explain that she stole the idols in order to force her father to renounce them as well, but the text gives little indication of that.

The text does hint, however, at a different reason for the theft. Rachel hides the idols beneath a camel pillow and sits on them—hardly a sign of respect or worship. When her father comes looking for what he calls his "gods," she explains that she cannot rise to greet him because "the period of women" is upon her (Genesis 31:35). What comes through in this scene is Rachel's utter disdain for Laban and his gods. Her menstrual flow, regarded as unclean in the ancient world, is, for her, a symbol of her power to shame her father in his beliefs. As strong-minded and determined as Ruth, she tricks Laban and mocks his gods even as she rejects them and all that they embody.

Trickery, a common theme in the Bible, has, of course, been a common theme in the lives of women in all societies and all times. Lacking direct power, women use other means to achieve their goals—shrewdness, verve, wit, and just plain smarts. And because power for women traditionally comes from their identification and association with men, the shrewdness and smarts have often been applied to winning or controlling a man. Certainly trickery plays an important part in the acquisition of a husband in both the narratives of Rachel and Leah and of Ruth and Naomi, and in both cases, the women's trickery allows them not only to marry but also to remain together.

The story of Rachel and Leah begins with a trick played on their husband (himself a trickster) and ends, as we saw, with the tricking of their father. It is the first trick that leads to their most competitive moments as well as their most cooperative ones and that fixes their life together until death parts them.

Immediately upon meeting her, Jacob singles Rachel out. He kisses her, identifies himself as her cousin, and soon after agrees to work for her father to gain her hand. On what is supposed to be Rachel's wedding night, Leah replaces her younger sister in the bridal chamber, forcing Jacob to work another seven years for his beloved. Amazingly, although we hear the women speaking to each other later, we hear not a word from them at this moment, perhaps the most critical in both their lives. Did Laban simply force Rachel to step aside while he substituted her sister for her? Was Rachel devastated? Was Leah triumphant? Or did both feel victimized by a father who had no regard for the feelings of either?

The latter seems closest to reality. Years earlier, when Isaac sought Rebekah's hand, her family asked her if she wanted to leave her parental home to wed him. Laban asked his daughters no questions. He acted out of his own interests. If the sisters resented their father's actions, the best they could do was join forces to help and support each other.

I have never read the descriptions of the marriages of Rachel and Leah without feeling deep inside me that the sisters colluded in deceiving Jacob. Loved by him, but not necessarily loving him back, Rachel knew that by helping Leah she could save her older sister from the shame of not marrying first. She could also guarantee that the two would not be separated and could continue their lives together in the same household. Leah knew that by taking Rachel's place and marrying first, she could save face and also serve as her younger sister's guide and mentor in the marital sphere, much as she may have in their earlier life.

The talmudic rabbis suspected collusion. They suggested that Jacob and Rachel, fearing that Laban would substitute his elder daughter for his younger, devised a signal whereby Jacob could recognize Rachel. But at the last minute, Rachel reneged and told Leah the signal to save her from the humiliation of being rejected. I imagine the collusion was more direct. Knowing Laban's intention, Rachel and Leah decided not to fight it but to help each other so that neither became simply a pawn of their father or of Jacob. They could not have known then that their trick would lead to bitter rivalry later.

The collusion of Ruth and Naomi in using guile to win over Boaz was forced on them not by another man, but by the realities of their society. Self-sufficient as they were in their journey from Moab to Bethlehem, they could not sustain that self-sufficiency forever. Boaz became for them a means of survival and a stepping-stone into the future. As Jacob did with Rachel, Boaz singled out Ruth from the other women gleaning in the fields, revealing his interest in her by giving her special privileges. Encouraged by that interest, Naomi devised her plot to have Boaz marry Ruth and serve as her own redeeming kinsman.

Their trick is quite astonishing and daring. In a scene reminiscent of the story of Lot's daughters, Ruth waits for Boaz to become sated with food and drink. Then she lies next to him on the threshing floor as he sleeps. Like Jacob, Boaz awakes surprised to find a woman at his side. ("There was a woman lying at his feet!" the text says [3:8]; "There was Leah!" says the Genesis text [29:25].) Whatever may have transpired after that—and the text is arch about whether Boaz and Ruth consorted that night—her act of lying down at his feet is bold, shocking, almost brazen for a single woman, not long widowed. Ruth could never have conceived of it alone; Naomi could never have carried it off by herself. But by conspiring, through wit and great courage the women force Boaz to face his obligations. By working together they boldly establish a marriage for Ruth, a home for themselves, and a future filled with promise.

The man Naomi and Ruth choose as their savior is a good man, a sincere man, and a man who doesn't hold a candle to the two women in wit or courage. Boaz does what is expected of him but takes no initiative. Although the whole town is abuzz upon Naomi's return to Judah, Boaz does not step forward or reveal himself as a kinsman. Only by chance, and not by invitation, does Ruth glean in his field, though he treats her generously when he learns who she is. And only after being forced to face his responsibilities does he undertake the legal procedures that designate him as the redeeming kinsman. Methodically, he goes about the job of presenting the unnamed closer kinsman with his choices. Efficiently, he enacts the ceremony through which he "acquires" Ruth as his wife.

Boaz does the right thing. But if he feels any passion for Ruth, we hear nothing of it. In fact, one senses that of the two women, it is Naomi with whom he most closely identifies. When he first meets Ruth, he praises her for her kindness to Naomi. After spending the night with her, he sends her home with barley for her mother-in-law. Left on his own, freed of the womens' manipulations, he might one day have asked Naomi for her hand in marriage, happy to have her as a companion in his later years.

Certainly, Boaz shows no interest in the son he and Ruth have, content to have the neighbor women name the boy. After the birth, he fades into the shadows as Naomi and Ruth care for his son. A good man, and dull.

Jacob is not dull. Shrewd himself, he can out-trick anyone. And he does love Rachel passionately. But he has little interest in having children and little knowledge about how to rear them. When the sisters get entangled in a fierce competition over children and conjugal rights, Jacob remains their passive tool, following their orders about whom to sleep with and when. He is the first patriarch who takes no part in naming his children—each wife names the children born to her and her handmaiden with names that have significance only to her. More important, when Rachel, barren, cries out, "Give me children or I shall die," Jacob answers unfeelingly, "Can I take the place of God, who has denied you fruit of the womb?" (Genesis 30:1–2). He doesn't care and he doesn't want to be blamed. He is a man who stands apart from family life, involved with himself and preoccupied with his own destiny.

In both narratives, it is the women—the sisters and the sisterly companions—who see destiny in broader terms. The women, like women in all times and places, are driven to have children, and, like women in

many times and many places, they view a son as a blessing and the lack
of one as a curse, a punishment. From a feminist point of view, we would
say that they have incorporated patriarchal values, and certainly their stories are presented from a male perspective. How we long to know more
about Dinah. How we long to hear Leah's voice when her only daughter
is raped. How we cringe at Ruth's being "acquired" by Boaz along with
Naomi's property. How we wish the line were not traced only through
the men.

Still, to dismiss these women simply as products of patriarchy is to
do them an injustice. For they, through their children, are the progenitors of the Israelite people and the kingdom of David. Is it not possible
that they truly sensed within themselves a divinely directed destiny? Is
it not possible that their drive for children came not only from society
but from some deep inner conviction about the role those children
would play in the shaping of a nation?

The matriarch Sarah overheard an angel announcing to Abraham
that she would have a child. Rebekah heard God tell her that two nations were in her womb. Leah and Rachel received no divine messages.
Yet time and again they invoked God in naming their sons. "This time
I will praise the Lord" (Genesis 29:35), said Leah in naming Judah, and
the rabbis said that she was the first person since the creation of the
world to give thanks to God. Without hearing God speak, these women
nevertheless felt a bond, an intimacy with the divine that perhaps lay at
the heart of their desire for children.

For Ruth and Naomi the wish for a child to perpetuate their line un-
derlies all their actions. From the day they leave Moab they seem to be
on a trajectory leading to the moment when Ruth gives birth to Obed.
Their own natures work hand in hand with a providential plan. If Naomi leaves Moab to return to her land and people, Ruth knows that she
must be part of that land and that people. If Ruth just happens to glean
in Boaz's field, Naomi knows how to turn that happenstance into history. Strong women, they sense their destiny and are driven to fulfill it.

As Ruth and Boaz wed, the people at the gate and the elders bless
them: "May the Lord make the woman who is coming into your house
like Rachel and Leah, both of whom built up the house of Israel!"
(4:11). The blessing is for Ruth, for fruitfulness and good fortune, and
it places her on a plane with the matriarchs of Israel. But the blessing
is also something more. It is a statement of recognition and relation-

ship. Aside from their own narratives in the book of Genesis, the names
of Rachel and Leah appear together only here in the Bible. And that is
fitting, for this is where they belong, here with Ruth and Naomi, with
whom they have much in common.

Like Rachel and Leah, Ruth and Naomi have a sisterly bond. If
theirs is more idealized than the bond between the real sisters, it still includes the realities of sisterly love and sisterly tensions. Like Rachel and
Leah, Ruth and Naomi abandon a land of idol worshipers, Naomi to
return home, Ruth to adopt a new homeland, another God. Like Rachel and Leah, Ruth and Naomi use courage and guile to achieve their
ends in a world in which women have few options for surviving on
their own. Like Rachel and Leah, Ruth and Naomi are driven to shape
the destiny of their people. They may not be fully aware of that destiny,
but their strength and determination bring it about.

In Genesis, the narratives of Leah and Rachel, intense though they
are, are secondary to the narrative of Jacob and his transformation into
Israel. In contrast, in Ruth, the narrative centers around two women
and the lives they pursue. Even when the child Obed is born, he is
hailed as the son of Ruth and Naomi, not of Boaz. Then suddenly, in
the last few sentences, the narrative switches, the women disappear, and
we are back in the world Rachel and Leah inhabited, the world of the
fathers—of Jacob who begat Judah who begat Perez, and from Perez we
follow the line to Boaz and Obed and David, who became king.

The Book of Ruth ends with the birth of David. But the story itself
has not yet ended. For, it is said, from the house of David will come
the Messiah. And when she does, she will be the descendant of Ruth
and Naomi and of Rachel and Leah and of the daughters of Lot, who
wanted to re-create humanity. When she comes, she, too, will shape the
destiny of her people.

Soldiers in an Army of Mothers

Reflections on Naomi and the Heroic Biblical Woman

Sylvia Barack Fishman

Authors who draw closely on Jewish tradition often extol interfering or manipulative mothers, provided that those women have at heart the good of their families and the Jewish people. For example, when the Yiddish novelist Sholem Asch depicts his heroine Rachel-Leah Hurvitz in the novel *Three Cities*, he glorifies her for engineering the lives of almost everyone around her and compares her explicitly and implicitly to many female biblical figures. Rachel-Leah takes responsibility not only for her family, but also for her husband's students and the sickly and impoverished among her neighbors. Asch names his heroine Rachel-Leah, after the two matriarchs who together gave birth to the Jewish people. When Rachel-Leah's children are exiled, she works fearlessly for their release; when she cannot free them, like the biblical Rachel she weeps for their distance and their suffering. Although she and her husband have joined the emancipated Jews of Warsaw and consider themselves to be apostates, Rachel-Leah's daily activities replicate the activities of the *eshet chayil*, the proverbial "woman of valor" who cares for her family and the community (Proverbs 31). Asch hastens to assure the reader that Rachel-Leah thrives on this regime, emphasizing her vigorous self-esteem.

The author used her own translation of the Book of Ruth.

None of these allusions to biblical matriarchs and female allegorical figures is surprising in the work of a Yiddish writer whose youthful education steeped him in biblical texts. But Asch gives an unusual military twist to the descriptions of his heroine: "Full-bosomed and ripe, she advanced like a soldier in an army of mothers, knowing her duty and her own value."[1] When her family and community are threatened, Rachel-Leah leads a hungry, angry, and frightened group of assorted poor people, patriots, and socialists in open confrontation with armed soldiers on horseback. Asch's curious comparison of his idealized Jewish matron to a soldier can be seen as an alternate reading of the term *eshet chayil*—usually translated as "woman of valor" or "worthy woman"—as literally a "soldier woman." When he called Rachel-Leah "a soldier in an army of mothers," Asch saw in biblical women and in the European women he knew soldiers in the army of divine providence, soldiers in the army of God.

In contrast, many modern American readers have had negative reactions to aggressive mothers. Societal standards influence how we respond both to living persons with whom we interact in daily life and to literary characters. Americans often regard people who accomplish their goals covertly with suspicion and disapproval. Many modern observers dislike both literary and real-life mothers who scheme behind the scenes. They are treated with satirical scorn by mid-twentieth-century misogynist authors, such as Philip Wylie and Philip Roth, who see manipulative mothers as power-hungry matriarchs who emasculate their husbands and sons.[2] They are also regarded with disdain by some feminist theorists, who see mothers' manipulative behavior emerging out of frustration with the real powerlessness of women.[3] This disapproval of behind-the-scenes engineering extends to women in the Bible. Influenced by a societal disapproval of manipulativeness and covertness, especially in women, some contemporary readers are impatient with biblical women who accomplish their goals by tricking or convincing others to carry out plots.

Biblical narratives, however, approve of women who plot—and control the plot—outwitting historical circumstance or defying human authority in the service of Jewish destiny. Thus, the Bible depicts women of very different types who act independently. They include Tamar, who uses her sexuality to take her rightful place in the lineage of the tribal dynasty through a complex scenario, compelling the autocratic Judah to see and admit his error; Hannah, who rejects her husband's insistence that his love should compensate for their infertility and prays to God on her own behalf most effectively; and Esther, the secretive beauty who, once challenged by her uncle Mordecai to save the Persian Jews, plots to outwit a powerful monarch and a Machiavellian villain. Each of these women, like Asch's Rachel-Leah Hurvitz, is challenged by destiny to come out and do battle. And each courageously follows her own personal, inner-directed yet divinely ordained goals.

This broad spectrum of enterprising women provides a context for women who exceed mere independence, such as Rebekah, Jochebed, and Naomi. These three women are not just soldiers but generals in the service of destiny. Faced with developments which they recognize as contrary to God's plan or the best interests of their families, they, rather than the men around them, analyze the situation, plot, plan, and direct others in order to bring about the desired future.

By acting vigorously to change unacceptable circumstances, Rebekah, Jochebed, and Naomi act very much within the Jewish ethos. Jewish tradition seldom rewards passive or docile acceptance of an unfair fate at mortal hands. Acceptance may be appropriate when God tests (Abraham, Isaac, Job) or punishes (Miriam, David, the Israelite exiles). But active opposition is rewarded within biblical narratives as a response to human attempts to thwart God's will. The nature of the human obstacle and the status of the activist determine the most effective response. Both force and deception are seen as appropriate, active responses to threatening situations in biblical texts. Ensuring the survival of those who serve God is seen as a primary virtuous act and the foundation upon which all other virtuous acts are based. When acting for purely selfish ends, however, even a heroic general is culpable and punishable. Thus, when David sends Uriah the Hittite to his doom in order to protect Bathsheba and keep her for himself, he earns the prophet Nathan's castigation and loses his beloved son.

"The deeds of the fathers are a sign of what will happen to their sons" is a primary principle of Jewish exegetical interpretation. Much more is revealed, however, if we invoke a parallel, feminine version of the same principle: "the deeds (experiences, concerns) of the mothers are a sign of what will happen to their sons and daughters." Rebekah, Jochebed, and Naomi take up arms against fate and change the shape of history, rather than passively accepting what they perceive as outrageous fortune. Their activism is rewarded in biblical and later traditional Jewish texts; they succeed in their goals, and their progeny become the Israelite people's most respected leaders.

Viewing the behavior of these female "generals" in the light of military strategy provides interesting insights into their status in biblical texts. Even those who demand that human relationships be consistently open and aboveboard would never require a strategist to dispatch soldiers to come out, stand in a row, and "fight fair"—only to be mowed down. Indeed, such a leader would be judged not only foolish but responsible for the failure of the mission and the destruction of the troops. Women such as Naomi, Rebekah, and Jochebed are gifted strategists whom history has placed in subordinate or compromised positions. They understand the factors which motivate people and are able to seize opportunities and act on them. Yet they are not opportunists, because they act to further not their own interests but the interest of Jewish peoplehood.

Rebekah's pregnancy becomes a nightmare. While her two sons are still in her womb, she feels them warring. Distraught over what she feels within her, alone and almost overwhelmed, she questions the very purpose of her existence: "If things are going to be this way, what am I here for?" Her response to this pain is to ask God what is happening to her. God answers her directly: "Two nations are in your womb, and two separate peoples will be separated from your innards, and one people will be stronger than the other people, and the older one will serve the younger one" (Genesis 25:23).

From her painful, intuitive, and God-given understanding of the spiritual chasm between her two sons, Rebekah later draws the strength to do what she sees needs to be done. Over the years, she observes differences in character between the two boys that Isaac either doesn't see, or chooses not to acknowledge or react to. Perhaps God's in utero revelation sensitizes her to clues and signals about their personalities and value systems; in any case, the things she observes reinforce her earlier experiences. The biblical text comments, for example, that both Isaac and Rebekah feel a "bitterness of spirit" because of Esau's two foreign wives, and yet Isaac does not seem to make a connection between his misgivings about Esau's marital choices and his appropriateness as a spiritual heir. Isaac's preparations to give the birthright to Esau follow immediately upon his "bitterness of spirit."

The situation which faces Rebekah is not one that she can confront directly because of the patriarchy and primogeniture which are fixed aspects of the social structure of her times. But she does not allow her status as a wife and Jacob's as a second-born son to intimidate her from acting on the realities she sees. She knows that Esau lacks qualities necessary to carry on the covenantal spiritual heritage, and she knows that without financial backing, those who are to spread the spiritual heritage cannot flourish. Rebekah believes that in her household only one son can inherit the covenant and be given the birthright blessing. The son appropriate to that responsibility is Jacob. God has told her the outcome but not how she can accomplish it. So Rebekah the strategist plans exactly what must be done. She gives Jacob his orders. She takes upon her head even the curse which he may be provoking in deceiving his father (27:6–13).

Rebekah's position as a proactive spiritual ancestor to future Jewish men and women is reinforced by the fact that many motifs in the biblical description of her life are paralleled in the descriptions of her son Jacob's life. The incidents and themes which unite the lives of mother and son are rich and multilayered, often resonating in ironic or poignant ways. For example, Rebekah's lonely confrontation with the painful wrestling within her womb leads her to a direct encounter with God; this encounter gives her the direction and strength to pursue a sometimes devious path to ensure the continuation of the covenantal line. Similarly, after a lonely night wrestling with an unknown force, Jacob is injured near his groin, but in the morning he encounters God. The Midrash says that the force with which Jacob wrestles, which leads to his encounter with God, may be Esau. Thus, Jacob and Esau wrestle in Rebekah's womb and again in Jacob's night vision, with each struggle leading to a revelation experience.

Several incidents, attitudes, and behaviors in Rebekah's life are paralleled by Jacob's dealings with his brother Esau and his uncle Laban, tying the characters of Rebekah and Jacob even more closely together. Just as Rebekah disguises Jacob so that he will appear to be his brother Esau and receive the desired blessing from his blind father, Laban veils Leah so that she will seem to be her sister Rachel and become Jacob's bride. Jacob, utilizing Rebekah's legacy of manipulating appearances to increase his gain, appropriately outwits Laban by causing the livestock to be born with special markings that define the animals as his property.

Later, Laban claims that Jacob's entire household, including the wives, children, and livestock Jacob has worked years to earn, should revert to him. Laban's angry attempt to rescind his previous agreement with Jacob evokes the earlier triangle of Rebekah, Jacob, and Esau; it recalls Esau's initial willingness to sell his birthright—ironically, Esau echoes Rebekah's words, *lama zeh li* (here meaning, "what do I need it for")—which Esau subsequently ignores when he angrily demands the same birthright which he had sold to his brother.

Jacob's difficult wanderings through a sometimes overtly and sometimes subtly hostile world resonated for Jewish readers. Jacob was not only renamed Israel, but became the symbol of the Jewish people in the minds of Jews. As a people more often than not in positions of subordination or vulnerability, Diaspora Jews could identify closely with Jacob's predicaments and his particular methods for dealing with a destiny which threatened him, his family, and his way of life. God's consolatory words to Jacob—"Do not fear, my servant Jacob," *al tira avdi ya'akov*—echoed and consoled his descendants.

Jochebed, along with her daughter Miriam, both of whom served as midwives, according to the Midrash, battle the brutality of an infanticidal Pharaoh and the depressed passivity of Jewish husbands who are afraid to produce more children. Through their efforts, not only Moses, the leader, but indeed an entire generation of Israelites who fled Egypt into the desert are born and sheltered. Jochebed sees immediately that her own newborn is "a good child" (Exodus 2:3). Facing the almost certain death of her infant after rescuing a generation of Jewish children, Jochebed devises a watertight boat of branches and reeds to cradle him. Against all odds, her scheme works. Although an Egyptian princess adopts Moses, with Miriam's help Jochebed is able to reclaim, nurse, and nurture her own infant.

As an adult, Jochebed's son, Moses, sometimes experiences and says things which echo his early life with his mother. Moses encounters God within the branches of an ever-burning bush. Later, he confronts God himself with a riddle: Who has been the mother to the Jewish people, Moses or God? "Did I conceive these people? Did I give birth to them? Why do you say that I should carry them in my bosom like a nursing father, carrying them to the land which you promised to their fathers?" (Numbers 11:12). When God offers to destroy the Jewish people and leave only the descendants of Moses, however, Moses declines vehemently. In the tradition of the mother who risked her life daily to save a generation of Jews, Moses tells God that he does not care to have his descendants survive unless God saves and protects the people themselves. Moses thus became, in the Jewish mind, the model of the selfless leader, a man totally devoted to his people, who risks all on their behalf.

Like Rebekah and Jochebed, Naomi plays a role closely tied to themes of childbirth and Jewish continuity. And like them, her contribution to the Jewish people begins with a terrifying episode which gives her the strength to act behind the scenes, directing a complicated and potentially dangerous sequence of action.

Almost from the beginning of the Book of Ruth, Naomi becomes the reference point of the narrative. Her name appears early; she is first mentioned as the wife of Elimelech (1:2), but by the third verse Elimelech is being identified as "Naomi's husband" (1:3). It is Naomi, we are told, who is bereft of her children and husband (1:5), who hears that the famine has ended and decides to return to her homeland (1:7), and who convinces one daughter-in-law but not the other to return to their own homes.

Ruth's attachment to the Jewish religion, the Jewish people, and the Jewish destiny is initially an attachment to Naomi. The language of her attachment echoes language often used to describe attachment to God: "And Ruth cleaved to her" and "[Naomi] saw that [Ruth] was strengthened [in the will] to go with her" (1:14, 18). It is significant that the word *davak* (cleave) is often used to prescribe how a human being should relate to God and is also used in Genesis to prescribe a man's successful transition from love of his parents to love of his wife (Genesis 2:24).

Naomi's motherhood and maternal bereavement is a recurring motif throughout the book. When Naomi returns with Ruth to Israel and is surrounded by her old friends and acquaintances, she tells them, "Don't call me Naomi, call me Mara—bitterness—for God has dealt very bitterly with me. I went out [of this place] full, and the Lord has brought me back empty. Why should you call me Naomi, since God has spoken against me and done evil to me" (1:20–21). A midrash suggests that Naomi was pregnant when she left her homeland. The evil which God has done to Naomi, albeit late in her life, is to make her childless—a condition which ties her closely to the infertility of the matriarchs and other biblical heroines.

Although Naomi moves behind the scenes for much of the narrative, she directs the action throughout. Each major character is identified through her (see 1:22, 2:1, 2:6). Ruth eagerly informs Naomi at each step of the plot, tells her what has transpired, and follows her advice about what to do next. When Naomi thinks it is time for Ruth to initiate action, she prefaces her detailed advice with a declaration that her motivation is concern not for her own but for Ruth's well-being: "My daughter, I would like to see you situated happily and safely." She then tells Ruth exactly what she should do: "Wash and perfume yourself, put on your cloak and go down to the threshing floor, but don't let Boaz know that you are there until he finishes eating and drinking. When he lies down, notice exactly where he is, then go in to that place, lift up the covering at his feet, and lie down." This is certainly unusual advice for a virtuous older woman to give an equally virtuous younger one, but Ruth answers unhesitatingly, "I will do whatever you tell me to" (3:1–5).

During the night Boaz wakes and is startled to discover the woman at his feet. Ruth reveals her identity to him and asks for his protection. He answers her in honorable fashion, praising her kindness because she has sought for a husband not a man closer to her own age, but himself, as a next of kin. He calls her *eshet chayil*, woman of valor, or soldier-woman, and urges her to be prudent, remaining safely until dawn but leaving before she can be seen and recognized. The scene's sexual possibilities are obvious, but the storyteller deliberately evokes and then dismisses them. When Ruth returns to Naomi with a gift of barley which Boaz has placed in her cloak, Naomi greets her with the question, *"Mi at biti?"* ("Who are you, my daughter?") While some contemporary translators read this as "How did things go, my daughter," Midrash Rabba on Ruth underscores Naomi's awareness of the riskiness of her plan. The Midrash says her question really means "You left here a chaste woman. Are you still a chaste woman?" Ruth immediately tells Naomi "everything the man had done," the biblical text continues, and then adds, "He gave me these six measures of barley . . . he wouldn't let me come home empty-handed to my mother-in-law." Naomi is satisfied and tells Ruth to bide her time quietly. "The man will not rest until he has completed the matter today," Naomi predicts (3:16–18).

When Ruth and Boaz are married and have a son, it is Naomi rather than Ruth who is restored as a mother in Israel. Her friends come to her and say, "Your daughter-in-law, who loves you, who is better to you than seven sons, has given birth [to a son]." And the narrative continues, "Naomi took the child, and laid it in her bosom, and became a nurse to it. And the women, her neighbors, talked about it and said, 'There is a son born to Naomi' " (4:14–17).

She who was bitter because she was bereaved of her sons mothers a new son, and this son is the grandfather of David, the psalmist and the king. David's life and poetry have interesting parallels to Naomi's experiences. Within the lyrical songs of David are echoes both of Naomi's dejection and of her restoration. David's early exile in and outside his land recalls Naomi's wanderings. Perhaps most strikingly, David's deep friendship with Jonathan parallels the deep friendship between Ruth and Naomi. David's passionate friendship with his brother-in-law is sweeter to him "than the love of women," just as Naomi's daughter-inlaw is "better to her than seven sons."

Each general in this biblical army of mothers makes it possible for the aristocratic line of the Jewish people to continue and flourish. But mothers such as Rebekah, Jochebed, and Naomi transcend their roles as enablers of future generations. The inner lives of these women as described in the biblical text, share in and foreshadow the divinely ordained trials of the men whose futures they guarantee. Jacob, Moses, and David are men whose images have been larger than life in the Jewish imagination, men who wander and struggle with morally difficult situations. Thus, when sly Laban's malevolent control threatens to rob Jacob and his descendants of freedom and their rightful payment for years of labor, Jacob's active opposition takes the form of deception and subversiveness—the only effective weapons against such hypocritical tyrants. When Pharaoh calls on magicians to oppose Moses (and God) and repeatedly goes back on his word, Moses indulges in magic tricks as well and does not tell the whole truth about his agenda for the enslaved people. Even David, a man certainly not lacking in military prowess and confrontational abilities, poses as a madman and hides in caves when these tactics will guarantee his survival. Each of these men displays the deep emotions and courage, and many of the survival skills, of his physical and spiritual mothers.

Historically, Jews as individuals and as a nation have often felt that their physical and spiritual survival depended on their battling an unfair destiny with any means at hand. Forbidden to study the Torah, they studied in secret. Barred from agricultural and artisan's guilds, they lent money, collected taxes, and worked as peddlers and middlemen. Op pressed, they fought back when they could and sometimes forfeited their own lives in active—if desperate—responses, outwitting human authorities to serve God's will and guarantee the survival of His word. When such Jews read and thought and sang about Jacob and Moses and David, their biblical ancestors, they saw their own lives foreshadowed. They identified with the biblical figures, and this identification made their lives more meaningful and more bearable.

Curiously, however, the parallels between the experiences and responses of Rebekah and Jacob, and Jochebed and Moses, and Naomi and David have been little noted. Perhaps even more significantly, women such as Rebekah, Jochebed, and Naomi have not attained places in the popular Jewish imagination commensurate with those occupied by their sons. Despite their poignant predicaments and valiant responses, they are seldom seen to symbolize Jewish history and the Jewish psyche. When Jews historically sat in the Succah, no brave biblical women were invited in among the honored historical guests, called *ushpizin*, who symbolize the suffering and triumphant survival of the Jewish people and the Jewish spirit.[4]

And yet the Bible and other traditional texts elevate motherhood and the maternal spirit. Biblical mothers are often blessed with a profound insight into people and events and the likely consequences of action. Within biblical narratives, this insight often grows out of initially painful experiences. For example, women such as Rebekah and Naomi experience a personal nadir, a crisis of belief, and then, with the guidance of God, emerge and direct a complicated sequence of events. The type of insight that these biblical characters exhibit, which grasps from the outset a situation's potential, prompts an extraordinary statement. According to the *Ethics of the Fathers*, a much studied and quoted tractate of the Mishnah, one definition of a person who has the wisdom to cleave to God's will is "the person who sees the newborn."

This is often interpreted to mean that true wisdom or discernment is impossible without the ability to see a situation and understand where it can lead, much as a parent understands the potential of a newborn child. But in ancient civilizations, it was the female midwife and the mother who first saw and assessed the newborn. The statement elevates female, maternal experience to a symbol of one of the primary conditions for wisdom and piety. Gifted mothers—and people who are like gifted mothers—have the capacity to enter into the potential of their children and of situations and the wisdom to guide both people and situations in the right direction.

This conception of a mother's insight—and the uses to which such insight should appropriately be put—illuminates a declaration in the story of Deborah. Deborah judges her people and supervises the military activities of her general, Barak. And yet, when Deborah chooses to praise herself, this paragon of military acumen says, "I arose, a mother in Israel" (Judges 5:7). Deborah sees herself in the tradition of a general in an army of mothers, mothers who, like Rebekah and Jochebed and Naomi, "see the newborn"—who have unique insights, act on them, and direct others on the basis of those insights.

The elevation of motherhood as the context of intellectual and spiritual excellence is used within the Bible to portray not only women but men and God as well. Maternal imagery appears in the words of such male heroes as Moses and of the prophets, especially Isaiah, who tells the Jewish people that God himself is their mother:

> Listen to me, Oh house of Jacob, and all the remnant of the house of Israel, You that are born from within my belly, you that are carried from inside my womb; I remain the same into old age, and even when my hair grows white I will carry you; I created you, and I will bear you, I will carry you, and I will deliver.
>
> —ISAIAH 46:3–4

Indeed the gift of "seeing the newborn" often seems, within later Jewish tradition, to have been subsumed by men, just as the maternal quality of mercy, *rachamim*, often came to be considered a masculine trait. Within Jewish texts and the popular Jewish imagination, maternal insight and activism—and insightful, activist mothers such as Rebekah, Jochebed, and Naomi—have often faded into the background, while sons became larger than life.

The texts themselves, however, yield fertile and liberating antidotes to such disenfranchisement of women. The Book of Ruth and the stories of many biblical women provide female models of cleverness, courage, resilience, and leadership. Similarly, biblical texts present models of nurturing, compassionate males. Such passages offer flexible and humane images of the ways in which both women and men may discover their own spirituality and act upon moral mandates.

6

"A Son Is Born to Naomi"

RUTH 4:17

*T*HE STARTLING DECLARATION by the women celebrating the birth of Ruth's son—"A son is born to Naomi"—has puzzled commentators for centuries. The three authors in this section extend the commentary on this extraordinary statement in new directions, reading it as the most prominent sign of the darker or problematic side of the connection between Ruth and Naomi. By focusing on Ruth's disappearance at the end of the story and her replacement by Naomi as the center of attention, they reveal the dilemmas for the reader in evaluating and responding to this extraordinary moment in biblical narrative.

For Vanessa Ochs this moment is the culmination of a text she finds "troubling" on many grounds, but most poignantly for its apparent endorsement of women's self-effacement. Longing for sacred texts "about real women and their survival and their relationships with each other," she is ultimately dismayed by the failure of Ruth to satisfy her "hunger."

Statements and actions that Ochs reads as essentially the annihilation of self, are turned on their head by Mona Fishbane, who reads them as indices of Ruth's faith in interpersonal connections. Drawing upon her professional and personal experience of family relationships and her training in family systems theory, Fishbane reads Ruth and Naomi as representative of "types" of women facing issues of separation and connection. For her the women's declaration is "jarring and startling" because it endorses "Naomi's obsessive focus on husband and sons" and explicitly reveals Naomi's "overidentification" with Ruth.

Marianne Hirsch sets the text and her own response to it in the context of our culture's stereotyped denigration and even fear of the mother-in-law. Ruth is one of the few texts in Western literature to present a relationship of love and affection between mother-in-law and daughter-in-law. By reflecting on the contrast between the cultural construction of the mother-in-law as despised competitor for the husband/son and her own relationship of respect and affection with her recently deceased mother-in-law, Hirsch is led to perceive Ruth and Naomi's story as one of mutual caretaking. In Hirsch's reading, Ochs' self-effacing Ruth and Fishbane's insecure and desperate Naomi are transformed into two women who "work hard to take care of each other as each takes care of herself."

Hirsch is also puzzled when the women seem to eliminate Ruth from the child's future by declaring him Naomi's son. But the personal experience she brings to bear on the text suggests a counterinterpretation of that ending. In distinct contrast to Ochs and Fishbane, she regards the bond between "grandmother" and "grandson" as one of sharing, not supplanting. Ruth the daughter-in-law remains present for Hirsch as part of a triangle in which two women do not compete over a male child; instead the child enables them to enlarge their relationship with each other.

Reading Ruth
Where Are the Women?

Vanessa L. Ochs

The questions that come to my mind when I read a text like the Book of Ruth have often differed from those the ancient commentators asked. I once imagined that if only I were more devout and better schooled in sacred texts, I would respond more conventionally. My own thoughts, I assumed, were pesky, impudent, irrelevant, and the result of limited knowledge. These discounted thoughts I kept to myself. And between my silence, my muzzled thoughts, and the closed text, dust gathered.

To overcome my reticence is to blow through that dust. My encouragement comes from the women scholars of Jewish sacred texts who have emerged in the last fifteen years. These scholars have convinced me that the old questions are not the only ones worth asking and answering. As I was once told by Chana Safrai, then director of the Judith Lieberman Institute for Learning for Women, in Ramat Shapira, Jerusalem, "If it's an issue to me, then it needs to be addressed." Encouraged by Safrai and by feminist scholars who are arriving at radically new understandings of ancient texts by daring to voice their very legitimate new questions, I can admit what I have felt all along: that the Book of Ruth troubles me. Before I allow myself to say precisely what troubles me, I should explain that my approach to the text is both like and unlike that of a traditional commentator such as Rashi. When schoolchildren begin to study Rashi's commentaries on scripture, they often learn

---

The author used *Tanakh: A New Translation of the Holy Scriptures* (Philadelphia, New York, and Jerusalem: Jewish Publication Society, 1985).

to make sense of his intellectual process by asking of each gloss, *Ma kashe leRashi?* (essentially, what is troubling Rashi here?). By looking at Rashi's commentary, the children try to guess what in the sacred text represented a "glitch" for Rashi—a confusion, a mystery, an anomaly. The children are trained to see how Rashi's glosses, documented by prooftexts he brings from other sources and by legends he discovers and creates, smooth away the irritants and restore happy coherence to the original text.

When I read the Book of Ruth, I, too, encounter glitches. Like Rashi, like any Jew who studies Torah, I can enter into dialogue with the text by stating what troubles me—the contradictions I perceive, the details I feel are missing. Unlike Rashi and his peers across the generations, I feel less motivated to rationalize the contradictions with fancy intratextual, legendary, linguistic, or historical footwork or to fill in what's missing with suitably pious and didactic details. (My example of the very fanciest footwork is the commentary called Zohar Chadash Ruth, which to the question "Had Ruth converted to Judaism while her husband Mahlon was still alive?" gives this answer: "God forbid that Mahlon married her while she was still a Gentile." Reduced to logical principles: How do we know that X is the case? Because it would be unthinkable for X not to be the case!) Perhaps, as a twentieth-century reader of secular texts of indeterminate meaning, I'm accustomed to living harmoniously alongside problematic, perplexing texts. The thought of entering into dialogue with a text and not coming to a clever or fudged resolution doesn't really rattle me.

Rashi's commentary is influenced by the skills and qualifications he brought to his task: his scholarly competence in scripture and language; his knowledge of the vineyards of medieval France; his social roles as son, husband, father of daughters, father-in-law. It goes without saying that who he is, where he lived, and what he believed determine the questions he asked and the answers he came up with. I don't mean to suggest that Rashi's particularity limited his understanding, but rather to acknowledge the obvious: that Rashi's commentary arose from the profundity and complexity of who he was, and not just of what he knew.

I am not a university- or yeshiva-trained biblical scholar. I can, however, struggle through the sacred texts in the original and sift through the Midrash, commentaries, and Targum (ancient Aramaic translation of the Bible). I write essays on feminist spirituality and on family life and have taught writing and literature in colleges in the northeastern United States. I am a daughter, a sister, wife, mother of daughters, and daughter-in-law. Like Rashi's, all my emotional and intellectual particularities influence the questions that I ask as I read the Book of Ruth. When I feel free enough to ask my questions, I engage with the text. I bring all my wishes and needs to it. And because this is a sacred text, I trust that the text—like a staid and infinitely wise parent whose love is unwavering—will not collapse under the weight of my questioning. How could I understand a text to be sacred if I didn't think it could stand up to my questioning? About this, I feel quite confident.

As I begin to read the Book of Ruth, I'm convinced that the text, like other finely crafted stories and dramas, spills many of the beans right off. My educated guess is that the story will be about human misery that either is or is not relieved. It is about a test of loyalty, one that may or may not be passed. It is about a journey that will result in either survival or extinction. Most certainly, it's about women: women's misery, women's loyalty, women's journeys.

Yet, just as I'm arranging myself to follow the plot that I think is about to unfold, I find myself straining to accept the book's premise. It's so implausible. In the abstract, of course, I can easily imagine a drama of devotion between human beings who share suffering, or devotion between two women who are bound to each other by circumstances. But the specific scenario of this text makes me raise my eyebrows. Really, now. What young widow would leave her country and her people and follow her mother-in-law to a place where she will find personal and national salvation through a night spent with an elderly uncle-in-law on a threshing room floor? What widow, even one who adores her mother-in-law, could be so foolish as to put herself at the mercy of that woman's clan if it means giving up her own people, her god, her country, her family, and her sister? An in-law relation, knowing no blood bond, is tenuous enough; it is not clear to me how Ruth could have dreamed that Naomi's people, famous for abhorring Moabites, might make an exception and accept her.

Perhaps the text intends for us to feel incredulous in the face of the premise. Perhaps that's just the point. We're supposed to be amazed by Ruth. No flesh-and-blood daughter-in-law would be so filled with *chesed* (righteousness, love beyond duty, love beyond reason) that she would march, unprotected by a husband, into the lion's den of in-laws. But that's who Ruth is; she is all irrational, undemanded love.

What's more, if Ruth and her sister-in-law were indeed Moabite princesses and sisters, as the Midrash claims, how could it be that their family of origin—the royal house of Eglon—would abandon them as they faced widowhood and famine? I understand that a woman in Ruth's patriarchal society was expected to leave her family and adapt to her husband's clan. But in switching allegiances, stepping outside the orbit of her original family, surely the woman didn't sever all ties to her own people for all time! Would her family stop loving her, stop caring about her well-being? Would they let her starve? This confuses me. In Ruth's society, if a woman's husband died, she *could* go back home to Mom and Dad and start over again. Under her parent's auspices, she would be supplied with a new husband to maintain her. I am not imposing twentieth-century thinking; this is Naomi's thinking. She sensibly advises Ruth and Orpah: "Go, return, each of you to her mother's house. . . . May God grant that you find security, each in the home of her husband." If this were socially bizarre, unheard-of advice, I don't think Orpah would have followed Naomi's instructions.

As for herself, Naomi knew life in Moab was hopeless: *va tishaer ha-isha* (the woman was left), we are told. That is, with the deaths of her husband and sons, the elderly Naomi was forever bereft—or so she had every reason to believe—of all possibility of love and regeneration. She knew that in her world, without men for protection, sustained human interaction, and baby making, she would know only grief and more grief.

I find myself wondering why any time at all passed before Naomi thought to send her Moabite daughters-in-law away. If her counsel to them is to start afresh, why didn't she suggest this immediately after their husbands died? Perhaps this sensible idea didn't dawn on Naomi until the three women had already set out together on the road back to Bethlehem. We might imagine that the sisters-in-law were merely accompanying Naomi as she got started on her trip, the socially correct biblical send-off. But it seems to me that the three are very much en route together, and when Naomi does choose to unbind herself from Ruth and Orpah and travel home alone, the decision comes to her suddenly and unexpectedly, as a mid-journey revelation.

In literature, as in life, certain ideas can become clear to us only when we loosen our ties to or break from customary roles and routines. We are often told we need a change of venue when we are befuddled, on the assumption that a new environment will unhinge us somewhat from our conventional patterns of thinking and seeing and enable us to perceive with greater clarity. Perhaps this is why so many recent short stories begin with a couple or an individual in a car on a highway, midway between someplace familiar and the unknown. Such stories rarely hinge on the physical question—Will the characters get to their destination?—as if they might be stopped by bandits, beasts, or inclement weather. Rather, these stories—psychological, rather than physical adventures—hinge on psychological questions: What will the characters learn en route? What does the journey require them to discard of their former selves? Can they be transformed in time to arrive deepened and altered by the experience? To be a courageous character in the context of a psychological journey is to see what needs to be seen (the truth) and to adapt.

I try to imagine just what it was that became so clear to Naomi midjourney. Did something happen on the way to make her realize that a mother-in-law and two daughters-in-law wouldn't be an effective "alternative family," able to provide sustenance, safety, or happiness? Certainly, they were not a procreative unit: was that the crucial definition of their impossibility? What, indeed, would have happened had these three women stuck together? Should we regard the choice to stick together as an ethically superior one that the women failed to make? Was it altruism that motivated Naomi to send off her daughters-in-law, or her wish to be free of excess baggage? Perhaps Naomi reasoned that it was going to be difficult enough for her to take care of herself en route, and a long shot to hope that someone would take mercy on her and care for her once she had returned to Bethlehem. Why have her difficulties compounded by having to look after and worry about these two widows? Surely she could anticipate that she and her entourage would not be well received by her former kin and townspeople. Perhaps Naomi was anticipating this poor reception and saying, in effect, "Let your own family worry about you; you are no longer my burden."

Another possibility: Naomi may have decided, mid-journey, that she needed to travel alone and return home alone to see how much more pain God could inflict upon her. Perhaps this was part of her grieving: If I feel alone, she may have reasoned, then let me be alone and know the fullness and depth of my grief. My daughters-in-law will eventually reattach themselves to husbands and abandon me. Let us cut the cords and be done with each other now.

Naomi, Ruth, and Orpah think of themselves as unfortunate, miserable women with no one to take care of them. A day doesn't go by when I don't imagine what this could feel like. As a mother of two young daughters, I am always worrying, "What would become of us if something were to happen to my husband? Who would take care of us then?" It is funny that I ask this so frequently, as I, a good enough mother, am the one who does so much of the caretaking: the feeding, the emotional comforting, the nursing through sickness, the instructing in academics and ethical behavior. I like to assume that when my husband tells me, "I need you," he tells the truth: that he, too, is sustained by my love and care. Yet when I imagine myself and my two girls alone, I see us as Naomi and the daughters-in-law, women unable and unprepared to constitute a viable unit, women who are inept and vulnerable, who need to be rescued. Though I know that we—that any group of women—should have it in ourselves to sustain and comfort one another, I look outward for a *goel*, a redeemer, to arrive on horseback and be moved by compassion to protect us, to take responsibility, to look after us. My confidence in our female self-sufficiency—which ought to be very high—is nil. (Has feminism gotten all of us only this far, or am I the lone woman who still can't recognize that I don't need to be saved? Do other women believe they can save themselves? A straw poll tells me they don't. So many women who do an enormous amount of caretaking, and do it with energy and competence, are still not confident they would be able to care for themselves without a loving man on the scene. So many women still feel that without men they would fall off the face of the earth. Maybe men feel they will disappear without women? Well, look on the bright side, I tell myself: this neediness, this longing for completion and assistance, makes us open to love and loyalty.)

The Book of Ruth, or so the title leads me to believe, is Ruth's journey too. She goes off to an unknown land as Naomi's sidekick, her guardian angel. Unlike Abraham, who goes to an unknown land that God says will yield promise and fortune for him, Ruth goes off without promise of happiness or fortune. She goes off without dreams or divinely inspired visions. And she goes off uninvited. Maybe in her gut she thinks her goodness will be rewarded, but I doubt it. She goes selflessly. It is simply the right thing to do; that's what the situation demands of her. Again, Miss Perfection.

Together on this journey, Naomi and Ruth are so capable. They are buddies who sustain each other, dividing the labor of living by drawing upon their differing strengths. Let's say that Ruth, the heartier of the two, provided the physical sustenance. Let's say that Naomi, who could affirm God, even after having been whacked three times by the hand of God, provided the spiritual sustenance. I imagine that they are buddies who are off to an auspicious start. They journey from one land to another and arrive unmolested, in one piece. They are poised for continued survival.

The text does not tell us Ruth's mental state upon arrival. Ruth seems, at this point, lacking in personhood. To say that she is returning to a place she has never been is to say that she has not only annexed herself to Naomi in friendship, but has made Naomi's history and memory her own. Ruth is witness to her own invisibility. She stands beside Naomi as the chorus of townswomen come to observe and confirm Naomi's downfall.

These are women who knew Naomi in better days. For Naomi to end her grieving and begin her surviving, she needs to reconnect with her "old crowd." Perhaps, back in Moab, no one really noticed Naomi and her plight. There, she was invisible, another hungry, barefoot wretch. There, she held her misery within her. Back home in Bethlehem, as she might have anticipated, the whole city goes into a tumult just at the sight of her. Embarrassing, maybe, but ultimately satisfying. Whatever her reasoning, Naomi wants her suffering, her mental state, to be known. She wants to be defined by it. She is so depressed that she chooses to change her name to "the bitter one," asking the women to join her in acknowledging the new identity that grief has imposed upon her. I wonder if Naomi is also telling them that she, like Ruth, is watching her identity drain away.

As Naomi tells the women that she went out of Bethlehem full and has come back empty, Ruth stands beside her. Were I Ruth, standing there, hearing my mother-in-law announce her emptiness, I know I'd have thought, "What? I left my people, my land, my God, my everything, to see you to safety, to protect you from loneliness, to be your Other—and as you make your grand entrance, you say you are totally empty? Am I invisible? Does my being here not matter at all? I should never have come."

Ruth apparently doesn't have my impure thoughts. Again, only a person of exemplary *chesed* would not take personal offense at Naomi's words. Ruth is quite the saint, isn't she? She is totally other-directed. Never self-absorbed. Flawless in generosity. While I am moved by the idea of an extremely kind, unselfish person, I am suspicious of a person so selfless that she essentially annihilates herself.

You might say that ultimately Ruth does well for herself in Bethlehem. She gets a baby, and through this baby, through the biological fiction of levirate marriage, she gets to bring her husband's soul back from the dead. She gets to see his name carried on. Or does she have a baby at all? Certainly a son comes forth from her womb, but is the baby hers?

While the townspeople compare Ruth to Rachel and Leah, I think she is more like Rachel's and Leah's handmaids, in that she essentially becomes a surrogate mother. No sooner does Ruth give birth than the townswomen burst forth in congratulations. No *mazel tov* to Ruth, but to Naomi. God gave *you* a redeemer, they tell Naomi. He will redeem *you*, sustain *you*. To confirm this alternative reality the townswomen propose, Naomi holds the baby to her bosom, and, figuratively, nurses him, making Ruth utterly unnecessary. The Book of Ruth closes with baby Obed at Naomi's bosom as the credits of genealogy roll: we don't even have a closing shot of Ruth. Once again, Ruth is negated, and if she doesn't do it herself, her mother-in-law or the townspeople will do it for her. Now—and this seems quite sad—her son Obed annihilates her by suckling elsewhere.

A modern commentator, Eliezar Kitov, looks at this scene and reflects (in his Sefer Hatoda'a), "The neighbors described the child as a 'son born to Naomi,' with reference to the legitimacy of the child, which some questioned, for he had been born from a Moabitess. That is to say, it is not the name of the Moabite mother which is called on this child, but the name of Naomi—a great-grand-daughter of Nachshon, the son of Aminadav, a prince among his people." Spin doctors are at work here; it is an ancient craft, I see. According to Kitov, the text is telling us, Don't connect the baby Obed to Ruth, because her past and her genes—regardless of her conversion, regardless of her noble life—are bad for his image. Connect him to the regal Naomi, who comes from unquestionably good stock. This kind of thinking truly disturbs me, for it confirms what I've long observed: Jews may say they honor the convert, but that is theoretical, wishfully ethical thinking. In Jewish communities that I know, Jews are always suspicious of converts to Judaism and rarely forgive them for their pasts. Ruth, our quintessential convert, gets the quintessential cold shoulder.

This is not a story about women surviving as I thought it might be at the outset. This is a story about one woman who survived: Naomi.

The townspeople who earlier came to witness Naomi's pain now show up to witness her good fortune. They don't really notice Ruth; so I will. I think of Ruth, postpartum, her baby called Naomi's baby, held at Naomi's breasts, as very lonely. Bitter, even. As the townswomen once asked, "Is this Naomi?" I ask, Is this the Book of Ruth, or is it the Book of Naomi?

I scan the ending of the book a last time. The genealogy: Boaz begat Obed. Obed, Jesse. Jesse, David. Even Naomi is obliterated. The women, I discover, have all been tangential to this story. Pawns.

This is not the Book of Ruth. This is not the Book of Naomi either. It is not even baby Obed's book. It is the book of King David. My initial take is wrong: this ends up being neither a story about women withstanding misery, nor a story about women's devotedness. It is not about God directing women to discover the strength to survive. It turns out to be one of those "how our hero was born" stories.

Of course King David needs a miraculous birth, and, what's more, so does his heir, the Messiah. Ah, so I was wrong all along. This is a story meant to justify the power of a particular kingship. On that level, this is as satisfying a legend as any other.

Where does this rooting around leave me? It leaves me hungry for the sacred text that I had thought this would be, the text this had originally appeared to be: one that is about real women and their survival and their relationships with each other. The Book of Ruth, despite its surface appearance, despite its female characters and female dialogue, happens not to be this book. The improbability of the premise, the nonhuman perfection of Ruth, should have alerted me. The clues were there all along, staring me in the face. This misreading alerts me to the intensity of my own hunger for the sacred text that does address women. That Book of Ruth remains elusive.

Ruth

Dilemmas of Loyalty and Connection

MONA DeKOVEN FISHBANE

When I was a girl and young woman the Book of Ruth spoke to me with a lyrical clarity of faith, courage, and the love of women. The character of Ruth offered me a model of a strong yet caring woman. As I reread the Book of Ruth in middle age, with the eyes of a psychologist, I find a more complex narrative. I am struck by tensions in the text that go beyond the sweetness and clarity I once found there. The text is remarkable in the boldness with which it confronts some of the most perplexing dilemmas we face as persons—then, in those biblical days, and now.

The story of Ruth grapples with such issues as separation and connection, emptiness and fullness, and, most especially, continuity and disruption of the generations. Ruth and Naomi face these issues in different ways.

The story begins with Elimelech, his wife, and sons leaving their home in Bethlehem for Moab, because of a famine in Judah. The ancient rabbis criticized Elimelech for abandoning his people and his obligations, especially since he was, in their view, a leader. Elimelech's journey is seen as an act of cowardice and a cutting off from his people. The tragedies that subsequently befall his family are considered by the

---

The author used *Tanakh: A New Translation of the Holy Scriptures* (Philadelphia, New York, and Jerusalem: Jewish Publication Society, 1985).

rabbis to be punishment for this abandonment. In fact, much of the story of Ruth can be seen as a reparation for this act of cutting off.[1] Elimelech is punished with both his own death and the deaths of his sons; his spirit is left with no heir to carry it on, say the rabbis. Only Ruth's journey back to Bethlehem with Naomi and their relationship with Boaz allows for the family to be redeemed, for the line to continue through Obed, the son whose son begets David.

But first let's look at the women in this story. Naomi, overcome with grief at the deaths of husband and sons, urges her daughters-in-law to return to their mothers' houses: This is clearly a woman's story. When Ruth and Orpah declare that they will stay with Naomi, Naomi answers that she has nothing to give them—no more sons for them to marry. In this way, Naomi tells them and us that as a woman she is nothing without a man. She doesn't see their devotion to her as sensible without a man in the middle of their relationship. Naomi finally convinces Orpah to leave by referring to her own bitterness at seeing her daughters-in-law without husbands. Orpah's departure reflects her empathy for Naomi's pain. But Ruth refuses to leave, and appeals to Naomi through yet another empathic twist. The language with which she begs Naomi not to make her leave (*al tifge'i bi*) can be read as either "Do not urge me to leave you" or "Do not hurt me to leave you." By using this double entendre, Ruth makes it clear that leaving Naomi would cause Ruth too much pain. In effect she asks Naomi to transcend her own pain over Ruth's pain, so as not to cause Ruth further pain! This elaborate "dance" of empathy involves a complex negotiation between the women—a negotiation process that is not centered on power, but rather on mutual concern and caring.

Ruth follows this appeal with her famous "Whither thou goest" affirmation. The language of this affirmation is striking. She does not say, "I choose the Israelite people and their God"; she makes it clear that she is choosing *Naomi's* people, *Naomi's* God. Ruth is making a relational choice. It is in the context of her relationship with Naomi, and as an affirmation of it, that she makes her statement of faith.

At one level, we see a new bond forged between the two women. At another, we see that Naomi's inner world has not been transformed by the relationship. When the two arrive in Bethlehem, Naomi tells her women friends, "Call me Mara [bitter]. . . . I went away full, and the Lord has brought me back empty." This is hard for us to hear, right after Ruth's testimony of faith and loyalty; for Naomi has not come back empty—she comes with a loving and devoted daughter-in-law! However, Naomi is so bitter and empty that she cannot see this gift for what it is. She is overwhelmed with grief—and sees herself as nothing without a man. But Naomi's emptiness goes deeper. She seems emotionally wounded, and self-centered in a way not unlike her dead husband—who chose for his own welfare over that of his community.

A different sort of woman, Ruth is decisive, making her choice of Naomi, Naomi's people, and Naomi's God freely and courageously. The two "types" which these two women represent can be seen in the meanings associated with their names. "Naomi" means "pleasant," but she renames herself "Mara," "bitter." Indeed, Naomi is pleasant under pleasant circumstances—married, with children—but turns bitter with the turn in her fate. Tradition associates the meaning of the name "Ruth" with "saturated" or "full"—a marked contrast with "empty" Naomi. Ruth's fullness is a woman's fullness; her choices are in the context of relationship. Hers is a journey with, a journey through empathy and caring.

In this regard, it is interesting to contrast Ruth's journey with Abraham's. Both leave their homes and go to a new land; and both become progenitors of our people. But there is a difference. Abraham is called by God, alone. He is commanded directly by God to leave his homeland. His leap of faith is a lonely one. As a reward for his faith, he is promised a future: progeny, a great nation. By contrast, Ruth is not called by God, and she is promised nothing. She undertakes her journey out of loyalty to Naomi. They go together. Her faith is contextual, in relationship.

The dyad of the two women expands into a triangle when Boaz enters the story. At the most basic level, Naomi attempts to find a husband/protector for Ruth, a redeemer for the whole family. However, the drama reveals more complex dynamics. When Boaz first sees Ruth gleaning in his field, he asks his overseer, "Whose girl is that?" At one level this question raises the issue of ownership of a woman: Whose daughter is she? Whose wife? But the overseer's answer points to another dimension. When he says, "She is a Moabite girl who came back with Naomi from the country of Moab," the question is transformed from one of possession to one of connection. For this, after all, is a story of connections: connections chosen and broken, natural and created. It is a story of contexts, of loyalties. "She is a Moabite girl" (the broken connection, the home she left) "who came back with Naomi" (a created connection, a chosen bond). The overseer goes on to describe Ruth's character: She works hard in the fields. And when Boaz first speaks to Ruth, he also speaks not of her beauty, but of her character— her loyalty to Naomi, her brave decision to join the house of Israel. In return, he offers her protection. Ruth is deeply touched by this meeting with Boaz and by his kindness. As the text stresses, he has spoken "to the heart" of her. He has understood her in her fullness.

What is the protection Boaz offers Ruth? On the one hand, he offers her access to his fields, so that she can glean for herself and Naomi. Ultimately, he will offer her the protection of levirate marriage, a redemption of her family. And he offers her protection from the young men who could "molest" her. The text points to the dangers lurking for a young woman on her own. Ruth is told to "Stay here close" or "cleave" (*tidbakin*) to the young women in the field for safety. In this female huddle the maidens provide each other with safety from the young men. Both the text and the rabbis emphasize over and over the vulnerability of a young woman alone in those times. She is in need of protection—the protection of a man, of God, of the female huddle. The rabbis suggest that Ruth was so beautiful that men had seminal emissions when they looked at her. What is striking about this comment is not Ruth's beauty as such, but the rabbis' preoccupation with it and with the sexual dangers to a woman in the world. This aura of fear and danger, and this sexualization of the relations between men and women, provide a striking backdrop that further highlights Ruth's courage and determination. She chooses to leave home; she walks alone to the fields; she works hard to feed herself and Naomi. In this context, we hear a fundamental question emerging from the story: Is a woman complete or safe without a man to protect her? Naomi says no, and the task she sets herself is to find a husband for Ruth, a man who will protect and redeem both women. Ruth, however, is much less conventional than Naomi. In reporting to Naomi her meeting with Boaz, Ruth makes an interesting slip of the tongue. Whereas Boaz tells Ruth to cleave to his maidens in the field, Ruth tells Naomi that Boaz told her to cleave (*tidbakin*) to his young *male* workers in the field. Naomi quickly corrects her, and reminds her to go with the maidens. Might Ruth's slip betray her desire to be bold and free like the men? Might it

express her own bravery and disregard for her conventional role as a
fragile woman?

Lest I imply that Ruth is a thoroughly autonomous, independent being, however, let's look at an earlier point in the text where Ruth does
indeed "cling." The same Hebrew word (*davka*) is used to describe
Ruth's cleaving to Naomi as she professed her faith and loyalty early in
the story. This clinging, this female huddling, does not seem to be
about mutual protection against dangerous men as in Boaz's fields. So
how may we understand Ruth clinging to Naomi? Is it desperate? Is it
chosen? A modern reader might be embarrassed by Ruth's refusal to
separate from Naomi, seeing her clinging as overemotional, unseemly.
Such clinging could be seen as a sign of instability. In a world like ours,
which overvalues autonomy and independence, such an intense need
for relationship can be disquieting. Naomi's model—as a vulnerable
woman who needs the protection of a strong man—is supplanted in
our culture by the model of the independent, strong man or woman
who doesn't need much from other people at all. But Ruth's stance offers us a third alternative—a view of woman as neither fragile nor
fiercely independent. She offers us the model of woman in relation, for
whom connection, loyalty, and caring are primary values. From this
perspective her clinging to Naomi is not an act of desperation, but
rather a passionate statement of her faith in interpersonal connection.
As Abraham makes his leap of faith, so does Ruth. Ruth leaps into her
choice with her whole being, her whole body. Every fiber of her self is
choosing. Ruth's faith is as much about her caring for Naomi as it is
about Naomi's God and people. At a more abstract level, it is a statement of faith in the importance of relationship itself. Ruth represents
woman as a relational creature, who finds and creates herself in relationships with other men and women.[2]

While Ruth appears confident in her choice, in her bearing, and in
her relational stance, Naomi strikes us as insecure, anxious for the future and for Ruth's safety. She experiences herself as powerless and relies
on an old tactic of powerless women to get what they need: manipulation. In the tradition of Rebekah, who tricks her husband into providing for her son, Naomi lays out a plot to ensnare Boaz into marrying
Ruth. She sends Ruth to the threshing floor at night, bedecked and perfumed, to lie secretly at Boaz's feet as he sleeps. But the snare turns into
another respectful meeting between Ruth and Boaz. She doesn't seduce

him but honestly asks him to protect and redeem her, according to his kinship obligation. We can only imagine Boaz's complex feelings as he finds beautiful Ruth at his feet in the middle of the night. The rabbis capture the tension in the scene as they discuss the erotic overtones. They suggest that Boaz struggles with his lust and prevails. He offers to redeem Ruth through levirate marriage.

When Ruth returns to Naomi, Naomi asks an odd question: *Mi at biti*, literally, "Who are you, my daughter?" This can again be understood as Naomi defining Ruth's status vis-à-vis a man: Do you belong to Boaz? Ruth seems to have understood Naomi's intent, for she answers by reporting the events on the threshing floor. Ruth and Boaz also understood Naomi's neediness, for Ruth brings barley to Naomi and reports that Boaz told her, "Do not go back to your mother-in-law empty-handed." Naomi's emptiness prompts her to cleave to Ruth in a disturbing way—indeed, she seems at times to be living through Ruth. This overidentification is apparent in Naomi's slips of the tongue when she instructs Ruth to go to the threshing floor at night. She tells Ruth to put on her dress and lie at Boaz's feet: "Bathe, anoint yourself, dress up, and go down to the threshing floor . . . and uncover his feet and lie down." These are Naomi's words as traditionally pronounced when the Bible is read aloud. But the text, as written in Hebrew, presents a striking variant at this point. Some of Naomi's words in the written version are in the first person: "Bathe, anoint yourself, and *I* will put on your dress, and *I* will go down to the threshing floor . . . and uncover his feet and *I* will lie down." The ancient coexistence of both versions underscores the conflation of identities in Naomi's mind. In contrast with Naomi's desperate scheming, it is remarkable that Ruth and Boaz develop a relationship of honesty and respect. In pursuing the marriage, Naomi seeks a conventional place of safety for Ruth. But the safety Ruth seeks is a personal centeredness and an interpersonal relationship based on mutual respect.

Why is Naomi so desperate? What is the urgency behind her plot? At one level Naomi is simply trying to ensure the family line, so that the name of Elimelech and Mahlon can continue. The tradition of levirate marriage, in which a brother or close male relative of a man who died without children marries the widow, could ensure this continuity. Such is Naomi's hope; and such is the task Boaz undertakes. But there is a deeper sense to Naomi's need for continuity. A suggestion of this

deeper meaning occurs when Boaz speaks to the elders of his intention
to marry Ruth and redeem the family line. Following the levirate law,
he offers to marry Ruth in order "to perpetuate the name of the deceased upon his estate, that the name of the deceased may not disappear
(literally, "not be cut off") from among his kinsmen." Such a cutoff
would be a disaster. The continuity of the generations is at the heart of
the survival of a family, and ultimately of a people. The notion of the
end of a family line, or of a person cut off from his or her family or
people, is anathema in the biblical and later Jewish world. In fact, when
a person commits a serious crime, such as profaning the Sabbath, the
punishment is death, and "that person shall be cut off from among his
kin" (Exodus 31:14). Such a cutoff represents the worst punishment a
person could endure. A medieval tradition has it that the souls of the
dead find rest in their heirs, whereas a person who dies with no children can find no rest. Naomi's anxiety over finding heirs for Elimelech
and Mahlon through the union of Ruth and Boaz is deeply rooted in
fear of such a cutoff.

To our modern ears, this fear of being cut off, this anxiety over continuity may seem odd. With the emphasis in our culture on autonomy
and personal fulfillment, cutoffs from difficult family members may
even be encouraged. Moreover, having children is often considered a
personal choice, not an obligation to continue the family into the next
generation. In fact, the thrust of much individual psychotherapy is to
encourage the patient to shed neurotic ties to parents, to shed old
guilts, and to re-create the self in the relationship with the therapist.
The implications of this for other family members are often not considered.

The Book of Ruth dramatizes complex familial tensions and anxieties
over cutoff and continuity—anxieties that our own culture has denied,
but which most other cultures, including the biblical one, understood
deeply. The myth of the individual, autonomous and free of family obligation, may be unique to our culture, and is based on a rejection of
tradition and legacy, as if they were so much excess baggage. Only in
recent years have new voices been heard, challenging the cult of the individual, reclaiming the wisdom of continuity and family loyalty. The
thrust of systemic family therapy is to see the individual in the context
of his or her family of origin, a multigenerational context. The destruc-
tiveness of cutoffs and the significance of family loyalty are taken very
seriously.

The emphasis on heirs, on continuing the family name and ensuring new generations, lies at the heart of the Book of Ruth. To be sure, this emphasis makes perfect sense in its time and, as we have seen, points to a more universal thirst for intergenerational survival. Yet one is still struck by the extent of Naomi's panic and her sense of urgency and fear that her family may come to an end, that the name of her dead husband and sons will be cut off utterly. Troubling anxieties or overly intense reactions can often be clarified by looking at family history. In this case, Naomi's anxiety becomes less puzzling if we study the family histories or legacies of the story's protagonists. Ruth is a Moabitess. Her ancestor, Moab, was the product of an incestuous union between Lot and his daughter (Genesis 19:30–38). The circumstances of this union are remarkable. Lot and his daughters had survived the destruction of Sodom. The daughters, thinking themselves and their father the only human survivors, were panicked at the thought that they might be the last humans on earth—the end of the line. So they got their father drunk and had intercourse with him during his drunken stupor. One product of these desperate acts was Moab. A remarkably similar series of events lies embedded in Boaz's family tree. Boaz is the descendant of Perez, the son of Judah and Tamar. Tamar was Judah's daughter-in-law; when her husband died and Judah did not provide a levirate husband for her, she tricked Judah, waylaying him in harlot's garb (Genesis 38:14–30). The product of their union was Perez. Although Tamar did not imagine herself the sole surviving woman on earth, she did see the end of her family line; and so she deceived Judah, manipulating him into providing her with a future, i.e., descendants. For in those days a future meant not one's individual future, but offspring and future generations.

Legacies in both Boaz's and Ruth's families thus included uncertainty over continuity, anxiety or panic about it, and a determination to ensure continuity, with means lawful or not. Ironically, in both these families the urge for procreation, for connectedness to the future, was achieved through false connection, through deceit. Naomi was Boaz's cousin; she shared this family legacy, this anxiety, and this determination. This multigenerational legacy in both families, which reverberates in the triangle of Ruth, Naomi, and Boaz, illustrates a central tenet in family systems theory: Current dilemmas often reflect old family legacies and unfinished business from prior generations.

In light of these traditions of anxiety and deceitfulness, the honesty of Ruth's and Boaz's encounters is striking. Perhaps Naomi did the worrying and the conniving for them, leaving the couple free to find each other graciously and respectfully! We often see in families that one person carries or performs a psychic function for another, freeing the other from having to own that part in him/herself. This process is called "projective identification" and is often not conscious or explicitly stated. In the Ruth-Naomi dyad, Naomi carries the worry and anxiety, while Ruth carries the confidence and calm. We might well wonder, if Naomi were not so busy hovering, whether Ruth would look so centered and calm.

There is yet another possible explanation for the honesty in Ruth and Boaz's relationship. Both Ruth and Boaz were loyal and caring toward family and family obligations. Ruth's chosen loyalty was to her husband's family; she honored the dead and cared for the living. For his part, Boaz was ready to fulfill his familial responsibility by redeeming Ruth's family, marrying her, and carrying on the family name. We might say that this couple, having expressed their loyalty to family in constructive and caring ways, earned for themselves the right to a constructive and caring relationship with each other. They had paid their filial debt, and so were free to build a solid relationship with each other.[3] We could imagine a much different version of the Ruth story, in which Ruth is rude to Naomi and out of spite or desperation seduces Boaz, who has shirked his levirate responsibility. Perhaps Ruth gets him drunk first, perhaps she plays the harlot. Such would be a story of "invisible loyalties," of unfinished business in the family reenacted yet again.

But our couple does indeed marry with the blessings and respect of the community. The elders witness their union and bless them with the wish for offspring—ironically, invoking the household of Judah and Tamar and their offspring, Perez. And Ruth does conceive, and bears a son. A happy ending would complete this picture with the proud parents caring for their baby, sharing their joy with Naomi. Instead, the ending is jarring and startling. With the birth of the child, Ruth and Boaz disappear from the text! The women surround Naomi, and they praise Ruth "who loves you and is better to you than seven sons." In this formulation the women implicitly understand Naomi's obsessive focus on husband and sons. They attempt to counteract it with their praise of Ruth—who is better than "seven sons." But the neighbor ladies don't pursue the point. They join Naomi in putting a male at the center of their world. They say to Naomi that Ruth's son "will renew your life and sustain your old age." Thus this son is to continue the process of redeeming, restoring, and soothing Naomi. We are startled to learn that Naomi becomes the baby's nurse! It is as if this son were born for Naomi, as if he were born to Naomi. Perhaps now her wound, the loss of her husband and sons, will be healed. The text continues to disturb us: The neighbor ladies name the son! And they declare him Naomi's son: "The women neighbors gave him a name, saying, A son is born to Naomi! They named him Obed." Once again we see Naomi's overidentification with Ruth, the blurred lines of identity and belonging between Naomi and Ruth. "Obed" (*Oved* in Hebrew) means one who serves; is Obed destined to be a "servant" to Naomi's needs? The description of his beginnings and his very name are a setup for him to be a "parentified child"—a child who parents his parents—or, in this case, his (quasi-) grandmother.

A question nags at me: Why doesn't Ruth mother her own son? Has her whole purpose been to heal Naomi's wounds, a job now taken over by Obed? Another possible explanation for why Ruth does not mother Obed relates to Ruth's relationship to her own family of origin, the one she left in Moab. The text does not ask these questions, but we might. What of Ruth's wound in leaving her family? What of her ambivalence? What of her loyalty to them? Perhaps she was badly mothered, and so was incapable of mothering her own son. Or perhaps she could not mother Obed, having turned her back on her own family, having cut herself off from her roots. Perhaps this is her invisible loyalty to her family in Moab: She cannot take care of her Israelite son.

In the last scene of the story, there is a final female huddle, the women surrounding Naomi and "her" baby. These women have taken over the drama; theirs is a sweet victory, a triumph, the power of women caretaking and ensuring the future.

And then, a postscript to the text—by a male editor, perhaps—in which all traces of women disappear. The image is one in which men beget men—as if by a variant of immaculate conception. "Perez begot Hezron, . . . Salmon begot Boaz, Boaz begot Obed, Obed begot Jesse, and Jesse begot David." In one stroke of the biblical pen, all the tensions and anguish and connections of the women heroines in this text are done away with, or seem as though they never existed. What

really matters is the reproduction of men and their power, resulting in
King David. A final tension—perhaps the most painful—in the Book
of Ruth.

Reading Ruth with Naomi

MARIANNE HIRSCH

For Rose

I never referred to Rose as my "mother-in-law." Not only did she fail to fit the stereotype, but in all the stories I had read and studied, I could think of only one or two accounts of affection and respect between mothers-in-law and daughters-in-law that could serve as models for our relationship.

Nowadays, mothers-in-law bear the brunt of the pervasive fear of and contempt for mothers—and therefore of women—that define our culture. The mother-in-law is the adult version of the evil stepmother in the fairy tales of our childhoods.[1] Our culture projects onto her all its discomfort with maternal power and powerlessness. She is a comic figure, the subject of sitcom humor, jokes, and bumper stickers (e.g., "mother-in-law in trunk"). The sociological literature unequivocally corroborates the clichés: "In American, British and other Western societies, surveys consistently have indicated mothers-in-law to be the most disliked of all relatives," says Lucy Rose Fischer in the most often cited article on the subject. She cites an earlier study which suggests that "across cultures relationships with mothers-in-law, for both men and women, are the 'principal points of tension in the situation created by marriage.' "[2] It is as though the contemporary nuclear family's very self-definition depended on the exclusion of the parental generation, and of

---

The author quotes from the New English Bible (New York: Oxford University Press, 1970).

the mother in particular, but we divide the labor and exclude, through humiliation and disdain, each others' mothers and not our own. That exclusion serves to reinforce a heterosexual marital bond that has become more and more strained. Men (husbands) come between women (mothers and daughters), and women (daughters-in-law) collude in the hatred of women (mothers-in-law). This ensures that the primary bond remains a heterosexual one, unthreatened by connections between women. The triangulation of these familial interactions reinforces traditional rivalries and gender stereotypes. The strain, sociologists report, tends to be particularly strong between mothers-in-law and daughters-in-law: "They are essentially strangers to each other whose relationship derives from the fact that they both have intimate bonds with the son-husband."[3] Because of the "diverging orientations toward maternal versus paternal kin," maternal in-laws tend to be more present, while mothers of sons tend to be more scorned and dispossessed. Our families are so constructed that two women end up competing over the attention and approval of one man, the husband/son. When one recent study finds that a high proportion of mothers-in-law and daughters-in-law report that they have "no problems" with each other, the researchers repeatedly express their surprise.[4] At a recent feminist psychology conference, I attended a workshop on mother-in-law/daughter-in-law relationships and was amazed at the terrible anxiety that pervaded the room; most of those in attendance were new mothers-in-law who had come because they so much wanted to "do it right." Even feminist writers and scholars have not attempted to demystify the negative constructions of this woman-to-woman relationship.

As someone who studies cultural representations of familial bonds, I have always been puzzled by the absence of mutually supportive mother-in-law/daughter-in-law relationships in our literature, especially given the connection Rose and I established over the few years of my marriage to her son. Rose was a diminutive, energetic, gray-haired woman whose eyes shone with her vital interest in everything that surrounded her. When she came to visit us in the college town where we teach, she accompanied me to lectures and poetry readings, to which she listened carefully, with openness and generosity. She often read my books and discussed them with me; she met many of my friends and joined in our talks with ease and curiosity. Much of our relationship revolved around the children—hers and mine—and we enjoyed sharing advice, worry, and reassurance. Little of our interaction was mediated by my husband/her son; we had our own issues to negotiate. We exchanged family stories and stories of her life: her childhood in Vienna, the escape from Hitler, life in Bolivia and later New York, raising four children, living as a widow for twenty years. We discussed movies and politics, but mainly we talked about people—her friends and mine, our relatives. I loved her cooking and her way of taking care of my household without ever intruding. She could play Sorry with our five-year-old with as much enthusiasm as she devoted to adult conversation. She loved to tell us about her travels and to listen to tales about ours. To me she was nothing like the "mother-in-law" of cultural representation, but she was also not simply a "friend"—after all, she mended my sweaters, shortened my pants, bounced my baby, and needed to be checked on several times a week. And when she died, very suddenly, three years ago, I knew, in spite of the deep pain I felt, that she was also not a "mother": that relationship may have many similar dimensions but it remains, nevertheless, unique, for reasons I find difficult to articulate.

When Rose died, I wanted very much to say something at her funeral and to write something about her and our relationship. I wanted to do it as a tribute to her and a gift to her family, but most of all I wanted, for myself, to focus the particular nature of our connection to each other. Writing about our relationship, I thought, would name it and make it real, since it seemed so much to stand outside the available discourses. Writing about it would give me a place in her memory since, as a "daughter-in-law" I was at a distance that made me sad and uncomfortable. Only two literary accounts of mother-in-law/daughter-in-law love and affection came to mind as possible models: Toni Morrison's *Beloved* and the Book of Ruth. They had a great deal in common with each other, but less with my story. In both texts, the daughter-in-law follows her mother-in-law to a foreign land—Morrison's Sethe to Baby Suggs's house, and freedom across the Ohio River, and Ruth from Moab to Judah and Naomi's home. In both, the mother-in-law/daughter-in-law bond is consolidated after the death or disappearance of the husband/son and evolves independently of him.[5]

Neither of these elements seemed to apply to me. Yet both texts show the mother-in-law as the figure who reconnects a family dispersed and fractured by circumstances, and this did echo Rose's role as mediator and link among her siblings, children, and grandchildren. Both speak of the deep connection between two women, of a mutual care, nurturance, and dependence that spoke to me and would, I thought, also speak to Rose's family. Both also describe the mother-in-law as a leader and teacher, someone who could show the daughter-in-law how to survive in the context of patriarchy and under the harshest conditions, and someone who was also willing to learn from the daughter-in-law's experience. Both describe the mother-in-law as someone who is willing to be literally inside and outside the law. These aspects appealed to me. As I came to prepare my short speech for the funeral, however, it was Ruth I chose, perhaps because, as a biblical text, it seemed more appropriate, perhaps because it is a story from my own tradition, perhaps simply because there were moments in the book that had always puzzled me and that, thinking about Rose, I was able to see in a new light. Seeing Ruth as a story about a mother-in-law was in itself new, since I had previously read it as a mother/daughter story, the only one in the Hebrew tradition. I had, until Rose's death, viewed the in-law relationship as metaphorical and chosen to disregard it. Rose's loss and the intense mourning that followed, along with my need for a story to define my relation to Rose and to explain my loss—a loss different from that felt by her children and grandchildren—suddenly made me see Ruth for what it had always been. And I knew from that moment on that I could only read Ruth through the lens of such a personal and deeply emotional response.

Ruth and Naomi are indeed, as the sociologists say, strangers to each other: they have different nationalities and religions. Ruth's decision to follow Naomi rather than to return to her own family is represented as radically unconventional, and it is this choice that has always fascinated me. For here a relationship between two women becomes the basis for the construction of family and social continuity. The unusual nature of Ruth's choice is underscored by its contrast to the choice of Orpah, the other daughter-in-law, who reluctantly returns to her Moabite family of origin. As the three women stand at the crossroads where Naomi urges her daughters-in-law to return to their own maternal families, they enact the fragility of female relationships in a world of compulsory marriage and heterosexuality. But as Ruth and Naomi return to Israel together, they transform the paternal family, mediated by the husband/son, into a maternal family of two women. Over time, they both come to realize that even though they have lost the men in the family, they have each other and therefore need not see themselves as barren or empty, as Naomi first thought. They also realize that their bond can indeed become the foundation of a new extended family—nothing less than the family of David—and that Boaz, the man Ruth will marry, and Obed, the son Ruth will have, need not divide them but can actually support and consolidate their own womanly relationship. The female family, which stands on the margin of a society whose law barely includes it by prescribing the charity on which Ruth relies for work and nourishment, can be made viable only through marriage and male mediation. But marriage, it turns out, can be a form of connection between mother-in-law and daughter-in-law rather than a form of disconnection between mother and daughter. Boaz serves as next of kin, as the representative of law and authority, what the French psychoanalyst Lacan calls the "name-of-the-father" who will allow Naomi and Ruth to own their land and have their child.

Throughout the process of their return to and reintegration into Israel, Ruth and Naomi work hard to take care of each other even as each takes care of herself. Ruth brings food to Naomi and never returns home empty-handed. Naomi advises Ruth on how to get Boaz to marry her. Although they are dependent on landowners like Boaz, they work slowly and steadily to reestablish a position commensurate with their former status, and they need to do this together. Ruth follows Naomi's advice and Naomi benefits from Ruth's dedication and hard work.

I have read the story many times and have always felt that Ruth is the one who believes most strongly in this relationship, who keeps it going—and needs to convince Naomi of who she is. Why did she choose to go with Naomi? Had Naomi been the mother Ruth never had, as Baby Suggs was for Sethe in Morrison's *Beloved*? Why did she protect Naomi to the point of lying to her, inserting her into the center of the relationship she was beginning to forge with Boaz? " 'He gave me these six measures of barley,' she said; 'he would not let me come home to my mother-in-law empty-handed.' " And why, when she gives birth to her son, is she content to disappear from the story and allow Naomi to be represented as the baby's mother?

It is this passage, in fact, that I have found the most ambiguous and troubling, especially since it seems to reinforce contemporary readings of the competition between mothers-in-law and daughters-in-law resulting from the birth of the daughter-in-law's child. ("The most frequent source of irritation with mothers-in-law focuses on issues around children," says Lucy Rose Fischer. "It is mothers-in-law, rather than mothers, who tend to be seen as subverting the daughter's right to manage her own child.")[6] And Naomi's neighbors say to her: " 'The child will give you new life and cherish you in your old age; for your daughter-in-law who loves you, who has proved better to you than seven sons, has borne him.' Naomi took the child and laid him in her lap and became his nurse. Her neighbours gave him a name: 'Naomi has a son,' they said; 'we will call him Obed.' " Although I realize that the laws of levirate marriage stipulate that the first son will carry the first husband's name, making Obed clearly Naomi's grandson, I have never understood why this paternal law is here also applied in the maternal realm, why the neighbors attribute the son to Naomi and seemingly eliminate Ruth, his mother, from the child's future.

During the brief period of Rose's illness and in the weeks following the shock of her death, I began to understand this passage and the unique quality of the relationship between mother-in-law and daughter-in-law. One moment, in particular, has remained with me to the point of obsession. It was in the hospital, on the eve of the surgery which Rose would not survive. We were all there—her four children, her sister, her brother, her sister-in-law, her son-in-law, and I, her daughter-in-law. I think now that on some level she knew she would not live and that she "told" me that through the intensity and utter sadness of her eyes. It was an intensity I could almost not bear, a gaze I had to force myself to return. But I also knew she could "tell" *me* because I was her daughter-in-law and not her child, or sister, or brother, because, she might have felt, I could bear the knowledge better than they but would still have the empathy to understand her sadness and fear. This was my role; her daughter would spend the night in the room with her, her sons would stand close to her the next morning, but I, her daughter-in-law, would bear her premature farewell message.

It was as she hugged me for the last time that she whispered, "Give the children a hug for me." It was a sentence I had heard so many times that I almost didn't hear it. But now it meant something different. Now that she would never be able to hug them again, I would have to give them a hug *for her* all the time. I have felt, in the years since her death, that I have to provide something of what they lost by losing her. Thus I have tried to incorporate some of the particular qualities she had, and perhaps I have become a better mother for it.

I also look at Gabriel, Rose's youngest grandchild, and I know that in many ways he is, like Obed, his grandma's son. He gained some of his warmth and his smile from the particular closeness he shared with her, from the secrets they discussed when he climbed into her bed every morning of her visits. There is a sparkle in his eye when he enjoys a game or looks forward to an activity that reminds me of Rose. As he has gotten older, he remembers Rose with a vividness that startles me, especially because his expression when he thinks of her is so much like hers. Through Gabriel I understand that the continuity of generations celebrated in Ruth can sometimes bypass the mother and be carried from grandmother to grandson. This need not exclude the mother; it need not result in conflict or competition. Naomi is Obed's nurse; she can transmit to Obed her own stories and values. By claiming Obed as her son, she has not supplanted Ruth but has shared him with her. The triangle established here is not one in which two women compete over a male child, but one in which a child enables the two women to enlarge their own relationship with each other. Gabriel certainly did this for me and Rose; we became closer through him. But he was a mediating figure, not the object of envy. He was and he continues to be the one who carries Rose's memory to me, just as I try to carry her memory to him. All of us together are the family Ruth and Naomi worked so hard to establish.

I have no daughters, a source of much regret in my life. But if my sons decide to marry, I will be able to experience the relationship between mothers-in-law and daughters-in-law. I hope I will have learned from Rose just how to enjoy that woman-to-woman bond.

A few weeks after Rose's death a small package arrived in the mail. My sister-in-law Elly sent me Rose's favorite necklace—a gold chain with a diamond-shaped garnet pendant. Her gift touched me deeply because it signaled her recognition of my place in Rose's memory. But, since Rose wore it every day, it seemed fitting to my sense of female transmission that her daughter should have it, and I regretfully told her so. Although, like me, Elly loves the delicate garnets and the connection to Rose that they bring, she urged me to keep it, since she was wearing the ring her mother had wanted her to have. We finally agreed to share the necklace: I would wear it for a few months, then give it back to Elly for a while. Through her garnets, Rose has taught us, posthumously, how to continue the network of relationships she fostered through her life.

7

"Ruth the Moabite . . . Begot David"

RUTH 1:22, 4:22

*U*NLIKE the other section titles in this volume, this section's title is not drawn from a single verse. Instead it brings together phrases from Ruth's beginning (1:22) and end (4:22) and thus highlights the connections between Ruth's Moabite origins and her place in the engendering of the Messiah, whom Jewish tradition envisions as the descendant of David. As a Moabite, Ruth is not simply an outsider, but the descendant of a despised people, a cruel, inhospitable enemy whose origins the Bible traces to a major sexual transgression. Both authors in this section probe the meaning of the tainted lineage the Bible ascribes to Israel's ultimate redeemer as well as Israel's ideal king.

For Tamar Frankiel the puzzle of the book centers on the "contradiction" of redemption achieved through a "crooked, twisted path" of sin and transgression. By using the concepts developed in Kabbala (Jewish mysticism) Frankiel reads Ruth as a story of *tikkun* (correction). The actions of Ruth, Naomi, and Boaz together prepare the world for the Messiah, but Ruth the Moabite, descendant of incest, cruelty, and inhospitality, particularly opens the way with her generosity, lovingkindness, and egolessness.

Frankiel's interpretation, though based in the complexities of the Jewish mystical tradition, remains comfortably within a religious language. Susan Reimer Torn poses some of the same questions to the text but from a radically different perspective. Like many of the writers in this volume, she contrasts her current understanding of Ruth to a childhood memory of a character closely resembling the selfless heroine Frankiel extols. Torn now imagines Ruth as a "highly charged, transformative field" who "brings forth a Messiah with the ingredients of incest." Rather than explaining the pervasive presence of this pattern in messianic history in religious terms, she uses comparative mythology and Jungian psychoanalysis. Whereas for Frankiel, Ruth's transformation of the sexual transgression in her ancestry consists of "egolessness," a humility expressed in the willingness to surrender to the needs of the other, Torn describes the same transformative energy as a search for "the fullest dimensions of Self."

These two writers assemble similar pieces of the puzzle into radically different configurations. Yet both are drawn to project their textual readings into lessons that speak to our psychological and spiritual needs. The very nature of the theme that fascinates them, the pathway to the Messiah, engenders motion forward into our own lives, since the concept of "Messiah" implies the ongoing need for and movement toward a redemptive goal in an imperfect world.

Ruth and the Messiah

TAMAR FRANKIEL

❧

The Path to the Messiah

Ruth, tradition tells us, is the "mother of the Messiah"—that is, the ancestress of David, who was the "anointed one," the king chosen by God to lead the Jewish people to its greatest heights in the land of Israel. David is regarded as at once the most pious of kings, author of most of the Psalms, and the greatest warrior, whose strategies won the citadel of Jerusalem and made it possible to unite the Israelite tribes completely. One would expect that such a man, even if he were but the youngest son of Jesse, would have an illustrious lineage.

But did he? The story of Ruth and her marriage to Boaz is the last in a history of strange liaisons, going back to the time of Abraham, that eventually led to the birth of David. This history began on Ruth's side, with the incestuous relationship of Lot (Abraham's nephew) and his daughters. After the destruction of Sodom and Gomorrah, Lot's daughters concluded that they were the only survivors of a worldwide devastation. To perpetuate the human race, they got their father drunk and became pregnant by him (Genesis 19:31–38). From them came the Ammonites and the Moabites, the latter being Ruth's ancestors.

As if being born in incest were not enough, the Moabites gained in infamy by their refusal to aid the Israelites during their trek through the wilderness on their way to the promised land, and by their hiring a famous non-Jewish prophet to curse them.[1] For this lack of concern for

---

The author used the Book of Ruth in Artscroll Tanach Series (Brooklyn, N.Y.: Mesorah Publications, 1989; orig. 1976).

others, this lack of *chesed* (kindness), it was decreed that Moabites could not marry Israelites (Deuteronomy 23:4–5).

Boaz's ancestors came from the union of Tamar and Judah. Judah was Tamar's father-in-law, having married two of his sons (from a Canaanite wife) to Tamar in succession, and betrothed the third to her as well. When Judah delayed the third marriage ceremony, fearing that Tamar was the cause of the first two sons' deaths, Tamar took matters into her own hands. Disguising herself as a harlot, she waited by the roadside for Judah, whom she knew to be traveling in the region, and induced him to visit her. She bore twins by him, named Perez and Zoar; from Perez's line came Boaz (Genesis 38).

Ruth and Boaz ended up marrying under less unusual circumstances, though they still did not follow typical marriage procedures. Ruth, following Naomi's advice, went at night to the threshing floor where Boaz was sleeping during the harvest season. When he woke, she asked him to "spread [his] skirt" over her and redeem her according to the laws of levirate marriage. Even if we understand the text as indicating that no sexual relations occurred until after the marriage was properly arranged the next day, Ruth's action was still a bit forward. The text acknowledges this by describing how her coming and going were designed not to attract attention. Nevertheless, from this union came Obed, father of Jesse, father of David.

Finally, the family for whom Boaz was performing a duty as redeemer was not untarnished. He married Ruth because he was a kinsman to Elimelech and thus to Elimelech's son Mahlon, who had been Ruth's husband. But Elimelech had blackened his family's name by leaving Israel at a time of famine. The biblical commentators, beginning with Rashi, regarded his departure as especially treacherous because he was known to have been a wealthy man who could have helped the poor and hungry had he stayed home. While it is permissible for a Jew to leave Israel in time of famine (on the model of Abraham and the sons of Jacob), Elimelech left not out of actual need but out of fear and selfishness. Naomi, when she returned to Israel, had declined greatly in social status because of the loss of her wealth and her family, losses which—as Naomi herself recognized—were themselves regarded as signs of God's disapproval: "I went away full, and God has sent me back empty" (1:21).

David's family background is, to say the least, problematic. Yet

David, the "Chosen One of Israel," known for his piety, artistry, and leadership, is supposed to be both the ancestor and the model of the Messiah whom Jews have awaited for centuries, the great leader who will reunite us and bring the history of creation to its fulfillment. Similarly, we are taught that the path to that ultimate fulfillment is the faithful observance of Torah law, as developed and applied through the tradition of the sages: laws of ritual and ethics to be kept to the letter as well as with an intense devotion of spirit. Yet the prehistory of the kingly Messiah, David, shows that rules were flouted left and right by his ancestors—including rules of sexual boundaries and purity, which were and are often considered of the highest priority. How can we reconcile this contradiction? Tradition prescribes one path to the goal, the straight path of observance; yet the same tradition attests historically to the fact that the goal is achieved through a crooked, twisted path, where observance of the law seems to play a minor role.

Some have argued that these transgressions, when understood in context, might not even be considered violations of law. For example, Lot's daughters were acting according to a mistaken, but well-intentioned, belief that they were the last living humans, so that preservation of the species would take precedence over incest prohibitions. Tamar acted within her rights, since she was required to marry a redeemer from her husbands' family; she simply chose the father instead of the brother. Ruth and Boaz committed no actual sin, only the minor indiscretion of meeting alone at night.

Context, however, could not explain away one of the violations: Ruth was a Moabite, and marriages with Moabites were forbidden to Jews. Indeed, the traditional view of the Book of Ruth is that Shmuel HaNavi (Samuel the Prophet) was inspired to write it specifically to deal with this problem: Shmuel had anointed David at God's decree, and he wrote Ruth to counter objections he knew would be made to David's qualifications for holding the throne of Israel. Indeed, one of David's opponents, Doeg, a brilliant man and an adviser to King Saul, repeatedly attacked David's reputation on the grounds that he was of Moabite ancestry, and encouraged Saul to kill David as a rebel (1 Samuel 22). He claimed that since David's great-grandmother was a Moabite, her marriage to Boaz was a forbidden union and therefore David was a *mamzer*, or bastard. David's supporters claimed that the law against intermarriage included only the men, not the women, of the

Moabite nation. The traditional commentaries on Ruth hold that this interpretation of the law was understood by Boaz, and this was why the elders of Bethehem accepted Boaz's marriage to Ruth, as described in the concluding scene of the book (4:11–12).

Yet none of the explanations is entirely satisfying. We still ask: Why did it have to be this way? Shouldn't the messianic lineage be pure and untainted? If scribes of Davidic times had wanted to invent a perfect lineage for the Messiah, they certainly could have done so, but they did not. And why not? One answer is that the questions in themselves are valuable: they leave room for mystery, and therefore for faith. Further, they encourage us to probe beneath the surface. Modern critical interpretations tend to view Ruth as a beautiful legend or interesting literary piece, but they ignore the deeper issue of its real significance. The guardians of Jewish tradition insisted that the story told in Ruth, with all its bizarre circumstances, is one of the traces in history of the path to the Messiah. They also insisted on its prophetic origins, in order to emphasize that it contains messages absolutely essential to the fulfillment of our destiny. We must take seriously that this book is one of the keys to the direction of history, a trajectory along the path of grace.

Good from Evil

If we take this viewpoint, we find that the Book of Ruth begins to speak to us more richly, offering beacons to guide our own path. Let us take our first clue from the kabbalistic tradition, as summarized by Rav Moshe Chaim Luzzatto in the eighteenth century:

> It is known to all who have been given understanding that the soul of David was clothed in the shell of Moab and that it was freed from Moab through Ruth. Concerning this, too, Scripture says: Who could withdraw purity from impurity? These were the intentions of the inscrutable wisdom of the Creator in guiding His world to bring every act to its proper path. Every act of God travels through byways, often in complex, crooked ones. . . . For such has occurred to all great souls as they go among the "shells" of impurity to capture and extract the good.
> —*Megilat Setarim*

The biblical quotation "Who can withdraw purity from impurity?"

comes from the book of Job (14:3). The Midrash on that verse expands
the scope of the question:

> Abraham came from Terach, Hezekiah from Achaz, Yoshiah from
> Omon, Mordechai from Shim'i, Israel from the nations, the world to
> come from this world. Who could do this? Who could command this?
> Who could decree this? No one but [God] the only One on earth!
>
> —BAMIDBAR RABBAH[2]

The rabbinic and mystical traditions assert that God can turn evil to
good—indeed, that God intends good to be born from evil in order to
"raise the sparks," to redeem the good that is hidden in every evil.
This is the *tikkun* or correction that will bring the world to perfection.

But to leave this lesson on the level of faith, even mystical faith, is incomplete. Why is it that, in David's prehistory, God chose these particular instances of evil: Lot's daughters' incest, the Moabite treachery,
Tamar's apparent harlotry, Elimelech's selfishness? Is there something distinctive about these sins that defines the aspects of the world which the
Messiah must redeem? At another level, perhaps it is possible to ask *how*
it is that the actors in Ruth bring forth the good. How do they transform the evil of previous generations into the foundation for the highest
level of human achievement, represented by the kingship of David?

We can begin by noting that the traditions surrounding Ruth and
the Davidic lineage attest to three different kinds of impropriety or sin
in which the forbears of David were involved. Then we can consider,
for each in turn, how it is that the primary figures of the book of
Ruth—Ruth, Naomi, and Boaz—acted as channels for the divine work
of "raising the sparks," how they created the *tikkun* that drew the good
out from the evil. The three areas of sin were (1) the cruelty of the Moabites (their inhospitality to the Israelites when they came out of Egypt,
and their attempt to have them cursed), (2) the sin of leaving the land
of Israel (Elimelech and family), and (3) sexual improprieties (Lot and
his daughters; Tamar and Judah).

The sins of the Moabites, mentioned in the book of Deuteronomy
and described more fully in the story of Balak (Numbers 22:2–24:25),
ranged from implicit hostility (their unwillingness to give the Israelites
even water) to preparing for war. They stopped short of actual violence

only out of fear of the Israelites' strength, which had just been demonstrated against the Amorites. Their hateful attitude is in the sharpest possible contrast to the character of Ruth and even of Orpah, Naomi's other Moabite daughter-in-law. For these women exemplify kindness (*chesed*). Indeed, kindness is mentioned repeatedly in Ruth as the greatest of virtues and an occasion for blessings.

Naomi expresses her appreciation to her daughters-in-law with these words:

> May Hashem deal *kindly* with you, as *you have dealt kindly with the dead and with me*! May Hashem grant that you may find security, each in the home of her husband. (1:8–9)

Boaz reiterates Ruth's virtues, again with a blessing, in 2:11:

> I have been fully informed of all that you have done for your mother-in-law after the death of your husband, and how you left your father and mother and the land of your birth and went to a people you had never known before. May Hashem reward your actions, and may your payment be full from Hashem, the God of Israel, under whose wings you have come to seek refuge.

Rabbi Yehoshua Bachrach has pointed out that this passage echoes the story of Abraham, who was told to leave "your country and your family and your father's house."[3] If Ruth imitates Abraham in going to a strange land, she also follows in his footsteps as an exemplar of *chesed*. Abraham was known for his hospitality, Ruth for her kindness to her adopted family. Ruth, like Abraham, would eventually be rewarded with righteous descendants.

Naomi praises Boaz in similar terms for his kindness. When Ruth reports to Naomi how Boaz not only allowed her to glean in his fields, but made sure she was well fed and had plenty to take home, Naomi exclaims: "Blessed be he of Hashem, for not failing in his *kindness to the living or to the dead*!" (2:20). Finally, when Ruth surprises Boaz by asking him to act as redeemer, he blesses her also: "Be blessed of Hashem, my daughter; you have made your latest act of *kindness* greater than the first, in that you have not gone after the younger men, be they poor or rich" (3:10). As the Midrash and later commentaries noted, kindness is a continual refrain in the text, and is directly connected with the bestowal of blessings.[4]

We know that *chesed* has always been considered a primary Jewish virtue, and not only because of Abraham: the sages said that kindness, mercy, and modesty are characteristics of the entire Jewish people. We are reminded repeatedly in the Torah that we should be kind to the stranger "because you were strangers in the land of Egypt" (Exodus 22:20, 23:9; Leviticus 19:33–34; Deuteronomy 24:17–18). Anyone who does not have family to provide and care for them—the widow, the orphan—is to be the focus of our special concern.[5] In the Book of Ruth, however, it is the stranger-widow-orphan Ruth, who has left her family and come to a new land, who is the exemplar of kindness.

Notably, Naomi praises not only Ruth but also Orpah and Boaz for going to extremes in *chesed*, specifically for their kindness "to the living and the dead." The kindness of the daughters-in-law refers not only to their taking over the responsibility of their dead husbands in caring for Naomi, but also, the Midrash tells us, to their arranging for their funerals (traditionally a masculine responsibility).[6] They go beyond the call of duty, showing an excess of *chesed*, as Jewish tradition holds that an act done on behalf of a dead person is at a very high level, since s/he cannot return the kindness. One who performs acts for the dead is on the level of Moses, following in the ways of God himself. Similarly, Boaz honors Ruth's dead husband by being kind to Ruth and showing honor to her, even though the favor can never be returned. Boaz praises Ruth for her kindness in selecting him, an old man, over a young one. This too is *chesed* toward the dead: she chooses to preserve her husband's lineage by marrying a relative rather than a younger man who might be more pleasing to her.

Because Ruth, Boaz, and even Orpah go to extremes in their kindness, always having in mind the dead as well as the living, they stand at the opposite end of the spectrum from the Moabites of a few generations before, who refused to offer bread and water to travelers through their land. The Moabite women, tradition tells us, did not participate in that sin; and it was in fact Moabite women like Ruth and Orpah who could transform that history by extending themselves in kindness. Where the earlier generation refused to do even the minimum to maintain life, Ruth does the maximum to honor even the dead. Here we can see explicitly how the evil "shell" of Moab, which clothed the soul of David, began to be broken. The Book of Ruth also poses a question for us as we seek to free the imprisoned sparks of the Messiah in our times:

while Jews everywhere emphasize *chesed,* how far does our kindness really extend?

The second sin was that of Elimelech's leaving the land. In contrast, the Book of Ruth stresses the theme of return: those who left the land return to it. Again, we find a number of references. In 1:6 the text states that Naomi, after the death of her sons, "then arose along with her daughters-in-law to *return from the fields of Moab,* for she had heard in the fields of Moab that Hashem had remembered His people by giving them food." The episode of their departure from Moab and arrival in Bethlehem concludes with an apparently repetitious statement: "And Naomi *returned,* and Ruth the Moabite, her daughter-in-law, with her, the *one who returned from the fields of Moab,* and they came to Bet lechem at the beginning of the barley harvest" (1:22). When Boaz's servant identifies Ruth to him, he explains that Ruth is "the *one who returned with Naomi from the fields of Moab*" (2:6).

Since Ruth had never been to the land of Israel before, it is quite remarkable that she should be repeatedly identified as one who "returns." Boaz proceeds to address Ruth in a welcoming tone:

> Hear me well, my daughter: Do not go to glean in another field, and don't leave here, but stay here close to my maidens. Keep your eyes on the field which they are harvesting and follow them. I have ordered the young men not to molest you. Should you get thirsty, go to the jugs and drink from what the young men have drawn. (2:8–9)

The Midrash interprets verse 8 allegorically: "Do not go to glean in another 'spiritual' field: 'Thou shalt have no other gods before Me.' " The allegorical interpretation reflects as well the emphasis on Ruth's new adherence. She has promised Naomi, "Wherever you go, I will go." Here she is explicitly told not to leave her newfound home. Even though she is a Moabite by birth, she is now treated as a "returner," one who belongs to the land and is under the stricture of not leaving.

Boaz's welcoming speech to Ruth is one of the highlights of the book. It concludes her search for a place in her new country and is a prelude to the next phase, in which she will approach Boaz directly as a potential marriage partner. The Midrash's introduction of another level of interpretation emphasizes the importance of this passage. Note that Boaz goes on to say, "Keep your eyes on the field." At a deeper level, we can understand him to be saying that the land is a feast for the eyes, reflecting the light of the Torah and the Jewish people. "Stay close to my maidens," he goes on—for the women of Israel represent the *Shekhinah* (presence of God) that rests there. "If you get thirsty, go to the jugs and drink." Water often symbolizes the wellspring of life and Torah itself, which is now available to Ruth through the labor of the "young men."

Ruth hears these words as "comfort," as words spoken directly "on her heart" (2:13), not merely as social acceptance or the assurance that she will get a meal. Rather, she experiences a deep sense of belonging, of coming home. She is then content to come near to Boaz and sit beside the "harvesters"—though she is merely a "gleaner"—sharing bread dipped in vinegar to cool herself from the heat. "She ate and was satisfied," the text concludes, echoing the biblical command that "you will eat and be satisfied, and bless the Lord your God for the good land which he has given you" (Deuteronomy 8:10). Ruth the returner is accepting the bounty that the land has to give her: not only physical sustenance, but spiritual refreshment and homecoming. In her grateful return we can see the arrogance of Elimelech, who abandoned the land when it was not bountiful, being rectified. Another shell, this time one that sometimes hardens the Jewish heart, is being broken. Again we can hear the echo for our times: How deep is our connection to our people and to the land? How heartfelt is our gratitude for our life, our history, the bounty God has shown us?

Ruth exemplifies kindness, in contrast to the harshness of her former people, and gratitude, in contrast to her father-in-law's arrogance. But she herself seems to be implicated in what comes close to a sin when she approaches Boaz in the dark of the night. How is it that the sexual sins of Lot and his daughters, on the one hand, and Tamar and Judah on the other, are transformed in this story?

Marriage and sexuality in Jewish tradition are directly linked with holiness. The exclusive partnership of husband and wife, the family unit, and the privacy and intimacy of the home as a physical locus of holiness—all these have deep significance. The woman often symbolizes this constellation of meanings. As I have suggested elsewhere, the archetypal woman, represented by Sarah, the first Jew, is connected by analogy with the Holy Temple in Jerusalem, for she is the recipient of the same blessings. Sarah is said to have had a blessing in her *challah* that made it stay fresh from week to week, her candles never went out, and a divine cloud hovered over her tent. Similarly in the *mishkan* (tabernacle) and later the Holy Temple, the shewbread was always fresh; the *ner tamid* (eternal light) provided a continual light; and the *Shekhinah* hovered over in the form of a cloud.[7]

Yet Ruth does not seem to be exemplifying this aspect of holiness, which is usually symbolized by a protected inner space: the Holy of Holies within the inner court, Sarah in her tent, Queen Esther in her palace chambers. Ruth, by contrast, goes out to the threshing floor. She encounters Boaz in his temporary sleeping quarters for the harvest season. Ruth's situation here echoes that of Lot's daughters and Tamar. The mothers of Moab and Ammon were in the wilderness, out beyond civilization, after the destruction of Sodom. Tamar played the harlot by the roadside in a temporary structure. These settings suggest that we are outside the boundaries that usually constitute the infrastructure, so to speak, of holiness.

The meeting between Ruth and Boaz shares the outsideness, almost the wildness, of the other strange liaisons. But at the same time the story manages to create an atmosphere of holiness in a unique way, very different from the more familiar symbolism of home and temple. In doing so, it raises to a new level our ideas of intimate relationship. What we notice above all in the planning of the meeting between Ruth and Boaz, and in the meeting that actually takes place, is a delicate humility and even surrender which each person shows to the other.

This becomes evident in three simple statements in the third chapter. First, when Naomi reveals her plan to Ruth, she advises Ruth to listen to Boaz: "He will tell you what you are to do" (3:4). Second, Ruth replies simply, "All that you say to me I will do" (3:5). Third, when Boaz wakes and discovers Ruth by his side, he turns the relationship around: "Do not fear; whatever you say, I will do for you" (3:11).

Each person completely yields to the authority of the other. It is as if each one, even though faced with an unusual suggestion or surprising turn of events, recognizes in it the will of God, and accepts it with utter egolessness.[8] As far as we know, Ruth had encountered Boaz only once during the harvest, and he had made no move to propose marriage. Yet at the end of the season of work, Naomi instructs her to go out in the

evening, lie down near him, and do whatever he says. Boaz finds a
woman sleeping next to him; not only does he immediately put the
most positive interpretation on her act, but he also assures her that he
will do everything possible to carry out her will in the matter of marriage.

Compare this relationship to the earlier questionable unions. Lot's
daughters took it upon themselves to overthrow their father's authority
and gave birth to nations of ill repute. Tamar was different—on a level
higher, so to speak. While she took it upon herself to assert her rights,
she ultimately placed herself in the hands of the other. When her pregnancy was discovered and reported to Judah, he ordered her killed. She,
however, had kept his staff and ring, which he left with her in place of
a promised payment. She now sent them privately to him with a message: the person to whom these belong is the father of my child. While
she could have exposed him publicly, she did not. Rather, she put herself in his hands: if he acknowledged paternity, he would make her his
proper wife; if he denied it, she would die (Genesis 38:24–26). While
Tamar had first bypassed Judah's plans, she showed him the ultimate
honor by placing her trust in him, hoping that he would prove to be
the godly man she believed him to be.

This extraordinary humility and faith in the other comes to its highest point in Ruth. Ruth had affirmed her willingness to follow Naomi;
now she risks her reputation, indeed her entire life, in this new society,
on Naomi's words. Moreover, she agrees to follow the directions of a
strange man. Certainly, she has already experienced him as kind and
welcoming, but she doesn't really know him. Instead of having her sub-
mit to his authority, however, he submits to her: I will do for you
whatever you tell me.

Implicit here is a remarkable perception of the dynamics of a male-
female relationship, one which will be echoed in rabbinic writings down
through the ages. Its first appearance was in the Chumash (Pentateuch),
when God advised Abraham to follow Sarah's advice: "In everything she
tells you, listen to her voice." There are other examples of biblical couples in which one member accedes to the other: Isaac accepts Rebekah's
plot (after Jacob stole the blessing); Jacob insists that Rachel face her
own relationship with God; Judah declares of Tamar that "she is more
righteous than I"; Moses agrees to the circumcision of his son by
Zipporah. In each of those stories, however, there remains a suggestion

of tension, a sense that there was or may have been a struggle. In Ruth, however, the partners achieve an extraordinary gracious and reciprocal relationship: what you say, I will do.

Deeds follow the words: Ruth accepts the burden of marrying an elderly man; Boaz exerts himself on her behalf among his townsmen, to ensure that she will be accepted in Israelite society. Moreover, each expresses deep gratitude to the other. Ruth asks, "Why have I found favor in your eyes?" (2:10). Boaz responds to her acts with, "Be blessed of the Lord, my daughter; you have made your latest act of kindness greater than the first" (3:10). In their repeated honoring of each other, we see the prelude to the understanding of marriage in the rabbinic tradition: "A man must love his wife as himself, and honor her more than himself" (Yevamot 62b). In the way Boaz and Ruth act toward one another, yet another level of the shell around the soul of David is broken. There could hardly be a more poignant message for us today, we who live in the era of "broken homes": can we imagine bringing egolessness back into our relationships?

The final, remarkable sequence brings home the point of the story. Boaz, having decided to marry Ruth if the closer kinsman will allow it, goes to the gate and waits. The text records:

> Just then, the redeemer of whom Boaz had spoken passed by. He said, "Come over, sit down here, 'Ploni Almoni,' " and he came over and sat down. . . . Then he said to the redeemer, "The parcel of land which belonged to our brother, Elimelech, is being offered for sale. . . . If you are willing to redeem, redeem!" . . . And he said, "I am willing to redeem it." Then Boaz said, "The day you buy the field, you must also buy Ruth the Moabite, wife of the deceased, to perpetuate the name of the deceased on his inheritance." The redeemer said, "Then I cannot redeem it for myself. . . . Take over my redemption responsibility on yourself, for I am unable to redeem." (4:1–7)

The name of the other redeemer is not mentioned—only a pseudonym, "Ploni Almoni," sometimes translated "so-and-so." The commentators tell us that his real name is withheld lest his reputation be lessened because he did not discharge his obligation. Otherwise he is only called "the redeemer."

But there is another level of meaning here. *Ploni* is said to mean "hidden"; *almoni*, either "nameless" or "mute." This is the redeemer who had to be hidden, who would be nameless because he failed to speak on behalf of one in need. This so-called redeemer would take on the redemption of the field, of the land, but not of the Moabite, the outsider. He is, the text tells us, a false redeemer, a failed redeemer.

Boaz, on the other hand, is the consummate redeemer. For him, the fullness of the field, the holy land, is meant to feed the hungry. He understands that a person has wealth and status in order to serve and to help, not to preserve his own name. Thus he is willing to father a child who will in a sense be Elimelech's child, not his own. Later it turns out that Obed is not called Elimelech's son—that name would do him no honor. Rather, he is called Naomi's son and also receives the title "redeemer," the restorer of her life. In the end, Boaz is acknowledged as Obed's father (4:14–21), but Boaz did not count on any of this. His kindness, openness, generosity, and willingness to stand up for those in need make him the true redeemer.

Ruth needed a redeemer, for she was left alone, adrift in society and separated from her homeland and her family. She was in a sense the new Abraham, who had also left his homeland and his father's house at God's call. On another level, David's soul needed a redeemer, because it had been wandering in some of the impure places of the spiritual world. Who could this redeemer be? It could not be one who focused only on what would be good by society's standards. Such a redeemer would hold back selfishly—like Elimelech at the beginning or the nameless redeemer at the end of Ruth. This false redeemer would be a hoax, truly no redeemer at all.

Rather, the redeemer had to be, like Abraham, a person of *chesed*. Boaz and Naomi each represent facets of this redeemer: a person of kindness, gratitude, and humility, a person who affirms God's grace and bounty and sees God's will in every event. These are some of the characteristics that make it possible for Ruth to be redeemed, and for David to be born. But Ruth, the redeemed, herself embodies many qualities of the redeemer. It is she who prepares the way, by acting with extraordinary *chesed* in her own life. Boaz, the redeeming kinsman, responds with the same level of *chesed*.

The extraordinary goodness and the selfless actions of Boaz and Ruth enable them, under Naomi's insightful guidance, to rectify the course of David's soul and prepare the world for the Messiah. The story of these three helps us answer the question of why David's lineage is so strange. Their actions display a *tikkun*, a correction, to the wanderings of earlier generations from the straight path: Lot's break with Abraham; his daughters' incest; his Moabite descendants' hostility; Tamar's resort to harlotry; Elimelech's desertion of his people. The figures in Ruth offer the *tikkun* for all those acts of selfishness, which eventually express themselves in the world as lust, treachery, and war. Only when such righteous people as Ruth, Boaz, and Naomi have arrived on the scene can the kingly soul of David come into the world.

From this we can begin to understand the possibility of redemption in our day, to open at least one gate along the path to the Messiah. These traces of the history of redemption which Ruth records for us provide hints as to how to prepare for redemption. The model is *chesed*—kindness at every level and every opportunity. Particularly, Ruth reminds us to be mindful of *chesed* for the dead as well as the living: to honor in memory and deed the past generations. Each of our ancestors had a "name," a lineage, a personal contribution to our tradition, which we too often belittle or neglect. As we rebuild Jewish life on the ashes of those who devoted themselves to Torah—as we have always rebuilt on the ashes—it is especially important to awaken this form of *chesed* in ourselves.

Second, we can be "returners," like Ruth and Naomi. If we have left to sow and reap in other fields, "the fields of Moab," we can return. This means that the Jewish people must turn their faces toward one another, like the cherubim on the ark. We can embrace one another, in appreciation of our traditional way of life and the land of Israel. In this kind of turning and returning, we can learn the powerful practice of gratitude: being grateful for the life and sustenance we are given, for the kindnesses we receive from others, for the special qualities of the Jewish people and our land. Yet at the same time, we cannot focus only on what will be good for us, for our "family." *Chesed* demands that we be ready to see the good in everyone, to recognize and encourage virtue in all, "outsider" and "insider" alike, and to extend to all the bounty we receive.

Third, and perhaps most difficult, we must learn to relate to others with humility, recognizing each person in our life as an agent of God, seeing everything that happens as a teaching from heaven. These lessons are sometimes harder to learn from strangers than friends, from spouses than strangers. Wherever our difficulties are, that is where we can learn most, and where we most need to be grateful. The sense of divine direction that we find in the Book of Ruth can enter our lives. Our task is to become less driven by ego, more willing to do the will of the other. Practicing this level of *chesed* can open our hearts, and can indeed make possible the redemption of which we have so long dreamed.

For we too await a *tikkun* for those acts of long ago which sent their ripples of evil across the earth: the arrogant desire for power, wealth, comfort, and pleasure, which have given us war, pornography, and oppression. Like Ruth, we can take steps to generate this *tikkun* in our own day.

Ruth Reconsidered

SUSAN REIMER TORN

༄

Ruth was never one of my favorite biblical heroines, certainly not back in the days when I first read her story in religious day school. Ruth, who put aside concern for herself in deference to her bereaved mother-in-law, was a model of the self-sacrificing woman we young girls were taught to emulate. But Ruth could not earn a place in my pantheon of heroines, as I was skeptical at an early age of women who were considered worthy because of a willingness to overlook their own needs. My distaste for Ruth's capacity for self-abnegation led me to neglect her for years.

Recently, however, I've rediscovered Ruth in a startling new perspective. No longer do I think of her as one-dimensional or bland. In Ruth, humanity's basest impulses and highest aspirations merge in a potent alchemy. Far from being some goody two-shoes, Ruth is a highly charged, transformative field, a mysterious terrain where taboo and redemption are reconciled.

In day school I was taught that Ruth was a forebear of the Messiah, her lofty destiny confirming that righteousness is duly rewarded. I also learned that she was a gentile and moreover, according to the Babylonian Talmud, a princess, granddaughter of the Moabite king Eglon. Moabites were a people excluded from the Jewish nation, because they originated from a disturbing incident of father-daughter incest.

Although it was never highlighted in school, Ruth came from a pariah tribe whose inception took place in the aftermath of the destruction of Sodom and Gomorrah. Lot's daughters, fleeing with their father,

---

The author used the Colbo edition of the Book of Ruth (Paris, 1986).

were convinced he was the only man left on earth. Consequently, they decided to have sex with him to ensure the survival of the human race. As told in Genesis, chapter 19, the act was initiated by Lot's older daughter, who lay with her father after getting him drunk. She conceived a son whom she would call Moab (derived from the Hebrew *meab*, from father), and urged her sister to take her turn the following night. Although the intoxicated Lot participated only semiconsciously and his daughters believed they were saving the human species from annihilation, the incestuous origins of Moab are a blemish on Ruth's pedigree. But in spite of this tarnish, not only is Ruth welcomed into the Jewish fold, she is singularly credited with insuring the birth of the Messiah. What began in incest passed through Ruth and reemerged as redemptive.

It is not immediately evident what message lies in this astonishing juxtaposition of moral polarities. I can't help thinking back to my school days when I first met Ruth, to the emphasis in our early education on the absolute dichotomy of right and wrong, sin and virtue. There were good girls (who were not selfish) and bad girls (who, of course, were); the light of faith versus the darkness of doubt; the rightness of the Jewish cause versus the criminality of our enemies. I always had trouble with the virtues-versus-transgressions worldview that crops up in the Book of Ruth: If Ruth was the devoted daughter-in-law, praised for staying with Naomi, she had to have a counterpart in Orpah, the daughter-in-law who lacked sufficient devotion and was disparaged for going home. Yet, surely, I thought, even then, the issue could not be black and white; some sympathy might be accorded a young widow, childless after ten years of marriage, who sought to start her life anew.

The revelation that Ruth brought forth a Messiah out of incest suggested that I could think about her in less categorical ways. The startling contrast between Ruth's origins and her destiny implied that the separation of high and low, right and wrong, laudable conduct and acts that are damned was not as rigid as a young yeshiva girl was trained to believe. Ruth, seen in a new light, reflects the idea that human experience can incorporate extremes.

Even if this moral paradox was overlooked by our teachers, surely the traditional biblical commentators had to address it. How did they explain why a Moabite, of all women, was chosen for this noblest of fates? What message or meaning could the rabbis derive from Ruth's dual identity as issue of an incest and progenitor of the Messiah?

In his introduction to the Colbo edition of the Book of Ruth, Rabbi Nosson Scherman faces the issue squarely. He relies on esoteric kabbalistic sources to explain that good and evil are not stored in separate compartments in God's world. On the contrary, the divine sparks of goodness are entrapped in outer shells of evil. This is why the righteous souls who are called upon to rescue the divine sparks must be willing to penetrate evil and understand its ways. They can do so and remain unblemished since this seemingly circuitous path is part of a divine plan culminating in redemption.

If the redemption of good that is trapped in evil is a prerequisite of the messianic era, it becomes less startling that the redeemer's origins could be sown in impure soil. Rabbi Moshe Chaim Luzzato explains in the Sefer Megillat Setarim (a kabbalistic text), "The pure soul of David was imprisoned in the evil shell of Moab." It seems that back at the beginning of this tale, on the eve of the destruction of Sodom and Gomorrah, the angel of God who visited Lot gave him a holy spark. "This spark," explains Rabbi Luzzato, "was passed along from Lot through his daughter through seven generations of Moabites until it was the destiny of Ruth, who carried the spark within her, to bring it into the fold of the Jewish nation."

It follows that a force for the good which is powerful enough to engender the Messiah has to be contained in an equally powerful medium of evil. What more appropriate act within this context than incest? No minor transgression could harden into a crust strong enough to imprison a divine spark of that potential. The harder you fall, the higher you soar: the more explosive the sin, the more resounding its ultimate liberation. If that's what the Book of Ruth can be said to be about, and I believe it is, then, Ruth is certainly a more compelling figure than I ever imagined in grade school.

The question remains: why, of all possible manifestations of wrongdoing on earth, was the act of father-daughter incest the specific dark medium in which the messianic spark had to be embedded? Can an illicit sex act, however shocking and distasteful, be considered the expression of evil incarnate? We will see that, however disturbing, a daughter's urge to "return to the father" is repeatedly associated with

messianic aims. Why does this theme play so important a role in redemptive schemes, and what are the implications for the virtuous figure
known as Ruth?

While the biblical authors tell us little about the women named in the
messianic lineage, all of them have in common the willful return to the
father. In the story of Ruth, incest is more than a haunting specter of
an ignoble past. The pattern of an irregular relationship between a
younger woman and an older father figure is set seven generations back
at the beginnings of Moab. In mutated and attenuated form, the theme
is echoed several times in connection with the Messiah's ancestry. Let's
start with a closer look at the story of Ruth and how her instrumental
marriage to Boaz came about.

After Ruth's return to Bethlehem with her impoverished mother-in-
law Naomi, she goes to glean the leftover wheat in the field of an elderly and distinguished kinsman named Boaz. He inquires as to her
identity during the harvest but loses interest in her once the harvest is
over. Realizing that the wealthy Boaz is a relative of her deceased husband (which means he bears some moral obligation to marry clan widows), Naomi urges Ruth to go back to Boaz's field. Despite the entirely
unsanctioned nature of the act, Ruth agrees to steal into Boaz's threshing floor under cover of night when he is sleeping among the stalks,
stretch herself out at his feet (which she will expose to the nighttime
chill), and hope that when he wakes to find her, he will act according
to scheme. He does indeed wake to find Ruth, bathed and perfumed,
by his purposefully uncovered feet and, after a few formalities, agrees to
make her his wife.

Ruth's tactics—while much tamer than those of her ancestresses,
Lot's daughters—bear some traces from the earlier tale of incest. Ruth's
is undeniably a story of a young woman deliberately seducing a kinsman old enough to be her father and, once married, lying with him
with conception urgently in mind. Like that of Lot's daughters, Ruth's
is a onetime union resulting in immediate conception. In both cases
there is a serious concern for the propagation of a family line, which the
women believe will be lost if they don't ensnare these men and produce
male heirs.

Midrash Rabba tells us that Ruth and Boaz's son Obed, who was the
grandfather of King David, was conceived on their wedding night,

which was to be the last of the patriarch Boaz's life. His and Ruth's was a brief couplehood fraught with destiny, and once the preordained union was accomplished, Boaz could die reassured that, thanks to Ruth's initiative, he had fulfilled his life's true mission.

Nonetheless, the rabbis are forced to examine the morality of an unmarried woman stretching herself out at the feet of a sleeping man. Under ordinary circumstances such immodest behavior could not have been condoned. But, the rabbis hasten to tell us, these were not ordinary circumstances. These were circumstances in which God's plan (concerning messianic genealogy) had to be brought about, even, if need be, by an unorthodox act.

Destiny aside, the biblical author of Ruth has to address the question of the heroine's highly irregular conduct in the field. This the author accomplishes with a subtle reference to a predecessor, the provocative Tamar. When the people of Israel come to congratulate Boaz on his impending marriage to Ruth, one of the blessings they offer is "May your house be like the house of Perez whom Tamar bore to Judah" (4:12). Tamar was yet another woman who took matters into her own hands and insured the survival of a lineage, not by the rape of her father, but by the unabashed seduction of her father-in-law.

Her story (told in Genesis 38) is particularly vivid. Twice widowed by Judah's two sons, Tamar is told by Judah to wait until his youngest son is old enough to marry her. But she suspects what is secretly in Judah's heart; despite the custom, he will never give her his third son in marriage. Tamar waits patiently until her mother-in-law dies and Judah emerges after the period of mourning. Tamar disguises herself as a prostitute and waits for Judah at a crossroad. It doesn't take much to persuade this presumably righteous patriarch to have sexual relations with a woman who, as far as he knows, is a random prostitute (providing another example of sexual transgression in the story of the making of the Messiah). Tamar, in disguise, agrees that Judah can pay for her services belatedly by sending her a kid goat, providing he leave her his ring, seal, and stick for security.

It turns out rather awkwardly for Judah, though, thanks to Tamar's clever maneuvering, it is all set right in the end. When Judah first learns that his daughter-in-law is pregnant "from having played the harlot," he decrees a death sentence. When it becomes undeniable that he and no other is the father—what with the production of his unmistakable seal, ring, and stick—Judah, of course, reconsiders the verdict.

Perez, progenitor of the mighty tribe of Judah from whom Boaz, King David, and eventually the Messiah descend, is born to Tamar, just, the rabbis hasten to comment, as he was meant to be. Judah was not intimate with Tamar again (Genesis 38:26). Divinely sanctioned destiny exonerates the whole cast of characters from any suggestion of wrong-doing. Tamar's seduction of her father-in-law was condoned because it served a divine purpose. So, too, the rabbis add, can Ruth's boldness be absolved, since it worked toward a greater, preordained good.

It is, as we can see, no easy process to insure the birth of a Messiah. It took three women acting on their own to get a father, a father-in-law, and an elderly father figure to sire their progeny, under circumstances that ranged from the shocking to the questionable. Tamar, invoked in the text of Ruth, stands as a link between Lot's daughters and the far more moderate—but thematically consistent—behavior of Ruth.

Looking for examples of father-daughter unions outside biblical culture, we find that such unions in the service of kingly lineage are not un-usual. It is a practice that James Frazer, in *The New Golden Bough*, traces to matriarchal times, when the power to rule was considered to reside in the female rather than the male. In his discussion of royal suc-cessions, Frazer reveals a singular connection between father-daughter incest and dynastic rule. The stories of such unions, he claims, are rooted in actual practice: in matriarchal cultures, "where the royal blood was traced through women only," the rule of descent dictated that the king relinquish the throne upon the death of his wife "since he occu-pied it by virtue of his marriage to her." This rule furnished a real-life motive for incest with a daughter. For as Frazer explains, "if the king desired to reign after his wife's death, the only way in which he could legitimately continue to do so was by marrying his daughter and thus prolonging through her the title that had originally been his through her mother."[1]

Our biblical heroines were, likewise, concerned with the perpetuation of a kingdom, even if not an earthly one but a preordained, heavenly one. This goal, too, had to be assured through the siring of children for and by their nearest blood relatives.

The stories of Lot's daughters, Tamar, and Ruth suggest that the women in question were behaving in accordance with some atavistic, matriarchal tradition. All of these women broke taboos without hesita-tion, acting as if in response to some inner voice guided by an unnamed source. Could this source be identified as a vestigial matriarchal memory concerning the importance of blood ties in matters of royal dynasties? This possibility is supported by the sudden disappearance of Lot's wife (who is turned into a pillar of salt) and the death of Judah's wife just before Lot's daughters and Tamar instigate their unlikely unions. In Ruth's case, Naomi, clearly a matriarchal figure, whispers instructions in her daughter-in-law's ears. Could Naomi have been passing along a "secret knowledge," which is never named or acknowledged? Even more surprising is that these women's irregular behavior is absolved and lauded! The story of the Messiah can be seen as a precious example of ancient matriarchal imperatives prevailing despite a stern patriarchal order. The all-important end could not have been brought about without reference to these ancient, matriarchal voices. We can consider these women all the more inspired for their exceptional attunement to its message.

A glance at comparable tales of father-daughter incest in other cultures further underscores the exceptional nature of the biblical women. Father-daughter incest tales are certainly abundant, but examples of daughters taking the initiative are strikingly rare. In the majority of tales, it is the father—often disguised as someone else—who ruthlessly pursues the daughter, while the young woman flees in panic. As Otto Rank explains in his famous study, *The Incest Theme in Language and Literature*, incest stories are inevitably told from a male point of view, or more precisely, "from the standpoint of the father." Since it was men who made the myths, these are all tales of a father's lust. Rank argues that even the exceptional stories, where women do take the initiative (citing the examples of Myrrha, who was "inflamed by Aphrodite with criminal love for her father," and Lot's daughters), are disguised versions of the father's own urge to trespass. As Rank wrote, "Even in the few mythological passages in which the loving passion is presented from the viewpoint of the daughter, this is only a justification of the father's shocking desires. An attempt is made to shift the blame for the seduction onto her."[2]

According to that argument, we can also view the stories of Lot's daughters and, later, Tamar and Ruth, as disguised tales of male-incited incest, as told—and distorted—by male writers eager to protect their fellows. As it happens, everyone is absolved of blame and the courageous women emerge heroic. In spite of the ultimate absolution of the act, the patriarchal authors may have preferred to shift the blame onto the women rather than write frankly of a man committing so heinous an act.

Yet these stories—even if ascribing initiative to women in order to exonerate men—may also bear traces of an earlier theme, that is, women acting in accordance with a once potent matriarchal tradition. Thus these biblical women, while fashioned partly out of the needs of male storytellers, retain an autonomous dimension.

Lot's daughters, Tamar, and Ruth differ from their nonbiblical counterparts in other significant ways. Not only are they among the rare initiators of incest, they also do not suffer any of the usual consequences.

Rank's essay confirms that most often, when the disgraceful act is consummated, the victimized daughters are transformed into nonhuman or inanimate objects, become eternal wanderers, or suffer severed limbs, that is if they don't die immediately of shame. Moreover, in the cases where they live to give birth, their progeny meet ghastly ends: they are exposed, dismembered, or even served up as pièces de résistance at banquets. In contrast, our biblical heroines thrive and have healthy children who not only survive but have lofty destinies. Furthermore (with the exception of Lot's daughters, who are considered marginal) the women's taboo-defying acts are highly praised.

As mentioned earlier, the midrashic tradition offers a religious explanation for the exceptional outcome of these irregular deeds: These individuals, however irregular their behavior, were accomplices to an inevitable process deemed necessary to engender a Messiah. But we might find another explanation for their conduct in the psyches of the human protagonists themselves. A psychological perspective would see these women's decisions and destinies not as arising from socioreligious imperatives but from the nature of the female psyche itself.

Jungian psychology provides the richest perspective for looking at the personality of the daughter who initiates (and gets away with) incest. In his introduction to *The Father: Contemporary Jungian Perspectives*, Andrew Samuels tells us that Jung did not regard the young girl's impulse toward her father in a literal manner. For Jung, the girl's unconscious incestuous feelings or fantasies were "a complicated metaphor for a path of psychological growth or development." Such feelings or fantasies can be understood "as unconsciously attempting to add enriching layers to personality by contact with the parent."[3]

Samuels understands the girl's yearning for her father in a symbolic sense, as an attempt to grow toward psychic wholeness by contacting the positive aspects of her own animus, or the masculine side of herself. For Jungians (and indeed for many contemporary women) the integration of both the so-called feminine and masculine elements within a woman's psyche is a prerequisite for individuation or growth into her full potential. In this sense, the yearning for the father is symbolic of the yearning for the fullest dimensions of Self.

Samuels insists that it is neither strict denial nor indulgence of incestuous longings that contribute to an optimal climate for growth. Rather, he suggests, fathers and daughters should acknowledge "a deep connection . . . that has its erotic tone" and together participate in "a mutual, painful renunciation of erotic fulfilment." Avoiding both "the absence of eros and its excess" will insure the daughter benefits from the father's "potential to stimulate an expansion and deepening of her personality."[4]

Seen in this light, the biblical heroines' personalities take on interesting contours. They become women who are seekers of greater enrichment, of deeper layers of inspiration in the service of their fullest potential. In their quest, they are willing to ignore ordinary boundaries. They seek the wholeness of spirit that comes from uniting the opposites within. It should be recalled that they return to the father but do not linger there. Rather than become fixated or stunted in their growth, once having returned they forge ahead in the search for successful individuation.

These women have not only returned to the father as a source of enrichment, they have been empowered by internalizing his strengths. While their counterparts in other stories are abused and raped, these women take matters into their own hands, even steering their male protagonists toward their chosen course of action. Rape is, of course, an imposition of male authority upon women. However, these biblical women, rather than bowing to some external, foreign authority embodied in the father, fully appropriate his prerogatives. They themselves seduce fathers and father figures. The importance of their directing— rather than submitting to—the father cannot be overlooked. It is they who are the decision makers, the "actresses-upon." The rabbis see these women's actions as divinely decreed. But even so, the courage it took to influence the course of history was indisputably theirs. That their actions are applauded by religious authority, and ultimately are redemptive, seems to underscore the wisdom of their course.

By now I have gone way past the grade school version of Ruth as a one-dimensional model of devotion and virtue. Ruth, lest we exaggerate, neither commits incest nor is a messiah. She is an unselfish woman, loyal and obedient to her elderly mother-in-law. But if Ruth must be re-evaluated, it is because of the new light her story sheds on the very meaning of the messianic.

Ruth carried within her a divine spark planted much earlier in the sullied womb of Lot's daughter. Her personal virtue was powerful enough to free the divine spark from a hard shell of evil. How different things would have been if my grade school teachers had used the example of Ruth to point out that the impulse to good can find a springboard in darkness, that virtue can be highlighted by its opposites, or that inner schisms are far from deplorable. Ruth, herself neither incestuous nor messianic, is nonetheless the transformative field, a figure in whom the highest and the lowest, the most shocking and the most exalted meet. A discussion of Ruth in her true state would have avoided much self-rejection among those of us who, as adolescents, were attracted to the unpermitted.

Ruth not only engenders the Messiah, she culminates a lineage of extraordinary women. Each of these women acted in defiance of an awesome taboo, in accordance with an inner prompting. Once again, I can't escape the implications that were passed over in grade school: trespassing boundaries and defying limits can sometimes be a prerequisite to personal achievement and possibly even redemption.

Mythology tells us that these women did not act without antecedent. I conjecture that they were informed by ancient matriarchal voices giving them "secret knowledge" about the acceptability of such acts. In school, Ruth was a role model presented within the limits of a male-legislated world. As young girls, we would all have been enriched by the mere suggestion that she was inspired by a source uniquely female.

If the women were enriched by their contact with the matriarchal, they were also forthright in their quest for the patriarch. It is significant that each of them, in her own way, returns to the father. Such an act—be it literal or symbolic—could never find a place in our religious education, its salient role in the birth of a messiah notwithstanding.

The reason for this is twofold: Courageous thrusts into the forbidden were never encouraged, since inner completion and self-empowerment were never valued. The permission to reach for both is something most women have only come to as adults, long after the Book of Ruth has been closed and nearly forgotten. A more probing reading of Ruth could have equipped us earlier with what we needed to hasten the Messiah, in both the deeply personal and truly universal sense.

Dialogue on Devotion

NORMA ROSEN

SCENE: Five women, their ages spanning the decades from late twenties to fifties, are meeting in a Manhattan living room. It is early evening; they have carried coffee to chairs and sofa. Comfortable with one another, they are members of an ongoing group facetiously acronymed WGTDTB: Women Gathered to Deplore the Bible. One or two of them secretly wish the initials more innocently connoted Women Gathered to Discuss the Bible. However, when mailings went out under the latter rubric, too few responded.

CHARACTERS: SHARON, the oldest, a psychologist. The meeting is in her apartment. According to their informal custom, the hostess acts as moderator. The others are BECKY, LAURA, MARION, and EVELYN, the youngest. Each is a member of a profession—social worker, lawyer, history professor, and doctoral candidate in English literature. All received religious school training in childhood; a few still read Hebrew. All recognize with pain that their training overlooked the fact that the bias of the Bible was masculine and they were female. The same blankness characterized the way, in secular schools, they were taught great works of English literature; the teaching never acknowledged that many of the works were anti-Semitic, and that they, the students, were Jews.

In each of the following sections two members are in dialogue, while the rest act as chorus. The scene should be visualized with speakers sit-

---

The author used her own translation of the Book of Ruth; she also consulted the King James Version, the Jewish Publication Society edition, the Anchor Bible (Garden City, N.Y.: Doubleday, 1975), and the Soncino edition.

ting in bright light, the others in dimmer light that brightens when they speak.

I. Letting off steam: Sharon and Becky

SHARON [glancing around]: It's a shame we're so few this month, because the Book of Ruth is so . . . Well, maybe the others didn't come because Ruth's not a book they like to deplore. It's one of the very few where we finally get some good lines! And they really are good lines, aren't they? (Declaims) "Wherever you go I will go!"

CHORUS [voices tinged with satire, speaking one at a time]:
—"Your people will be my people!"
—"Your God will be my God!"
—"Where you die I will die!"
—Yes, indeed!

BECKY: Of course there isn't a single unblemished man portrayed in the Bible, not even Moses. When it comes to Ruth, she has to be dehumanized into someone who's always unselfish, loyal, and in perfect control of herself.

S: I thought you believed people were basically good, Becky. Isn't that why you became a social worker?

B: I think people would be good if circumstances allowed them to be—don't you?

S: Maybe. In any case, it takes extraordinary people to be good when circumstances aren't conducive. In fairness to the story, we have to say that everyone here is virtuous, especially Boaz! I admit I love the virtue of Boaz, though I find Ruth's tiresome. I suppose I could try to analyze why that's so, but I think I'll just ease into this slowly tonight.

B: Anyway, for once it's women who make the story move; yet they still need men to redeem the property, to redeem them. Boaz even says [she consults one of the books open on a small table beside her chair]—yes, here it is—he will "buy" Ruth along with the property! This other translation doesn't use the word "buy." It says "acquire." That's splitting hairs.

S: If you're looking for faults, Ruth has them, though the Bible doesn't count them as faults. You could just as easily describe Ruth as passive, subservient, waiting to be reclaimed—bought—however you translate! I still want to be fair, though. In those days progeny and family affiliation really were the most important things in life.

CHORUS:

    —In those days progeny and family, now it's our therapist!

    —Now it's our aerobics class!

    —Without them, everything collapses, soul and body. We don't dare miss a session!

S: It's a simple story that's very complex! We already have two conflicting sets of qualities to define Ruth. Is she a symbol of passive, unquestioning virtue or a brave partner in adventure? A third pattern suggests itself; variant of a folktale. Mother and daughter-in-law set out into the world to seek their fortune, defenseless, like Hansel and Gretel. Will they meet a witch who wants to eat them? No, they meet a dear, grandfatherly man who feeds them.

B: Not exactly out into the world. Back to Naomi's home, though she's been away long enough to feel a stranger. Her husband, some sort of important Jew, dragged her and the kids out to Moab when there was famine in their own land. How will the folks at home feel about her coming back now that things have improved in Judah? Oddly enough, they don't seem to resent it at all. They don't say sarcastically, "Well, Naomi, so you've decided to come back to us now that there's food on the table!" They say, "Is this Naomi?" Everyone's incredibly forebearing. Where do you find people like that? In the Bible, I suppose, is the answer. But don't we need to make some connection to ourselves here? Right away, Naomi tells them her troubles—her sons died. Never mind how many of *their* children died in the famine! The text leaves that out. In fact, the text leaves too much out. I can't connect with this story unless we put a few things back.

S: Shouldn't we try to follow the chronology of this so-called simple tale?

B: All right, but first I want to say it's a story I do not trust.

S: Don't trust! Why?

B: The whole world takes this story to its heart. But only because it leaves out reality. Like nastiness. And ulterior motives. Spend a day with any of my caseload families!

CHORUS:

> —Spend a day with me in any courtroom!
> —Spend a day in the history department of my university.
> —Or the English department of mine!

S: Spend a day in my therapy office! But you haven't stopped believing that *virtue* is part of reality, have you?

B: No, of course not. But the story makes me aware of the devil lurking behind the lines. Naomi says, "Go, my daughter, to the gleaning in the fields." Later we get a good idea of what the dangers are, when Boaz tells his workers not to harm Ruth, the unprotected female. So in what spirit does Naomi send Ruth out on these errands?

S: Now you make it sound as if Naomi is sending Ruth to destruction, deceiving Ruth the way Abraham deceived Isaac. Do you really think that the minute you get a parent-child story, somewhere there's a sacrifice? Another *akeda*?[1] I can't believe the goodness of the story doesn't move you!

B: Of course it moves me—that's why I don't trust it! It's trying to put me to sleep, like all stories about virtuous women! I'm not speaking as a social worker, I'm speaking as myself. I can't afford it. Part of me would love to go into that world and close the door! Such a lovely world, where people behave like ideal beings. But maybe that's going too far, calling them ideal beings, when all that's on their minds is procreation and property!

S: What about Ruth's loyalty to Naomi? What about Naomi's concern for Ruth? What about Boaz's respect for Ruth's goodness toward her mother-in-law? That's not just procreation and property!

B: A young woman gives herself to an old man in exchange for food. That teaches us something about female survival! On the other hand, it's also a story of redemption! Of the property of a widowed woman, and of life, through acts of unselfishness and virtue. I know I keep going around and around here. But I don't think it's entirely my fault. There's great beauty and virtue in the story, and there's great ugliness and shame.

S: Yes, I agree we can't get away from the double reading. There's the positive one, but we also get female subjection and humiliation. Boaz's warning to his men in the fields only points up the terrors that must have been the usual thing. In that world women had to be pragmatists. Naomi's husband and sons have died so she calls herself empty, meaning her womb. She's too old to bear again. Her daughters-in-law can still bear sons, and she tells them, Go back to your families, hurry up and get fixed up with new husbands. Don't hang around with me, I'm finished! Well, where could a woman go in those biblical days, what could she have, without the protection of a man? Nowhere. Nada. The daughters-in-law have to find new husbands and bear sons. That's their function, their whole value in that society. Why should that make us feel bitter? Things have changed!

B: The Book of Ruth talks about taking possession of women and of property. If Ruth weren't a widow, her virginity would be very much to the point. As it is, her virtue is attested to, if I remember, by her having stuck close to Naomi. In fact, Boaz comments that Ruth has not been fooling around with the young men in the field. Nobody gives sexual purity credentials to the other possible redeemer or to Boaz, either. Is Boaz a widower? Does he have children? Does he fool around with gleaners in the fields? The text doesn't bother to tell us. And we tell ourselves how much things have changed!

CHORUS:

—How can we speak of change?

—Nothing has really changed!

—And the text doesn't even bother to tell . . .

—Oh, those texts, they're hopelessly fragmented, garbled . . .

—And shaped to keep women in line . . .

—Or worse, not in line at all. Out of line, pariahs, actually warned against . . .

—Why do we bother, what is the point?

S [standing]: I hope we'll find one. If we take a brief break to get more coffee or tea—then, when we come back, can we look at some important themes we haven't touched yet?

II. Seeing the loss: Sharon and Laura

LAURA: Sharon, you like us to be chronological, so let's go back to leaving Moab. I think we should be very strict with the text. A fine-print reading wouldn't hurt. Ruth says her piece, "Where you go, I go." Then she adds something very strange: "Your God will be my God." Now, Naomi has just judged God very harshly. She says [checks her book], "My lot is far more bitter than yours, for the hand of the Lord has struck out against me." So why, at this moment, should Ruth proclaim allegiance to a God that even Naomi seems to be withdrawing from? Even more important, why, at this moment, is she so tactless as to mention God at all, when she knows what a painful point it is for Naomi? Why should Ruth in effect be saying, "Now that I see how cruelly your God has treated you, I will follow your God"?

SHARON: But sense or no sense, when Ruth says that, it's a stunning moment. Naomi, follower of God, has just all but denounced God, and look!—a young woman with choices chooses Naomi's God!

L: I don't think she does choose Naomi's God—not yet. Here's how I read Ruth's statement: "You and I," she is saying, "have loved the same people for so many years, and then suffered their loss together. My emotional life is bound up with yours. I can't see any other life for myself than with you, and that includes, for better or worse, even staying with the God I now hear you denounce. Your God will be my God, and if we must denounce God, we will do it together." Ruth then adds, "Where you die, I will die, and there I will be buried." She may actually expect, as the remnant of this ill-fated family, that she and Naomi will both be struck dead next! Though Ruth's bravery at that moment is extraordinary, I see her embracing Naomi's God not out of love of God—how could she?—but rather with an existential stoicism. And it is this stoical going on, this determination to bestow human kindness in a world blasted by God, that gives Ruth greatness.

S: So you think Ruth and Naomi go back in resignation, possibly expecting more terror from this punishing God? Naomi then figures out how to get food, the way Elimelech had figured it out before, when there was famine and he took his family to Moab. People act, and no one knows ahead of time whether God will smile on those actions or not. In Naomi's case, God does smile, after a while, as God smiled on Abraham, Joseph, and Jacob, who also left the land when there was famine. Poor Elimelech doesn't get smiled on; he dies.

L: The commentators love to insert their must-have-beens. They slip in that Elimelech must-have-been a stingy man who didn't want to share his wealth in hard times, so he went to Moab, and God zapped him and his sons. This is the sort of commentary that makes me want to sue for libel! Ishmael must-have-been shooting arrows into people; that's why Sarah wanted him out of the house. Cain's sacrifice to God must-have-been done in the wrong spirit; that's why God rejected it. And on and on—apologetics for God. Better to have commentaries that tell the truth. Elimelech tried his best and died. Cain's sacrifice was as good as Abel's, Ishmael was a boy like Isaac or any other boy, Elimelech did what Abraham, Joseph, and Jacob all did—went to another land when there was famine. "I will be gracious to whom I will be gracious to," God said to Moses. Weren't the commentators listening? With their pietistic interpretations, their zeal to teach a moral order, they commit the absurdity of saying that everything bad happens as punishment for sin. Where is existential chanciness? As post-Holocaust Jews, we have no right to say Naomi's plans are rewarded because they are better plans than Elimelech's. We should symbolically empty ten drops of wine from our glass of joy at Naomi's triumph, and remember what befell people of virtue and ingenuity who by prayer or plan struggled to save themselves and their little ones but earned no protection from God.

S: But for now, for Naomi and Ruth, can't we agree, at least, that things worked out? It's a story of Jewish rebirth after terrible suffering, symbolized, as in Job, with a new family. God gives no answer to the question of why such suffering happened. Just—start again. Nature's answer and God's answer turn out to be exactly the same. Start again with fresh-planted seed. That's why I think we should address the two characters in the story who "defect." The other daughter-in-law, Orpah, who doesn't go with Naomi, and later the male relative who won't redeem. The defecting male relative creates a certain narrative suspense: Will Boaz get his turn to redeem? But Orpah does nothing for the narrative line, except, of course, to lighten it. One daughter-in-law less to schlepp back to the land of Judah.

L: What if Orpah had also gone with Naomi? Then we might have had a Leah and Rachel situation between sisters-in-law. At the end, people say to Boaz, "May the Lord make the woman who is coming into your house"—meaning Ruth—"like Rachel and Leah." That almost sounds as if the two, Orpah and Ruth, were meant to come back. Boaz, old as he is, would take both widows as wives. Ruth produces the line that leads to King David. Orpah, let's see—I know there's a legend that Goliath was a descendant of Orpah and her new Moabite husband. Doesn't that sound like what might have happened if she'd married Boaz, carrying on the tradition of enemies born of the same father, like Isaac and Ishmael, Jacob and Esau, Joseph and his brothers? Or, wait—why couldn't Orpah have borne a *daughter* to Boaz? From her descends Queen X! She, too, turns out to be a wonderful psalmist. It's those Moabite genes. After David seduces Uriah's wife, Nathan the prophet ought to tell David that God is deposing him the way God deposed Saul when he displeased God. Queen X would be annointed in David's place, ruling more justly than David, and never seducing anyone's wife!

S: Instead of that, Orpah and the defecting redeemer lose their places in the story. The man who won't redeem is never named at all, and Orpah is merely not-Ruth. I can just hear Orpah complaining to her therapist: Why is it other people know when to say yes or no and I never do? I'm always on the wrong foot! Why couldn't I have gone with Naomi instead of Ruth? You know why? Because I always felt Naomi favored Ruth's husband, not mine, but I should have gone anyway! Why am I always putting myself down? Why do I let other people write the script for me?

L: Those two defectors sound like people I know. Maybe I'm even like them. I pride myself on being able to think through a situation and not let emotion carry me away. I want to behave decently, but not be a self-sacrificer. In short, I don't want to be my mother. All of a sudden, I think the story is saying that logic and practicality aren't enough. You need something closer to passionate generosity, to reasons of the heart, not the head.

S: Is this the legal mind of Laura speaking? Anyway, I gather neither of us would want to be Orpah. How about Ruth? Speaking for myself, I'd like to have her serenity, her unwavering sense of choices.

L: Back to your mother and father or stick to your mother-in-law, and no such thing as going it alone? You call those choices?

S: But look what these women did with their no-choices! At the end, people say to Boaz, "May your house be like the house of Perez whom Tamar bore to Judah." The text invites us to pair Ruth and Tamar, two women who dove into the adventure of their own stories and made themselves part of biblical history.

L: It's true that both Tamar and Ruth lure an older man into impregnating them. But unlike Tamar's father-in-law, Judah, Naomi can't impregnate her daughter-in-law. Maybe we ought to say that Boaz is Naomi's chosen surrogate!

S: Now you want us to think of Naomi as Judah in drag?

L: Look at it this way—Tamar is both the inventor of her own story and its passionate actor. In Ruth, inventor and actor are divided between two women. Naomi is the strategist—what a brilliant trial lawyer she would have made! Ruth acts. Tamar was obsessed with having progeny, if necessary even with her father-in-law. Ruth is obsessed with being with her mother-in-law, who is obsessed by her grief at being "empty." Naomi finds a way to fulfill covenant with a "covenanted" relative, someone in the circle of family redeemers. She can fill up her own emptiness through Ruth's child, and find safety for Ruth in Boaz's house. It's a dramatic summing-up!

S: One thing I keep coming back to—in biblical life, it's progeny and inheritance that count. Family clusters are like beads on the covenantal string. From this Jewish string of beads God chooses, here and there, a Moses, an Abraham, a Sarah, a Rebekah, a Tamar, a Naomi, a who knows which one next? At least the sense of stretching toward the future is a change from Eastern thought, where the tragic wheel of life rolls its cycles over each generation till it, too, is broken.

L: Broken strings of beads are no less terrible than broken wheels! Creatures capable of comprehending their own tragedy deserve better. On the other hand, if we hadn't been given tragedy for our lot—if we had, say, eternal lives or eternally bland lives—we wouldn't have the Book of Ruth, would we? No death, no poetry. No legal system, either.

S: I'm not as stoical as you, Laura. I find it interesting—comforting, I suppose—to think of the kabbalist view here. Creation is broken. God is shattered into the ten *sefirot*, or attributes. God takes up residence in one, then another, then another. Like the old Jewish joke-curse, do you know it? May you be a millionaire and own beautiful mansions.

L: How is that a curse?

S: Aha, wait! And in each mansion, may there be spacious rooms, gorgeously furnished, with luxurious beds.

L: What's bad about that?

S: And may you go from mansion to mansion, from luxurious bed to luxurious bed, turning and tossing, unable to sleep!

L: Wait a minute, you think that's what God is doing?

S: I exaggerate. But the kabbalist idea divides God into personae—wisdom, mercy, justice, judgment, pity, some of them male and some female. It's up to human beings to bring those attributes into a single focus, like in some giant stereopticon. Through virtue, goodness, and fulfilling the law. And that ties in with why it's important for the characters in Ruth to choose the right way. Those who act out a vigorous virtue can alter the world. The kabbalist idea is sexy, too. The male aspect of God has intercourse with the female element, the *Shekhinah*, to achieve One-ness. Look how important the female is! And that, in a way, is what Ruth is about, too. Imitatio dei on the humblest threshing floor level.

L: Is this what you mean by a hopeful idea? Thinking of God in pieces? I find that really depressing! Not to mention pagan!

CHORUS:

—Most views of God are depressing.

—And avoiding the pagan is as skittery as balancing on a skateboard!

—Either God is responsible for evil . . .

—Which is depressing . . .

—Or some other force, like the Devil, is responsible for evil . . .

—Which is probably pagan.

—It's certainly not a monotheistic idea.

—And it's still depressing!

S [standing]: Maybe it's time to take another break? Stretch, move around the room? A little liqueur? It's harvest time in the bible, after all. Have some fruit! [She takes up a platter and moves about the circle.]

III. Mother-daughter: Sharon and Marion

MARION: What would we say if Naomi were not a mother-in-law but a mother?

SHARON: [laughing]: We'd say, "Doesn't Ruth know the importance of separating from her mother, of developing an autonomous life?" We'd quote Margaret Mahler![2] We'd say, "Ruth was led by the nose! When does she develop a will and purpose of her own, instead of going wherever her mother goes!"

M: Here's another question. Did the daughters-in-law worship their own gods all the time they were married to Naomi's sons? Laura's commentators probably say somewhere that a virtuous woman like Ruth must-have-been converted to God already. But Naomi tells Ruth, "Your sister-in-law has returned to her gods. Go follow your sister-in-law." Why would one daughter-in-law convert to the Hebrew God and not the other? That's unlikely. And if Ruth had converted, would Naomi be so wicked as to urge her back to pagan gods in Moab? No—Ruth has either gone on worshiping her pagan gods all during her marriage, or she's been indifferent to religion altogether—recognizable to some of us! Ruth shows tact by not saying to Naomi, "Your God has given us no protection; why don't we try the ones they've got back in Moab?"

S: Personally, I worry a bit about Ruth's family. Won't her own mother be hurt when she hears? How old is Ruth, anyway? Childbearing age, that's all we know. Maybe a teenager? The culture was different, but some things may not have changed. We know the pull of other people's mothers, more attractive than our own. Relations with ours are too complicated. Come to think of it, I don't believe there's a single scene of mother-daughter relationship in the entire Bible!

M: This one wouldn't be there either if the Bible weren't trying to say something about tolerance for conversion. Ruth's a Moabitess. Historically we should place this story just after the Babylonian exile. Jews were urged to abandon their non-Jewish wives before going back to Jerusalem. The Book of Ruth may have saved marriages! But about helping women like Naomi control their own property, the text has nothing to say! Or about anything else to do with furthering the autonomy of women! To think how women beg for favors, tiny changes in the liturgy that will let them feel a little bit like covenanted Jews—"Oh, please, don't always translate *b'nei Yisrael* as sons of Israel; please say sons and daughters sometimes, or at least children." It makes me sick!

S: Let's not dwell on it, then. Tell me if you agree with a notion I have that Ruth's attraction to the Jewish husband and to somebody else's mother share a certain tendency? It's going toward the genetic outsider, the Other. Ruth, the Moabite, seems always attracted outside the immediate "family." That tells me something about her character. As a teenager, I adored my friends' families! Food, sleepovers, shopping trips, all without having to fear or resent too much or too little protectiveness. Friendly detachment—perfect! Naomi reminds me of the mother of the French writer, Colette, who was also somewhat detached. Sido was unable to visit when Colette was ill—she had to watch a rare cactus bloom! Of course, Naomi's distractions are the sorrows of two dead sons and a dead husband. "I left full, I return empty." Since she can't dismiss Ruth, she accepts her coming along, but without enthusiasm.

M: And that's what's fascinating! Naomi feels almost dead. What wakens her to new life? It's not because Ruth loves her! She's far too unsentimental and life-toughened for that. Ruth's presence stirs Naomi to responsibility. "I must find rest for you, my daughter." She thought she could never be a mother again, and then she finds herself taking on a mother's concerns for needy Ruth! So the text tells us that what keeps people alive is not passively waiting to be loved, but having tasks to perform that show your own love.

S: I ought to get my abused women's groups to read Ruth!

M: But there's also a dark note here. When Naomi does come to life, I find her, frankly, anything but noble. More like controlling and manipulative. Why does she reveal her plan only tiny bits at a time? Does that show respect for Ruth? Naomi treats Ruth like a dimwit!

S: Could that be because Naomi hasn't herself figured out the whole plan in advance?

M: But Naomi could have known everything from the start. I have this property, she might have said to herself. I am in deep grief but not destitute. If I can't get a kinsman of my dead husband to redeem my land and my life, I've got this nubile girl to offer. I don't think Naomi is Laura's trial lawyer. She's Robespierre!

S [laughing]: Madame DeFarge and Lady Macbeth come next! But I don't see any of that. To me, she seems without hope and without plan at the beginning. She heads toward home with Ruth, despairing and grief-stricken. She feels life has shut down. Gradually on this journey, her despair-frozen brain thaws out. Maybe she's *not* a brilliant strategist, maybe she never reveals everything to Ruth because she doesn't know the whole plan! She's trying one piece at a time. Only after Ruth returns successful from each task does Naomi intuit the next one. Ruth by chance—if we can say anything in the Bible is by chance—gleans in Boaz's field. Then Naomi works out a use for the kinship connection. She tells Ruth to lie on the threshing floor at Boaz's feet and uncover them.

CHORUS:

—Oh, I remember those feet, those feet!

—We know about patriarchal oaths. Put your hand under my thigh turns out to mean swear on my testicles.

—It shouldn't be too hard to figure out those feet! Feet, knees, thighs, and upward?

M: As far as I'm concerned, it's a bold enough act even if they are feet. She gets into Boaz's bed and uncovers a part of him so he'll get cold, wake up, and find her there, where she can declare her kinship and his responsibility. Cover and protect me, she is saying, as your covering warms and protects you. I believe that some Arabs still keep that wedding gesture, the man placing a corner of his cloak over the woman. Notice, though, that Ruth says this to him in his bed at night, not in the field during the day!

S: She's shy. She's modest. Maybe. She also understands perfectly that Naomi's suggestion is so daring and dangerous that it's not even to be spelled out at this point. As if Naomi is saying—like Macbeth, not Lady Macbeth—"Be ignorant of the deed!" I think it's generous, not manipulative, of Naomi. If her plan fails, Ruth can save face by saying, "I had no idea what was supposed to happen." Of course there is an incredible intuitive resonance between the two women. Ruth never puts a foot—speaking of feet!—wrong.

M: Fine, we disagree. I still say Naomi is orchestrating this, using the only power available to her. When men bully women, women bully their daughters or daughters-in-law. Nowadays, Naomi would write one of those *Cosmo* articles: "Getting Your Man to Propose." She thinks daylight doesn't do it. How right she is! It's the *legalities* of the marriage agreement—the levirate marriage, if that's really what it is—that get spelled out in a public way, at the village gate in daylight with witnesses.

S: Yet that little whispered, nighttime encounter between Boaz and Ruth on the threshing floor is so unbelievably real!

M: The question is—Did they or didn't they have sex? Naomi sent this poor child out with instructions: Go as far as you have to, Ruth, to get what I, Naomi, want!

S: I think that once Boaz remembers there's a nearer relative who might redeem, he gallantly puts his feet, so to say, back in his pocket. So even if no intercourse took place—and there's plenty of ambiguity— the scene already shares the intimacy of marriage, the human one-to-one.

M: I'm glad to hear your upbeat view of marriage, Sharon! But we know there's treachery in gleaning fields and threshing floors. Boaz has to warn his male workers not to—wait—[she opens her book] yes, this says "molest." "I have ordered the men not to molest you." That's how we know she would have been fair game, an unspoken-for female! How far would they go? Rape? No mother would send a daughter into such danger!

S: But sending Ruth also tells us about alternative dangers. If Ruth doesn't go, what would those two women be? Truly empty! Still— you may be right, maybe Naomi is a little detached.

M: This may work, thinks Naomi, or it may not. Let's see how far we get. She places Ruth here, then moves her somewhere else. Ruth's a chess piece Naomi uses while she plays out her game against Boaz and the other male kinsman, who are such lovely legal redeemers they'd probably swallow up Naomi's property if no one was looking.

S: You're saying Ruth is a pawn? For what? Look, when Ruth returns from her night on the threshing floor with Boaz, Naomi asks a question. Because the Hebrew is ambiguous, translations differ. Some say Naomi asks, "How is it with you, my daughter?" and some say, "Who are you, my daughter?" Both questions are wonderful. Oh, I agree with you that when Naomi sends Ruth to Boaz and says, "He will tell you what to do," you might hear an ominous tone, a combination of the menacing "You'll find out!" and the contemptuous "Don't ask questions or even think. Let yourself be abused, if that's what's needed." When Ruth returns, Naomi's question surely means, "How did things go with Boaz?" but she is also asking Ruth a great many other things. It's as if the strong, decisive Naomi is suddenly afraid, and she's asking Ruth, "How has this changed your outer condition? Who are you now? Are you a dishonored woman? A spurned one? Or are you on the way to becoming an honored wife? And how have you changed within yourself? Are you still the open, loving creature you were, or has the experience altered and embittered you forever? Who are you now? Still my loving daughter, or my enemy?" What mothers teach, pass on, to their daughters is what daughters come back to confront their mothers with. Naomi's vulnerability to Ruth's answer is as important to me as anything that happens in the story.

M: You make a case for all the meanings of Naomi's question. But the story doesn't unravel them. It hurries on to the near redeemer, to whether he will marry Ruth. In the end he doesn't, because Ruth's child would inherit the land he redeems. He's not feeling very brotherly.

S: There's actually ambiguity about who would get Ruth. Some translations have Boaz say to the redeemer, "On the day you acquire the property, I acquire Ruth." This implies that Boaz and Ruth already made it in the maize. Either way, Ruth's child would inherit the bought land in the end.

M: A kinsman refuses to "raise up seed," as they say, for his dead brother. But Ruth raises up seed for her mother-in-law! When Ruth's child is born it's placed in Naomi's arms. The women say, "A son is born to Naomi!" There are rewards all around. Ruth gets rest and a baby, marriage to a kind man, and an honorable place in that society. A nice enough picture. But gloomy, too, since that's all there is to the woman's covenant. Women aren't directed to go anywhere, to do anything. Only their minds and emotions move, physically they're planted.

S: But not in this case. Naomi and Ruth walk into a new life, and between them they get a baby! A progenitor of David! And a few generations later King David, descended from that threshing floor encounter, will ascend stairs to a roof, where he will gaze lustfully at naked Bathsheba, the wife of another man. When we compare the fate of those babies, we see that Ruth's, the child of honorable intentions, thrives in his grandmother's arms and in history. Bathsheba and David's child, born of a love that betrays Bathsheba's husband and David's faithful follower, Uriah, is stricken and dies. We're in a world ruled by God's moral order. But we don't have more mother-daughter stories. Maybe because powerful women in groups have worried the rabbis. They were fearful of those old goddess religions from which some of these Bible stories may have emerged, carefully Hebraized. If you start thinking of Naomi and Ruth as Demeter and Persephone, with their terrific power over the land, the seasons, the ability of earth to renew itself, then the whole story dances around

the edges of the fertility goddess. One false move and there goes
monotheism! As if we couldn't have a system of laws, of moral order,
without suppressing the female.

CHORUS:

—You see? Bring in powerful women and everyone starts to worry.

—Paganism again!

—Quick! they say. Close the gates! Idolatry! The goddesses are coming!

M: There are plenty of other stories echoed here. Ruth sets out like
Abraham. Both leave the place where they were born and go to a
strange land. And both Ruth and Abraham are progenitors of a line
of covenant-inheritors! But only the male descendants hold the keys
to the citadel! I really wish I could stop going on about that! But I
can't. As far as I'm concerned, that's the top of the agenda.

S: But if you say only that, you've fallen into a trap of your own making. Then there's no way to reclaim our texts. Their glory is withheld
from us!

M: I give up, if you want glory at any price!

S: Women have been kept outside the palace and starved for centuries.
When we finally get inside, we don't want to just look at crumbs
under the table, do we? We want to see the whole banquet, even if
we're not allowed to taste it all.

M: I hate to say it, but that's slave mentality, taking pride in the pos-
sessions of the big house, even though . . .

S: I understand and empathize with you! But we can't just always lash
out, can we? Just mock and satirize and be negative and angry? Then
we ourselves will have lost the gifts these stories have brought to
human life!

M: What gifts, Sharon? I can't understand how you let yourself roman-
ticize!

S: Even if some stories are formulaic, teaching behavior that's simplis-
tic or narrow, these tales have touched our hearts, moved us, taught
us values. Oh, don't make me drag it all out! You know perfectly
well . . .

M: I'll do without it.

S: Will you? Can you? I don't think I can, or want to. I can't go
through literature with an ax, smashing things because women are
badly portrayed.

M (half rising): If you're going to say that critical thinking is only smash and destroy . . .

S: No, of course I don't mean that. . . .

CHORUS:

—We seem to be getting further and further from the story of Ruth and Naomi!

—I feel tears welling up whenever I read or even think about it.

—That's nothing to be ashamed of.

—Why can't we talk about the welling-up of tears?

M [bursts out again suddenly]: But it's such a rotten age!

S: You mean the biblical one?

M: No—ours!

S [stands quickly]: I have some absolutely no-fat chocolate ice cream in the freezer, and I think we should break to indulge ourselves—we've all earned it!

IV. No going back but by going forward: Sharon and Evelyn

SHARON: [with sympathy]: Tell us what parts of the story make you cry, Evelyn.

EVELYN: It's when Boaz says to Ruth, "I have been told of all that you did for your mother-in-law after the death of your husband." He's heard of her kindness to the dead and to Naomi. I took care of my father when he was dying for two years, and my sisters say to me, "What did you ever do for Daddy?" I can't bear to defend myself or remind them of what I did. But not to be understood, not to be known—that's when I feel a true absence of God! Boaz understands, remembers, values what should be valued. Boaz sees and hears, he knows. He rewards goodness, he's like God, or like what we want God to be.

S: Yes, all right, but why take what's clearly for once a woman's story and turn it into a man's? Boaz like God! Why not Naomi like God?

E: No, she's too poor, too stripped, she has no largesse to bestow. She's exactly not God. She's quintessential human, using brains, shrewdness, energy, to attract God's attention—or get away from God's attention. All right, no one is like God, but everyone comes close to godlike actions. Everybody does the right thing—for once! And when Ruth tells Boaz, "Now spread your wing over your maidservant for you are a redeemer." Don't ask me why that makes me cry. Maybe because Boaz says to Ruth, "May you have a full recompense from the Lord, the God of Israel, under whose wings you have sought refuge!" Boaz makes the connection, through language, to Ruth. He may not be like God, but he knows how like God a man should be. And that brings me close enough to tears.

S [sighs]: A perfect husband?

E: Don't joke!

S: And don't think tears don't well up for me, too. For me it's that question Naomi asks Ruth when she comes back from her night with Boaz.

E: When Ruth eats in the field, she takes from her own meal to bring to Naomi. I can't help thinking of Lear, who begs his daughters, "Oh, reason not the need," when they ask why he requires so much for his upkeep. Ruth is always adding more than good measure. So much of the text is about food, subsistance, gleaning, grain. Enough and more than enough, which is what generosity is about. Here there's more generosity, more love, more courtesy than any ordinary family can give. What the story tells me is that here at last is enough to feed the soul. Made-up stories invent characters that fill the need reality can't fill. Characters can treat one another with tenderness, courtesy, and care. Ruth and Boaz are like my favorite people in all of English literature—Elizabeth Bennett and Mr. Darcy—though without any of their defensive wit. The expectations of a person of purity and virtue are met with purity and virtue. Ah, God, when was the last time that happened on earth? And why did it stop?

S: Maybe it never started. Maybe it happens only in fantasy, invention, art. Or in religion. Be careful, Evelyn.

E: Two seconds in the Garden of Eden, maybe. Then it stopped.

S: And that was invention, too. Maybe it's invention we have to be careful not to stop!

E [becoming tearful]: Don't be clever. I want to go back to ideas of loyalty, devotion, honorableness! Mothers and daughters who care for one another, men who feel responsible. I want to talk about continuity in a world where everything is getting lost.

S: Poor Evelyn! You're the youngest of us, it's worse for you.

E: We've lost all that. We're barely willing to recognize what we're read-ing—plain, unironical goodness and virtue. [Laughs shakily] "Honk if you love your mother!" I actually saw that on a bumper sticker on the Hutchinson River Parkway! A little red Saab that everyone, in-cluding me, was passing! I wanted to see who was driving, but I couldn't. I didn't hear anybody honk, and I didn't honk, either!

S: You think it's entirely our fault that we don't identify with Ruth? I'm not so sure! Ruth may be timeless, but it's not for our times. Noth-ing, no one is satirized. That's intolerable to modern temperament.

E: What in God's name is there to satirize here?

S: Everything can be satirized if you look at it a certain way.

E: I challenge you on that. I don't see how you can, with Ruth.

S: With very little effort. Here—we all suspect that Naomi really hates her daughters-in-law, don't we? Obviously, she blames them for the deaths of her sons. The story doesn't say how the sons died, but if the women had been better wives, would this have happened? And we know about Naomi sending Ruth out to seek fortune for both of them. A real mother wouldn't have sent her own child, never! Naomi doesn't mind risking Ruth. She's got no clear plan. She just lets her daughter-in-law out like a monkey on a string, as lure, as bait, to see who she can trap. And what's beautiful about this old man, this Boaz, who's perfectly willing to use up a young woman's life?

E [crying out]: Oh, stop it! Are we so willing to give up the beauty of our texts because we're women? On Shavuot, we celebrate the giving of the Torah!

S: To men, I'm tempted to say! Should we ignore the taking away of it from women?

E: But in revolt against that theft, must we empty ourselves of our own stories?

S: The truth is, men are as bereft as we are. Men or women—we live in the same sour, skeptical age. We've lost our absolutes.

E: Worse than lost. We bad-mouth them, act as if to believe in them robs us of our right to lay claim to intellect.

CHORUS:

—Our age has lost it all.

—The beauty.

—The purity.

—The innocence.

E: The love!

S: The willingness even to believe in it!

CHORUS:

—Our lawyers love to find loopholes.

—Our literary critics love irony and satire.

—We're used to sniffing out ulterior motives.

—To hearing about betrayals.

—We love to think about unconscious motives.

E: Our writers punish characters in their stories with their own worst suspicions. They find decay everywhere, but never explain their own thriving.

S: We put on the mantles of prophets and castigate, castigate, but then the mantles fall from our shoulders because we know no standards to uphold.

CHORUS:

—If we knew them we wouldn't believe in them.

—We'd think they were too soft, too beautiful.

—Too pure, too unlikely.

—Too innocent, too soppy and cloying.

—Too sentimental, going on about "love."

—We'd miss the satire.

—We'd miss hearing about betrayals.

—We'd want to think about everybody's unconscious motives.

—We'd want to show how ridiculous and awful everybody is, compared to something or other, but we can't remember what.

—We scoff at stories of unselfish love.

—But even while we scoff we feel the tears come.

—That is our hope.

E: That is our salvation.

S: No, not salvation, only a sign that we may still thaw.

E: Yes, that's the necessary, the only sign.

[All five women stand, heads bowed, fists striking their hearts, as in the chorused *Al chet* recitations on Yom Kippur.]³

CHORUS:

—for the sin of suspecting self-interest in all virtue,

—for the sin of skepticism toward love,

—for the sin of knowing Freud,

—for the sin of not knowing Freud,

—for the sin of breaking with the past,

—for the sin of not breaking with the past,

—for the sin of subservience to a man,

—for the sin of not living up to being a woman,

—for the sin of thinking children are our only fulfillment,

—for the sin of thinking children are not even necessary to our fulfillment,

—for the sin of thinking only of self-fulfillment,

—for the sin of not living for the good of community,

—for the sin of living only for others and forgetting self,

—for the sin of letting relatives dominate one's life,

—for the sin of forgetting family,

—for the sin of abandoning love of God and substituting romantic, erotic love,

—for the sin of not embracing romantic, erotic love and longing only for God-like love.

[The women now speak singly, each starting the moment the previous one stops.]

SHARON: Oh hear us, God whose masculine, paternalistic form we can't believe in.

MARION: Oh answer us, God whose anthropomorphic condition we could not believe in, even if presented to us in female form.

BECKY: Oh guide us and make us whole, fractured God who requires human deeds to fuse the scattered attributes . . .

LAURA: Judgment always joined with mercy, with beauty, with knowledge, with wisdom, with law, with goodness.

M: Oh stay with us, unlikely God, as Ruth stayed with Naomi.

B: Help us to remember the secret syllables that revive our encounter on the threshing floor.

EVELYN: Oh, stay with us, unlikely God, stripped of power and impoverished, as Ruth stayed with Naomi, who was stripped of power and impoverished . . .

L: Though it hardly seems worth Your while, or Ruth's while, or Naomi's while . . .

B: Yet who knows whether we might, after irretrievable losses, encounter once more . . .

S: Oh, stay with us, unlikely God, as Ruth stayed with Naomi, though it hardly seemed worth her while, until she awakened in Naomi's withered life new energy for encounter, which in the end brought both to redemption. [Raises her head] I guess we stop now.

[One by one, the women embrace Sharon and leave.]

S [circles the room collecting cups and glasses, then looks up, meditative]: The Book of Ruth closes with celebration of a boy's birth, a living bead on the covenantal string that's meant to reach us from our ancient past. Yet it's Naomi's question that stays with me. "How is it with you, my daughter?" "Who are you, my daughter?"
What is my answer?

[Sharon exits, bearing away her burden of assorted vessels and food.]

Notes

Verse by Verse: A Modern Commentary

RUTH H. SOHN

1. In rabbinic literature, *Shekhina* refers to God's Presence, or the aspect of God which is most accessible to us. The phrase "under the wings of the *Shekhina*" is an image of God's protective and nurturing love for the Jewish people, and since rabbinic times has been used to express welcome to Jews by Choice and to refer to the act of conversion itself. (See for example Sanhedrin 96b in the Talmud.) In later kabbalistic literature, *Shekhina* refers to the feminine aspect of God.

Finding Our Past: A Lesbian Interpretation of the Book of Ruth

REBECCA ALPERT

Many thanks to Christie Balka for her thoughtful editorial suggestions, and to Linda Holtzman and Faith Rogow, who first challenged me to think about Ruth and Naomi.

1. Becky Butler, ed. *Ceremonies of the Heart: Celebrating Lesbian Unions* (Seattle: Seal Press, 1990), 13.

2. The story is based on a novel by Fannie Flagg, *Fried Green Tomatoes at the Whistle Stop Cafe* (New York: McGraw-Hill, 1988), 191.

3. Jody Hirsch, "In Search of Role Models," in *Twice Blessed: On Being Lesbian or Gay and Jewish*, ed. Christie Balka and Andy Rose (Boston: Beacon Press, 1989), 84–85.

4. There is no mention of sexual activity between women in the Hebrew Bible. Some discussion of lesbian behavior occurs in the Talmud; see Rachel

Biale, *Women and Jewish Law: An Exploration of Women's Issues in Halakhic Sources* (New York: Schocken Press, 1984). By the Middle Ages, lesbian sexual behavior was recognized as something women did. Women who engaged in such practices could be identified, and men were admonished to be sure that their wives were not involved with other women known to engage in this behavior.

5. See Jody Hirsch, "In Search of Role Models," 84–85.

6. See *Ruth: A New Translation* [Anchor Bible], with introduction, notes, and commentary by Edward F. Campbell, Jr. (Garden City, N.Y.: Doubleday, 1975), 22–23.

Her Mother's House

GAIL TWERSKY REIMER

1. See Esther Fuchs, "The Literary Characterization of Mothers and Sexual Politics in the Hebrew Bible," in *Feminist Perspectives on Biblical Scholarship*, ed. Adele Yarbro Collins, 117–36 (Chico, Calif.: Scholars Press, 1985). Fuchs provocatively argues that "the biblical narrative spares no effort in describing woman's desire for children" but overstates her case, I believe, when she insists that "women's reluctance to give birth or to assume maternal responsibility is an option that is completely excluded from the represented reality of the Bible."

2. Ann Snitow, "Feminism and Motherhood: An American Reading," *Feminist Review*, no. 40 (spring 1992), 32–51.

Language as Female Empowerment in Ruth

NEHAMA ASCHKENASY

1. See Nehama Aschkenasy, *Eve's Journey: Feminine Images in Hebraic Literary Tradition* (Philadelphia: University of Pennsylvania Press, 1986), 86–88, 251–52.

The Journey Toward Life

PATRICIA KARLIN-NEUMANN

1. Dr. Ziony Zevitt, "Wherefore Is the Night Different from Other Nights," *Direction*, University of Judaism (April 1980).

2. The repetition of this phrase was discussed by Evelyn Strouse and Bezalel Porten in "A Reading of Ruth," *Commentary*, February 1979.

3. See Strouse and Porten for an elaboration of the number seven in the Book of Ruth.

Fullness and Emptiness, Fertility and Loss: Meditations on Naomi's Tale in the Book of Ruth

LOIS C. DUBIN

It is my pleasure to thank Professors Benjamin Braude, Bruce Dahlberg, Edward L. Greenstein, Warren Zev Harvey, and Carol Zaleski for their helpful advice and suggestions. I am also grateful to the Yad Hanadiv/Barecha Foundation for financial support and the Institute of Advanced Studies of the Hebrew University of Jerusalem for making its facilities available to me while I wrote this article.

1. For Jewish perspectives on pregnancy loss and infertility, see Judith R. Baskin, "Rabbinic Reflections on the Barren Wife," *Harvard Theological Review* 82, no. 1 (1989):101–14, and Michael Gold, *And Hannah Wept: Infertility, Adoption and the Jewish Child* (Philadelphia, New York, and Jerusalem: Jewish Publication Society, 1988), especially chaps. 2, 3, and 6. For a ritual designed to cope with pregnancy loss and infertility, see Peninah V. Adelman, *Miriam's Well: Rituals for Jewish Women around the Year* (Fresh Meadows, N.Y.: Biblio Press, 1986), 84–90.

2. Yair Zakovitch, *Ruth* [Mikra le-Yisrael, Perush Mad'ai le-Mikra] (Tel Aviv and Jerusalem: Am Oved and Magnes Press, 1990), 9, 30–31, compares Naomi to Job.

3. *Torah Neviim Ketuvim 'im Perush Da'at Mikra* (Jerusalem: Mossad Harav Kook, 1973) on Ruth 1:5.

4. Phyllis Trible offered the formulation "from mother to 'no-mother' " in "Human Comedy," in *God and the Rhetoric of Sexuality* (Philadelphia: Fortress Press, 1978), 167. The Hebrew Bible has no word specifically for such a

woman, though in other books it does use the root *sh,kh,l* to mean a parent—either male or female—whose child has died.

5. *Torah Neviim Ketuvim 'im Perush Da'at Mikra* on Ruth 1:5.

6. On the motif of journey as growth, see Barbara Gail Green, "A Study of Field and Seed Symbolism in the Biblical Story of Ruth," Ph.D. thesis, Graduate Theological Union, 1980, 101–30.

7. *Midrash Rabbah* (London: Soncino, 1939).

8. On the crucial role of the female friends and neighbors, see Zakovitch, *Ruth*, 30–31, 63–64, and Trible, "Human Comedy," 173–74, 193–96.

9. For traditional commentaries, see *Mikra'ot Gedolot* and *Torah Neviim Ketuvim 'im Perush Da'at Mikra* on Ruth 1:21, and *Midrash Rabbah 'im Perushim* 3:7 ("full of sons and daughters"—see the commentary *Yefe 'anaf* especially on daughters). For convenient English translations of Rashi, Ibn Ezra, and other medieval commentaries, see D. R. G. Beattie, *Jewish Exegesis of the Book of Ruth* [*Journal for the Study of the Old Testament*, Supplements Series 2] (Sheffield: Sheffield Academic Press, 1977), 60, 105, 119, 132, 138. On the theme of fullness and emptiness throughout Ruth, see D. F. Rauber, "Literary Values in the Bible: The Book of Ruth," *Journal of Biblical Literature* 89 (1970): 27–37, and Trible, "Human Comedy."

10. On the various interpretations, see *The Jewish Encyclopedia* (New York and London: Funk and Wagnalls Company, 1901–1906), 9:162, "Names of God"; *Encyclopedia Judaica* (Jerusalem: Keter Publishing House, 1972), 7:676–77, "God, Names of"; *The JPS Torah Commentary*, 1: Genesis, commentary by Nahum M. Sarna (Philadelphia, New York, Jerusalem: Jewish Publication Society, 1989), 384–85; *Ruth: A New Translation* [Anchor Bible], with introduction, notes, and commentary by Edward F. Campbell, Jr. (Garden City, N.Y.: Doubleday, 1975), 76–77; and Jack M. Sasson, *Ruth: A New Translation with a Philological Commentary and a Formalist-Folklorist Interpretation*, 2d ed. (Sheffield: Sheffield Academic Press, 1989), 34.

11. The *Encyclopedia Judaica* 7:677 notes a possible connection between the Akkadian word *sadu*, mountain, and the Hebrew *shad*, breast; thus " 'El Shaddai would mean 'El-of-the-mountain, i.e., of the cosmic mountain. . . . The semantic development from rounded 'breasts' to 'hills' and 'mountains' would not be impossible [sic]." For interpretations of El Shaddai as God of the breast or fertility, see Trible, "Human Comedy," 61, 70; Frank Moore Cross, *Canaanite Myth and Hebrew Epic: Essays in the History of the Religion of Israel* (Cambridge, Mass.: Harvard University Press, 1973), 55–56; and David Biale, "The God with Breasts: El Shaddai in the Bible," *History of Religions* 21 (1982):240–56.

12. Zakovitch, *Ruth*, 17, 59, 65; Campbell, *Ruth*, 77, 83.

13. Trible, "Human Comedy," 174.

14. Po Chu, in Janet L. Sha, *Mothers of Thyme: Customs and Rituals of Infertility and Miscarriage* (Ann Arbor: Lida Rose Press, 1990), 71.

15. *Pesikta Rabbati: Discourses for Feasts, Fasts and Special Sabbaths*, trans. William G. Braude, Yale Judaica Series, vol. 18 (New Haven: Yale University Press, 1968).

16. *Torah Neviim Ketuvim 'im Perush Da'at Mikra* on Ruth 1:21 notes that the initial "I" contributes to the sense of lamentation.

17. Adelman, *Miriam's Well*, 87.

18. Commentary of Zev Wolf, son of Israel Isser Einhorn of Grodno, in *Midrash Rabbah 'im Perushim*.

19. On levirate marriage—the marriage between a widow whose husband died without offspring and the brother of the deceased—see Deuteronomy 25:5–10 and *Encyclopedia Judaica*, 11:122–31. On the complicated relations between these concepts in the Book of Ruth, see Campbell, *Ruth*, 83–84, 109–10, 126, 132–37; Sasson, *Ruth*, 60–61, 81–83, 90–92, 126–40, 158–64; and Zakovitch, *Ruth*, 21–24.

20. Zakovitch, *Ruth*, 112–13.

21 *Genesis Rabbah* (London: Soncino, 1951).

22. On Naomi's role, see *Torah Neviim Ketuvim 'im Perush Da'at Mikra* on Ruth 4:14–17; Zakovitch, *Ruth*, 114–15; Sasson, *Ruth*, 170–72; and Campbell, *Ruth*, 164–65.

23. Campbell, *Ruth*, 168; Zakovitch, *Ruth*, 12.

24. Trible, "Human Comedy," 194.

25. Campbell, *Ruth*, 164, 168.

26. This instance of women ceremoniously naming a child is unique in the Bible. See Trible, "Human Comedy," 192–94, who reads this naming as the reassertion of the women and their concerns after the all-male legal ceremony at the gate of the city in Ruth 4:1–12. Sasson, *Ruth*, 172–75, 233–40, sets the female naming ceremony against the backdrop of ancient Near Eastern literature and symbolism and discerns the vestigial motif of birth deities: "Ancient Near Eastern literature assigns female deities the task of establishing the fate, hence the future, of a newborn male; and . . . such a newborn, if human, is invariably a future king," 235.

27. Zakovitch, *Ruth*, 17, 115; Sasson, *Ruth*, 176–77; Campbell, *Ruth*, 166–67.

28. For a feminist reading of the Book of Ruth, which stresses the role of Ruth and Naomi in creating the Davidic monarchy, see Gillian Feeley-Harnik, "Naomi and Ruth: Building Up the House of David," in Susan Niditch, ed., *Text and Tradition: The Hebrew Bible and Folklore* [The Society of Biblical Literature, Semeia Studies 20] (Atlanta: Scholars Press, 1990), 163–91.

At the Crossroads
MERLE FELD

1. *Shiva*: the first seven days of mourning after the burial of a close relative.

2. *Tisha B'Av*: a day of mourning and fasting commemorating the destruction of the first and second temples in Jerusalem.

3. *Tzitzit*: ritual undergarment traditionally worn by males.

4. *Ivrit*: Hebrew.

5. *Licht bensching*: lighting of the Shabbos candles.

6. *Kefiyah*: headscarf worn by Arabs.

7. *Machane Yehuda*: market area in West Jerusalem.

Women at the Center: Ruth and Shavuot
JUDITH A. KATES

1. David Hartman, *A Living Covenant: The Innovative Spirit in Traditional Judaism* (New York: Free Press, 1985), 26.

Circles of Kinship: Samuel's Family Romance
SUSANNE KLINGENSTEIN

1. Sigmund Freud, *Moses and Monotheism*, Pelican Freud Library, vol. 13, *The Origins of Religion* (Harmondsworth: Penguin Books, 1985), 246–52.

2. Like Freud, the sages of the Midrash could not resist the family romance. They revise Samuel's provocative view into a more conventional direction: "R. Bibi said in the name of R. Reuben: Ruth and Orpah were the daughters of Eglon" (2:9). Eglon was a king of Moab (Judges 3:12). *Midrash Rabbah: Ruth*, 3d ed. (London: Soncino Press, 1961). All references to the Midrash are to this edition and will be cited in the text.

3. From Samuel's arguments in *Megillat Ruth* the rabbis learned that Deuteronomy 23:3 should be understood as "[the exclusion of an] Ammonite but not [an] Ammonitess, [of a] Moabite but not [a] Moabitess" (*Ruth Rabba* 4:1, 6; 7:7, 10; etc.).

4. *Ruth* (Jerusalem: Mossad ha-Rav Kook, 1973), 15.

5. The Midrash stresses Ruth's modesty in public. "All the other women bend down to gather the ears of corn, but she sits and gathers; all the other women hitch up their skirts, and she keeps hers down; all the other women jest with the reapers, while she is reserved; all the other women gather between the sheaves, while she gathers from that which is already abandoned" (*Ruth Rabba* 4:6).

Ruth

CYNTHIA OZICK

1. Latter-day scholarship avers that Elimelech is a run-of-the-mill name in pre-Israelite Canaan, "and is the one name in the Ruth story that seems incapable of being explained as having a symbolic meaning pertinent to the narrative" (*Ruth*: [Anchor Bible] with introduction, notes, and commentary by Edward F. Campbell, Jr. [Garden City, N.Y.: Doubleday, 1975], 52). The rabbis, however, are above all metaphor-seekers and symbolists.

2. The rabbis' notion of Elimelech as a man of substance is of no help to his widow. She has not been provided for; we see her as helpless and impoverished.

3. "Boaz and Naomi talk like older people. Their speeches contain archaic morphology and syntax. Perhaps the most delightful indication of this is the one instance when an archaic form is put into Ruth's mouth, at 2:21—where she is quoting Boaz!" (Campbell, *Ruth*, p. 17).

Soldiers in an Army of Mothers: Reflections on Naomi and the Heroic Biblical Woman

SYLVIA BARACK FISHMAN

1. Sholem Asch, *Three Cities*, "Warsaw" (G. P. Putnam's Sons, 1933; New York: Carrol and Graf Publishers, 1983), 313–14.

2. Philip Wylie, *Generation of Vipers* (New York: Holt, Rinehart and Winston, 1955); Philip Roth, *Portnoy's Complaint* (New York: Fawcett Crest, 1967). Wylie accuses "dear old Mom" of tying male America to her apron strings through heavy-handed emotional manipulation.

3. See Phyllis Bird, "Images of Women in the Old Testament," in *Religion*

and *Sexism,* ed. Rosemary Ruether (New York: Simon and Schuster, 1974), 41–88, 63; and Dorothy Dinnerstein, *The Mermaid and the Minotaur: Sexual Arrangements and Human Malaise* (New York: Harper and Row Publishers, 1976), 112, 275.

4. The *ushpizin* include Abraham, Isaac, Jacob, Judah, Moses, David, and Elijah.

Ruth: Dilemmas of Loyalty and Connection

Mona DeKoven Fishbane

1. "Cutoff," in the language of family therapy, refers to the action of people who remove themselves totally from their family of origin, rejecting contact with them. Clinical data suggests that such cutoffs create havoc in the family system, especially for the person who cuts off, and may negatively affect subsequent generations if not resolved.

2. Our understanding of woman as fundamentally a relational creature, with her own line of development, has been enormously enhanced by, among others, Carol Gilligan at Harvard and the researchers at the Wellesley College Stone Center. Their work has revolutionized the field of adult development and of psychotherapy. In their research and theory building, these women have allowed us to go beyond autonomy and separation as the hallmarks of adult mental health, to an appreciation of the importance of connection and caring in mature functioning. Although this is described as a new understanding of women's development, it may well point to a new understanding of male and female development in terms of the capacity to connect and care. Indeed, Ivan Boszormenyi-Nagy, a family therapist, has suggested that autonomy be redefined (for men and women) as involving the capacity for relational responsibility. Boszormenyi-Nagy focuses on the healthy role of caring and loyalty in family relationships.

3. This interpretation reflects Boszormenyi-Nagy's claim that we are only free to build our own lives, to love and work creatively, if we have found a way to express our loyalty to our parents and, thus, to repay our filial debt to them. If we do not find a constructive way to express this loyalty, Boszormenyi-Nagy suggests that we will do so negatively, in a self-destructive way, through "invisible loyalties."

Reading Ruth with Naomi

MARIANNE HIRSCH

1. Note, for example, the slip in a recent article on the relationship between mothers-in-law and daughters-in-law: "Mothers-in-law have been viewed as problematic at least since the days of Hansel and Gretel." Ramona Marotz-Baden and Deane Cowan, "Mothers-in-law and Daughters-in-law: The Effects of Proximity on Conflict and Stress," *Family Relations* 36, no. 4 (October 1987): 389.

2. Lucy Rose Fischer, "Mothers and Mothers-in-law," *Journal of Marriage and Family* 45, no. 1 (February 1983): 187. The citation is from A. R. Radclyffe-Brown, Introduction, in *African Systems of Kinship and Marriage*, ed. A. R. Radclyffe-Brown and Darryl Forde (London: Oxford University Press, 1950).

3. Fischer, "Mothers and Mothers-in-law," 188.

4. Marotz-Baden and Cowan, "Mothers-in-law and Daughters-in-law," 387.

5. In her "Patterns of Support among In-Laws in the United States," *Journal of Family Issues* 11, no. 1 (March 1990): 67–90, Ann Goetting reports on a number of studies of African-American welfare families where a support network is established and perpetuated between the child's mother and the father's mother and sister, even in the absence of the father himself. These welfare families diverge consistently from middle-class families, which evidence less support among in-laws.

6. Fischer, "Mothers and Mothers-in-law," 189.

Ruth and the Messiah

TAMAR FRANKIEL

1. The Torah states that the Moabites refused to give the Israelites bread and water, although it also states (Deuteronomy 2:29) that the Moabites did allow them passage through the land.

2. Quoted by Rabbi Nosson Scherman, "Overview" to *The Book of Ruth*, trans. Rabbi Meir Zlotowitz, Artscroll Tanach Series (1976); (Brooklyn, N.Y.: Mesorah Publications, 1989), xlii–xliii.

3. Yehoshua Bachrach, *Mother of Royalty* [Ima Shel Malchut], revised ed. (New York: Feldheim and the Jerusalem College for Women, 1973), 86.

4. Midrash Lekach Tov, cited by Bachrach, *Mother of Royalty*, 155. The full citation: "Why is the Book of Ruth read on Shavuoth, on the anniversary of the giving of the Torah? / Because this Book is permeated with *hesed*, and the Torah is permeated with *hesed*. / As it is said (Prov. 31.26): 'The Torah of *hesed* is on her tongue.' " See the entire chapter, pp. 155–89, for Rabbi Bachrach's rich compilation of commentary on the theme of *chesed*.

5. See Bachrach, *Mother of Royalty*, 69–77, for a discussion of these obligations.

6. Cited in the Artscroll commentary to *Ruth* 1:9, p. 73.

7. Tamar Frankiel, *The Voice of Sarah: Feminine Spirituality and Traditional Judaism* (San Francisco: Harper Collins, 1990), 83–86.

8. This interpretation is reinforced by the Iggeret Shmuel, who comments on the fact that the phrase "to me" does not appear in the Hebrew, although it is read when the book is read. This suggests that Ruth cast herself completely on Naomi's instructions, and removed "herself" from making any decision in the matter. Similarly, M'lo ha'Omer holds that the omitted "to me" shows how Ruth trusted everything to God, excluding "herself." See the Artscroll commentary to 3:5, p. 111.

Ruth Reconsidered

Susan Reimer Torn

1. Sir James Frazer, *The New Golden Bough*, ed. Theodore Gaster (New York: New American Library, 1959), 359.

2. Otto Rank, *The Incest Theme in Language and Literature* (Baltimore: Johns Hopkins Press, 1975), 300.

3. *The Father: Contemporary Jungian Perspectives*, ed. Andrew Samuels (New York: New York University Press, 1986), 29.

4. Ibid., 30–31.

Dialogue on Devotion

Norma Rosen

1. *Akeda*: literally, "binding"; refers to Abraham's preparation to kill his son, Isaac, at God's command. The miraculous appearance of a ram for slaughter saves Isaac's life.

2. Margaret Mahler: author of works on early childhood developmental psychology, with special emphasis on separation from the mother.

3. *Al chet*: literally, "for the sin"; refers to a list of transgressions for which one asks pardon of God on Yom Kippur, the Day of Atonement.

Contributors' Biographies

REBECCA T. ALPERT is codirector and assistant professor of women's studies at Temple University in Philadelphia. For many years she served as dean of students at the Reconstructionist Rabbinical College.

ROBERTA J. APFEL is a physician, psychiatrist, and psychoanalyst who practices in the Boston area and teaches at Harvard Medical School, Cambridge Hospital. She lives with her husband in Newton, Massachusetts, and is the mother and stepmother of five young adult children.

DR. NEHAMA ASCHKENASY is director of the program in Judaic studies and Middle Eastern affairs at the University of Connecticut at Stamford, where she also teaches English literature and women's studies. Her book *Eve's Journey: Feminine Images in Hebraic Literary Tradition* (University of Pennsylvania Press, 1986) won the 1988 Present Tense Literary Award for "best book in the category of religious thought." Her book *War and Siege: Reflection of Israel's Geopolitics and Society in the Works of Amos Oz* will be published by SUNY Press next year, and she is currently completing *Woman in the Window: Paradigms of Female Existence in Biblical Civilization.*

ADELE BERLIN is professor of Hebrew Bible at the University of Maryland, College Park. She is a former director of the Myerhoff Center for Jewish Studies. She has published numerous articles and books, most recently a commentary on Zephaniah as part of the Anchor Bible series.

LOIS C. DUBIN is assistant professor of religion and biblical literature at Smith College. She specializes in Jewish thought and history. She is married and the mother of two daughters.

MERLE FELD is an award-winning playwright whose credits include *The Gates Are Closing* and *Across the Jordan.* She is also a widely published poet, a lecturer on spirituality and Jewish feminism, and an activist for social and political change. She lives in New York City with her husband Eddie and children Lisa and Uri.

MONA DEKOVEN FISHBANE, PH.D., is a clinical psychologist in private practice in Chicago, and is on the faculty of the Chicago Center for Family Health. She is married to Michael Fishbane. They have two sons, Eitan and Elisha.

SYLVIA BARACK FISHMAN is assistant professor of contemporary American Jewish life in the department of Near Eastern and Judaic studies at Brandeis University. She is the author of *A Breath of Life: Feminism in the American Jewish Community* (1993), *Follow My Footprints: Changing Images of Women in American Jewish Fiction* (1992), and *Changing Jewish Life: Service Delivery and Planning in the 1990's*, coauthored with Lawrence Sternberg and Gary Tobin (1991).

TAMAR FRANKIEL holds a Ph.D. in history of religions from the University of Chicago and has taught in a number of universities including the University of California at Berkeley and the University of Judaism in Los Angeles. She has published articles and books on religion for both academic and general audiences. Her most recent book is *The Voice of Sarah: Feminine Spirituality and Traditional Judaism.*

GLORIA GOLDREICH is a writer living in New York. The author of several novels chronicling Jewish experience and a series of children's books on women in the professions, Goldreich won the National Jewish Book Award for her novel *Leah's Journey*. Her short fiction and critical essays have appeared in numerous magazines and have been widely anthologized. Her most recent novel, *Years of Dreams*, was chosen as a Literary Guild selection.

LISE M. GRONDAHL, M.D., M.P.H., is completing a psychiatric residency at Stanford University. Upon graduating she will be a clinical instructor in psychiatry at Stanford Medical School and in private practice in the San Francisco area. Dr. Grondahl previously trained at Cambridge Hospital, Harvard Medical School, where she was supervised by Dr. Roberta J. Apfel. Dr. Grondahl grew up in Oslo and received her medical degree from the University of Bergen School of Medicine in Norway. She currently resides in Palo Alto, California.

KATHRYN HELLERSTEIN, a poet, translator, and scholar, teaches Yiddish at the University of Pennsylvania. Her poems have appeared in *Tikkun, Bridges, Poetry,* and the anthologies *Without a Single Answer* (Jewish Magnes Museum, 1990) and *Four Centuries of Jewish Women's Spirituality.*

MARIANNE HIRSCH teaches French, comparative literature, and women's studies at Dartmouth College. Most recently, she is the author of *The Mother/Daughter Plot: Narrative, Psychoanalysis, Feminism* (1989) and coeditor of *Conflicts in Feminism* (1990). She is completing a book entitled *Family Frames: Narrative and Photography in the Postmodern*.

BARBARA HELFGOTT HYETT has written four books of poetry: *In Evidence: Poems of the Liberation of Nazi Concentration Camps* (University of Pittsburgh Press, 1986), *Natural Law* (Northland Press, 1989), *The Double Reckoning of Christopher Columbus* (University of Illinois Press, 1992), and a forthcoming collection on endangered wildlife. Director of the Workshop for Publishing Poets, she teaches English at Boston University and lives in Brookline, Massachusetts.

PATRICIA S. KARLIN-NEUMANN was ordained as a rabbi at Hebrew Union College-Jewish Institute of Religion, New York, in 1982. She is the rabbi at Temple Israel in Alameda, California, and is interested in religious pluralism, Jewish feminism, and the relationship between text and experience.

JUDITH A. KATES received her Ph.D. in comparative literature from Harvard University, where she taught for eleven years. She now studies Bible and Rabbinics and teaches at Hebrew College in Brookline, Massachusetts, and in many programs of adult education in the Jewish community. She has published in the areas of Renaissance studies, women's studies, and Jewish studies.

FRANCINE KLAGSBRUN writes and lectures on Judaism, feminism, and social and family issues. Her most recent book is *Mixed Feelings: Love, Hate, Rivalry, and Reconciliation Among Brothers and Sisters*. Among her other works is *Voices of Wisdom: Jewish Ideals and Ethics for Everyday Living*.

SUSANNE KLINGENSTEIN was born in Germany in 1959. Her mother was a Swiss-born Catholic, her father a German Jew. From 1973 to 1982, she received an education in centrally Jewish texts in Mannheim's Jewish community. She received her Ph.D. in American studies from the University of Heidelberg in 1990 and converted to Judaism in the same year. She now lives in Boston and is an assistant professor in the program of writing and humanistic studies at MIT. Her publications include essays on American Holocaust literature and American Jewish history, and the book *Jews in the American Academy, 1900–1940: The Dynamics of Intellectual Assimilation* (1991).

VANESSA L. OCHS is the author of *Words on Fire: One Woman's Journey into the Sacred* (Harcourt Brace Jovanovich, 1990) and a forthcoming book (Viking) about protecting children in a dangerous world. She has written for *Lil-*

ith, Moment, Tikkun, Congress Monthly, the *New York Times, Newsday, Woman's Day, Redbook, Child, Health Confidential, Croton Review,* and the *Melton Journal.* She is the recipient of an NEA Fellowship in nonfiction writing. Ochs has taught at Colgate, Hebrew University, and Yale and now teaches both writing and religion at Drew University in Madison, New Jersey.

ALICIA OSTRIKER is a poet-critic, author of seven volumes of poetry, including *The Imaginary Lover,* which won the William Carlos Williams Award of the Poetry Society of America. Her writing on women's poetry includes a volume of essays, *Writing Like a Woman,* and the controversial *Stealing the Language: The Emergence of Women's Poetry in America.* A new book of essays, *Unwritten Volume: Rethinking the Bible,* is forthcoming from Blackwell's.

CYNTHIA OZICK, author of novels, short stories, and essays, has published, among many other works, a volume of essays called *Metaphor and Memory* (Knopf, 1989), the stories "The Shawl and Rosa" (Knopf, 1989), and the novels *The Messiah of Stockholm* (Knopf, 1987) and *Cannibal Galaxy* (Knopf, 1983). Her most recent project is a play called "Blue Light," about Holocaust denial.

MARGE PIERCY is a poet and novelist who has also contributed essays and reviews to many periodicals. Her most recent works include the volumes of poetry *Available Light* (Knopf, 1988) and *Mars and Her Children* (Knopf, 1992), and the novel *He, She and It* (Knopf, 1991).

RUTH ANNA PUTNAM has taught philosophy at Wellesley College since 1963. She has published numerous articles in moral philosophy and in American philosophy. "Friendship" is her second paper in Jewish philosophy.

NESSA RAPOPORT is the author of a novel, *Preparing for Sabbath,* and of *A Woman's Book of Grieving.* With Ted Solotaroff, she edited *Writing Our Way Home: Contemporary Stories by American Jewish Writers.*

GAIL TWERSKY REIMER is associate director of the Massachusetts Foundation for the Humanities, the state-based program of the NEH. She holds a Ph.D. in English and American literature from Rutgers University and has been involved in the study and teaching of Jewish texts in *chavurot,* synagogues, and women's study groups. She has published scholarly and popular articles in Victorian studies, women's studies, and Jewish studies.

NORMA ROSEN has published four novels, a volume of stories, and most recently a book of essays, *Accidents of Influence: Writing As a Woman and a Jew in America,* published by SUNY Press. Her novel, *Touching Evil,* which treats the response of Americans to the Holocaust, has been reissued in paperback by

Wayne State University Press. She teaches fiction writing at the Tisch School of Dramatic Writing at NYU.

SYLVIA ROTHCHILD has explored relationships between the generations in the novel *Sunshine and Salt*; in the short story collection *Family Stories for Every Generation*; in two works of oral history, *Voices from the Holocaust* and *A Special Legacy*; and in *Keys to a Magic Door*, a juvenile biography of the Yiddish writer I. L. Peretz.

RUTH H. SOHN was ordained as a rabbi in 1982 at Hebrew Union College-Jewish Institute of Religion. She currently lives in Los Angeles with her husband and three children, where she teaches commentary, midrash, and Talmud to high school students and adults. She has published several articles as well as creative midrash and poetry.

SUSAN REIMER TORN is a free-lance journalist, writer, and editor. Formerly a New Yorker, she lives in Paris with her husband and two sons, where she directs Creative Consultants International, a communications company specializing in the English language. She is working on her first novel.

RUTH WHITMAN is the author of eight books of poetry, the most recent of which is *Hatshepsut, Speak to Me*, published in 1992 by Wayne State University Press. The same press published *Laughing Gas: Poems New and Selected 1963–1990* (1991) and her third book of translations of Yiddish poetry, *The Fiddle Rose: Poems 1970–1972* by Abraham Sutzkever (1990). She has received numerous awards and honors and has taught in the Radcliffe College Seminars and at the Massachusetts Institute of Technology.

AVIVAH ZORNBERG received an education in traditional Jewish texts from her father, Rabbi Doctor Zeev Gottlieb, and at the Gateshead Seminary in England. She holds a doctorate in English literature from Cambridge University. She lives in Jerusalem where she teaches *shiurim* (Torah classes) in institutions of higher Jewish learning.

About the Editors

JUDITH A. KATES holds a Ph.D. in comparative literature from Harvard University and teaches Jewish Women's Studies and Bible in adult education programs in the Jewish community.

GAIL TWERSKY REIMER received her Ph.D. in English literature from Rutgers University and is associate director of the Massachusetts Foundation for the Humanities.